MW00713597

LEGAL CULTURE IN THE UNITED STATES

AN INTRODUCTION

Kirk W. Junker

Routledge
Taylor & Francis Group

LONDON AND NEW YORK

First edition published 2016
by Routledge
2 Park Square, Milton Park, Abingdon, Oxon, OX14 4RN

and by Routledge
711 Third Avenue, New York, NY 10017

Routledge is an imprint of the Taylor & Francis Group, an informa business

© 2016 Kirk W. Junker

The right of Kirk W. Junker to be identified as author of this work has been asserted by him in accordance with sections 77 and 78 of the Copyright, Designs and Patents Act 1988.

All rights reserved. No part of this book may be reprinted or reproduced or utilised in any form or by any electronic, mechanical, or other means, now known or hereafter invented, including photocopying and recording, or in any information storage or retrieval system, without permission in writing from the publishers.

Trademark notice: Product or corporate names may be trademarks or registered trademarks, and are used only for identification and explanation without intent to infringe.

British Library Cataloguing in Publication Data
A catalogue record for this book is available from the British Library

Library of Congress Cataloguing in Publication Data
Names: Junker, Kirk W.
Title: Legal Culture in the United States : An Introduction / Kirk W. Junker.
Description: Abingdon, Oxon; New York, NY : Routledge, [2016]
Identifiers: LCCN 2015037719 | ISBN 9781138642454 (hbk) |
ISBN 9781138194304 (pbk) | ISBN 9781315629940 (ebk)
Subjects: LCSH: Law–United States–Methodology. | Culture and law–United States. | Justice, Administration of–Social aspects–United States. | Adversary system (Law)–Social aspects–United States. | Sociological jurisprudence–United States.
Classification: LCC KF380.J85 2016 | DDC 340/.1150973–dc23
LC record available at http://lccn.loc.gov/2015037719

ISBN: 978-1-138-64245-4 (hbk)
ISBN: 978-1-138-19430-4 (pbk)
ISBN: 978-1-315-62994-0 (ebk)

Typeset in Bembo by
Out of House Publishing

Printed and bound in the United States of America by
Edwards Brothers Malloy on sustainably sourced paper

For Robert D. Taylor,
who in dedicating himself to teaching law through its humanities
has brought humanity to the law.

CONTENTS

ACKNOWLEDGEMENTS

I first want to thank my colleagues on the Law Faculty at the University of Cologne for having granted me research leave in order to bring this book forward. Thanks especially to colleagues Prof. Stephan Hobe for the suggestion to write the book and Prof. Claus Kress for characterizing the focus on culture. Dr. Keith Wilder's perspective of the historian helped to keep any claims regarding the past from wishful wandering. Dean Kenneth Gormley of Duquesne University School of Law and Dean Markus Ogorek of the EBS School of Business and Law generously agreed to review the entire book. Prof. Bruce Ledewitz of Duquesne University School of Law and Amy Sugin, formerly Dean of International Students at Cardozo Law School provided helpful commentary on the Social Reference Frame chapter. I am especially grateful to those colleagues from other disciplines who made sure that my expansion of law into other disciplines left those other disciplines at least recognisable to their own scholars—Prof. John Poulakos of the Department of Rhetoric and Communication at the University of Pittsburgh, Dott. Alessandro Galli, linguist and lecturer at the Sapienza University of Rome, and Prof. Barbara Tuchańska of the Philosophy Faculty of the University of Łódź. I especially want to thank Maria Peiou for her support and her patience in explaining to me all things Greek. I am grateful to all those who work or have worked with me at the University of Cologne to give me insights into how others view U.S. legal culture—especially my assistants, Ass. jur. Anja Meutsch and Ryan Kraski Esq., and student assistant Kristine Hörmann. I thank P. Matthew Roy Esq., with whom I had collaborated on an earlier book and who took on the tasks of proofreading, indexing and editing this book. I would also like to thank two lawyers who conducted essential early research on the book, Matthew Rudzki Esq. and Peter Kern, RA.

I am grateful for Dr. Sonja Frenzel's discussions on notions of culture, which helped to frame the whole project. I would also like to thank Fiona Briden of

Routledge, who supported the idea of publishing this book since she first read my proposal, as well as her colleague Emily Wells, whose responsiveness and patience made the production easy. I thank Deborah Renshaw for her close reading and editing of the entire text. My thanks are due to Marcel Buckan for finding and designing cover images that demonstrate that law is formed from culture. And finally, I am grateful to the students of the University of Cologne, who remain interested in and receptive to foreign legal cultures, and who continually provide an engaged audience for the ideas in this book.

FOREWORD

There is nothing like a dream to create the future.

-Victor Hugo[1]

This book is a gift for comparative law – it is badly needed as a matter of confidence. The world of law is global, in no small part due to the Internet: domestic rules cannot be seen in isolation any longer. The meeting of minds demands a deeper understanding of cultural backgrounds; thus, comparative law becomes a central position.[2] It requires all our senses to find a way somewhere between cosmos and chaos, between order and disorder. To what extent can we trust each other, where can we "meet"?[3] Different concepts of "rationality" and of "time" compete with each other. We meet the strange in the familiar and the familiar in the strange. We lose our language-, letter- and even number-based feelings of security.

That is a mighty challenge: As "global neighbors" we have to know what we and they regard as being "in order", what we and they regard as legitimate norms in our patterns of organization. Comparative lawyers are often lonely riders and they often have an identity problem: what is law at home and abroad, what are legal rules here and there? As my teacher Myres McDougal[4] explained it: "The greatest confusion continues to prevail about what is being compared, about the purpose of comparison, and about appropriate techniques."[5]

---

[1] Victor Hugo, *Les Miserables*.
[2] Bernhard Grossfeld, "Global Accounting: A Challenge for Lawyers," in *Liber Amicorum for Professor Roberto MacLean*. London: British Institute of International and Comparative Law. 2007. 143.
[3] Bernhard Grossfeld, *Recht als Begegnung*. Paderborn: Schöningh, 2015.
[4] Bernhard Grossfeld, *Rechtsvergleichung*. Westdt. Verlag, 2000. 67.
[5] Myres McDougal, "The Comparative Study of Law for Policy Purposes: Value Clarification as an Instrument of World Order," 1 Am. J. Comp. L. 24, 28 (1952).

Answers require a sensitive approach: Law is more than letters and institutions. It grows from cultural backgrounds which we are often not aware of. It is a "distinctive way of imagining the real" from the past to the present into the future.[6] I would call it "a social dream that is stirred by our senses' everyday experiences, past and present."[7] It demands more than a functional approach.

But how can we master the challenge? How can outsiders from abroad cope with it? Are they just dreaming their local views into a foreign chaos? We are all tempted to see foreign laws according to our own experiences and assumptions. Thus, we often do not meet the underground dynamics – as a consequence – we do not find the answers: What are the economic and emotional pictures behind the text? What stitches on the back of the carpet create the patterns on the front?[8] Can we rely on the hope that the human heart beats to the same measure everywhere?[9]

Kirk W. Junker brings us into the center of these questions and thus into the heart of Comparative Law. He starts with the problems and develops his answers in a way that is always down to earth – written in a language that is up to the standards of the issue but also open to the reader. I am not giving an indication of his answers, but I would like to give my general opinion: this book is a wonderful stronghold of Comparative Law.

Bernhard Grossfeld

---

[6] Bernhard Grossfeld, "Dreaming Law," *Comparative Legal Semiotics* 4 (2010).
[7] *Ibid.*
[8] Bernhard Grossfeld, „Ordnungsmuster", in: *Festschrift 50 Jahre ZfRV*, Wien, 2013. 25.
[9] *Cf.* Bernhard Grossfeld, "Comparative Law: Meeting Cultures," in: *Liber Amicorum*, René de Groot, 2016.

PREFACE

Seeing Law through the Reference Frames of Culture

It is vulgar error to suppose that America was ever discovered. It was merely detected.

— Oscar Wilde[1]

The Exigency

This book has come about as my attempt to address a problem. The problem was that when I spoke to lawyers and law students from around the world about the law in the United States of America, there were moments when the sense of U.S. legal practice just seemed to be ungraspable to people living and educated outside the U.S. They could learn and memorize the sources of law well enough, and many had notions of legal practice from popular film or television, but still there were those moments when the legal substance or procedure just did not sensibly orient the student to the norms meant to solve the corresponding social problems. So I considered what the reason could be for the difficulty of seeing the foundations of the norms. Then, while teaching in the United States, I experienced a related, but more precise phenomenon. Foreign law students would enroll to take the same courses as the U.S. law students—contracts, torts, property, criminal law, constitutional law, civil procedure and so forth. But I noticed that even the best foreign students had the greatest problems when working with the less-globalized norms, such as the constitutional rights to bear arms and to separate the church from the state. These are difficult enough legal concepts for those native to the system, and a proper legal

---

[1] Oscar Wilde, *The Complete Works of Oscar Wilde: The Picture of Dorian Gray: the 1890 and 1891 Editions*, Clark Wilde MS W6721M3P576. Oxford: Oxford University Press, 2005. 433, fn. 26–7.

understanding requires quite a bit of cultural knowledge that U.S. legal education assumes the students have, if the students are born in the United States. But then come the even more challenging issues in legal education such as the constitutional issues of U.S. "horizontal" federalism and the associated problems of federal diversity jurisdiction of the courts. And in more everyday matters of practice, it was also obviously difficult for many of the civil law students to understand the role of the advocate in an adversarial system in which the lawyer, and not the judge, controls the presentation of evidence, while balancing the responsibility to advocate on behalf of the client and with the constraints on a sworn officer of the court. Other phenomena also presented cultural-understanding challenges, such as lay juries, class actions, punitive damages, plea bargaining, pre-trial discovery, the *stare decisis* doctrine, the lack of a separate constitutional court or prohibition of fact revision on appeal. By comparison, when it came to commercial matters, foreign students made the connections more readily, presumably due to the more globalized commercial norms based upon a more globalized commercial culture.

Thus it occurred to me that when U.S. law professors teach U.S. law to U.S. students in their own country, the educational atmosphere unconsciously makes all sorts of presumptions about the students' recognition of social problems in their own culture. And while teachers and students may have a variety of different opinions as to how one solves those problems, the problems are nevertheless familiar enough, even if unarticulated, to create a common touchstone. Not so for the foreign lawyer or student in that same lecture. Thus I set myself to write an introduction to the U.S. legal system with the agenda of connecting U.S. norms to U.S. legal culture for a foreign audience. The discipline of ancient rhetoric teaches its practitioners to distribute attention in communication equally among the speaker, the audience and the text. With this in mind, one is reminded when teaching U.S. law that foreign students are a different audience than domestic students. And recently in the United States, perhaps due to the abundance of foreign lawyer LL.M. programs, the foreign student audience for U.S. law has grown significantly.[2] Texts have begun to recognize this different audience when they are concerned with practice skills[3] and legal writing.[4] This book addresses the different audience in order to help it to understand U.S. legal culture. For example, from the cultural perspective of history alone, the American literary critic Kenneth Burke provides us with a helpful image when, in thinking about the U.S. Constitution, he writes that if one does

---

[2] American Bar Association, "ABA Section of Legal Education Reports 2013 Law School Enrollment Data," www.americanbar.org/news/abanews/aba-news-archives/2013/12/aba_section_of_legal.html (last accessed 8 January 2015).

[3] See Anne M. Burr and Howard Bromberg, *U.S. Legal Practice Skills for International Law Students*. Durham, NC: Carolina Academic Press, 2014.

[4] See Laurel Currie Oates and Anne Enquist, "Grammar and Rhetoric for ESL Law Students," in *The Legal Writing Handbook: Analysis, Research, and Writing*, 4th ed. New York: Aspen Publishers, 2006 827–79; Deborah B. McGregor and Cynthia M. Adams, *The International Lawyer's Guide to Legal Analysis and Communication in the United States*. New York: Aspen Publishers, 2008; Amy Krois-Lindner and Translegal, *International Legal English: A Course for Classroom or Self-Study Use*. Cambridge: Cambridge University Press, 2006.

not understand the problems that the writers of the constitution were attempting to solve in the eighteenth century, then reading the text of the Constitution today is like unearthing a broken statue with half missing—a man in the pose of a fencer parrying. Against what thrust was he parrying?[5]

Using the Word "Culture" and a Sense of Orientation

From Bismarck's resistance to the Catholic Church (*der Kulturkampf*) to the political divide in the United States, there is a history of disputes over the word "culture" and what it might mean. The concern over culture has even produced "culture wars." When I explained this book's idea to a faculty colleague, he said "ah, so what you are writing is not an introduction to the sources of law, but to legal culture, right?" I had not previously thought to distinguish the book through the use of the word "culture," but upon reflection came to believe that he was correct. However with the word "culture" comes other problems.

First is the problem that far too often in everyday discourse, "culture" is treated as though it is limited to so-called "high culture," and even then, only in its most over-inflated constructions. Second is the example of associating "culture" with enemy ideology. Although we may not know the play *Schlageter* by name, most of us are familiar with the infamous line that the title character delivers: "Whenever I hear of culture … I release the safety on my pistol!"[6] The line of the character Schlageter not only shows the politics of culture, but also has resonance with those whose tastes run counter to "high culture."

A third problem comes about by placing too much faith in the notion of definition. The concept of definition began in western culture as a common topic of invention (Latin, *inventio*; Greek, εὕρεσις) in the art of rhetoric. From just one of many common topics of invention, the common topic of definition seems to have evolved into something often mistaken for being reified or nearly tangible. In his poem, "Law, Like Love," the English poet W. H. Auden eventually tires of trying to say what "law is" by definition. He tells us instead:

> Yet law-abiding scholars write:
> Law is neither wrong nor right,
> Law is only crimes,
> Punished by *places* and by *times*.[7]

---

[5] Kenneth Burke, *A Grammar of Motives*. Berkeley, CA: University of California Press, 1969. 365.

[6] The line was written by pro-Nazi author, Hans Johst, in his play, *Schlageter*. ("*Wenn ich Kultur höre … entsichere ich meinen Browning!*") (Act 1, Scene 1), my translation from original German text, now available at http://forum.axishistory.com/viewtopic.php?f=44&t=148927 (last accessed 17 September 2014).

[7] W. H. Auden, "Law, Like Love," in *Collected Shorter Poems, 1927–1957*. London: Faber and Faber, 1969 (emphasis added).

xvi Preface

Definitions also can be quickly dated or biased. For example, back in the nineteenth century, when cultural anthropology smacked of a colonialism that may make one wince today, British anthropologist Edward Burnett Tylor defined "culture" as "that complex whole which includes knowledge, belief, art, morals, *law*, custom, and any other capacities and habits acquired by man as a member of society."[8] One must admit that this definition shows that "culture" is not limited to "high culture," but Tylor's thinking is embedded in a time when one could speak of "civilized" and "primitive" cultures, as the title of his work indicates.

By the latter part of the twentieth century, the word "culture" became so politically charged that one dared not use it unless with polemic intent. I hope to avoid much of this vinegar with the following simple disclaimer. The process of defining is to make something finite from among that which is infinite. Thus it is a chalk line that at the same time creates two categories—that which is included in the definition and that which is excluded from the definition. Here, with my discussion of U.S. legal culture, the first thing to realize is simply that with the use of the word "culture," one is usually drawing a line between that which is called "culture" and that which is called "nature." With this distinction, my main message is that law is a function of culture, not a function of nature, and insofar as it is, law changes from time to time and place to place.[9] This is not a statement for or against legal positivism or legal naturalism. A legal naturalist might insist there are universal norms precisely because the norms are somehow part of our nature. But the concept of a natural law, understood biologically, becomes more and more doubtful because the idea of a permanent human nature is fading away as we expand our knowledge of biological evolution. And if that is true, then law must either be dependent upon its cultural character or have a divine foundation for human rights or universal norms. Cross-cultural norms, even to the extent of having become universal, can be accomplished through broad agreement as well. All norms must be expressed in language and they need social institutions for their factual and actual working. So even if we agree that universal norms do or can exist somewhere in the ideal world, one cannot prove that they are expressed in all languages in the same way because we do not have any measure of the sameness of linguistic expressions. Consequently, even natural law theorists often disagree on the basic, "natural" norms.

Applied to the case at hand, one should note that the legal culture of the United States today is not the legal culture of elsewhere at any time, or even the same as the legal culture of the United States in the past or in the future. Thus a lawyer from another place cannot use his or her other-place conceptions of legal culture "in general" to understand U.S. legal culture in its time and place specifics.

---

[8] E. B. Tylor, *Primitive Culture. Researches into the Development of Mythology, Philosophy, Religion, Language, Art and Custom.* 2 vols. 1871. 7th ed. New York: Brentano's, 1924 (emphasis added).

[9] See E. H. Carr, "History, Science, and Morality," in *What is History?* New York: Penguin, 1964 56–86.

So far, in considering the word "culture," I have only said that legal culture would not include nature, but what else can one say? Cultural anthropology today of course has changed from what it was in the days of Edward Burnett Tylor and sees its role and definitions differently. My use of the word "culture" is not meant to be that of the anthropologist, past or present. Instead, I am *using*[10] the word "culture" not as the *terminus technicus* of the anthropologist, but simply to address the problem I have identified: lawyers and students of one legal system cannot study another legal system without knowing something of the culture that produces that system. The problem is most pronounced to the lawyer or student from outside the United States, but by focusing on cultural connections rather than just the mechanics of the law, even a U.S. student can benefit from reflecting on these issues. The U.S. reader may find that this sort of approach helps one to see U.S. law in the light of U.S. culture, rather than passively allowing the culture to rest as unexamined wallpaper in the background, or worse—as a set of static facts.

This book attempts to help students and lawyers from outside the United States make sense of an unfamiliar culture—U.S. legal culture. Understood that way, were one to resist my insistence on the distinction between usage and definition, and demand at least a working definition[11] of the word "culture" for this book, it would seem that the definition of Siegfried Schmidt comes closest: culture is "*Sinnorientierung*";[12] that is, either sense orientation or meaning orientation, with the use of the word "sense" as in "to get a sense of something" and the use of the word "orientation" as in aeronautic attitude. One might dwell longer on the problems of using the word "culture," but that could infinitely deflect from treating the *topos* of the study of culture—in this case, legal culture. Thus although this book could be characterized as part of a longer tradition of treating law as culture, it is limited to the attempt to present U.S. legal culture to those for whom it is foreign.[13] My emphasis on culture may tip the reader that I come from a common law system. By comparison, according to comparativist John Henry Merryman, the civil law's legal scientist "is concerned only with the law and with purely legal values. The result is a highly artificial body of doctrine that is deliberately insulated from what is going on outside, in the rest of culture."[14]

---

10 In Chapter 3, comparing civil law and common law, as well as in Chapter 6 on language, more will be said about the difference between usage and definition.

11 As the reader will see in Chapter 3 on comparative law and Chapter 6, the language reference frame, reliance upon definition is itself a questionable road to understanding the meaning of any word, including "culture."

12 Siegfried J. Schmidt, *Kognitive Autonomie und soziale Orientierung*. Berlin: Suhrkamp, 1996.

13 One may also speak of a culture of legal comparison, as well. See e.g. Maurice Adams and Dirk Heirbaut, *The Method and Culture of Comparative Law: Essays in Honour of Mark Van Hoecke*. Oxford: Hart Publishing, 2014.

14 John Henry Merryman and Rogelio Pérez-Perdomo, *The Civil Law Tradition: An Introduction to the Legal Systems of Europe and Latin America*. 3rd ed. Stanford, CA: Stanford University Press, 2007 65.

I anticipate that a student or, even more so, a practicing lawyer might object that a study of legal culture is impractical. My response to that objection is that the profession of law is practiced by people. There is nothing more practical in the study of law than to understand those people. Understanding an Australian, Canadian, English, Irish, Indian, U.S.[15] or any other common law lawyer, who may sit across a courtroom, negotiation table, or email link from you, requires more than understanding the mechanics of the sources of law. Such an understanding also requires that a lawyer outside the United States understands how his or her counterpart was educated and trained, what methods of thought were explicitly or implicitly exercised and developed during that education and training, and what expectations a non-lawyer might have of that legal culture. Once a lawyer outside the United States understands how a U.S. lawyer thinks, then the sources of law can be researched and better understood, whether now or at some later date. The foundation of this book is, therefore, the fact that the most practical thing a non-U.S. student can learn about U.S. law is the way that the U.S. lawyer is thinking, not the words of the sources of law.

The cultural problems raised in understanding U.S. law have come to me from students and lawyers from every continent whom I have had the pleasure to know. The book has benefitted from proofreading and draft-circulation among lawyers from the United States, but also from Germany and Italy, and law students from Germany, Greece, France, Turkey, Spain, China, Switzerland, Serbia, Moldavia, Russia, Israel and Japan (as well as others) for whom English is usually not the first language. Their insights into how foreign lawyers read legal English and understand U.S. law have been extremely valuable. In addition, lawyers from India, Peru, Uruguay, Brazil, Nigeria, Cameroon and Ethiopia have provided valuable feedback and input on various ideas in the book.

The "Law as Culture" Category

As a product, if one were to place this book in an existing category of thought, it would most likely be that of the tradition of "law as culture." As such there are some differences between the treatment of what is often called "U.S. legal culture" in this book and the literature in the law-as-culture tradition.[16] First

---

[15] There are of course other common law countries and many other countries in which common law is mixed with either civil law or domestic indigenous law, such as Ghana, Nigeria, Cameroon and South Africa. Those mixed legal systems produce and are produced by mixed legal cultures.

[16] Lawrence Rosen, *Law as Culture: An Invitation*. Princeton, NJ: Princeton University Press, 2008; Naomi Mezey, "Law as Culture," 13 *Yale J.L. & Human.* (2001) 35–67; and the entire series *Law as Culture* edited by Werner Gephart, from The Käte Hamburger Center for Advanced Study in the Humanities, Bonn; Kathy Laster, *Law as Culture*. 2nd ed. Sydney: Federation Press, 2001; as well as Roger Cotterrell, "Law in Culture," 17 *Ratio Juris*, 1, (March 2004) 1–14; and Hendrik Hartog and William E. Nelson (eds.) *Law as Culture and Culture as Law: Essays in Honor of John Phillip Reid*. Madison, WI: Madison House Publishers, Inc., 2000.

is the difference understood and meant between law *as* culture and law *in* culture. The meaning of the former is that one understands the workings of law in and of itself as cultural workings, perhaps somewhat as an anthropologist would, rather than simply as detached sources of legal rules and institutions. The meaning of the latter is for lawyers to understand the role that law plays as part of the larger culture. By including this second meaning, this book includes law in culture—specifically, the culture of the United States—in addition to discussing law *as* culture. For example: "I know my rights!" exclaims the protagonist in a Hollywood movie. It is a common statement in U.S. culture. The statement is in fact so common that it is not interrogated. How does a person know his or her rights? Was it through formal education—high school classes in social studies or "civics" perhaps? Does she know her rights from having prepared for a state-sponsored citizenship test? Has this person learned what he believes to be his rights from film and television? In the United States, the answer to the question is likely to be all of the above.[17] And when a student comes to the formal study of law in order to be a lawyer, which can only happen in postgraduate education in the United States, the student believes that he already has some sense of knowing what his rights are, and proceeds with the formal study of law from that informal basis. A student who did not grow up with these domestically learned U.S. cultural pieces does not have even this informal sense, and no amount of studying the sources of law from a book will give the student that sense. And so I offer this book to the non-U.S. student to fill that gap and to remediate the lack of prior shared cultural experience, as well as to help the U.S. student to reflect on his or her own legal culture.

Does law influence the larger culture in which it is practiced, or does the larger culture influence the practice of law? The arrow of causation points in both directions.[18] Whereas we might have traditionally felt that the combination "law and culture" was a consideration of how a culture formed a particular legal system, we now must take note of how the legal system also produces or maintains aspects of the culture, sometimes with direct, intentional acts, other times with indirect unintentional acts or what one might call attitude, orientation or even ideology. This may be particularly true of U.S. culture. In his *Democracy in America*,[19] Alexis de Tocqueville claimed that the fate of the United States "depended on the moral and political leadership provided by the lawyers who inherited the responsibilities

---

[17] For a consideration of the role of law in the education of the citizen, with particular emphasis on environmental norms, see Kirk W. Junker, "'What We Could Do Is …': The Relation of Education to Legal Obligations to Protect Public Health and the Environment," 4 *Umwelt und Gesundheit Online* (2011) 18–29, www.electronic-health-journal.com/ (last accessed 19 November 2015).

[18] See e.g. Dorothy H. Bracey, *Exploring Law and Culture*. Long Grove, IL: Waveland Press, 2006. 8: "This book's underlying premise is that the relationship between law and culture is a two-way relationship."

[19] Alexis de Tocqueville, *Democracy in America*. Cambridge: Cambridge University Press, 1863.

of the abolished aristocracy."[20] One could also argue that in a common law system that, unlike that of the British, establishes a separate chief executive of the law—the president—that person ought to be one who is well versed in the law. It is thus not surprising that until 1920, all U.S. presidents had been lawyers, except for several military leaders.

A final point regarding culture is in order. Above, I noted that a U.S. student may have first acquired a sense of his rights from film or television. The role of popular culture should not be dismissed during the study and practice of law. In the United States, for example, criminal prosecutors report the phenomenon of juries acquitting criminal defendants because the state failed to produce DNA evidence or other evidence from natural science to prove simple crimes for which no scientific evidence had ever been used in the past. These jurors, when polled, report that they see such evidence made available in criminal prosecutions on television shows and in film.[21] There is a further point on popular representations to be made here. Of course it is true that U.S. popular culture is exported, even globalized for all sorts of reasons, but it is also true that when it comes to culture, the nature of an adversarial common law trial makes far more appealing drama than a univocal inquisition or administrative legal proceeding.

Using the Words "United States"

In addition to my disclaimers on the word "culture," I should explain my insistence on writing "United States" instead of the word more commonly used in everyday speech—"America." I use the term "U.S. law" to mean the law associated with one of the states or the federation of the United States of America. The name "United States of America" is especially significant for lawyers for three reasons. First, it is a plurality, not a unitary state and thus the name alone, when reflected upon, provides an orientation to the sense or meaning of U.S. federalism, which is a peculiar legal animal. Second is a related but separate idea. Within the federation known as the United States of America, the fifty separate states are called "states" because like other countries, they are in fact independent entities with the sovereign ability to raise their own taxes, arm themselves for defense, and make their own laws. Journalists, politicians and talk-show hosts say "America" but it is really inappropriate shorthand for lawyers. The "United States of America," "U.S.A.," "the U.S.A.," "United States," "the U.S." or even "the states" are all preferable because they indicate the united plurality of independent legal entities that, for limited purposes,

[20] Paul D. Carrington, *American Lawyers: Public Servants and the Development of a Nation.* Chicago, IL: American Bar Association, 2012 vi. Carrington observes that it is no coincidence that de Tocqueville, himself an aristocrat, found the lack of aristocracy in the United States to be a void in need of filling.

[21] For scholarly treatments of U.S. law in film, see Michael Asimow and Shannon Mader, *Law and Popular Culture: A Coursebook.* New York: Peter Lang, 2007; Paul Bergman and Michael Asimov, *Reel Justice: The Courtroom Goes to the Movies.* Kansas City, KS: McKeels Publishing, 2006.

constitute the federal legal entity. And third, the use of "America" can be ambiguous or even offensive. Canada, the countries of Central America and the countries of South America all are, in the geographic sense "America" as well, and as a matter of usage, it might be confusing as to whether one is or is not including them when one uses the words "America" or "American."[22] Persons in the United States might not see this, but I have been painfully reminded by those from the other Americas while in conversation with them. The points that I have just made do produce a small problem of language. It is true that one can write "American," but not "United Statesian" as an attribution. I consider this a small price to pay for getting the cultural concept right, so I shall simply use the terms "United States" or U.S. as an attribution to solve the problems.

And while I am discussing the words chosen for the title of the book, I should add a few words on the word "introduction." As an introduction through what I call the "reference frames" of history, philosophy, social studies, language and disciplinarity, I make no claim to be dispositive of any of these topics. A full, in-depth analysis of any of these topics would turn each chapter into at least a long book of its own. Instead, the goal is for the student to see how all of these reference frames interact with one another and together build a cultural construct capable of producing law in the United States.

Reference Frames

Practicing lawyers and law students far too often come to understand the law only in reference to itself, which is to say, looking through its own frame of reference. This problem is exacerbated when the law student or practicing lawyer takes that self-referential understanding to a different culture. A lawyer licensed in one of the United States works under obligation to his or her state's rules of professional responsibility. The state rules often follow the Model Rules of Professional Responsibility. Even if the lawyer remains limited to understanding law through its own reference frame, under Rule 2.1 of the Model Rules of Professional Responsibility, titled "Advisor," the following is stated:

> In representing a client, a lawyer shall exercise independent professional judgment and render candid advice. In rendering advice, a lawyer may refer not only to law but to other considerations such as *moral, economic, social* and *political* factors that may be relevant to the client's situation.[23]

---

[22] Consider, for example, such legal examples as the "Inter-American Bar Association" and the "Organization of American States," both of which include members for all of South, Central and North America.

[23] American Bar Association (A.B.A.) Model Rules of Professional Responsibility 2.1 (emphasis added). While states like California have not expressly adopted the model rule promulgated by the A.B.A., its courts have explained the obligation of its lawyers using language similar to the model rule. See e.g. *Wolfrich Corp. v. United Services Auto. Ass'n* (1st Dist. 1983) 149 Cal.App.3d 1206, 197 Cal.Rptr. 446: "Attorneys act as counsellors, and

Note the use of the word "shall." For lawyers, "shall" is always interpreted to mean "must." It is a command. A lawyer must exercise judgment and render advice, and in so doing, is invited to refer to moral, economic, social and political factors. That said, it would behoove the lawyer to be acquainted with those factors beyond the tourist level. The commentary to Rule 2.1 then states:

> Advice couched in narrow legal terms may be of little value to a client, especially where practical considerations, such as cost or effects on other people are predominant. Purely technical legal advice, therefore, can sometimes be inadequate. It is proper for a lawyer to refer to relevant moral and ethical considerations in giving advice. Although a lawyer is not a moral advisor as such, moral and ethical considerations impinge upon most legal questions and may decisively influence how the law will be applied. A client may expressly or impliedly ask the lawyer for purely technical advice. When such a request is made by a client experienced in legal matters, the lawyer may accept it at face value. When such a request is made by a client inexperienced in legal matters, however, *the lawyer's responsibility as advisor may include indicating that more may be involved than strictly legal considerations.*[24]

This American Bar Association (A.B.A.) Model Rule provokes me to a discussion of what I call "reference frames," which form the method and outline of this book. The reference frame can help students from both outside and inside the United States but is for the most part left unexamined, even in the U.S. classroom. By comparison, the objects of study such as sources and institutions of law are heavily discussed in other available books, so this book moves rather lightly through these, precisely because information is readily available elsewhere.

Most of this book's chapters are devoted to one reference frame each, but each chapter is also explicitly tied to other reference frames where appropriate. Each reference frame is a way of seeing U.S. law as a set of responses to perceived problems, which can then be studied through a variety of frames, or lenses. Reference frames are related to the notion of law as culture. Echoing the sense of the A.B.A. Model Rule mentioned above, the French jurist, Maître Pierre Lepaulle, wrote that "The significant forces that frame new law are not only legal forces, but also moral, economic, religious, etc.; in a word, all social forces, in different proportions, come into play in each social phenomenon."[25] The social forces, which I call "cultural" forces, and

---

in rendering advice to their clients may, and when appropriate should consider social, economic and even political factors as well as legal. ... Clients have a right to expect their attorneys to render complete and candid advice." (Page citations omitted.) Supporting this notion is the scientific finding through Eurobarometer research that concluded that people are more motivated by moral concerns than calculations of risk. Commentary, *Nature* 387, 845–7 (26 June 1997).

[24] A.B.A. Model Rules of Professional Conduct, Rule 2.1 Advisor – Comments 2 and 3, "Scope of Advice" (emphasis added).

[25] Pierre Lepaulle, "The Function of Comparative Law with a Critique of Sociological Jurisprudence," 35 *Harv. L. Rev.* (1922) 838, 853.

which are included as reference frames in this book are: historical (Chapter 4), social (Chapter 5), language (Chapter 6), philosophy (Chapter 7), disciplinary (Chapter 8) and mechanistic (Chapter 9). To study law through the lawyer's own lens is only one way to study law and the self-referentiality of that approach leads one down a narrow path of problems. In his critique of the enterprise of comparative law, German jurist Günter Frankenberg refers to law's self-referential problems as "legocentrism":

> By legocentricism I mean that law is treated as a given and a necessity, as the natural path to ideal, rational or optimal conflict resolutions and ultimately to a social order guaranteeing peace and harmony. Most of legal scholarship and practice centers around law—how it works or ought to work, and how it can be made to work better. Jurists—legally educated and socialized, intrigued by legal techniques, overwhelmed by the legal vision of life—think and talk and act in terms of the law.[26]

Studying a foreign legal culture is always an exercise in comparative law. Were comparative law so simple an exercise as comparing sources, it would amount to a mechanical juxtaposition that would neither give a person sufficient insight into the legal solution of conflict, nor provide sufficient understanding for making agreements that avoid conflict. To understand the law one must see it not just from the perspective of the lawyer, but from the perspective of the culture of which the law is a part. None of the reference frames seeks to provide a list of facts and call it knowledge; that would be an anathema to the spirit of the law, especially[the]common law. Common law thinking treats knowledge as a product of experience (empiricism), rather than a body of facts at which one arrives through abstract[rational] thought (rationalism). I take it as always and already the case that if the reader of this book is not a U.S. lawyer, then any consideration of the U.S. legal system will be by way of comparison, and thus ought to be conducted under the umbrella discipline of comparative law. Comparative law as a critical practice "recognizes the problems of perspective as a central and determinative element in the discourse of comparative law."[27] The reader will explore this and other problems of comparing other legal cultures to that of the United States in Chapter 2.

In treating history, social theory, philosophy and language as "reference frames" in this book, no chapter claims expertise in any of these fields any more than a practicing lawyer must claim to be expert in any of these fields in order to practice law. But, in fact, a lawyer does employ ideas from all of these fields, consciously or not, in constructing his or her representation of a client in conflict before the court and it is in that sense that the reference frames are explored.[28]

---

[26] Günter Frankenberg, "Critical Comparison, Re-Thinking Comparative Law," 26 *Harv. Int'l L. J.* (1985) 411, 445.

[27] Ibid.

[28] Here I am reminded of the Model Rule of Professional Responsibility that allows lawyers to include economic and moral advice to clients rather than just advice on the technical rules of law, as discussed above.

Finally, one might well question why I chose these reference frames and not others when discussing law and culture, when it is more common, for example, to include economics or politics. That is precisely why I did not include those reference frames. There is no shortage of extant literature on law's connection to politics or economics. An additional reason not to include either of those enterprises is that they tend to swallow the whole discussion once they enter. As a result, if one talks about the economic reference frame, the discussion too easily slips into "law and economics," an established category from which it is just a short slide to understanding law *as* economics, as does the so-called Chicago school of thought, represented most familiarly by Richard Posner.[29] Similarly, public law (a category not nearly as separate in common law as it is in civil law) is often criticized as being politics and not law, and therefore discussed *as* politics. To the non-lawyer, politics and law are either the same thing or are so interwoven that one cannot discuss one without the other. Not so in this book—I will discuss law without politics. The tendency to conflate law and politics might be because in the United States, "in numbers far disproportionate to the population, many of the nation's political leaders are lawyers."[30]

Framing Issues and Checking, Furthering and Challenging Your Understanding

Each chapter of this book begins with "Framing Issues" for the reader. The purpose of raising the issue is not simply to direct the reader to find information and call the information an answer to a question, but to use the issue as the red thread to guide one's reading through the themes of the chapter. Just as each chapter of the book begins with Framing Issues to guide a reader through the issues under consideration in that chapter, each chapter will end with questions that do one of three tasks: check, further or challenge the reader's understanding of the chapter. Questions for checking one's understanding should be answerable from having read and understood the chapter alone. Questions for furthering one's understanding are based upon what was discussed in the chapter, but then take those concepts and incline the reader to go forward with more thinking. Challenge questions are those that assume the reader has read and understood the chapter, and is now ready to think in related but new ways about the topic.

In this Preface, I hope to have explained the goal of this book to discuss legal culture as well as to have presented the method of reference "enframing."[31] The most difficult notion of legal culture—to know the "spirit" (per Harvard Dean James Barr Ames), the

---

[29] See Richard A. Posner, *Economic Analysis of Law.* 8th ed. New York: Aspen Publishing, 2010.

[30] William M. Sullivan et al., *Educating Lawyers: Preparation for the Profession of Law.* Hoboken, NJ: John Wiley and Sons, Inc., 2007 82. (Also known as the "Carnegie Foundation Report".)

[31] See Martin Heidegger, "The Question Concerning Technology," in *Basic Writings.* Ed. David Farrell Krell, trans. William Lovitt. New York: Harper & Row, 1977 325. Krell has translated Heidegger's concept regarding technology, "*das Gestell,*" as "the enframing."

"soul" (per French jurist Edouard Lambert) and as it has been "experienced" (per U.S. Supreme Court Justice Oliver Wendell Holmes, Jr.) is the theme of Chapter 1.

Literature

Auden, W. H., "Law, Like Love," in *Collected Shorter Poems, 1927–1957*. London: Faber and Faber, 1969.

Bracey, Dorothy H., *Exploring Law and Culture*. Long Grove, IL: Waveland Press, 2006.

Burke, Kenneth, *A Grammar of Motives*. Berkeley, CA: University of California Press, 1969.

Burr, Anne M. and Howard Bromberg, *U.S. Legal Practice Skills for International Law Students*. Durham, NC: Carolina Academic Press, 2014.

Carr, E. H., "History, Science, and Morality," in *What is History?* New York: Penguin, 1964 56–86.

Carrington, Paul D., *American Lawyers: Public Servants and the Development of a Nation*. Chicago, IL: American Bar Association, 2013.

Cotterrell, Roger, "Law in Culture," 17 *Ratio Juris* 1 (March 2004) 1–14.

Frankenberg, Günter, "Critical Comparison, Re-Thinking Comparative Law," 26 *Harv. Int'l L. J.* (1985) 411.

Gephart, Werner, ed. *Law as Culture* series. Bonn: The Käte Hamburger Center for Advanced Study in the Humanities. 2012–15.

Hartog, Hendrik and William E. Nelson (eds.), *Law as Culture and Culture as Law: Essays in Honor of John Phillip Reid*. Madison, WI: Madison House Publishers, Inc., 2000.

Junker, Kirk W., "'What We Could Do Is …': The Relation of Education to Legal Obligations to Protect Public Health and the Environment," 4 *Umwelt und Gesundheit Online* (2011) 18–29, www.electronic-health-journal.com/ (last accessed 19 November 2015).

Krois-Lindner, Amy and Translegal, *International Legal English: A Course for Classroom or Self-Study Use*. Cambridge: Cambridge University Press, 2006.

Laster, Kathy, *Law as Culture*. 2nd ed. Sydney: Federation Press, 2001.

Lepaulle, Pierre, "The Function of Comparative Law with a Critique of Sociological Jurisprudence," 35 *Harv. L. Rev.* (1922) 838.

McGregor, Deborah B. and Cynthia M. Adams, *The International Lawyer's Guide to Legal Analysis and Communication in the United States*. New York: Aspen Publishers, 2008.

Merryman, John Henry and Rogelio Pérez-Perdomo, *The Civil Law Tradition: An Introduction to the Legal Systems of Europe and Latin America*. 3rd ed. Stanford, CA: Stanford University Press, 2007.

Mezey, Naomi, "Law as Culture," 13 *Yale J.L. & Human.* (2001) 35–67.

Oates, Laurel Currie and Anne Enquist, "Grammar and Rhetoric for ESL Law Students," in *The Legal Writing Handbook: Analysis, Research, and Writing*. 4th ed. New York: Aspen Publishers, 2006 827–79.

Posner, Richard A., *Economic Analysis of Law*. 8th ed. New York: Aspen Publishing, 2010.

Rosen, Lawrence, *Law as Culture: An Invitation*. Princeton, NJ: Princeton University Press, 2008.

Schmidt, Siegfried J., *Kognitive Autonomie und soziale Orientierung*. Berlin: Suhrkamp, 1996.

Sullivan, William M., Anne Colby, Judith W. Wegner, Lloyd Bond and Lee S. Shulman, *Educating Lawyers: Preparation for the Profession of Law*. Hoboken, NJ: John Wiley and Sons, Inc., 2007.

de Tocqueville, Alexis, *Democracy in America*. Cambridge: University Press, 1863.

Tylor, E. B., *Primitive Culture. Researches into the Development of Mythology, Philosophy, Religion, Language, Art and Custom*. 2 vols. 1871. 7th ed. New York: Brentano's, 1924.

1

THE GOAL: KNOWING THE SOUL AND SPIRIT OF U.S. LEGAL CULTURE THROUGH THE EXPERIENCE OF THE COMMON LAW

1.1 Framing Issues

1. How might the spirit of professional legal practice in a legal culture differ from the spirit of professional legal practice in another legal culture?
2. Through what method can one learn what the spirit of legal practice is within a particular legal culture—in this case the legal culture of the United States?

In this book, a lawyer or student will have the opportunity to explore the comportment by which the U.S. lawyer approaches the law, and recognize that the process of study in the common law is not to memorize a list of norms. The common law lawyer is an advocate, and the legal process is one of partisan advocacy, not neutral inquiry. This very fact changes everything about the way in which lawyers inside the legal system use and avoid the legal system in their culture. This fact also changes the expectations that citizens have of their legal system. As U.S. Supreme Court Justice Oliver Wendell Holmes, Jr. famously said of the common law, "the life of the law has not been logic; it has been experience."[1] If this is true, the student who wishes to learn the law is confronted with a problem: One can study logic from a book or a website, but how does one study experience? This is a great challenge even to the U.S. student of law, who begins his or her study from the perspectives of general cultural experience and formal education prior to law school.[2] Although one

[1] Oliver Wendell Holmes, Jr., *The Common Law*. Boston, MA: Little Brown and Co., 1881, 1.
[2] The study of law that qualifies one to be licensed to practice law only begins in "law school" in the United States. To enter law school, one must have completed a university education in some other field of study first. At the first level of university education, called the undergraduate or bachelor program, the study of law is not possible in license-qualifying courses. Much more will be said on U.S. legal education in Chapter 5.

might expect that the experience of U.S. culture at home may be an advantage to the student of U.S. law, it could also be a hindrance to that student's self-reflection by fostering unexamined prejudices. Either way, it is of course difficult for the foreign law student who must study a legal system that claims that its life is experience, when that student does not have the shared culture from which to know that experience. This book attempts to make that sense of shared experience a bit more recognizable to the non-native by exploring various aspects of U.S. legal culture.[3] In a "post-factual"[4] age, education must teach judgment, not only facts, and I hope to enable students to recognize the basis from which the U.S. lawyer exercises judgment.

For the reader to understand the focus of this book's topic—U.S. legal culture—one can raise a simple question: How can a person predict the outcome of a conflict? In the common law system, the experience of judges and lawyers is to some extent recorded in case decisions. Those recorded experiences help to predict the outcome of conflicts with sufficiently similar facts and law. But that record, enabling the doctrine of *stare decisis* to be put into practice, provides limited help to one needing to predict a legal outcome. In addition, the individual experiences of the judge or lawyer, drawn from memory that is woven into the full texture of psychological fabric, guides him or her in daily practice. Experience is formally recognized in the system, as demonstrated in the U.S. federal judiciary, where the measure of practice experience qualifies one to be a judge, either officially through local bar association recommendations to voters, or unofficially in the cultural values expressed in voting patterns. Among the various U.S. state judiciaries, some states appoint judges and others elect them. And when judges are appointed, those who make the appointments (governors for state courts and the U.S. president for federal courts) also rely on the experience of the judicial candidate as the evidence upon which to choose.

Insofar as legal systems are designed to provide method, process and substance to conflict resolution, we ought to be able to look to the legal system to answer the question of how one can predict the outcome of a conflict. In the study of law, a student is presented with mechanical processes that, when taken together, form a type of social science by which the student can predict a conflict's resolution within a given legal system. But these mechanics do not enable the lawyer to predict with anywhere near the certainty of the natural sciences, where the physicist, chemist or engineer, using mathematical extrapolation and prediction, can send a satellite into a useful orbit, calculate the forces and materials needed for a bridge to carry

---

[3] Of course, given the nature of experience, some things one can only learn through personal experience, not through the communication of experience from others. For a thoughtful reflection on the difference between the two, see John W. Gardner, "Commencement Address Delivered at the Stanford (University) 100th Commencement Ceremony, 16 June 1991, available at http://jgc.stanford.edu/docs/JWGCentennialCommencementSpeech.pdf (last accessed 4 February 2015).

[4] For a discussion of life in the "post-factual" society, see Farhad Manjoo, *True Enough: Learning to Live in a Post-fact Society*. Malden, MA: John Wiley and Sons, 2008.

trains, or bind materials stably together in extreme temperatures and pressures. The prediction of human behavior is weak in comparison. Yet there certainly is a desire to call at least part of the legal process "predictable," and there is evidence that some prediction is possible.

Nevertheless, despite this desire and evidence, there is also much that is not predictable. Take for example the U.S. constitutional law professor who is explaining U.S. Supreme Court decision-making in which the Court develops various "tests" to determine whether the conduct in question has violated some section of the U.S. Constitution. These tests have names based upon the factors that the Court believes should be included when interpreting particular sections of the constitution. So, for example, when determining whether the federal government has expressed an interest in maintaining jurisdiction over a matter that shares jurisdiction with the states, the Court has invented the "countervailing federal interest test." Under that test, even when a state has indicated that it wishes to exercise jurisdiction over the subject matter, a court may find that the federal government has indicated that its interest in the matter is sufficiently countervailing to keep jurisdiction before the federal courts. Other tests used by the U.S. Supreme Court include those known as "the strict scrutiny test" and "the rational basis test," just to name a few. In the law school classroom, just when the student thinks that he or she sees how the court invents and applies these tests, the student reads a new case and applies what seems to be the applicable test, only to be told by the professor that the student is wrong because in this case, "the court invented a new test applicable to such facts." The novice student will cry "foul!—arbitrary decision method!" thereby insisting the entire process is not scientific because it cannot offer the predictability of the physicist. Could a legal scholar or judge—or perhaps more importantly, the parties' lawyers—have predicted this new test or new application? Maybe. Most important here is to see that the professors' sense that they *know* is not due to practices of mechanical legal analysis (more on this when we return to mechanics in Chapter 9), but due to a feel for the law, or what one might call "local legal knowledge." Used in this sense, the word "local" can mean as broad as the United States or as local as a small town, depending on the sense of cultural identity that one has. It is cultural knowledge—to be more precise, legal cultural knowledge—that is unconsciously acquired through the experience of study and practice.[5] The local person in that culture knows it without trying—maybe even unwillingly. But to understand that legal culture, this local knowledge acquired through experience is essential. In a 1991 address to the Allegheny County Bar Association, U.S. Federal District Judge Donald E. Ziegler opened by saying:

> The practice of law in Western Pennsylvania has been marked for generations by civility, restraint, mutual respect and a sense of professionalism. The

[5] Compare all the articles in the volume called "*Das sogenannte Rechtsgefühl*" ("The so-called feel of the law"), *Jahrbuch für Rechtssoziologie und Rechtstheorie*. Ed. Ernst-Joachim Lampe, Westdeutscher Verlag, 1985.

unwritten rules of professional conduct were passed from preceptors, experienced lawyers and law firms to young lawyers to preserve the traditions of the Allegheny County Bar Association.[6]

Judge Ziegler is pointing out here that even within formal civil, criminal, or ethical rules of practice, a lawyer practices discretion. The discretion may come in the form of not filing an opposing motion even if technically one can or in the form of notifying an opponent of an intended action, even though one is not required to do so. The pattern of discretion cannot be predicted from the rules themselves, but, if at all, from observation of practice in actual cases. For an outsider, this local knowledge can be studied and must be studied and acquired in order to be able to predict the resolution of the conflict. The *way* in which we might "know" the local sense of the law could be through customary practices, including customary law, or more interestingly through rule-following behavior that could not be predicted from legal rules alone.

Sometimes rule-following behavior becomes formal custom. For the Viennese philosopher, Ludwig Wittgenstein, "[t]o follow a rule is to act or make a decision in accordance with communal practice and is established as such by training and regularity of use. Wittgenstein wants to argue that rule-following is customary."[7] Rule-following, in this sense, means neither obedience to the law due to fear of punishment, nor due to a desire to follow a norm. Furthermore, rule-following in this sense is not obedience to the law due to a shared understanding of the rationality of the law as applied. Rule-following means obedience to the law as a habit without asking why. Habits provide their own psychological, social and perhaps even economic comforts and advantages. Looking forward to the historical reference frame (Chapter 4), one would see that in history, this sense of custom comfortably fits among the recognized sources of law:

> [I]t used to be said, and not long ago, that there are four sources of law: legislation, precedent, equity, and custom. In the formative era of the Western legal tradition there was not merely so much legislation or so much precedent as there came to be in later centuries. The bulk of law was derived from custom, which was viewed in the light of equity, (defined as reason and conscience). It is necessary to recognize that custom and equity are as much law as statutes and decision, if the story of the Western legal tradition is to be followed and accepted.[8]

---

[6] Donald E. Ziegler, "The Unwritten Rules of Professional Conduct," reprinted in *The Federal Legal Forum of the Western Pennsylvania Chapter of the Federal Bar Association*. Ed. Sylvia Denys. Vol. 1 (May 2003) 1–2.

[7] Jonathan Langseth, "Wittgenstein's Account of Rule Following and its Implications," 1 *Stance* (April 2008) 38.

[8] Harold J. Berman, *Law and Revolution: The Formation of the Western Legal Tradition*. London: Harvard University Press, 1983 11.

Custom has been recognized as a source of law in civil law, common law and other jurisdictions. At its base are the common elements of a set of practices that are handed down and respected by a community as norms coupled with the notion that these norms are law.

1.1.1 Spirit

There are many fine books on U.S. law that introduce their readers to the sources of law in the United States' legal system. Indeed, it would make sense for one interested in U.S. law to read one of those books, but to do so *after* reading this book, because for the foreign reader—that is, the person not born into U.S. culture—it is not the sources of law or institutions of law that are difficult to grasp, but rather something more abstract about U.S. legal thinking that seems to be foreign. In 1907, at the same time that French jurist Edouard Lambert was reporting on the new project of comparative law at the Paris Exposition, James Barr Ames, the Dean of Harvard Law School, reported to the American Bar Association that "the great law schools try less to give the knowledge of the law than to infuse in the mind of the student the 'spirit' of the common law."[9] In 1921, Roscoe Pound, who would later also be a Dean of Harvard Law School, carried the notion of "spirit" further when he published a set of lectures that he had been giving to various universities and bar associations around the country. In print, he called the volume *The Spirit of the Common Law*. He advocated that his audience of United States lawyers must learn, among other things, the "spirit" of their legal system if they are to guide the judicial administration of justice.[10] Pound's lectures reject legal formalism and instead trace common law from its feudal element to Puritanism and the law, the courts and the crown, the rights of Englishmen and the rights of man, the pioneers and the law, the philosophy of law in the nineteenth century, and finally, to judicial empiricism and legal reason. Usually identified as the founder of sociological jurisprudence, Pound wrote:

> The fashion of the time calls for a sociological legal history; for a study not merely of how legal doctrines have evolved and developed, considered only as juridical materials, but of the social causes and social effects of doctrines of the relations of legal history to social and economic history. I should be the last to deny the great importance of this feature of the program of the sociological jurist.[11]

[9] Dean Ames, 31 Reports United States' Bar Association, 1025 (1907) (as quoted in Pierre Lepaulle, "The Function of Comparative Law with a Critique of Sociological Jurisprudence," 35 *Harv. L. Rev.* 838, 857 (1922)).

[10] Roscoe Pound, *The Spirit of the Common Law*. Francistown, NH: Marshall Jones Co., 192110. See also Bernard G. Weiss, *The Spirit of Islamic Law*. Athens, GA: University of Georgia Press, 2006; Alan Watson, *The Spirit of Roman Law*, Athens, GA: University of Georgia Press, 2008 and Geoffrey MacCormack, *The Spirit of Traditional Chinese Law*. Athens, GA: University of Georgia Press, 1996.

[11] Pound, *supra* note 9 at 10.

1.1.2 Soul

The French jurist and legal comparativist Pierre Legrand reminds us that none other than Montesquieu wrote that "it is not the body of the law that I am looking for, but their [sic] soul."[12] And according to German jurist and comparative law scholar Mathias W. Reimann,[13] the need to understand foreign "mentalities" had already been emphasized by the old guard of Ernst Rabel,[14] Rudolph B. Schlesinger,[15] Konrad Zweigert[16] and René David.[17] According to the scholars Jack A. Hiller and Bernhard Grossfeld, "[l]aw is largely culture-specific. At least to a great extent it is shaped by the culture out of which it arises."[18] Hiller and Grossfeld go on to quote the Canadian legal scholars J. C. Smith and David N. Weisstub, who write that "[l]egal systems emerge from cultural contexts. … In categorizing legal systems it is important to realize at the outset that law is a seminal institution in any given culture and that, therefore, in unpacking the cultural contours of a civilization we may hope to detect relations between the world view of that culture and its concepts of law."[19] I would add here that law—even positive law—is not only related to the world view of the culture, but contributes to shaping it. This is all the more true in a pluralistic culture such as that in the United States, where law has played a culturally unifying role among generations of immigrants and their descendants from a variety of legal cultures.

1.1.3 The Spirit and the Soul of Advocacy

To get a feel for the common law in practice, especially as compared to the civil law in practice, one must remember that the common law lawyer is foremost an advocate, although he or she also remains an officer of the court. The English legal system, as well as some other common law systems, such as that of the Republic of Ireland, continue to formally divide the profession of lawyers into counselors and advocates, known as "solicitors" and "barristers" respectively. A U.S. lawyer learns advocacy in the culture in which he finds himself before ever studying law. Much of the world is familiar with popular cultural representations of the U.S. lawyer in film

---

[12] Pierre Legrand, "European Legal Systems are not Converging," 45 *Int'l & Comp. L.Q.* (1996) 52, 81.

[13] Mathias Reimann, "The Progress and Failure of Comparative Law in the Second Half of the Twentieth Century," 50 *Am. J. Comp. L.* (Fall, 2002) 671, 673, fn. 40.

[14] Ernst Rabel, "Aufgabe und Notwendigkeit der Rechtsvergleichung," in 3 *Gesammelte Aufsätze* 1 (1967) 18.

[15] Rudolf B. Schlesinger, *Comparative Law, Cases and Materials.* Brooklyn, NY: The Foundation Press, 1950, XII (quoting Roscoe Pound).

[16] Konrad Zweigert, "*Zur Methode der Rechtsvergleichung,*" 13 *Studium Generale* (1967) 193.

[17] René David, *Major Legal Systems of the World Today.* 3rd ed. Trans. J. Brierley. London: Steven & Sons, Ltd., 1985 16.

[18] Jack A. Hiller and Bernhard Grossfeld, "Comparative Legal Semiotics and the Divided Brain: Are We Producing Half-Brained Lawyers?" 50 *Am J. Comp. L.* (2002) 175, 178.

[19] J. C. Smith and David M. Weisstub, *The Western Idea of Law.* London and Toronto: Butterworths (1983) (as quoted by Hiller and Grossfeld, *supra* note 17 at 178).

and television.[20] Unless he has been exposed to the actual practice of law through friends or family members who are lawyers, or through personal conflicts in need of a lawyer, before he enters the study of law, the U.S. lawyer would also think that being a lawyer in the United States is something like the portrayal in popular media, even though we all know that popular media is not bound to actual representations of any profession, including lawyers. A law course that qualifies one for practice only begins at the postgraduate level in the United States. Therefore, to prepare for the study of law as a study in advocacy, U.S. undergraduate students are often advised by their undergraduate university to join debate teams. After a student begins the study of law, courses in advocacy at both the trial level and the appellate level are a standard part of the regular curriculum, as are moot court exercises. But perhaps most revealing is the fact that substantive areas of law are taught through the position of the parties, not the position of the court. Students are taught that there are at least two perspectives to any dispute that has made its way to court, and that they must be prepared to argue from either of those, plus from the perspectives of additional interested parties. In some exercises, they are even taught to argue one side and then immediately turn around and argue the other side, and are rewarded for their ability to argue persuasively, not for arriving at the "right" answer, reminiscent of the *dissoi logoi* taught by ancient rhetoricians. (There will be more to say about this in Chapter 6, which concerns itself with the reference frame of language.) This kind of training may appear at first blush to be an exercise in pandering, as Socrates might have accused the sophists of teaching more than two millennia ago. However, the idea behind this advocacy format is that the court is most likely to see the best possible evidence and interpretations of the law, if the parties themselves, with the aid of their lawyers, are researching and presenting the evidence and law in the way that is most advantageous to them within the rules of evidence, procedure and professional responsibility, without being directed by an individual judge to do so.[21] Throughout history, law has generally claimed that it could offer a remedy for every wrong that had actually occurred,[22] but the common law has added that it does not provide a remedy until the wrong has actually occurred. This condition means, among other things, that common law judges could not offer advisory opinions on hypothetical wrongs. The U.S. Constitution formalizes that position in Article III, Section 2, Clause 1, which has been interpreted to limit U.S. federal courts to adjudicating

[20] Thus, for example, at the University of Cologne, I recently offered a law course in popular legal culture, focusing upon U.S. film. The German, Iranian, Turkish and Japanese students in the audience knew most of the U.S. films in advance, having already seen them in their own countries.

[21] Lon L. Fuller and John D. Randall: "Professional Responsibility: Report of the Joint Conference," Joint Report to the American Bar Association, 44 *A.B.A.J.* (1958) 1159.

[22] See James Williams, "Latin maxims in English law" in *Law Magazine and Law Review*, 4th Series, xx (1895) 283–95, (as cited by Donald F. Bond, "English Legal Maxims," 921 *PMLA* (51) 4, 921–935 (December, 1936)). According to Bond, Williams points out that some of these maxims are traced to Roman law, but that others, such as *Ubi jus ibi remedium* and *Mobilia sequunter personam* are indigenous to England. *Ubi jus ibi remedium* is usually paraphrased as: "There is no wrong without a remedy," according to Bond.

only actual cases or controversies. In the spirit of the common law, with its great dependence on the facts of the case, it would not be possible for a judge ever to have sufficient facts from a hypothetical problem from which to write a concrete adjudication, particularly not one that could be useful as case precedent.

1.2 Conclusions from Experience

In Chapter 2, the student will work through some issues in the theory of comparative law. Readers of this book are of course concerned with comparing U.S. law to that of their own country. But as one reflects on what is meant by comparing "law," the reader will be prompted to think more abstractly than one does in the relatively simple mechanics of comparing sources of law. In doing so, one is brought to the question of this chapter—beyond sources of law, how does one understand the spirit or soul of law, in particular the common law of the United States? To answer this question, Roscoe Pound made the point above that the role for lawyers and their practices differs from culture to culture.

One begins to understand legal culture through history, sociology, language, philosophy, and other aspects of culture. Moreover, one begins to understand the methods of experience through which those aspects make law and law makes them. When it comes to experience in the law, the role of judges and lawyers is to say "because of these experiences, the conflict between these parties should be resolved as follows." The experience of court practice, not the rationality of legislators, is woven through the spirit of resolving conflicts in the common law. Thus, even with the simple example of recording a judge's decision-making process in conflict resolution, one can see a record being made of experience. From these many recorded experiences, one may induce a common rule of law. But more than that, one can begin to induce an attitude toward the resolution of conflicts that helps one to know the spirit and soul of the law in such a way as to enable one to predict outcomes and help parties in litigation make choices in a more nuanced way than they would simply by reading the legislation to determine the outcome.

The English judge has "in general considerable confidence in his own powers of judgment and in his own way of expressing things. One has the impression that, by and large, society regards this self-confidence as justified. The appointment of someone as High Court judge in England is still seen as a considerable vote of confidence in the powers of judgment of the person concerned."[23] Common law wisdom requires what Sir Edward Coke described as "an artificial perfection of reason, gotten by long study, observation, and experience, and not of every man's natural reason."[24] Indeed, natural reason or logic may be outweighed by experience. In the U.S. Supreme Court's opinion in the case of *Michelson v. United States*, Justice

---

[23] Sir Konrad Schiemann, "Common Law Judge to European Judge," 4 *Zeitschrift für Europäisches Privatrecht* (ZEuP) (2005) 741–9, 743.

[24] Theodor Viehweg, *Topics and Law*. Trans. W. Cole Durham. Frankfurt am Main: Peter Lang, 1993 xxviii.

Jackson, in considering that character evidence is built on the otherwise inadmissible evidence of hearsay, wrote: "Thus the law extends helpful but illogical options to a defendant. *Experience* taught a necessity that they be counterweighted with equally illogical conditions to keep the advantage from becoming an unfair and unreasonable one."[25]

Oliver Wendell Holmes, Jr. is often quoted as defining law to be experience, not rationality. This experience is the experience of the law in contact with the society it serves:

> Although social conditions, constantly changing, are the context within which law develops, it cannot validly be claimed that they are solely responsible for legal change. Ever since the legal profession developed the thinking of lawyers about the law has been the main source of change. In some historical periods lawyers' thinking about law was, it seems, totally isolated from social conditions. Thinking about law was sometimes nothing more than a game for its own sake, and law so developed as theoretically logical derivations from accepted legal propositions. ... Lawyers are not necessarily dominant in the legislative process. The thinking of lawyers, however, does affect the way statutes are interpreted [during litigation]. Lawyers describe this process with the aphorism that "The law changes with its application."[26]

Thus the common law as practiced in the courtroom involves both lawyers and the real experience of society, one case at a time, in the law-making. This courtroom practice was likely in Holmes' mind as distinguished from the legislative practice of trying to anticipate harms and catch them in a covering net when he says that law is not "mathematical theorems."[27] Holmes had himself studied Roman law as practiced in Germany, but rejected what he considered to be the metaphysical presuppositions behind the German systematic formulation.[28]

CHECK YOUR UNDERSTANDING:

1. What features of U.S. law, or even common law in general, could one say represent the "spirit" and the "soul" of the law, such that one can study them to get a feeling or sense of the way lawyers practice in that system?
2. What are the roles played by a lawyer's experience in the U.S. legal system?

---

[25] *Michelson v. United States*, 335 U.S. 469, 478–79 (1948) (emphasis added).

[26] Frederick G. Kempin, *Historical Introduction to Anglo-American Law*. St. Paul, MN: West, 1936 5–6.

[27] Keith Wilder has observed that the German law student (whom one might allow to be representative of civil law students) is like a theologian: he is considered a "good" student and is most revered when he can quote line and verse of the German Civil Code, just as a dutiful theologian could quote his holy book.

[28] Viehweg, *supra* note 23 at xxxi.

FURTHER YOUR UNDERSTANDING:

1. What features of *your own legal system* would you say represent the "spirit" and the "soul" of the law, such that one could study them to get a feeling or sense of the way lawyers practice in that system?
2. What are the roles played by a lawyer's experience in your own legal system?

Literature

Berman, Harold J., *Law and Revolution: The Formation of the Western Legal Tradition*. London: Harvard University Press, 1983.

Coquillette, Daniel, *The Anglo-American Legal Heritage*. 2nd ed. Durham, NC: Carolina Academic Press, 2004.

Hiller, Jack A. and Bernhard Grossfeld, "Comparative Legal Semiotics and the Divided Brain: Are We Producing Half-Brained Lawyers?" 50 *Am J. Comp. L.* (2002). 175.

Kempin, Frederick G., *Historical Introduction to Anglo-American Law*. St. Paul, MN: West, 1936.

Pound, Roscoe, *The Spirit of the Common Law*. Cambridge, MA: The Marshall Jones Company, 1921.

Rabel, Ernst, "Aufgabe und Notwendigkeit der Rechtsvergleichung," 3 *Gesammelte Aufsätze* (1967). 1.

Reimann, Mathias, "The Progress and Failure of Comparative Law in the Second Half of the Twentieth Century," 50 *Am. J. Comp. L.* (Fall, 2002). 671.

Viehweg, Theodor, *Topics and Law*. Trans. W. Cole Durham. Frankfurt am Main: Peter Lang, 1993.

Zweigert, Konrad, "Zur Methode der Rechtsvergleichung," 13 *Studium Generale* (1967). 193.

2

THE ALWAYS AND ALREADY COMPARATIVE NATURE OF "FOREIGN" LAW

Framing Issues

1. When one compares the legal systems of the world, what exactly should one be comparing?
2. If the purpose of comparing two (or more) particular legal systems differs from the purpose of comparing two (or more) other legal systems, should the method of comparison also differ?
3. Can one study a foreign legal system without making comparisons to one's own legal system?

2.1 Introduction

Before looking at U.S. legal culture through the various reference frames that comprise Chapters 3–9 of this book, it is important to become conscious of one's method of study. When a student or lawyer from outside the United States looks at U.S. legal culture, he will be drawn to compare U.S. legal culture to his own legal culture, even if unconsciously. That is the nature of how our innate and learned sense of comparison works. Our physical senses that locate our bodies in spatial relationships function at the same time to understand other physical objects and spaces relative to our own. When we understand the methods by which we see, hear, and smell, we can understand how it is that we construct things in space. In the same way, when we locate other legal systems, it is important to see that we have constructed them from our base abilities of comparison relative to our own legal systems. And so it is important to give serious consideration to method in comparative law study. Further, we might well be making comparisons because we must! Comparison is inherent in the study of anything determined to be the other. This is not just an observation of abstract reasoning, but a fact of our neurological functioning.[1]

There is a way—a fundamental way—in which all of the social sciences, all of the liberal arts,[2] and even most of the natural sciences are practiced through a method of comparativism. How can I make such a sweeping claim? Well, to the natural scientist, for whom there is one and only one truth about a given phenomenon, and for whom that truth is determined by nature, which the scientist cannot influence or change, one's knowingness, that is, *scientia*, is the search for that one thing. Even here, however, science historian Steve Fuller would point out that there is choice—why search for this one thing and not that one thing?[3] But for the others, the social scientists and the liberal artists, the search is readily acknowledged to be one of choices because it is the socially constructed world of the human that is under investigation. And so it is for law.

In reviewing the literature that is categorized as comparative law, one too often finds that which is presented as "legal comparison" is little more than juxtaposition, and perhaps worse, a juxtaposition limited to sources of law. An equally important point to be made is that a student or lawyer outside the United States *cannot* study U.S. law from the same cultural perspective that a native would study U.S. law in his home. Even a person raised in the United States who does not study the law as a legal specialist began his or her understanding of the law through living in the culture. Some of the things a native of any culture learns about his legal system might even be wrong, but if it is generally believed in that culture, it is a force that forms general cultural expectations among the natives and cannot be discounted. Equally important is the fact that a student of law *should* not study U.S. law as though it is just another substantive law course among the domestic substantive law courses in his own educational system. Therefore, by studying U.S. law from outside the cultural context of the United States, one studies U.S. law in a way more similar to the way in which an anthropologist would study U.S. law, rather than as a U.S. law student would study his own law. I present these reflections on comparative law in a way to solve a real problem in comparative law, and that is to introduce persons who study or practice outside the United States to U.S. law in a way that makes cultural sense, rather than through the mechanics of norms in texts. Comparative law is not simply academic musing. It will affect how a student regards his or her own law as well as other legal systems in practice.

---

[1] See e.g. *Neurobiology of Comparative Cognition*. Eds. Kesner and Olton. Hillsdale, 1992 (as cited in Bernhard Grossfeld, *Core Questions of Comparative Law*. Durham, NC: Carolina Academic Press, 2005 51).

[2] For a helpful description of the history and function of the liberal arts in the university, see Linda Ardito "The Science and Art of Music: Cultural Perspectives," in *The Philosophy Of Culture*. Vol 1. Ed. Konstantine Boudouris. Athens,: Ionia Publications, 2006. 25–34; Janet M. Atwill, *Rhetoric Reclaimed: Aristotle and the Liberal Arts Tradition*. Ithaca, NY: Cornell University Press, 1998.

[3] Steve Fuller, *Philosophy, Rhetoric and the End of Knowledge: The Coming of Science and Technology Studies*. Madison, WI: University of Wisconsin Press, 1993 *passim*.

I call this chapter "always and already comparative" for several reasons. In its purest category, this book is really an introduction to foreign law, in which the author assumes the readers are not U.S. lawyers. The extant literature and categories of literature would place such work generally under the category of comparative law. But there are some reasons why one might rightly distinguish the study of foreign law from comparative law. Two leading German scholars in the area of comparative law, Konrad Zweigert and Hein Kötz, have alleged that the "mere study of foreign law falls short of being comparative law,"[4] but I am afraid I must disagree with this statement, at least in part. Anyone who is studying something that he would call "foreign" must be doing so while standing in his own legal system. While an author of such a study may not explicitly talk of comparison, he or she is of course comparing. We can do no other when studying a foreign legal system but compare it to our own, at least initially. Successful comparative law study must bring one's comparisons to consciousness and not act as though they are not in play. The U.S. comparative law scholar, John Henry Merryman, has noted that the study of foreign law is what "most comparatists do in fact most of the time."[5] Post-modern critique would say that the evidence that an author is aware of his comparative practices is found in the preface, foreword and other marginalia. Bringing these realities to consciousness has distinct advantages:

> Once the comparatist asks herself how she came to be what she is in terms of the law (an 'individual' with 'rights' and 'duties,' a 'tenant,' 'taxpayer,' 'parent,' 'consumer,' etc.) and how she came to think as a 'legal scholar' about her own law and the other laws the way she does, notions of normality and universality begin to blur. It becomes clearer then that any vision of the foreign laws is derived from and shaped by domestic assumptions and bias.[6]

A survey of comparative law literature, both among the legal practice-oriented authors and among the legal theory-oriented authors makes two things rather clear: First, there is no agreed-upon set of practices or concepts by which one can clearly denote "comparative law," and second, despite (or because of) the lack of agreed-upon practices or concepts, many writers spend much of their comparative law studies commenting on the nature of comparative law. In the context of human

---

[4] Konrad Zweigert and Hein Kötz, *An Introduction to Comparative Law*, 3rd ed., trans. Tony Weir, Oxford University Press, 1998 [Einführung in die Rechtsvergleichung, 3e Aufl., Tübingen, J.C.B. Mohr, 1996].

[5] Mathias Reimann, *The Progress and Failure of Comparative Law in the Second Half of the Twentieth Century*, 50 AM.J.COMP.L. 671, 675 n.18 (2002) (citing John H. Merryman, *The Loneliness of a Comparative Lawyer* 4 (1999)). In that same footnote, Reimann notes that "Looking through the volumes of the *American Journal of Comparative Law*, one quickly recognizes that almost invariably, the articles about foreign law outnumber (often by a huge margin) those explicitly comparing two or more systems."

[6] Günter Frankenberg, *Critical Comparison, Re-Thinking Comparative Law*, 26 *Harv. Int'l L. J.* (1985) 411, 443.

thought, perhaps the first observation is not unique to comparative law—physics does not have a unified theory of everything, nor does medicine or psychology or any other field of study. So why do we expect one of comparative law? Perhaps it is not the brass ring we need, but just something more unified or more useful than that which we have now. Part of the reason for the lack of agreement in comparative law might well be that like medicine, law is a scholarly area of study for the purpose of knowledge production, but is also professional study for entry into its practice. Thus when someone writes from one perspective to say what law "is" in his or her culture, the author might be comparing practice in that culture to practice in another culture, but ignore or even confuse the comparison of scholarship in those two cultures.

2.2 Cognitive Status Quo

While preparing the manuscript for this book and researching ideas of comparative law, I came across some wisdom regarding the process of learning from German legal scholar, Günter Frankenberg, that is even more important as the digital information age continues. Frankenberg wrote:

> Learning itself demands a change in a person's cognitive status quo. Basic prerequisites for a cognitive transformation are that one (1) become aware of her assumptions, (2) no longer project characteristics of her own way onto the objects of her scholarly attention, and (3) decenter the personal point of view so that through the vantage the new allows her she can consider not only the new, but the truthfulness of her own assumptions. In other words, it is crucial how we select the information we are exposed to and how we relate new knowledge to settled knowledge. *Unless we assimilate* what we get to know to what we know already and accommodate what we know to what we get to know, *we merely accumulate information. The new information has to be* processed, that is, to be *integrated and contextualized* with the known to make sense to us. And what we already know has to be connected with what we get to know in order for the latter to make a difference.[7]

Thus in some important ways, much of learning is, in general, a process of comparison. Using comparative law as one's method brings the process of comparison to the fore.[8]

---

[7] *Ibid.* at 413 (emphasis added).
[8] More recently, this distinction between accumulating knowledge and changing a person's cognitive status quo, or more conventionally, wisdom, was applied to the digital arena by Farhad Manjoo in his book, *True Enough: Learning to Live in a Post-fact Society.* Malden, MA: John Wiley and Sons, 2008.

2.2.1 Why Compare? A Brief History of Comparative Law

Comparative law is usually said to have begun as a discipline in 1900, the year of the *Exposition Universelle* (World's Fair) in Paris.[9] Thus, the first one hundred years since the Paris World's Fair produced a discipline that focused almost exclusively on Western Europe and North America in its comparisons. As a result, if there were successes of comparative law in the latter half of the twentieth century, they can largely be characterized as a tool for the "Europeanization of private law."[10] One might well ask, why was criminal law or other areas of public law not part of the study? For example, when it comes to various substantive areas of legal study, in "The Treaty of Lisbon: an impact assessment, 10th report of session 2007–08," published by the European Union Committee of the British House of Lords, the authors stated that "[o]ne problem we have is that little is known about continental systems of criminal justice. It is an area that has hardly ever been studied. There are no university chairs of comparative law that specialize in comparative criminal procedure anywhere in the British Isles."[11] And when it comes to different geographic regions of the world, while one must admit that new forays in comparative law may be happening recently in Asia, "Latin America continues to be understudied and Africa is almost ignored,"[12] even by such flagship comparative law journals as the *American Journal of Comparative Law*.[13]

To understand the spirit of a type of legal thinking—such as the *spirit* of common law thinking discussed in Chapter 1, one may also need to consider concepts in the law that are not settled categories in all systems. For example, even before comparative law had a disciplinary status or a name, there were practices in various systems that one could only collectively call "a *sense* of resolving difference." The author of the 1231 *Liber Augustalis*, a codification of the law of the Kingdom of Sicily, was:

> moved by the *spirit* of scholasticism that informed the intellectual life of the age to resolve differences within the existing legal tradition of the *regno* and to distill his legal knowledge and that of his associates, probably practical men of the courts, into a unified body of law.[14]

---

[9] K. Zweigert and H. Kötz, *An Introduction to Comparative Law*. Trans. Tony Weir. 3rd ed. Oxford: Oxford University Press, 1998 2.

[10] Mathias Reimann, "The Progress and Failure of Comparative Law in the Second Half of the Twentieth Century," 50 *Am. J. Comp. L.* (Fall, 2002) 671.

[11] House of Lords, European Union Committee, "The Treaty of Lisbon: An Impact Assessment, 10th Report of Session 2007–08. London: Stationery Office, 2008. E-131.

[12] Reimann, *supra* note 8 at 674.

[13] One count of articles published from 1952 to 1997 of that journal contained 41.12% about Europe, 8.6% about Asia and only 1.79% about Africa, as reported by Frank K. Upham, "The Place of Japanese Studies in American Comparative Law," 639 *Utah L. Rev* (1997) 641 (as reported by Reimann, *supra* note 8 at 674, fn. 12).

[14] James M. Powell, ed. and trans. *The Liber Augustalis or Constitutions of Melfi, Promulgated by the Emperor Frederick II for the Kingdom of Sicily in 1231*. Syracuse, N.Y.: Syracuse University

Even within comparative law, understood in its most concrete sense, in the century or so that it has been researched and practiced as such, its goals and theories have changed. Early comparative law, conceptualized at the Paris Exposition and reported by Edouard Lambert, had the noble, if Eurocentric aim to "eliminate differences." Even after the First World War, French jurist Pierre Lepaulle, *avocat* at Paris the Court of Appeal, while writing in the *Harvard Law Review*, remained optimistic regarding the abilities of comparative law: "divergences in laws cause divergences that generate unconsciously, bit by bit these misunderstandings and conflicts among nations which end with blood and desolation."[15] The second of two Eurocentric world wars may have been enough to convince comparatists to rethink their aims, however. After the Second World War, lesser aims that were more commercial in nature began to take hold. This change of focus is important to note because one must remain conscious of one's stated focus and goal in any comparative law enterprise. With every new "crisis" in the European Union people would ask José Manuel Barroso, who served as European Commission President for ten years, whether the E.U. was successful. He consistently answered without hesitation that it was, and equally as quickly emphasized that Europe has not had a world war since the E.U. began. Barroso remained conscious of the original stated focus and goal of the union. A similar though lesser claim could be made about the League of Nations and its successor, the United Nations.

A standard work in the field of comparative law today remains that of Konrad Zweigert and Hein Kötz, simply entitled *An Introduction to Comparative Law*.[16] The book has received such a wide readership that it would not be an exaggeration to refer to it as the orthodoxy of comparative law. In Part I, the authors lay out what they call "general considerations," which include a discussion of the concept of comparative law, the functions and aims of comparative law and the history of comparative law. These various categories are not wholly discrete, however. To discuss the concept of comparative law, for instance, means to look at when and why it came into being as a separate discipline of its own. And here we learn that since the great Paris Exposition, at the height of the world's love affair with industrial progress, it was thought by Edouard Lambert and the others present that it was not only possible to distill a world private legal system from comparing all those existing already, but that it was desirable to do so. The optimism of that purpose eroded with the passage of time during which a world system was not forthcoming, soured by the discordance of two world wars and a lengthy cold war among superpower

Press, 1971 xxi. (as quoted by Harold J. Berman, *Law and Revolution: The Formation of the Western Legal Tradition*. London: Harvard University Press, 1983, 427).

[15] Pierre Lepaulle, "The Function of Comparative Law with a Critique of Sociological Jurisprudence," 35 *Harv. L. Rev.* (1922) 838, 857.

[16] Zweigert and Kötz, *supra* note 7. The treatise was translated by the late Tony Weir from the original *Einführung in der Rechtsvergleichung*. 3rd ed. C.H. Beck, 1995. In the preface to the third edition of the English language translation, Hein Kötz generously noted that in this case, "Thanks to the pith, poise and precision there are places where it might be thought to read better than the text in German." *Ibid.* at vi.

states.[17] Nevertheless, the orthodox approach established by Zweigert and Kötz does provide a replicable method, known as "functionalism," which one might employ as a social scientific tool to achieve respectable comparisons.

Social unrest in much of the world in the 1960s made its way to comparative law as well, eventually bringing such thinking as the "critical legal studies" movement in the United States. This movement applied social thinking and post-modern cultural theory to the law with the expressed aim of expanding the scope of comparative law to include marginalized and repressed persons' legal cultures. Now, still near the beginning of a new century, there is considerable evidence to conclude that comparative law has reached a new era. Mathias Reimann avers that "comparative law has moved way beyond ... relatively rudimentary models in at least three regards."[18] First, according to Reimann, we understand that categories and classifications are not exact, but rather are approximations of reality. In addition, we now recognize that legal traditions are dynamic, rather than static or isolated systems. Finally, and related to the second point, we now recognize that part of the dynamic process of legal traditions is that they interact with other legal families, traditions, and cultures.[19]

The concept of comparative law is often assumed to be understood, and that assumption entices us to jump directly to questions of "how" we go about comparing, right from the very start, just as we might get new software and think we know what software is, so just tell us how to use it. Before we can answer the question of *how* to compare, we must be conscious of *why* we are making a comparison in the first place.[20] This short, almost childlike question—"why?"—seems to be the most powerful source of disgruntlement among those who propose to compare. There are several common, distinct and concrete reasons why we might wish to compare. A first example comes from the time not long after the recognition of comparative law as a discipline, when Pierre Lepaulle wrote:

> If I may state a personal experience, I never completely understood French law before coming to the United States and studying another system. History of law seems inadequate to give the student this sense of relativity, because in

---

[17] Although it should be noted that as recently as 1989, physicist Werner Heisenberg still wrote: "If one looks around in history as to what great capacities human societies hold, next to the primitive same-race feelings that are prevalent already in the animal kingdom, is the shared language. But in addition to these strengths are two more still, which are stronger and can bring together even peoples of different races and languages: a common faith and, strongest of all, a common law." Werner Heisenberg, *Ordnung und Wirklichkeit*. Munich, 1989. 152 (as cited in Grossfeld, *supra* note 1 at 232).

[18] Reimann, *supra* note 8 at 676.

[19] *Ibid.* at 677–8.

[20] The readers of this book are most likely studying foreign law by choice, not because they have been forcibly exiled. Nevertheless, there have been such lawyers in forced exile in history who have shed great light on what it means to enter a foreign legal culture. For them, one could answer the question by saying "because I must—I have been forced out of my native legal system." See Bernhard Grossfeld and Peter Winship, "The Law Professor Refugee," 18 *Syracuse J. Intern. L. & Comm.* (1992) 3 and Kyle Graham, "The Refugee Jurist and American Law Schools," 1933–1944, 50 *Am. J. Comp. L.* (2002) 777.

history we often deal with forces which are not yet dead, which still unconsciously bend the mind of the student in a certain direction. To see things in
a true light, we must see them from a certain distance, as strangers, which is
impossible when we study any phenomena of our own country. This is why
comparative law should be one of the necessary elements in the training of all
those who are to shape the law for societies. ...[21]

From my own personal experience, I fully agree with Lepaulle; I better understand
U.S. law from having had the opportunities to have lived and worked in other countries.

Frankenberg asserts that "[t]he ultimate aims of comparative law [are]—to reform
and improve the laws, to further justice and to better the lot of mankind."[22] But
prior to all such intentional goals are the more pedestrian practices of comparison,
even in the law. There are conscious and unconscious comparisons. Many human
comparisons are done in unconscious ways so as to make decisions from choice, as
for example whether one hurries when crossing the street or whether one smiles
at another person when passing. Some human comparisons are done in conscious
ways and also serve to help make choices, for example everyday choices such as
when and what to eat for lunch or very big commitments like whether to become
a lawyer. But not all of comparison is done to make a choice. Why might one compare phenomena within the law?

According to legal scholars René David and John E. C. Brierley, by 1978 the
utility of comparative law could be analyzed under three complete headings, which
in some ways, were built upon Lepaulle's 1922 observation. Comparative law:

is useful in historical and philosophical legal research; it is important in order to
understand better, and to improve, one's national law; and it assists in the pro-
motion of the understanding of foreign peoples, and thereby contributes to the
creation of a context favorable to the development of international relations.[23]

Most students of the law go on to be practicing lawyers, and most of those in their
own domestic (or "national") system. Therefore I would add a variation to the
standard point made by David and Brierley for the practicing lawyer. Within the
United States, lawyers are often exposed to the law of different U.S. states. It is often
the case that from his or her observation of practice in other states, a practicing
U.S. lawyer may change and improve his or her own practice.

---

[21] Pierre Lepaulle, *supra* note 13 at 858.

[22] Frankenberg, *supra* note 4 at 412–13 (citing Zweigert and Kötz, *supra* note 7 at 12–14
and 19–23); André Tunc, "La contribution possible des études juridiques comparatives
à une meilleure compréhension entre nations," 16 *Revue internationale de droit compare*
[*R.I.D.C.*] (1964) 47; André Tunc, *Comparative Law, Peace and Justice in the Century*. 3rd ed.
Leiden: A. Mehren and J. Hazard, 1961 80; Ferdinand F. Stone, "The End to be Served by
Comparative Law," 25 *Tul. L. Rev.* (1951) 325; René David, "The Study of Foreign Law as
a Contribution towards International Understanding," 2 *Int'l Soc. Scie. Bull.* (1950) 5; H. E.
Yntema, "Comparative Law and Humanism," 7 *Am. J. Comp. L.* (1958) 493.

[23] R. David and J. Brierley, *Major Legal Systems in the World Today*. 2nd ed. London: Steven and
Sons, 1978 4 (emphasis added).

That leads me to another reason one would wish to conduct comparison. Frankenberg makes a point closer to the cultural focus of this book that also places the utility of the comparative work in the domestic practice of law. "To cope with ethnocentrism we have to analyze and unravel the cultural ties that bind us to the domestic legal regime."[24] Frankenberg then suggests, in a manner consistent with postmodern literary theory, that the comparatist conduct is the practical task of focusing on the marginalia of legal texts such as forewords and prefaces. In doing so, says Frankenberg, one can gain a realist's insight into the fact that the comparatist author is inspired and organized by his or her legal education, exposure to legal cultures, conference participation, and professional and personal travel experiences. According to Frankenberg, marginal remarks indicate how and *why* what an author purports to be an objective discovery and comparison of the compared legal culture can be undercut by the comparatist's own assumptions.[25]

One might also make comparison in order to develop the realization that one's observations must be from some perspective or other. All observations are made from some point of view—one cannot be standing[26] nowhere or everywhere, so we are best advised to become conscious of where we stand when we make our observations.[27] And where we stand as comparative lawyers or law students is usually within our own legal culture, from the perspective of looking out upon other legal cultures.[28] Once we realize that we must be making our observations from some point of view, we are then better positioned to examine and understand what our own point of view might be. As Goethe famously said: "*Wer keine fremde Sprache spricht, weiß von seiner eigenen nicht.*"[29] So we might make comparisons so as to learn something of our own legal culture.

Also within the realm of comparative legal practices, one might want to compare in order to create private law choices for a client.[30] Comparison might also broaden one's own creativity: new ideas about possible remedies, norms, causes of action or procedures might come up. And the final reason that might drive one to compare

---

[24] Frankenberg, *supra* note 4 at 443, citation omitted.

[25] *Ibid.*

[26] Kenneth Burke provides an excellent etymology of the related set of words that he calls the "stance family," including a comparison of the Greek "*hypostasis*," German "*verstehen*" and English "substance," while working his way from standing to understanding. Kenneth Burke, *Grammar of Motives*. Berkeley and Los Angeles, CA: University of California Press, 1969 22–4.

[27] Even the study of comparative law itself is from some cultural position. Here, we are presenting comparative law in order to study U.S. legal culture, and in addition, are doing so from the U.S. perspective. See, for example, Ugo A. Matei, Teemu Ruskola and Antonio Gidi, *Schlesinger's Comparative Law: Cases-Text-Materials*. 7th ed. New York: Thomson Reuters. 2009.

[28] Penelope Pether, "Language," in Austin Sarat et al. (eds.), *Law and the Humanities*. Cambridge: Cambridge University Press, 2014.

[29] J. W. von Goethe, *Maximen und Reflexionen, Aus Kunst und Altertum*. 1821. Translated as: "Whoever speaks no foreign languages, knows nothing of his own."

[30] See James Gordley and Arthur Taylor von Mehren, *An Introduction to the Comparative Study of Private Law*. Cambridge: Cambridge University Press, 2009.

is that exercising intelligent critical comparison helps lawyers to work in a more informed manner with clients, colleagues or adversaries from different legal cultures. By understanding the orientation, attitude or perspective of a foreign lawyer, one is better able to work with him or against him in the representation of a client to resolve a conflict.

Regardless of the reason why one compares parts or whole legal systems, one must proceed methodically in order to compare intelligently. If one fails to proceed methodically, one has made a weak comparison. Austrian legal historian Paul Koschaker warns us that "bad comparative law is worse than none."[31] For example, bad comparative law might simply look to compare texts (and often at least one country's texts are only readable by the comparativist in translation). Texts alone, especially statutes, are not sufficiently representative of how legal systems resolve conflict. European Court of Justice Judge David Edwards has noted:

> [c]odes and treatises on the law of evidence are, at best, unreliable guides. Superficially, the rules of two systems may appear very similar. For example, some aspects of Dutch procedures bear a striking resemblance to recent proposals for new procedures in the Scottish courts. Yet we can be certain that if the Scottish proposals were to be implemented, the Scottish courts would still work very differently from the Dutch courts.[32]

Mathias Reimann has renewed the 1978 list constructed by David and Brierley, by summarizing the reasons to compare that are advocated by some of the most influential authors in comparative law—Mary Ann Glendon, John Henry Merryman, Max Rheinstein, Rudolph Schlesinger, as well as Zweigert and Kötz—as follows:

1. Foreign models may improve domestic law.
2. Legal comparison promotes international unification or at least harmonization.
3. Legal comparison reveals the common core of all law.
4. Legal comparison teaches basic skills of international legal practice.
5. Legal comparison provides an overview of law on a worldwide scale by introducing the major legal families; or
6. It at least provides knowledge of foreign legal families.
7. Legal comparison familiarizes students with foreign rules, concepts, and approaches and thereby facilitates communication with foreign lawyers.
8. By forcing students to compare foreign law with their own, it forces them to be critical of their own system.

---

[31] Grossfeld, *supra* note 1 at 14 (quoting Paul Koschaker, "Was vermag die vergleichende Rechtswissenschaft zur Indogermanenfrage beizusteuern?", in Helmuth Arntz, ed. *Germanen und Indogermanen*, Festschrift für Herman Hirt, Heidelberg (1936) 149–50).

[32] David Edwards, "Fact-Finding: A British Perspective," in D. L. Carey Miller and Paul R. Beaumont (eds.), *The Option of Litigating in Europe*. London: United Kingdom Committee of Comparative Law, 1993 44 (as quoted in Jeremy Lever, "Why Procedure is More Important than Substantive Law," 48 *Int'l & Comp. L. Q.* (April 1999) 285, 301).

9. Legal comparison helps students to understand law as a general phenomenon, in particular its contingency on history, society, politics, and economics.

10. By providing critical perspectives and explaining alternatives, legal comparison fosters tolerance toward other legal cultures and thus overcomes parochial attitudes.[33]

Only once we have reflected upon the fact that we must ask why we are comparing, and found that there are a number of different reasons to do so, are we in the proper position to consider what the methods might be for conducting the comparison.

2.2.2 Comparative Method

When it comes to the methods of comparative law, one may begin rather simply. Consider this: you are reading this text in the English language and it is possible that English is not your first language. Remember the process of learning English (or any second or third language.) It was mechanical—one learns the structure of grammar and then inserts as much vocabulary as one can memorize. But that is not how we learn our native language. The same is true for law. We learn our own legal systems first by living in them as a part of the whole culture, not by studying them as a specialist. In addition, when learning second languages, we do so by comparison to our own first language. When learning legal systems after learning our own, we do so by comparison to our own. Furthermore, we accomplish this practice of comparison by *creating*—not finding—relationships that we say are equal. In the same way that we cannot learn a second language in the way that we learned our mother tongue (with the exception of course of those who have learned a second language at an early age and are truly bilingual), we must at least become conscious of these realities of learning by translation, and not fool ourselves into believing that we can learn another culture, even a legal culture, simply by reading the same sources of law that a native reads. So when we learn a second legal system, it is through the non-native practice of establishing something like a grammar and adding vocabulary to it. And although all grammars operate as rules of language structure, the particular rules themselves differ. For example, how does one make sense of declined pronouns if one's own language has pronouns that remain the same, regardless of the case? How does one make sense of abstractions such as "yes" and "no" if one's own language does not have single words used to affirm or deny something?

Some areas of the law, such as commercial law, are less culturally connected than others.[34] These areas of the law therefore tend to be more easily transferred from legal system to legal system and may be understood by lawyers in multiple cultures without the need for translation or immersion in another culture. But other areas of the

---

[33] Mathias Reimann, "The End of Comparative Law as an Autonomous Subject," 11 *Tul. Eur. & Civ. L.F.* (1996) 49, 54.

[34] Gordley and von Mehren, *supra* note 28.

law are more attached to a culture—constitutional law,[35] family law or criminal law,[36] for example. These more culturally dependent areas cannot so easily be understood without translation or immersion. In short, the study of any foreign legal system is *not* the same process as the study of one's own system. Differences include history, language, social structures, politics and philosophy; things that a person learns in his own culture—formally or informally—before even beginning to study a foreign legal culture. In subsequent chapters, the institutions, persons and sources of U.S. law will be studied through these reference frames using a comparative method.

The method of comparing "law" has developed into an entire discipline of its own. As with other comparisons, when comparing legal systems, one must distinguish uncritical comparison from critical comparison. (Here, I am using the word "critical" in its original Greek denotation—*kritiki* means judgment.) Judgment does not inherently carry a negative connotation, as popular usage of the term might suggest. The study of any foreign law is inherently a study carried on through comparative law. Therefore, in order to properly study U.S. law as foreign law, one must understand critical comparison and apply it through the scholarly study of comparative law. Comparativism is the formal study of comparison rather than the more common informal or even unconscious practice of comparing.

2.2.3 Functionality

The discipline of comparative law is a little more than a century old. In that century the discipline has moved through phases of focus, from formalism to functionality to critical legal theory. Each focus managed to correct problems but at the same time created some of its own problems. Formalism thought it appropriate only to compare things with the same legal form, such as statutes with statutes and constitutional courts with constitutional courts. Formalism treats foreign law as a topic of domestic law; that is to say, just another course in a student's domestic curriculum, like taxation or wills and estates, such that he then uncritically and unreflectively takes what he knows already of law, and plugs in foreign law as though it were just new rules within his own system. "Formalism proposes a narrow conception of law that, in a comparative perspective, is informed by the domestic legal culture and

---

[35] See e.g. Michel Rosenfeld et al., *Comparative Constitutionalism.* 2nd ed. St. Paul, MN: West, 2010; Vicki Jackson and Mark Tushnet, *Comparative Constitutional Law.* 2nd ed., New York: Foundation Press, 2006.

[36] Discussions with practicing professional German lawyers who have obtained their masters degrees in law (usually the LL.M degree) have indicated that they chose their curricula based upon cultural interest—hence family law and criminal law—and not just practical, commercial interest. After all, is legal education not intended to be a complete education, not just formal training, or in German concepts of educational reformer, Alexander von Humboldt: Should legal education be *Bildung* and not just *Ausbildung*? See for example Thomas Nipperdey, *Deutsche Geschichte 1800–1866: Bürgerwelt und starker Staat.* Vol. I. Munich: C.H. Beck, 1994. 58.

then projected onto what in other historical or social contexts is, looks like or may be taken as law."[37]

Functionality overcame that limitation by pointing out that different legal cultures use different forms of legal sources or institutions to accomplish the same function; therefore the function and not the form should be compared. However, functionalism also has its problems. For example, functionalism focuses far too often only upon sources of law as its objects of study, and not upon institutions or persons. As a consequence, were one to ask a functionalist what to compare, the answer would most often relate to the function of different sources of law. Private practitioners, who wish to represent the interests of their clients, are likely to use the functionality approach. "Functionality becomes the pivotal methodological principle determining the choice of laws to compare, the scope of the undertaking, the creation of a system of comparative law, and the evaluation of findings."[38] Other related areas of private comparative law follow the functionalist approach. So, for example, legal origins scholarship—which is "produced primarily by economists, not legal scholars—has a close affinity with functionalist comparative law."[39]

Public law might make use of functionalism as well, as with, for example, the function of a criminal sentence. I once worked for an appellate judge who, prior to being an appellate judge, had been a judge on a criminal trial court bench. Although he was known as being somewhat conservative as a criminal court judge, he once participated in an exchange with China back in the early 1980s, and learned about the Chinese criminal sentencing theory of the time. He believed that Chinese sentencing dichotomized criminals, rather than sentencing them over a continuum that ranged from a simple fine to life imprisonment (or even death). The theory behind the dichotomy was that if a criminal had made a mistake but might otherwise be a contributing member of society, he should not be exposed to prison life for too long. On the other hand, if a criminal was incorrigible, lock the door and throw away the key. So the medium-term sentences were eliminated. Given that judges in the jurisdiction that my judge sat in, like most jurisdictions, could exercise discretion in setting the duration of a sentence, the exposure to another system could well have led to a change in the sentences he issued. He certainly talked as though it had.

Further criticism comes from several directions against functionalism. Already back in 1922, long before functionalism was introduced, Pierre Lepaulle made the case that "comparison restricted to *one* legal phenomenon in two countries is unscientific and misleading. A legal system is a unity, the whole of which expresses itself in each part; the same blood runs in the whole organism. Hence each part must necessarily be seen in its relation to the whole."[40] It would be difficult to imagine comparing all parts of two or more legal systems simultaneously. But it is a good

---

[37] Frankenberg, *supra* note 4 at 422.
[38] *Ibid.* at 436.
[39] Christopher A. Whytock, "Legal Origins, Functionalism, and the Future of Comparative Law," *BYU L. Rev.* (2009) 1879, 1880.
[40] Pierre Lepaulle, *supra* note 13 at 853.

start to first ask what relationship to the whole any piece of that same legal system has, rather than looking only at that part in isolation. As a corrective measure, rather than compare sources of law or single legal phenomenon, one could conceivably compare the spirit of the law. For example, in his assessment of legal writing, Sir Konrad Schiemann, a judge on the European Court of Justice (E.C.J.), and formerly on the High Court in England, made a subtle but scientifically important conclusion. "All that said, it seems to me that the E.C.J.'s practices have the advantage over English practices—at any event for the task that this court has to fulfill. I have the feeling that there is a genuine attempt to arrive at the best common solution that the brains of the court can reach."[41]

An additional criticism of functionalism is that it favors the comparativist's own system. Returning to what Zweigert and Kötz explicitly present, it is precisely in the functionality principle that one sees a "hometown bias" in their approach. While it might seem beyond most students' confidence to critique published scholarly books, if we apply an important lesson from comparative law itself to Zweigert and Kötz, we can legitimately examine the perspective from which they see the discipline of comparative law. Part II of their work is divided into contracts, unjust enrichment and torts. Most German readers will readily recognize these divisions as being borrowed directly from the German Civil Code, the *Bürgerliches Gesetzbuch*. Why, for example, is a newer area of the law, such as environmental law not included?[42] Thus in attempting to provide a science and a method for comparative law that is above or beyond any one system, even the powerful work of Zweigert and Kötz demonstrates that it is impossible to compare without having a point of perspective from which one compares. We cannot step out of the hermeneutic circle, but rather can at best become conscious that we are in the circle, that we see the world from our place in the circle, and that we try to make observations of other things in the circle knowing that we are only one perspective.[43] Thus a common law lawyer writing on comparativism might need to invite a civil law lawyer to present the picture from civil law. Who might we invite to speak about the civil law who is at home in the civil law?[44]

Bias is not always obvious. Reimann, a well-respected comparatist trained in Germany and teaching in the United States, after surveying comparative law literature concludes that "[t]he problem is that these books, articles, ideas, and critiques do not add up to a sum that is larger than its parts. Instead, they constitute a potpourri of disparate elements that coexist side-by-side but rarely relate to any overarching themes."[45] If one thinks for a moment about the distinction in the ways

---

[41] Sir Konrad Schiemann, "From Common Law Judge to European Judge," 4 *Zeitschrift für Europäisches Privatrecht* (ZEuP) (2005) 741–9, 747.

[42] See e.g. Nicholas Robinson, ed. *Comparative Environmental Law and Regulation*. Dobbs Ferry, NY: Oceana Publications, 2006.

[43] See Rainer Hegenbarth, *Juristische Hermeneutik und linguistische Pragmatik*. Königstein im Taunus: Athenaeum, 1982.

[44] See Klaus Adomeit, "Was ist Recht"? in Klaus Adomeit and Susanne Hähnchen, *Rechtstheorie für Studenten*. 6th ed. Heidelberg: C.F. Müller, 2011 5.

[45] Reimann, *supra* note 8 at 686.

that civil lawyers proceed compared to common law lawyers, one might recognize the need to deduce from an overarching theme or a covering law, when common law lawyers would be satisfied to solve problems as they arise, finding a remedy for the wrongs that arise, but not creating remedies for which there is no wrong. So it is possible that Reimann's dissatisfaction is due to his civil tradition expectations of the comparative enterprise.

Weak comparisons begin with the assumption that what one already does is natural or normal, and if another person or culture does things differently, then that other person or culture is therefore unnatural or abnormal. This seems to be a rather common error among non-comparativists and even among non-comparativist non-lawyers, such as the German television broadcaster who phoned me when Dominique Strauss-Kahn was arrested in New York and demanded to know why, what he called "American" law allowed Mr. Strauss-Kahn to be shown on television in handcuffs and why were there allowed to be cameras in the courtroom? In the broadcaster's own culture, both were prohibited, which to his thinking made the prohibitions either natural or normal. I told him that I could explain why the U.S. Constitution permitted them, and asked whether he could explain why German law prohibited them. He could not, but it nevertheless seemed to be normal to him that these things were prohibited, so one need not have asked why:

> The similarities that surface in the course of such comparisons are mirror images of the categories of the conception of law in the comparatist's own culture. Ambiguities are defined away or adjusted to fit the model; thus the 'home' law is positioned as natural, normal, standard.[46]

Consequently, rather than look for an introduction to comparative law written from our own perspective, so as comfortably to ignore the fact that we are viewing the phenomenon from only one perspective, we can benefit from the perspectives of others who react to and analyze the orthodoxy presented by Zweigert and Kötz. At the same time, we must remain observant of the functionality principle, even while criticizing it. While functionalism may have problems and faults, the fact remains that if we want to compare legal traditions, there must be something we are comparing, and for the comparison to be worthwhile, the things compared should in some way be justifiably comparable. But as Reimann points out, whereas Professor James Gordley, for example, would compare black-letter law and say civil and common law cultures are converging, Pierre Legrand would compare the mentalities of the lawyers in those systems and say there is no convergence.[47] Judge Schiemann's

---

[46] Frankenberg, *supra* note 4 at 423. In the spirit of the critical legal studies, which features self-reflexive thinking, one can turn this critique back on Frankenberg and note that he too is too much wed to continental civil law when he says, "[i]n order to find, compare and evaluate these effects, the comparatist has to move back and forth between texts and their application." *Ibid.* Such a characterization of law omits both customary law and the oral tradition, and assumes that at its foundation, law is a text.

[47] Reimann, *supra* note 8 at 690, fn. 109.

position is evidence in support of Gordley's position at the level of European practice, if one allows the E.C.J. to be considered a civil court.

2.2.4 How to Compare

After having seen the issues concerned with the questions of why we compare and what we compare, we finally arrive at the issue of how we compare. As we have learned, how we compare is a function of why we compare. When addressing how one compares, again one needs to distinguish between unconscious and conscious comparison. In order to compare, one must acknowledge a commonality of reference frames. Consider the English simile that admonishes one not to compare X with Y because "that would be like comparing apples with oranges." However, one might want to ask, who has created the categories from which the two things were compared, why the categories are set, why focus upon colors—a category that would, for example, distinguish an apple from an orange, and not the category of shapes, or even the category of "fruit," both of which would put an apple and an orange in the same category. Further, one should inquire whether the categories are set consciously, how the categories are set and whether they may be intentionally changed. In this text, for example, the reference frames are being set by the author in an attempt to put law in cultural types of frames so that indeed one may cross cultures, in an effort to understand what is French about French law, Japanese about Japanese law, or in this case, American about U.S. law. But if the purpose was different, then the reference frames would change according to the different purpose. Because we are insisting that law is a cultural phenomenon, we are borrowing reference frames from cultural anthropology through which to compare U.S. law to other law, generalized as "civil law." German law is often used to represent civil law because of the relatively large size of Germany and its historical influence on the civil codes of other countries in Africa, Asia and Europe.

Professor Bernhard Grossfeld goes so far as to say that the notion of "comparative law" itself, therefore, is European and to get a step removed from it in an attempt to have a broader basis from which to conduct comparison, one should speak instead of a "comparison of orders."[48] Therefore, Grossfeld says that he only examines "how the environment and a view of reality guided by images and signs (world 'view;' world 'perception;' even better, world 'experience') mark legal cultures and legal institutions—and what that means for comparative law."[49]

Nevertheless, if one is to attempt this process, it is Zweigert and Kötz who systematically lay out a method for how one does it. Behind the Zwiegert-Kötz method is a presumption, however—the *praesumptio similitudinis*—that asserts that if one has inserted oneself into the foreign surroundings, one will recognize that people share a human nature with one another, and have a common core of experience

---

[48] Grossfeld, *supra* note 1 at 10.
[49] *Ibid.* at 13.

and cognition.[50] The first step in the method provided by Zweigert and Kötz is to lay out the basics of the systems being compared. In their text, they follow their own prescription and first turn to presenting a sketch from public law of the legal families of the world: The Romanistic Legal Family, The Germanic Legal Family, The Anglo-American Legal Family, The Nordic Legal Family, Law in the Far East, and Religious Legal Systems. It is only in the second step that they present their signature move—not to compare the norms from one legal system to another, but rather to compare the *functions* of various legal tools to achieve the norms. This is where the principle of functionality becomes the defining moment in the Zweigert and Kötz system. Once one has laid out the basics and compared the functions, it remains for the comparatist to give meaning to the functions that one has compared. The creation of meaning is accomplished in many different disciplines, including sociology, anthropology, psychology, theology, literature and linguistics. The creation of meaning from a text is the focus of a subset of these disciplines. For the purposes of this book, the reader will explore the creation of meaning from a text through the language reference frame in Chapter 6.

2.2.5 What Comparative Law Is Not

Matthias Reimann has observed that "outside of a small hard core, most of those engaged in comparative work of one sort or another do not even think of themselves (primarily) as comparative lawyers but mainly as Asia specialists, Russian law scholars, constitutional lawyers with comparative interests, etc."[51] I would add that if these scholars and lawyers are specializing in legal cultures other than their own, they must be doing so by way of comparison with their own legal culture. One might respond to my assertion by saying that one is not a legal scholar, but rather an anthropologist when looking at the foreign legal system, so that one is not in fact necessarily comparing the foreign system with one's own. That response fails to recognize that even before one is a lawyer or scholar in one's own legal system, he is a citizen, and therefore always and already begins from a citizen's understanding of the law in his own system.

Indeed my own informal survey found that among many well-known scholars, their institutions list their areas of research as including comparative law, but a review of the titles they publish does not support that moniker. Instead, the titles usually indicate that the scholar is active in one or more foreign languages and one or more foreign legal systems that practice law in that language, but nowhere do these entries or titles talk about "comparison" per se. To underscore the point that comparison is a set of practices and a method, and does not just happen in some obvious way, it would be helpful to call this scholarship something other than comparative law,

---

[50] Konrad Zweigert, "Die praesumptio similitudinis als Grundsatzvermutung rechtsvergleichender Methode," in Mario Rotondi, ed. *Inchiesta di diritto comparato—Scopi e Metodi di Diritto Comparato volume 7: L'abuso di diritto*. Palermo: CEDAM, 1979 735.

[51] Reimann, *supra* note 8 at 687.

such as "foreign law," where persons trained in one tradition and language report on other traditions and language to persons for whom that is foreign.

Comparative law is inherently interdisciplinary. "When comparatists go beyond blackletter rules and consider the historical background and social realities, or the political and economic environments, they need to cooperate with specialists from other fields."[52] There are other disciplines that have also institutionalized the sense of what it means to compare—comparative literature being perhaps the most prominent among them. One might therefore expect that there is something general to the notion of "comparativism" as a science that speaks across disciplines, but a review of the texts demonstrates that not to be the case.[53] And it seems that across the disciplines, when comparativism is practiced assumptions are made. Perhaps assumptions are necessary. Thus, even when an esteemed think tank in the U.S. like the Carnegie Foundation reports on legal education and the profession, it makes comparisons without reflection on comparativism. "[L]ike all the professions, engineering is finally about doing—exercising practical judgment under conditions of uncertainty."[54] What method was used for this comparison? Were the authors looking for similarities or differences and why? What assumptions are made upon which one can build the overarching abstraction known as "professions?" The same report continues in a similar vein when it states "compared to medicine or engineering, the particular social position of the legal professions and the nature of law as a field of study together create a unique situation for legal education. … Unlike physicians or engineers, legal professionals act as social regulators."[55] Even among—or especially among—the well-known scholars in the field of comparative law, there appear many assumptions. So when German jurist Rudolph B. Schlesinger taught comparative law to U.S. audiences, he used cases.[56] The common law lawyer or student, such as I was, might find it to be normal because when he or she studies common law, it is through the case method.

2.2.6 Further Critiques That Generate New Schools of Comparativism

Regardless of whether comparative law is conducted as a scholarly pursuit or a practical pursuit, the ideology remains that the subject is a disinterested neutral

---

[52] *Ibid*. at 698.

[53] Law is often compared to literature and sometimes even discussed as literature. But even here, even when literature's comparative element is used, it is not connected to the law. See Robin West, "Adjudication Is Not Interpretation: Some Reservations About the Law-As-Literature Movement," 54 *Tennessee Law Rev.* (1987) 203.

[54] William M. Sullivan et al., *Educating Lawyers: Preparation for the Profession of Law*. Hoboken, NJ: John Wiley and Sons, Inc., 2007 79 (also known as the "Carnegie Foundation Report").

[55] *Ibid*.

[56] Rudolph Schlesinger, *Comparative Law: Cases, Text, Materials*. New York: Foundation Press, 1950). This famous book has been published many times, including a seventh edition that was published posthumously in 2009.

observer, objectively and evenly studying several legal systems, their histories, pieces of their practices or elements of their sources of law. The well-founded critique of such an erroneous approach to comparative law, however, is that "The comparatist's own 'system' is never left behind or critically exposed to the light of the new. ... The comparatist travels strategically, always returning to the ever-present and idealized home system."[57] This book has the reverse relationship between the author and his legal culture. I am not reporting to my own culture on a foreign legal system, as is usually the case in comparative law, but rather am reporting to the foreign legal systems on my own legal culture. Thus, because this book is written from the reverse perspective, I am saved from even the pretense of trying to write as the neutral or objective observer. This book is written by a lawyer who was born and raised in the United States and who is licensed to practice law in one of the states. I would maintain that the book remains inherently comparative because I expect that in writing for law students and lawyers from outside the United States, it will be the reader who will necessarily be practicing comparative law in learning the legal culture of the United States. And insofar as the reader is doing that, he or she should be aware not only of the orthodoxy in comparative law, but of newer theories as well, some of which are borne out of critiques of the orthodoxy, just as the reader will learn that some common law norms are borne out of the dissenting opinions of judges, recorded as such after the majority opinion is expressed in a case report.

In response to functionalism, Professor Vivian Curran features instead the notion of immersion[58] as method and Bernhard Grossfeld mobilizes all the metaphorical meanings of translation as a method for comparative law.[59] Curran not only offers her own method that focuses upon immersion, but also offers a critique of Zweigert and Kötz's use of the functionality principle. She points out that in relying upon functionality, they assume away the object of inquiry. The question "*is* there a similar function?" is not asked, according to Curran, but rather it is assumed there is and the method launches itself from this assumption into determining *what* function is in operation. More importantly, she says Zweigert and Kötz are assuming that it is possible to carry out the old goal of comparative law—to distill a global, common, and unified system of private law—and to do so, they begin by assuming they will find similarities. This critique is like that of the old-time magician, who claims to be able to pull a rabbit from his hat, only because he knows he has already put the rabbit in the hat. One could level that same critique, to a limited extent, against Grossfeld, who states:

> [w]e must not in comparative law first and foremost fix on 'differences,' and even exaggerate them as 'exotic.' It is more important to perceive commonalities. They form intercultural 'bridges,' enabling agreement across borders. If

[57] Frankenberg, *supra* note 4 at 433.
[58] Vivian Curran, *Comparative Law: An Introduction*. Durham, NC: Carolina Academic Press, 2002.
[59] Grossfeld, *supra* note 1 at 89–104.

we total up the differences, we distort the picture. Comparative law first and foremost must be 'bridge seeking' and 'bridge building.'[60]

The "must" in that statement is of course a matter of choice.

If one is attempting something like an objective or neutral science of comparison, it is indeed peculiar to advocate beginning from a perspective that is admittedly biased toward finding similarities, just as it would be to acknowledge and employ a bias in search of differences. Yet there does not seem to be much reflection on the quick abandoning by many comparativists of both the attempt at a neutral scientific vantage point of observation and an exploration of the biases of their own vantage point. In this book, it is not necessary for me to try to claim the neutral observer vantage point because the explicit goal of the book is to introduce the student or lawyer to law in U.S. culture. To that end, I acknowledge that "[t]he comparatist's own 'system' is never left behind or critically exposed in the light of the new."[61] But here, it is you the unknown reader who are doing the comparing. I might, at worst, be accused of assuming I know who you will be. If so, I would rather accept that accusation as a positive and necessary characteristic of a writer conscious of an audience, than be the Romantic poet who just exudes text, forcing the audience to conform to his own conceits. The desire to find bridges can result in some odd construction of reference frames, as when U.S. Professor Peter Baldwin compares passenger kilometers in Europe for trains with freight kilometers in the U.S. for trains, and from that comparison concludes that both Europeans and Americans use trains approximately as often.[62]

Curran's critique is related to a more general critique based upon the identity-difference principle. In the identity-difference principle, it is said that for any two phenomena, one can of course find one basic similarity (they exist, they are both made of molecules and so on), and also at least one difference (even two pencils, mass-produced and side-by-side, do not exist in the same physical space, for example).[63] Curran's preferred alternative mode of comparison is through immersion in the new legal culture.

Like Curran, Bernhard Grossfeld not only offers his own method, but presents a critique of orthodox comparison method. In Grossfeld's critique, he unequivocally states that "[t]o give order to connections and to render them comprehensible also is

---

[60] *Ibid*. at 12.

[61] Frankenberg, *supra* note 4 at 433.

[62] Peter Baldwin, *The Narcissism of Minor Differences: How America and Europe Are Alike*. Oxford: Oxford University Press, 2009. In this case, while looking for similarities, Baldwin is led to structure his reference frames to exclude Sweden from Europe and Vermont from the United States because they do not fit the patterns that he would like to claim for each.

[63] Here one must be careful not to engage in the sophomoric practice of "compare and contrast," as a substitute for comparative method. Simple juxtaposition is not the comparative method. I am reminded of a colleague who once observed that most papers presented at academic conferences could be boiled down to one of two themes: "X and Xa may appear to be similar, but I will show you how they are really different," or "X and Xa may appear to be different, but I will show you how they are really the same."

the scholarly duty of comparative law."[64] He says that "we should not take the functional method too narrowly."[65] He goes on to write that comparison in the mode of translation has all the advantages of immersion over functionalism, but has the added advantage of being more easily executed than immersion by the comparativist.

By using the metaphor of translation, "[c]omparative law goes beyond textual comparison into order and relationship comparison."[66] Grossfeld argues:

> [t]he reading of a foreign legal text often gives us a false picture. Misunderstanding is programmed. In order to avoid this, we need to recognize the context of the text. Yet we are not able to observe foreign contexts in an unbiased way, for each system responds to observation, observes itself. Just as in the natural sciences, social reality is different if we observe it from when we do not.[67]

Grossfeld connects the science of comparativism to the natural sciences when he cites physicist Werner Heisenberg: "the connection between two different closed conceptual systems always must be a very painstaking analysis."[68] Grossfeld observes that comparative law "is not for 'clever boys' or 'clever girls.' It requires patience and the capacity to empathize. As in the natural sciences."[69] He adds: "Only rarely does one read anything about the execution [of law] in practice. We remain thus always at risk of taking the representation for life, and dead law for living law."[70] From this critique, he eventually arrives at the position of recommending that comparing legal systems is like translating natural languages.

Like natural languages, we all begin our lives doing everyday things within our own legal system. We typically spend years in that system, accumulating knowledge of it in the same way as other laypersons before we ever begin to study it scientifically or professionally. Thus the categories in our mind called language or legal system are in fact biased by the fact that we have learned *our* language and *our* legal system, not some neutral category called language or legal system, and we thus learn any second language or legal system by translating it into our own. This is not a disastrous state of affairs, so long as we remain conscious of it. But if we assume that our legal system is in some way *the* legal system, with some sort of natural or objective connection to the world, then we have made the same error as if we had assumed the same about our spoken language. We will take up this theme again later in the book when we discuss the perspective of language as a reference frame. Although I might say that in general comparative law is equal to comparative

---

[64] Grossfeld, *supra* note 1 at 93.
[65] *Ibid.* at 7.
[66] *Ibid.* at 125.
[67] *Ibid.* at 90–1.
[68] Werner Heisenberg, *Physik und Philosophie*. Berlin: Piper, 1984. 77 (as quoted in Grossfeld *supra* note 1 at 110).
[69] Grossfeld, *supra* note 1 at 110.
[70] *Ibid.* at 95.

language, Grossfeld would say, for example, that Eastern law, like pictograms, is not comprised of language, but is instead right brain thinking and therefore not comparable to other legal systems in which law is language-based.[71] Elsewhere, Grossfeld notes that law arises in ways similar to language, as was so clearly pointed out by the great legal historian Friedrich Karl Savigny, who stated early in his classic work:

> In the earliest times to which authentic history extends, the law will be found to have already attained a fixed character, peculiar to the people, like their language, manners and constitution. Nay, these phenomena have no separate existence, they are but the particular faculties and tendencies of an individual people, inseparably united in nature, and only wearing the semblance of distinct attributes to our view. That which binds them into one whole is the common conviction of the people, the kindred consciousness of an inward necessity, excluding all notion of an accidental and arbitrary origin.[72]

In order for systems to be compared, they need to be recognized as being separate. Imagine the two widest possibilities—every single person is his own legal system or there is only one legal system for the whole world. Step one is easy—law is a set of rules for social relations, so each having his own is silly. Now, we must thus ask what social features should make one want to be part of another's legal system? Unfortunately, too often it is assumed in secular systems that economics is the commonality that unites a legal system. Thus internationally, custom counts under Article 38 for similar states, and the first example of what counts as a "similar state" is whether the subject states are all economically "developed" or "developing." And of course the World Trade Organization has as its *raison d'etre* the handling of economic affairs. But if we compare the European Union, we find that entry in the European Union requires not only measureable economic stability, but also European human rights standards. Do senses of justice differ? What about retribution cultures versus forgiveness cultures? After all, some would cut off a thief's hand, which is a permanent punishment; others would just use prison, which is temporary. One could simply identify each state as a separate legal system. If one wants larger, more general categories, one might well find oneself addressing what Zweigert and Kötz call "legal families," rather than separate countries.

The Europeanization of private law that is mentioned above has led to a too-common tendency to treat the difference between common law and civil law as the "obvious" point of departure. Perhaps in the past, when "comparative" meant between North America and Europe, or even just within Europe, the others (such as Asian or African or South American legal systems) were only academic curiosities anyway. But now westerners go east and easterners go west and the twain meets

---

[71] Jack A. Hiller and Bernhard Grossfeld, "Comparative Legal Semiotics and the Divided Brain: Are We Producing Half-Brained Lawyers?" 50 *Am J. Comp. L.* (2002) 175, *passim*.

[72] Friedrich Carl von Savigny, *Of the Vocation of Our Age for Legislation and Jurisprudence*. Trans. A. Hayward. 1975. 24 (as quoted in Hiller and Grossfeld, *supra* note 69 at 178–9).

when they marry, have children, own property and conduct business. Global intercourse, whether social or business, makes comparative law a practical pursuit. For some, it might even be termed a necessity.

According to U.S. legal historian Frederick G. Kempin, "[a] realistic point in time to begin a discussion of Anglo-American legal history … is with the common law as it stood when it first became the object of study by a distinct legal profession."[73] Civil law begins with the establishment of a code, whether one takes the code as that of Rome or Napoleon or another. Common law continues with treating the facts as important and elevating judges to power, therefore. Common law focuses on process, and only after the independence of lawyers and legal process does it come to focusing upon texts. So immediately we are presented with a problem when comparing common law to civil law because the starting points of each system, respectively, are different; so to begin with either belies a prejudice. The risk of misunderstanding is great in comparative law, because here too we naturally are fixated on words, and begin with texts as our sources. If one begins a comparative law study by comparing sources of law, one has already demonstrated a prejudice. Equating the study of a legal system with a reading of its sources would certainly be misguided if the sources were customary law, for example. The Roman civil family of law features sources as its flag of identity and so many trained in the Roman civil system uncritically begin a comparison with sources. If, as suggested by Kempin, we treat the independence of persons as a legal profession, not the writing of a text, as the beginning point for a legal history, we might well identify that legal system, for the sake of comparison, by its various practitioners and other persons, not by its texts. Indeed, if one considers the notion of customary law broadly as a genus, common law is a species thereunder, and leads one to think differently about legal comparisons.

> European-style comparative law, due to its cultural imprints is even 'language-conditioned' and 'language-trusting.' … [B]ut how reliable is that with respect to other cultures? Perhaps we miss what is in the foreign order if we fixate on legal words or legal texts. Language may count as less 'order-generating' abroad; its relation to reality may be different. How can we ascertain its position?[74]

First, one must ascertain the role of language in that culture. Anthropology would not assume one compares law, or what Grossfeld calls the "legal order" by comparing texts.[75] "The 'misery of an order' is almost never to be found in the books used and displayed for internal use."[76] Having come this far, we are reminded also of

---

[73] Frederick G. Kempin, *Historical Introduction to Anglo-American Law in a Nutshell*. 3rd ed. St Paul, MN: West, 1990. 3.

[74] Grossfeld, *supra* note 1 at 90–1.

[75] See for example Jan M. Broekman, *Recht und Anthropologie*. Freiburg/Munich: Karl Alber, 1979.

[76] *Ibid.* at 91.

another assumption in our method—namely, that other cultures are open to being investigated or are at least neutral about the possibility. "In general, no culture wants to open up its inner core to the foreigner, to reveal its secret code, the one by means of which it grasps reality."[77]

2.3 Conclusions—What Is Learned or Gained from Comparative Science?

"It is worth noting, however that English judgments nowadays, by reason of the incorporation of Community law and the European Convention of Human Rights use such abstract concepts [as principles, freedoms and rights] more than in the past,"[78] writes Judge Schiemann. Matthias Reimann and others have noted the increased interest in comparative law in Europe as part of the Europeanization process of the Single European Act, the Maastricht Treaty and the Lisbon Treaty, but they have also cautioned that the process is concerned largely only with black-letter law, viewed positivistically, and advancing private interests. "As a result, there is no better theoretical framework in Europe than there is in the United States."[79]

As a bridge into subsequent chapters, one can combine the lessons of comparativism with those of other reference frames. For example, Frankenberg provides his critiques from the perspective of what became known as "critical legal studies," which will be explained further in the philosophy reference frame. He makes the most persuasive and continued rejection of the Europeanization of comparative law and all of its Eurocentricities.[80]

A second example comes from the language reference frame, in which one might ask the question: If linguists and translators find it absurd that treaties end with statements about official versions of the text being the same in multiple languages, how on earth could we expect other legal texts to be the same in different languages? It is "utopian to believe that two words which belong to two different languages have exactly the same meaning."[81] Furthermore:

> In reality it is truly that the real world is produced largely unconscious of the language habits of the group. There are no two languages that could be sufficiently similar to each other for them to represent the same social reality. The

---

[77] *Ibid.* at 96, with reference to Wilhelm Emil Mühlmann, "Ethnogenie und Ethnogenese," 1 *Studien zur Ethnogenese*, 57 (1985) 9.

[78] Schiemann, *supra* note 39.

[79] Reimann, *supra* note 8 at 694.

[80] To see the target of his critique, see e.g. Prof. Ulrich Drobnig, "A Memorial Address for Rudolf Schlesinger," in *The Common Core of European Private Law*. Kluwer, 2003. 29–34.

[81] Ortega y Gasset, cited in Werner Ross and Rudolf Walter (eds.), *Im Haus der Sprache*. Freiburg: Herder, 1982 205.

worlds which different societies inhabit are different worlds, not nearly one and the same world with different labels.[82]

Swiss jurist Rudolf Gmür wrote "It is clear that the European, geometrical mathematized view of the world is not easy to transplant"[83] and shows this with the example of the modern, systematic effect-of-law thinking in relation to medieval German private law. He concludes that one cannot grasp non-European cultures for the most part in the forms of European legal thinking. It is not amenable to being transplanted into Asian cultures: "[w]hile we in Europe are imprinted so as [sic] analyze mathematically-geometrically, and to dissect (individualism), in Asia we run into a much more wholistic [sic] thought and restraint (the group view)."[84]

I began the chapter promising to answer whether comparative law was in fact at all possible. If you have been reading along with all the warning language of social and linguistic constraints in comparative law practice, you might well be expecting that the chapter would conclude by saying that comparative law, at least in the "common sense" understanding of the project, is not possible. Not so. Comparative law is possible as a science, but it does not enable one to see other systems as a native of those systems would see his own system of order. Rather, a scientific practice of comparative law allows one to do what is possible from the most intelligent foreign perspective. A large part of that intelligent perspective relates to the themes of the spirit and soul of the law that were explored in Chapter 1. Bernard Grossfeld begins the final chapter of his excellent work on comparative law by infusing the notions of spirit and attitude into the method of comparative law. He begins by warning us not to conduct comparativism by looking only in a mirror, so to speak. He writes that "[g]reat tasks lie ahead for comparative law; it must let itself be challenged if it wants to win the future in a world that is not European in imprint."[85] His criticism is equally valid for comparativists in the United States as it is in Europe. Then he adds the point regarding attitude or spirit, in conducting a comparative study, by quoting the twelfth century abbot and scholar, Bernhard of Clairvaux, who wrote "*Res tantum intelligitur quantum amatur*"[86] (A matter is understood to the extent that it is loved.) Grossfeld applies that sense to comparative law and concludes that "[a] technical-functional comparison without a study of national customs, without cultural-research and without loving empathy, ... remains a study of words, letters and numbers, touches only the superficial level and leads into error."[87]

---

[82] Edward Sapir (cited in George Steiner, *Nach Babel.* Frankfurt: Suhrkamp, 1983 102).
[83] Rudolf Gmür, *Rechtswirkungsdenken in der Privatrechtsgeschichte. Theorie und Geschichte der Denkformen des Entstehens und Erlöschens von subjektiven Rechten und anderen Rechtsgebilden.* Bern: Stampili, 1981 310.
[84] Grossfeld, *supra* note 1 at 195 (citing Gmür, *supra* note 80).
[85] Grossfeld, *supra* note 1 at 245.
[86] Bernhard of Clairvaux, *De diligendo Dei,* (On Loving God), *circa* 1128.
[87] Grossfeld, *supra* note 1 at 245.

With that attitude in mind, one might move to the problem of hierarchy. The U.S. literary theorist Kenneth Burke includes in his rather famous characterization of humans the fact that we are all "goaded on by a spirit of hierarchy," and that spirit of hierarchy is borne of status and order. Related is the fact that all comparison creates hierarchy, regardless of how innocent it claims to be.[88] So if one applies Burke's observation to Frankenberg's critique of Schlesinger et al., one can see the danger that private law comparisons can easily become instrumental in the foundation and maintenance of hierarchies of legal systems and the cultures that make use of them.

Applying the orthodoxy of Zweigert and Kötz, one must begin by asking why one compares. In the early United States, the answer was comparatively simple: American judges had to compare the facts in their cases with norms in Britain because the United States had not yet developed law in many areas. During the decades before the American Revolution, disputes in commercial law and admiralty law, for example, were not decided in the colonies. This practice is not limited to the United States. The story is told of Irish revolutionary and first prime minister (*Taoiseach*), Éamon de Valera, who, when told shortly after independence from Britain that his own country had no copyright law, asked for a copy of the British copyright law. It was brought to him, he crossed off "United Kingdom" from the top of the page, inserted "Republic of Ireland" and said "there, now we do."

Kempin asserts that "[l]egal history can dispel many commonly held misconceptions. One is that the common law is held in the iron bands of tradition through the doctrine of precedent. But precedent is little more than comparing present cases with past cases."[89] Here then we see an effective and necessary practice of comparative law that is not commonly included in discussions of comparative law—comparison across time, rather than space. To Kempin, the practice of making and applying common law is constituted by comparison. One might even use this point as the point of departure to note that comparative law, as a discipline, cannot approach its topic from a neutral or omnipresent position, and insofar as common law lawyers approach comparative law itself, they will do so differently than civil lawyers will.

A weak point in the functionalist method, including that of Zweigert and Kötz, is that it begins from a presumption that legal systems of the world are sufficiently similar such that one can find similar functions among them: "[t]he proposition [of functionalism] rests on what every comparatist learns, namely that the legal system of every society faces essentially the same problems and solves these problems by quite different means though very often with similar results."[90] As a result of this

---

[88] Kenneth Burke, *Language as Symbolic Action*. Berkeley and Los Angeles, CA: University of California Press, 1966 15–16.

[89] Kempin, *supra* note 71 at III.

[90] Zweigert and Kötz, *supra* note 7 at 25. See also Zweigert, *supra* note 48 at 735. Critiques of this presumption of similarity are found in Léontin Constantinesco, *Rechtsvergleichung*. Vol. III. Cologne: C. Heyman Verlag, 1975 54–68 and Vivian Curran, *supra* note 56.

presumption, Zweigert and Kötz go so far as to say that if at the end of research one finds that there are:

> great differences or indeed diametrically opposite results, he should be put on notice to go back to check again whether the terms in which he posed his original question were indeed purely functional, and whether he has spread the net of his researches quite wide enough.[91]

With this in mind, analyses can only be conducted if the questions used are capable of yielding similarities, regardless of how well those similarities represent the practices of lawyers in those systems. It would be equally as logical to begin from the presumption that legal systems are dissimilar enough that no similarities can be found. If the Zweigert and Kötz introduction is a milestone in the scholarship of comparative law, the *International Encyclopedia of Comparative Law* is a mountain. The *Encyclopedia*, a project in which Zweigert was involved as one of the editors and authors, is a massive undertaking in both its attempt to corral a world of factual knowledge about the law, but also in its necessary attempt to operationalize a particular view of comparative law in order to carry out the project of organizing and recording the world of factual legal knowledge. For the student who peruses the *Encyclopedia*, two things ought to jump out immediately—why is it written in English and why is it arranged and divided as it is? The point is not to argue that the *Encyclopedia* should be written in another language, but to recognize that a choice has been made to present comparative law in a particular language, just as all presentations of comparative law are made from a particular conceptual perspective. That brings the reader to the second point. Why do the volumes discuss the topics they do, and not some other topics? Here too, choices have been made as to the topics that can or ought to be presented. This set of topics is not the "normal" or "natural" one, but rather, a set of topics chosen to serve the needs and uses of a particular view about comparative law. In Volume I, the state reports, what would happen, for example, if categories were used for which there was nothing to say for some states? If we say that those states are not comparable, we have concluded a priori that some features of state systems are of no interest outside that state. But is the comparativist not precisely the person outside a state who would like to know how law works in that state, including its unique aspects? Therefore, when I worked on the index for the *Encyclopedia* for years, the categories all seemed to make reasonable sense until, late in the exercise, I came to the letter U and the entry for the United States. When I saw the Procrustean result of fitting U.S. law, as I understood it, into these categories, I realized that the peculiar-looking result was likely felt by practitioners in other cultures regarding the descriptions of their own systems as well. Another example: in German law, based upon the traditional divisions of the legal world during study at university into private law, public law and criminal law, a German might be puzzled if a lawyer from another system saw

---

[91] Zweigert and Kötz, *supra* note 7 at 31.

criminal law as just one aspect of public law and who, in turn, was puzzled as to why criminal law and public law would be separated.

Frankenberg alleges that comparative law from the U.S. perspective might be inherently deficient. He says that Zweigert and Kötz infer that only the continental systems develop "grand comprehensive concepts," while the common law, owing to its inductive and case-by-case approach, produces "low-level legal institutions especially adapted to solve isolated, concrete problems."[92] Frankenberg continues that despite allusions on the European continent to a universal legal science, "the comparative functionalist should not be mistaken for a philosopher, her ideal is rather practical: to devise the most efficient legal system to order the reasonable expectations. In the end the neutral observer reveals herself as a lawyer in defense of the status quo."[93]

Further, functionalism lends itself to, and perhaps even leads to, an instrumentalist view of law in which law is seen as a technology. Peter G. Sacks makes a useful analogy to television to make this point:

> Just as television technology has nothing to do with the quality of the program sent, but only with the technical perfection of its recording—so that it can be employed to communicate all kinds of messages—so, this view holds, can law be used to implement any conceivable political, social or economic goal. What distinguishes one form of law from another, it maintains, is not its content or its purpose, but the degree of its technical sophistication. Consequently, the adoption of, for instance, English law by an African tribe is seen as being no more problematic than the use of Japanese television sets in British households.[94]

In conclusion, one can indeed see that there have been disappointments in the project of comparative law. Frankenberg cites British historian E. P. Thompson and concludes: "Tired and wary of truths, the teachers and students of comparative law should develop fresh enthusiasm in analyzing law as an omnipresent and ambiguous phenomenon, and in focusing on what the dominant discourse leaves out, suppresses or marginalizes."[95] Yet even at the height of critical legal studies, and after a long and convincing critique of the weaknesses of comparative law in practice, Frankenberg goes on to say that now would be the wrong time to abandon comparative legal studies, for it would "freeze the tradition and current conditions into an eternal pattern."[96] He quickly adds, however, that continuing in the current

---

[92] Frankenberg, *supra* note 4 at 440 (citing Roscoe Pound, "Comparative Law in Space and Time," 4 *Am. J. Comp. L.* 1 (Winter, 1955) 70–84).

[93] *Ibid.*

[94] Peter G. Sacks, "Law & Custom: Reflections on the Relations Between English Law and the English Language," 18 *Rechtstheorie* (1987) 421, 422.

[95] Frankenberg, *supra* note 4 at 453–4 (citing E. P. Thompson, *The Poverty of Theory and Other Essays.* London: Merlin Press, 1978 96).

[96] Frankenberg, *supra* note 4 at 441.

tradition would be equally as wrong. He then refers to Roscoe Pound, who insisted, as discussed in Chapter 1 above, that legal scholarship should investigate the "spirit" of the law. Frankenberg calls Pound's "Comparative Law in Time and Space," a "highlight" in the field from which one may:

> infer that it is not just a more complex and longer process of comparison that is needed. Comparative Law never had too little baggage in the overhead compartment. To this very day it is crammed with thoughts and oughts, with aims and claims.[97]

There have indeed been further investigations and theories in comparative law, but the point here has been to introduce the student to what has been and still is considered to be the orthodoxy and to provide just a few substantial alternatives. Those who are really taken with avant-garde comparative theory will need to read much more to keep up with current trends.[98] It is now time to take the orthodoxy and some alternatives and apply them to U.S. legal culture to see what difference they make.

CHECK YOUR UNDERSTANDING:

I have presented the position of Curran as a response to the functionality principle of Zweigert and Kötz. Based upon what you know of the Zweigert and Kötz functionality principle, if Zweigert and Kötz were to continue the conversation, how would they respond to Curran? Does Grossfeld address the issues you have raised for Zweigert and Kötz in their response?

CHALLENGE YOUR UNDERSTANDING:

If one adopts the positions of Grossfeld as outlined in this chapter on comparative law, how can one know that one is in error, as he warns us?

EXTEND YOUR UNDERSTANDING:

The notion of comparative legal science developed at the Paris Exposition in 1900 was established during a period of industrialism in which most people saw history as a story of progress. What other ideas of history exist, and how might the science of legal comparison differ if it were practiced under one of those alternative ideas, rather than based upon a belief in history as a narrative of progress?

---

[97] *Ibid.*
[98] See, for example, Jaakko Husa, *A New Introduction to Comparative Law.* Oxford: Hart Publishing, 2015.

Literature

Adomeit, Klaus, "Was ist Recht"? in Klaus Adomeit and Susanne Hähnchen, *Rechtstheorie für Studenten*. 6th ed. Heidelberg: C. F. Müller, 2011. 5.

Burke, Kenneth, *Language as Symbolic Action*. Berkeley and Los Angeles, CA: University of California Press, 1966.

Curran, Vivian, *Comparative Law: An Introduction*. Durham, NC: Carolina Academic Press, 2002.

David, R. and J. Brierley, *Major Legal Systems in the World Today*. 2nd ed. London: Steven and Sons, 1978.

Frankenberg, Günter, Critical Comparison, Re-Thinking Comparative Law, 26 *Harv. Int'l L. J.* (1985). 411.

Fuller, Steve, *Philosophy, Rhetoric and the End of Knowledge: The Coming of Science and Technology Studies*. Madison, WI: University of Wisconsin Press, 1993.

Gordley James and Arthur Taylor von Mehren, *An Introduction to the Comparative Study of Private Law*. Cambridge: Cambridge University Press, 2006.

Grossfeld, Bernhard, *Core Questions of Comparative Law*. Durham, NC: Carolina Academic Press, 2005.

Hegenbarth, Rainer, *Juristische Hermeneutik und linguistische Pragmatik*. Königstein im Taunus: Athenbaum, 1982.

Husa, Jaakko, *A New Introduction to Comparative Law*. Oxford: Hart Publishing, 2015.

Kempin, Frederick G., *Historical Introduction to Anglo-American Law in a Nutshell*. 3rd ed. St. Paul, MN: West, 1990.

Lepaulle, Pierre, "The Function of Comparative Law with a Critique of Sociological Jurisprudence," 35 *Harv. L. Rev.* (1922). 838, 857.

Pether, Penelope, "Language," in Austin Sarat, Matthew Anderson and Cathrine O. Frank (eds.), *Law and the Humanities*. Cambridge: Cambridge University Press, 2014.

Reimann, Mathias, "The End of Comparative Law as an Autonomous Subject," 11 *Tul. Eur. & Civ. L.F.* (1996). 49.

Reimann, Mathias, "The Progress and Failure of Comparative Law in the Second Half of the Twentieth Century," 50 *Am. J. Comp. L.* (Fall, 2002). 671.

Sacks, Peter G., "Law and Custom: Reflections on the Relations Between English Law and the English Language," 18 *Rechtstheorie* (1987). 421.

Schiemann, Konrad, "From Common Law Judge to European Judge," 4 *Europäisches Privatrecht* (ZEuP) (2005). 741.

Sullivan, William M., Anne Colby, Judith W. Wegner, Lloyd Bond and Lee S. Shulman, *Educating Lawyers: Preparation for the Profession of Law*. Hoboken, NJ: John Wiley and Sons, Inc., 2007.

Whytock, Christopher A., "Legal Origins, Functionalism, and the Future of Comparative Law," *BYU L Rev.* (2009). 1879.

Zweigert, Konrad, "Die praesumptio similitudinis als Grundsatzvermutung rechtsvergleichender Methode," in Mario Rotundi, ed. *Inchiesta di diritto comparato volume 7: L'abuso di diritto*. Palermo: CEDAM, 1979. 735.

Zweigert, Konrad and Hein Kötz, *An Introduction to Comparative Law*. Trans. Tony Weir. 3rd ed. Oxford: Oxford University Press, 1998.

3

COMPARATIVE LAW APPLIED: THE SUBTLE DIFFERENCES BETWEEN CIVIL LAW AND COMMON LAW IN STUDY AND PRACTICE

Framing Issues

1. What makes common law "common"?
2. How does customary law differ from statutory law?

3.1 Why Compare Common Law with Civil Law?

With the criticisms of the functionalist method in mind from Chapter 2, we turn to a consideration of common law by comparing the legal "families"[1] of civil law and common law. Within the history of comparative law, as soon as one mentions common law, the traditional literature jumps to the dichotomy of common law and civil law. Even in such a scientific approach as legal anthropology, one would find an assumed and unexplained discussion of what appears to be the full experience of *anthropos* encapsulated by the "Anglo-Saxon tradition" and "continental legal thinking."[2] Moreover, since a majority of the world's legal cultures identify themselves as civil law cultures, it makes sense to assume that the reader of this book is a law student or lawyer from the civil law legal family who is interested in U.S. legal culture and thereby, the common law.

To begin the comparison, one should consider how it is that any person in the U.S. culture becomes acquainted with the law, whether he is a student of the law or not. "I know my rights!" exclaims the protagonist in a Hollywood movie. It is a common statement in U.S. culture. It is in fact so common that we do not bother to inquire further. *How* does this person know his or her rights? Was it through formal

---

[1] Zweigert and Kötz use the term "families" in Konrad Zweigert and Hein Kötz, *Introduction to Comparative Law*. Trans. Tony Weir. 3rd ed. Oxford: Clarendon Press, 1998.

[2] Jan M. Broekman, *Recht und Anthropologie*. Karl Alber, 1979 11.

education—high school, perhaps? Is there a state-sponsored citizenship test? Has this person learned what he believes to be his rights from film and television? In the United States, the answer for any one person is likely to be a combination of more than one of the above, and more. And when a student comes to the formal study of law, which only happens in postgraduate university education in the United States, that student believes that he already has some sense of knowing what his rights are from one of the informal means, and proceeds with the formal, professional study of law from that informal basis. A non-U.S. student who has not had personal experiences in the culture does not have this sense, and studying the statutory or judicial sources of law, whether from a book or electronic database, will not give the student that sense.

3.1.1 What Should One Compare? The Range from Hand to Math

Elsewhere in the book, the reader will find lengthier discussion of legal "things" through various reference frames. The point of this chapter is only to use those things to illustrate subtle distinctions between common law and civil law. Between the civil law and common law traditions, there appear to be some obvious and commonly discussed differences, such as the sources of law. If the simple distinction between cases versus statutes as sources of law is overused, why do so many authorities focus upon it to characterize the two systems? To answer this question, there is the story of the police officer who is walking his patrol one evening and comes upon a man in a dark alleyway, crawling on his hands and knees. The policeman approaches the crawling man, suspecting that something is not right, and asks what he is doing. The crawling man replies that he is looking for the keys to his house. The policeman asks whether he dropped the keys near the spot where he is crawling. The man answers, "No, but this is where the light is shining." Similarly, the focus upon written legal texts as being the distinction between the two legal families may be more simply defined and easy to see, and therefore often cited,[3] but it is not the key that enables one to understand the differences in legal practice between these two legal families. The more important differences are more subtle and less sharply defined, but once these are grasped, they provide far more insight into the soul and spirit of legal cultures, and therefore the practice of law in those cultures.

Why else would one choose sources of law as the first ordering category for comparison? That choice alone may be a tip that the comparativist comes from the civil law tradition, in that civil law thinking features the source of law as a foundation for its system. To the student who has never practiced law, "the law" is equivalent to the rules that he or she reads in a book. But to the society living under the law, "the law" is a network of persons who observe

---

[3] See for example Buckland and McNair, *Roman Law and Common Law*. 2nd. ed. Cambridge: Cambridge University Press, 2008.

human behavior and are empowered to interpret whether that behavior is pro-
scribed or establishes liability. Perhaps with the civil law process of subsuming
the facts of individual cases under covering legislation in mind, Learned Hand,
an influential U.S. Court of Appeals judge wrote that "statutes should be construed, not as theorems of Euclid, but with some imagination of the purposes
which lie behind them."[4] As a corrective to bias from either common law
or civil law practitioners, Günter Frankenberg points out:

> Once the comparatist asks herself how she came to be what she is in terms of
> the law (an 'individual' with 'rights' and 'duties,' a 'tenant,' 'taxpayer,' 'parent,'
> 'consumer,' etc.) and how she came to think as a 'legal scholar' about her own
> law and the other laws the way she does, notions of normality and universal-
> ity begin to blur. It becomes clearer then that any vision of the foreign laws is
> derived from and shaped by domestic assumptions and bias.[5]

In comparing the "*mentalité*" of legal families, one might consider a juxtaposition
of two legal scholars, one French and one English. Pierre Lepaulle, writing in the
Harvard Law Review in 1922, began by stating:

> One of the first things to strike a foreigner who comes into contact with
> American lawyers is the general lack of interest in questions of comparative
> law. This indifference seems to be chiefly due to a failure to understand the
> real functions of that science in the modern world.[6]

Perhaps this indifference is due chiefly to the Americans' failure to understand the
real functions of comparative law in the modern world, as Lepaulle claims. But it
could also be the case that what Lepaulle considers to be proper comparative law
is only one way of seeing comparative law, and that is from a French or continental
perspective. If so, it would not be surprising to find *that* sense lacking among the
Americans. Comparativists themselves are not above seeing the legal world through
the reference frames of their own legal cultures, even while practicing comparisons.
So while Lepaulle is speaking of comparative law, he is doing so from the position
of the French lawyer, who would expect comparative law to function as his native
domestic law wishes to do—as a science, however one defines that.

Equally, on the other side, we have common law lawyers expecting comparative
law to have something akin to common law method. Basil Markesinis, Professor

[4] Justice Learned Hand, *Lehigh Valley Coal Co. v. Yensavage*, 218 F. 547, 553 (2nd Cir.
1914) (quoted by Justice John Paul Stevens in *Connecticut Nat'l Bank v. Germain*, 503 U.S.
249, 255 1 (1992)).
[5] Günter Frankenberg, *Critical Comparison, Re-Thinking Comparative Law*, 26 Harv. Int'l L. J.
(1985) 411, 443.
[6] Pierre Lepaulle, "The Function of Comparative Law with a Critique of Sociological
Jurisprudence," 35 *Harv. L Rev.* (1922) 838.

of Comparative Law at Queen Mary and Westfield College, University of London wrote in the *Modern Law Review* in 1990:

> [m]any years of teaching foreign and comparative law mainly—but not exclusively—to common law lawyers have convinced me of the value of presenting a foreign legal system to an unfamiliar audience primarily through its case law rather than by means of an exegesis of codal provisions.[7]

In both of these instances—Lepaulle and Markesinis—it is unsurprising that comparativists find that their own legal family's orientation is the best one for approaching comparative law. So, the Frenchman claimed the Americans knew nothing of, nor cared for legal science and the Englishman claims that the legal science that is constituted by an "exegesis of codal provisions" is less valuable than teaching cases.

What should one compare for the purpose of understanding the culture in which U.S. law is practiced? To answer this question, I refer to a discussion I had with a colleague during a conference about the word "policy." Often the word is used to label political talk about what *should be done*. I proposed instead that policy should be understood from empirical observations of what a government or other institution *has done*. In this sense, policy is an observable set of practices, not a wished-for plan. When it comes to law, one might make a similar observation and say that "law *is* what law *does*." Specifically, "[t]he law is not merely a bureaucracy or a set of rules, but a community of speakers of a certain kind: a culture of argument, perpetually remade by its participants."[8]

Legal historian Frederick G. Kempin introduces Anglo-American law by saying the history of Anglo-American law "tells a continued story of development of its institutions: courts, juries, judges and lawyers; the sources of law: custom, cases, legislation and doctrinal writings; and traces the beginnings and development of selected legal concepts."[9] A reader will notice not only that the order of categories places institutions before sources of law, but that the list of institutions itself does not even include legislative bodies. Moreover, within the sources of law, when legislation is mentioned, it is third. In the same way that these features may tip us off that the comparativist whom we are reading comes from the common law tradition, a comparativist from the civil law tradition shows his colors when his work features sources of law first, or even places legislatures first among his institutions. Even when "sources of law" are discussed as such, a common law lawyer may well feel that they are best considered after one investigates institutions, as when Kempin deflects sources of law to Chapter V in his book introducing Anglo-American law. He writes: "for a technical body of law to exist, some distinct group of persons,

---

[7] Basil Markesinis, "Comparative Law—A Subject in Search of an Audience," 53 *The Modern Law Review* (1990) 1.

[8] James Boyd White, *Law as Rhetoric, Rhetoric as Law: The Arts of Cultural and Communal Life*, 52 *U. Chi. L. Rev.* (1985) 684, 691.

[9] Frederik G. Kempin, *Legal History: Law and Social Change*. Englewood Cliffs, NJ: Prentice-Hall, 1963 Preface at 1.

a legal profession, must develop it. Such a profession emerges slowly; and in the beginning of any legal system, law is nothing more or less than the customary rules of the community."[10] Thus, although in some contexts one might take a "top-down" approach to describing a legal system, and do so through sources of law, starting with a constitution and continuing with the legislation and administrative regulations that cascade from it, one might alternatively take a "bottom-up" approach and begin instead with everyday conflicts and the persons and institutions that resolve the conflicts. In this manner, the latter approach would be consistent with the common law's inductive patterns of reasoning, whereas the former would be more consistent with the civil law's deductive patterns of reasoning.

It would seem that there is at least one additional answer to the question of why one would study sources of law for comparison. The additional answer is that we tend to think chronologically, so we assume there can be no discussion of the law, including no comparative study, until we have "made law." There are, however, two questionable assumptions in that answer. The first assumption is that when one proceeds chronologically, one begins with law-making. A bit of reflection on social history would show the weakness in that assumption. First, conflicts had to be resolved through whatever means were available, including force and violence, before one could say that law was made. And then one should ask at what point in legal history did humans begin changing their own behavior due to anticipating the result of conflict resolution? That is the point at which a system of law can be said to have begun—as a predictable pattern of conflict resolution. Only after that moment when patterns of conflict resolution could be observed, can the notion of legislation be introduced as a secondary act. A civil law practitioner may disagree and say that one's rationality is sufficient to anticipate conflict and legislate norms of conflict resolution before any conflict has occurred. A second assumption flows from the first: even if we first look to institutions, rather than texts, we first look to law-making institutions, rather than institutions that resolve conflict. Legal historian Harold Berman explains:

> The conventional concept of law as a body of rules derived from statutes and court decisions—reflecting a theory of the ultimate source of law in the will of the lawmaker ("the state")—is wholly inadequate to support a study of a transnational legal culture. To speak of the Western legal tradition is to postulate a concept of law, not as a body of rules, but as a process, an enterprise, in which rules have meaning only in the context of institutions and procedures, values, and ways of thought. From this broader perspective the sources of law include not only the will of the lawmakers but also the reason and conscience of the community and its customs and usages ....[11]

---

[10] *Ibid.* at 95.
[11] Harold J. Berman, *Law and Revolution: The Formation of the Western Legal Tradition.* London: Harvard University Press, 1983 11.

Although it must be noted that Berman is making his claim only regarding what he calls the "western tradition," he provides a sound basis from which to consider more than statutes and also more than court decisions when comparing legal systems. He states for example that beyond the sources of law, a legal system is comprised of the bodies or institutions of law. Therefore, for a start in the process of escaping the usual and narrow source of law comparison, the bodies and institutions should be compared.

3.1.2 Comparing Institutions

In his historical introduction to the Anglo-American legal tradition, Frederick Kempin lists lawyers, judges, juries and courts as institutions to be studied. Beginning with the institution of the lawyer, what can one observe? The advocate is an extremely important institution of the common law. As was mentioned in Chapter 1, the fact that a common law lawyer is educated and trained to be an advocate makes him or her a different kind of lawyer. To be an advocate does not mean the wild theatrics that one might see on television or in film. It does mean, however, according to the Rules of Professional Conduct that governs the practitioner's license, one must accept the client's decision to litigate, so long as it is a legally defensible position, and take the client's position even if the lawyer disagrees with it, and advocate that position using one's full energy and skills as a lawyer. In an adversarial system, even those lawyers who do not regularly litigate before the court, and who might do the work of conveying property, drafting wills and conducting transactions will always use as a guide, the answer to their conveyancing, drafting and contracting questions, "how will this work against an opponent in court?" For this reason, the skills that were historically set aside for the barrister in the English tradition, are part of every U.S. lawyer's training in advocacy. (There will be more to say on the role of the barrister when looking at U.S. legal culture through the Historical Reference Frame in Chapter 4.) Advocacy training includes drafting documents as an advocate, courses in trial advocacy and appellate advocacy, moot court competitions and the case method of substantive law instruction. The daily routine for the U.S. law student in the classroom was to have read dozens of reported judicial opinions each day in preparation for a question-and-answer classroom "lecture." Ex-cathedra lecturing was frowned upon by the academic community and the standard-setting American Bar Association through its education division. Reading "the law" means reading the cases and recognizing the merits and errors of the various adversarial positions. It is not an exercise in finding the one right answer, a position that ultimately infers that one of the parties is wrong.[12]

---

[12] Lon L. Fuller and John D. Randall: "Professional Responsibility: Report of the Joint Conference, Joint Report to the American Bar Association," 44 *A.B.A.J.* (1958) 1159.

Oliver Wendell Holmes, Jr. wrote a dissent in the case of *Abrams v. United States*, in which he says "[t]he ultimate good desired is better reached by free trade of ideas ... the best test of truth is the power of the thought to get itself accepted in the competition of the market."[13] This free trade of ideas has woven into its fabric a position regarding legal issues—justice does not lead to one answer only, and needs to be determined on a fact-dependent, case-by-case basis within predictable limits.

It is the presentation of evidence by an advocate that leads us to our next major area of distinction between the two systems. The advocacy discussed above is practiced within a jurisprudential world that revolves around evidentiary matters. If the distinction between "judge-made" common law and "statutory" civil law has become blurred over time, the dramatic disparity between the two systems' handling of evidentiary matters is still very much intact. Therefore, anyone wishing to gain a true understanding of the U.S. legal system must acquire an appreciation of the gathering, presentation and weighing of evidence within it. From the initial decision to take on a client to the final resolution of the conflict before a judge and jury, the U.S. legal system would be seen, at least in the eyes of many civil jurists, as being obsessed with the issue of evidence. There will be more to say about lawyers in Chapter 5.

Another function of advocacy that is worth mentioning brings us to another institution: the judge:

> In contrast to most continental systems, the English judge's jurisdiction is very wide. He will try civil, administrative, and criminal cases. Because of this breadth of jurisdiction, it is accepted by everyone that the judge may well not have a detailed knowledge of the law which he is supposed to be applying in a particular case. This he will openly acknowledge in court – to the astonishment of any German litigant who happens to be there! It is seen as the function of advocates to explain the law to the judge and to draw to his attention any relevant statute or case law even if this may well to [sic] lead to a decision against his client.[14] The trial process is founded on the belief, in general justified, that each side will competently say all that is honestly to be said on their side of the argument. The judge is expected to have a quick mind which can understand and perhaps develop positions which are new to him.[15]

---

[13] *Abrams v. United States*, 250 U.S. 616, 630 (1919).

[14] In the United States, the Model Rules of Professional Conduct, Rule 3.3, "Candor toward the Tribunal," in fact requires that one disclose to the court those sources of law contrary to one's position.

[15] Sir Konrad Schiemann, "From Common Law Judge to European Judge," 4 *Europäisches Privatrecht* (ZEuP) (2005) 741–9, 745–6. Schiemann adds: "There is no denying that the UK court process demands and receives a lot from advocates and, partly because of this, costs a lot of money to the litigant." *Ibid.* at 747.

The influence of the notion of advocate does not stop on that side of the courtroom bar. In most common law systems, including that of the United States, judges are selected from practicing lawyers, usually with some years' experience as litigators. Thus, the woman or man sitting on the bench was first an advocate, and perhaps an advocate for much longer than she or he has had the current role of adjudicator:

> The approach to the judicial task which prevails in the United Kingdom appeal courts has been greatly influenced by the fact that traditionally all appellate judges have practiced as advocates for many years, were appointed as one of the seventy odd judges of the High Court, usually after a successful career and aged about 50. The style of judgments tends to be influenced by this. They will have sat alone as first instance judges for a number of years before they were asked to join the Court of Appeal. ... Traditionally, each judge states in his own words, often instinctively employing the style of advocate, his reasons for coming to his decision.[16]

In comparing institutions, one notes that the institutions clearly differ between common law and civil law countries, such as between the U.S. Supreme Court and the dedicated constitutional courts in France, Italy or Germany. Moreover, the institutions even differ among the common law countries. Among those differences would be the different law-making institutions needed for a presidential system, as in the United States, compared to a parliamentary system, as in the United Kingdom, or the constitutional review power of the U.S. Supreme Court compared to the U.K. Supreme Court. An obvious institution of the common law that popular culture likes to see and discuss is the lay jury. The lay jury will be discussed in Chapter 9.

If one truly wants to understand the role of law in any culture, in addition to the institutions and instrumentalities one must also compare the reception of a legal order by the citizens who live with it. Do the citizens have affordable and open access to the courts? If they do have access, do citizens consider the courts decide fairly and according to the rule of law, or do they feel that the courts are biased or corrupt and therefore resolve their conflicts in other ways? As was mentioned in the Preface, in order to understand the reception of a legal system, the role of popular culture should not be dismissed during the study and practice of law as a profession. In the United States, for example, district attorneys report the phenomenon of lay juries acquitting criminal defendants because the prosecutor failed to produce DNA evidence or other technical evidence, even in cases of simple crimes for which no such technical evidence had ever been used in the past.[17] These jurors, when polled, report

---

[16] *Ibid.* at 743.
[17] See for example Katie L. Dysart, "Managing the CSI Effect in Jurors," American Bar Association, Section of Litigation, May 28, 2012. Available at http://apps.americanbar.org/litigation/committees/trialevidence/articles/winterspring2012-0512-csi-effect-jurors.html (last accessed 8 July 2014).

that they see such evidence made available in all criminal prosecutions in television shows and in movies. And as if that were not enough, the influence of U.S. popular culture, even in things legal, is not limited in its influence to persons in the United States. Several years ago a lawyer in Germany attempted to make an objection during the questioning of a witness at trial. This is noteworthy for two reasons: first, the trial practice of objecting that is commonly seen on U.S. television shows throughout the world is not an available practice in Germany. Second, and perhaps more striking was that everyone in the courtroom reportedly smiled at the failed effort, because they too knew what the objecting lawyer was trying to do and why—they too watch U.S. television and film.[18] There is a further point to be made here. Of course it is true that U.S. culture is exported—even globalized—for all sorts of reasons, many of which may well be economic. But in addition to that is the fact that the nature of an adversarial common law trial that makes for appealing drama in ways that the inquisitorial and administrative legal practices of many countries do not:

> In the common law system all that matters is what happened at the trial. That is indeed true and the corollary is that what actually happened is irrelevant unless it was accurately depicted at the trial: the common law trial is like a dramatic production; the audience, whether it is a judge and jury or a judge alone, delivers its verdict on the basis of what it hears and sees on the stage.[19]

On a recent flight, I was struck by the fact that two of the movies on offer were *The Judge* and *The Attorney*. There was no film about legislators.

There is a subtle but important difference between even the symbols for law that booksellers, university websites and public buildings use for law in the common law and civil law cultures. In the civil law culture of Germany, for example, the symbol often employed is the paragraph symbol ("Use the proper § symbol."). This would suggest that law is known by the words of the text of the statutes, denoted by their paragraph numbers. By comparison, the common law displays a figure, usually female, usually blindfolded and wielding a sword in one hand, but holding scales in the other hand. The scales are to weigh and compare something between two parties, two explanations of fact, or two interpretations of the law. Justice is not inquiring, justice is weighing, unbiased, and doing so under threat of the punishment of the sword, that is, *subpoena*. One could of course easily attack this iconic model with questions of interpretation—how is one argument given greater "weight" than another; how is the interest of a particular party or group given weight versus another; do multiple interests "weigh more" than single interests. But although with such questions we begin to see the obvious limits to notions of

---

[18] For scholarly treatments of U.S. law in film, see Michael Asimow and Shannon Mader, *Law and Popular Culture: A Coursebook*. New York: Peter Lang, 2007; Paul Bergman and Michael Asimov, *Reel Justice: The Courtroom Goes to the Movies*. Kansas City, MO: McKeels Publishing, 2006.

[19] Jeremy Lever, *Why Procedure is more Important than Substantive Law*, 48 *Int'l & Comp. L. Q.* (April 1999) 285, 297.

mechanical adjudication,[20] the juxtaposition of the woman with scales next to the paragraph symbol is a telling one.

Before leaving this discussion on subtle differences, there are a few further points to be made about comparing institutions. One can and should compare the more obvious institution of conflict resolution in courts, for example. When looking for the differences that matter to the legal practices of conflict resolution in different legal cultures, it is necessary to look beyond the broad categories one might rationally notice in the literature and make observations of conflict resolution in action as an anthropologist would.[21] In this way, one has the opportunity to test whether there are indeed any differences worth bothering about. After all, the stereotypes of "lawyers" seem to cross cultures, so it would seem from the broad comparative perspective of non-lawyer citizens that lawyers are all much the same! The goal here, however, is to get a sense of the feel, the local knowledge and the "soul and spirit" of U.S. law, as an example of the common law in practice.

3.1.3 Comparing Processes

Harold Berman said that to speak of the Western legal tradition, one must speak not only of rules, but of processes. There are obvious procedures, such as those governed by criminal, civil or administrative rules, but there are also more subtle processes. The famous nineteenth-century British legal historian Henry Sumner Maine was a bit more abstract when he wrote:

> A general proposition of some value may be advanced with respect to the agencies by which Law is brought into harmony with society. These instrumentalities seem to me to be three in number, Legal Fictions, Equity and Legislation. Their historical order is that in which I have placed them.[22]

While Maine does include legislation in his historical analysis, he does not begin there. He begins instead with fictions and then moves to equity. In short, if one wants to understand U.S. legal culture—an understanding of which forms the basis for all practitioners of U.S. law—history demonstrates that one will need to understand a history whose legal fictions and sense of equity precede any notion of legislation.

Despite what seems to be the widespread popular presence of the common law trial in film and television that was mentioned earlier, the notion of what

---

[20] For a more complete attack on the weighing and weighting of social interests, see Lepaulle, *supra* note 6 at 843–6.

[21] This process is similar to that of sociologists Bruno Latour and Steve Woolgar in *Laboratory Life: The Construction of Scientific Facts*. Princeton NJ: Princeton University Press, 1986, in which they themselves worked as laboratory technicians in order to observe, record and analyze the behavior of laboratory scientists, rather than accept descriptions of science practices from textbook theories.

[22] Henry Sumner Maine, *Ancient Law*. 10th ed. London: John Murray, 1884 15.

U.S. lawyers mean by the term "trial" does not seem to be fully understood outside the United States. Judge David Edwards states it well when he writes:

> [t]he technique of the civil law systems is archetypally "judicial" in that it involves a professional lawyer applying the rules, the methods and the outlook of the law as a science to a problem submitted by the parties to the judge, as a *lawyer*, for a solution. This, of course, is quite unlike the technique of a jury trial which relies on the capacity of the common man to "detect falsehood or receive an assurance of truth" and treats the process of fact-finding as a necessary and logical precursor of applying the law. It is pointless to look in the civil procedure of France, Germany or Italy for anything corresponding to a "trial" in the common law sense, since there is no place and no need for such an event.[23]

This description by Judge Edwards is much more than saying that the civil law relies upon statutes as sources of law and the common law relies upon judicial decisions as sources of law. First of all, we ought to note that he is looking to a judge, not to a legal scholar, to pronounce on the character of the law. Second, Judge Edwards feels that the common law process turns much more on the "common" person's determination of facts than it does on the legal professional's interpretation of the law, which he regards as the mark of the civil law process. And third, he makes a point of emphasizing the word "trial."

When a civil lawyer translates a term from his culture into "trial" or "litigation," he has brought a very different concept into the conversation from what a common law lawyer means by the words "trial" or "litigation." There will be more to say on that later in this chapter. If in fact the common law does not see itself as a science, what does that mean for the legal knowledge that one might obtain in an individual trial or in the construction of common law generally? Simply put: how is there knowledge if there are no absolute or permanent truths? "In the medieval period, and dating back before the Conquest, a common method of fact-finding in civil cases was wager of law. This was also known as a 'compurgation' or 'canonical compurgation,' particularly in ecclesiastical courts."[24] Trial by battle was later imported by the Normans. It was used in two types of case: private accusations of felony, and disputes involving ownership of land.[25] Ultimately the jury was developed in both criminal and civil cases.[26] It is this sense of trial that defines what U.S. lawyers mean when speaking of "litigation." It has the sense of an adversarial contest with a winner and loser, and those winners and losers are championed by their lawyers, using not physical weapons, but substantive law, rules of procedure and all the senses of persuasion they know. Metaphors from

---

[23] David Edwards, "Fact-Finding: A British Perspective," in D. L. Carey Miller and Paul R. Beaumont (eds.), *The Option of Litigating in Europe*. London: United Kingdom Committee of Comparative Law, 1993 54 (as quoted by Lever, *supra* note 19 at 296–7.

[24] Kempin, *supra* note 9 at 49.

[25] *Ibid.* at 51.

[26] *Ibid.* at 49.

war and sports abound. This can all be properly criticized as being taken over by those metaphors, leaving justice as a mild theory in the background of the trial, operating largely by implication only.

Again one is reminded that a commonly discussed feature of the U.S. legal culture is the jury trial. A television or film viewer would believe there is a lay jury in every trial. Not so in the United States, and even less so in the United Kingdom. It will be discussed in detail as the aspect of the U.S. legal culture that fulfils the desire of the public to be an active part of a legal system, and not be content to just vote for lawmakers indirectly and through party politics. But although many other systems do not have lay juries, some do, including in civil systems. If one keeps in mind that the role of the jury is to maintain an active and participatory role for the laity in the legal system, and not just in politics, this should come as no surprise. The laity has the role of judge in Germany and Austria (the *Schöffen*).

In many countries, it is not required that a person be a lawyer to be a law-maker. My recent survey showed that only about one third of the German federal parliament are lawyers and approximately 43 percent of the U.S. federal representatives are lawyers. One is also not required to be a lawyer to be a law enforcement officer, all the way from the top (a governor or president, for example) to the police officer in the street. In Belgium, the lay jury is still used in most serious cases. Decisions of the jury may not be appealed. The Russian Federation and the Kingdom of Spain still make limited use of lay juries. And it was in fact the French idea of a jury that William brought with him to England as part of Norman administration, after he defeated Harold in the Battle of Hastings in 1066. I will have more to say about that historical moment in Chapter 4. One may mark the pedigree of the U.S. jury by noticing that the concept of the "grand" jury still exists alongside the petit jury. The mechanics of how the jury functions in the U.S. system today will be discussed in Chapter 9, the Mechanical Reference Frame.

Before leaving this discussion of the trial it is worth pausing for a moment on the notion of an oath. It is a central component of what a U.S. lawyer considers to be a trial. As a descendent of a legal culture in England that for centuries depended solely on the veracity of oath swearing to determine truth or innocence, it is perhaps not surprising that a legal system infused with evolutionary legal culture would still have a residue of it. However, within the U.S. system, the disparity between the evidentiary worth of statements made under oath as opposed to those not made under oath remains dramatic. Within the U.S. system, evidentiary value hinges on the merit of oath swearing. Therefore, it is not surprising that oaths continue to be administered in relation to both spoken and written documents within the U.S. legal system. In addition, the somber formality of the oath-swearing process has changed little over the centuries, with oaths in many U.S. states remaining relatively unchanged since before the war of independence from Britain. While oath swearing exists within the civil law tradition, the lax method of administration and its discretionary use seems to reflect a lower faith in a peremptory oath's ability to persuade a witness to distinguish truth from fabrication.

Treating the adjudicative process as one of mathematics raises doubts within common law thinking whether in the previously mentioned broad critique of Judge Learned Hand, who in simile cautions against treating statutes as theories of Euclid, or in the more literal sense of using mathematics to determine conflict outcomes as Professor Lawrence Tribe of Harvard discusses. Beginning with a discussion of the explicitly admitted inability of the defense (and probably the judge) to understand the mathematics of probability offered in the infamous Dreyfus trial in France (1899),[27] Tribe goes on to critique both the use of mathematics in a court of law and in the design of the trial system as a whole. He points out the difficulties and weaknesses of using mathematical probability to determine the likelihood of occurrences, identities of persons, and most importantly, the intention of actors.[28] Much of a trial is for the purpose of determining what happened in a different place in the past, and then assessing what the facts of that narrative mean in the present:

> Twentieth century logic took enormous strides when logicians discovered, or decided, that the subject matter of logic is not truth but validity. Previously, we might *axiomatize* geometry, arithmetic, or logic itself, and the chief question would be whether the axioms were true.... In our century the right question to ask of an axiom system became not whether its axioms are true, but whether its theorems are well-derived from them according to explicit rules of inference.[29]

One might do well to consider what is meant by "science" or "truth" or any of the other important terms used to talk about the inquiry that occurs in legal proceedings. I say "legal proceedings," because, as previously discussed, what a common law lawyer would call a trial is not really experienced in civil law, at least not in Germany. Thus, when teaching students from other legal families, it takes some time to make clear what the term "litigation" means for the common law trial lawyer. There will be more to say about litigation and alternatives to litigation in Chapter 9, when the discussion turns to the mechanics of trials. The science of subsuming facts under covering models of law suits the process of solving individual conflicts, but it is not a research science capable of amplifying knowledge. As David Hume quite rightly noted, induction has no causal warrant and deduction does not amplify knowledge.[30]

---

[27] Lawrence H. Tribe, "Trial by Mathematics: Precision and Ritual in the Legal Process," 84 *Harv L. Rev* (1971) 1329. Tribe relies upon the person report by a student of the Dreyfus case, Armand Charpentier, *The Dreyfus Case.* Trans. J. May. BLES, 1935.

[28] *Ibid.*

[29] Peter Suber, "Legal Reasoning After Post-Modern Critiques of Reason," 3 *Legal Writing* (1997) 21–50, 24.

[30] David Hume, *An Enquiry into Human Understanding.* New York: P. F. Collier & Son Company, 1909–14.

Rather than being founded upon rationalism, induction is founded upon empiricism, as is the case with much of Anglo-American thought.[31] The U.S. legal historian Robert W. Gordon, an important figure in the critical legal studies movement, wrote that "any profession that attempts to legitimize existing procedures or rules will be tempted to demonstrate that such systems are inevitable, or are justified by 'universal rationalizing principles.'"[32]

And in the landmark case of *Erie Railroad Company v. Tompkins*, Justice Brandeis of the U.S. Supreme Court wrote that "[t]he common law so far as it is enforced in a State, whether called common law or not, is not the common law generally but the law of that State existing by the authority of that State without regard to what it may have been in England or anywhere else."[33] In that decision, Brandeis then went on to quote Oliver Wendell Holmes, Jr., and wrote that "the authority and only authority is the State, and if that be so, the voice adopted by that State as its own should utter the last word."[34]

If in fact the common law does not see itself as a science, what does that mean for the legal knowledge that one might obtain in an individual trial or in the construction of common law generally? Simply put: how is there knowledge if there are no truths? Holmes explains the inductive process of common law science:

> [t]he object of study, then, is prediction, the prediction of the incidence of the public force through the instrumentality of the courts … Far the most important and pretty nearly the whole meaning of every new effort of legal thought is to make these prophecies more precise, and to generalize them into a thoroughly connected system.[35]

Holmes goes on to say:

> The danger of which I speak is not the admission that the principles governing other phenomena also govern the law, but the notion that a given system, ours, for instance, can be worked out like mathematics from some general axioms of conduct. This is a natural error of the schools,[36] but it is not confined to them. I once heard a very eminent judge say that he never let a decision go until he was absolutely sure it was right. So judicial dissent is often blamed, as if it meant simply that one side or the other were not doing

---

[31] Mark C. Suchman and Elizabeth Mertz, "A New Legal Empiricism? Assessing ELS and NLR," 6 *Ann. Rev. of Law and Social Science*, (2010) 561.

[32] Daniel Coquillette, *The Anglo-American Legal Heritage*. 2nd ed. Durham, NC: Carolina Academic Press, 2004 628 (citing Robert W. Gordon, "Historicisim in Legal Scholarship," 90 *Yale L. J.*, (1981) 1017, 1018–24).

[33] *Erie Railroad Co. v. Tompkins*, 304 U.S. 64, 79 (1938) (quoting *Swift v. Tyson*, 41 U.S. (16 Pet.) 1 (1842), Holmes, J. dissenting).

[34] *Ibid.*

[35] Oliver Wendell Holmes Jr., "The Path of Law," 10 *Harv L. Rev.* (1897) 457.

[36] One should keep in mind that Holmes is speaking to law students and faculty at Boston University in this address.

their sums right, and, if they would take more trouble, agreement would inevitably come … But certainty generally is an illusion, and repose is not the destiny of man. Behind the logical form lies a judgment as to the relative worth and importance of competing legislative grounds, often an inarticulate and unconscious judgment, it is true, and yet the very root and nerve of the whole proceeding. You can give any conclusion a logical form. You can always imply a condition in a contract. But why do you imply it? It is because of some belief as to the practice of the community.[37]

3.1.4 Comparing Sources … from the Bottom up

With all the above said about institutions, processes, reception and custom, one still cannot simply ignore the sources of law. But rather than just assuming them to be universally identical categories, one can and should consider the sources critically. Common law is faithful to the custom in which it, like all legal systems, began.[38] As such the entire dynamic of custom as a source of law would alone make common law radically different from civil law. This dynamic means more than pointing to a written text after the fact and in one case saying a legislature wrote it, and in the other case saying a judge wrote it. There is, in addition, a large social difference in the making of these sources. In civil law countries, law-making means statute-making by the state. But:

> the state can *only* legislate. The state cannot create "custom," it can only create [statutory] laws. It cannot rule "custom" nor can it rule society. It can only rule and legislate for individuals. There is no room for society under "the rule of law," only for individual, legal persons. Perhaps this is the origin of, and the price to be paid for, English individualism?[39]

It helps to reflect for a moment on just why it is called "common law." Common law is a species of the genus customary law. If one thinks about the procedure through which a lawyer establishes evidence of custom in public international law, one finds a similar process in domestic customary law, beginning with William sending out his men to record and report on all the customary dispute resolution

---

[37] Holmes, *supra* note 35.

[38] See Leopold J. Pospisil, *Anthropology of Law*. London: Harper and Row, 1971. According to legal historian Frederick Kempin, a profession such as law "emerges slowly; and in the beginning of any legal system, law is nothing more or less than the customary rules of the community." Kempin, *supra* note 9 at 95.

[39] Peter G. Sack, "Law & Custom: Reflections on the Relations Between English Law and the English Language, 18 *Rechtstheorie* (1987) 421, 432 (citing Alan McFarlane, *The Origins of English Individualism*. Oxford: Oxford University Press, 1978 170 and 206). Or it is simply evidence of Sack's bias in favor of his native German system? Cf. Larry Cata Backer, "Reifying Law—Government, Law and the Rule of Law in Governance Systems," 26 *Penn St. Int'l. L. Rev.* (2008) 521.

norms and processes throughout his newly conquered England in the eleventh century. Thereafter, in the reign of Henry II (1154–89) a series of events occurred that ultimately led to a system of royal courts and a law *common* to all of England.[40]

Properly categorized, common law can be seen as a form of customary law. Berman makes the observation that:

> It is not easy to know what this means. The English common law is usually traced back to the Assize of Clarendon and other twelfth-century royal enactments; these constitute enacted law, which is the opposite of customary law. What is meant, no doubt, is that the royal enactments established procedures in the royal courts for the enforcement of rules and principles and standards and concepts that took their meaning from custom and usage. The rules and principles and standards and concepts to be enforced—the definitions of felonies, the concepts of seisin and disseisin—were derived from informal, unwritten, unenacted norms and patterns of behaviour. These norms and patterns of behaviour existed in the minds of people, in the consciousness of the community.[41]

In the discussion of the language reference frame that follows in Chapter 6, we will return to this notion of how one can say that norms and patterns of behavior existed in the minds of people and in the consciousness of the community. For approximately the first one hundred years after William took control of England, customary law continued to rule, and insofar as William was able to find things common among the customs of the various tribes of the island, one can say the law was inductively made common by observation, recording and bringing the records together. But with the reign of Henry II (1133–89), the observation of customary law began to lose its legitimacy to royal law. "[A] substantial part of property law and tort law which had previously been a matter of local custom became a matter of royal law, just as a substantial part of local criminal law had been 'royalized' through the device of the accusing jury. It is this historical expansion of royal jurisdiction in the reign of Henry II that marks the origin of the English common law,"[42] but not by direct legislation of his own, which did not cover many areas of the law, but rather indirectly "Henry II created the English common law by legislation establishing judicial remedies in royal courts."[43] The codification of the law of the Kingdom of Sicily, known as the *Liber Augustalis* (1231) uses the phrase "common law" to refer both to Roman law and Lombard law.[44] Philippe de Beaumonoir's *Books of the*

---

[40] John W. Baldwin, *The Scholastic Culture of the Middle Ages, 1000–1300*. Long Grove, IL: Waveland Press, Inc., 1997 8.

[41] Berman, *supra* note 11 at 480–1. "It seems highly probable that the 1152 peace statute of Frederick I was influenced by his knowledge, or the knowledge of his advisers, of the Sicilian legislation of Roger II, or at least by the common education and experience of Frederick's and Roger's advisers." *Ibid.* at 497.

[42] *Ibid.* at 456.

[43] *Ibid.* at 457.

[44] Berman, *supra* note 11 at 427.

Customs and Usages of Beauvaisians (written around 1283) and the earlier French and Norman "*custumals*" raise similarities to Glanvill and Bracton's work in England at nearly the same time, and that of Sicily:

> [T]he customs of Beauvais, as conceived and organized and rationalized and applied by the royal courts, were quite similar in general to the customs of the other regions of France, as sifted by the royal courts…. Periods of pre-scription differed, excuses for nonappearance differed, required formalities for transfer of land differed, and many other things differed; nevertheless, the permissible limits of differences in detail were set by the royal courts in the localities and indeed, in the time of Beaumanoir, by a supreme court in Paris. In addition, there were some uniform customs throughout France, and these were expressly referred to as "the common law."[45]

As Glanvill's first "systematic" treatise of English law (about 1187) shows, "[t]he king was not yet in a position to legislate many substantive norms of the law of contract, property, tort, or crime."[46] So although the judges had the legitimacy of the crown to sit in adjudication, the norms they applied were those of custom. Natural law theory would suggest that common law could be seen to function as custom—*jus gentium?*—to "fill in" the code gaps of the *corpus civilis* even in Rome.

So at the height of European population during the Middle Ages, just before the great famine and the black plague halved the number of Europeans, England, France, Sicily and Germany, through common influences and persons, were in the early period of transition from customary law to royal law, begun by the notion of royal courts determining the norms from local customs. So why did England retain a system that is at least fundamentally arranged in this power balance while the others and the rest of Europe did not? First, one must acknowledge the continuity of a thousand-year monarchy. Even though England underwent a revolution and had eleven years of Cromwellian rule without a monarch, the monarch was restored and continues to the present. Second, the fact that Great Britain is an island should not be underestimated. Daily intercourse at the border with other cultures, including legal cultures, as would be the case on the European continent, did not occur.

Customary law is older than the notion of a code, and its use as a source of law is a mix between societies that maintain a set of practices because they have always done so without knowing why,[47] and those that believe their practices

---

[45] *Ibid.* at 480.

[46] *Ibid.* at 458. According to Berman, the Dialogue of the Exchequer was written nearly a decade before Glanvill, but was not nearly as systematic. Glanvill's *Tractatus de Legibus et Consuetudinibus Regni Angliae* (Treatise on the Law and Customs of the Kingdom of England) "ranked the king's laws with his armies as a basis of his authority. Thereby, he legitimated royal power." *Ibid.* at 457.

[47] See Peter Berger and Paul Luckmann, *The Social Construction of Reality*. London: Penguin Books, 1991; see also chapter 4 of Wittgenstein on custom's origins in language,

have the common foundation of creating or maintaining justice. Even today, in international law, Article 38 of the Charter of the United Nations tells the International Court of Justice that one of its three primary sources of law for settling disputes is custom. Rather than ask why the English began following something called "common law," we should ask why other parts of the world stopped.

Legal education and practice in the United States do not divide substantive sources of law into private law and public law. Thus they comfortably insert questions of constitutionality and states' rights into a private conflict.[48] But for the sake of the civil lawyer reading this book, let us imagine for a moment that U.S. law could be divided into public and private law. What can be learned from such an exercise? One might notice, for example, that public trade law does not exist in the way a civil lawyer might understand it.[49] Similarly, environmental law to a common law lawyer usually involves both public and private interests, as with the numerous cases brought by an administrative agency of the state against the private citizen. In the somewhat famous case of *Boomer v. Atlantic Cement Company*, it is the judge who, when writing his judgment of the conflict, points out that private law will not solve some problems—in this case, one of the natural environment—and that public law must do so. He writes:

> It seems apparent that the amelioration of air pollution will depend on technical research in great depth; on a carefully balanced consideration of the economic impact of close regulation; and of the actual effect on public health. It is likely to require massive public expenditure and to demand more than any local community can accomplish and to depend on regional and inter-state controls. A court should not try to do this on its own as a by-product of private litigation and it seems manifest that the judicial establishment is neither equipped in the limited nature of any judgment it can pronounce nor prepared to lay down and implement an effective policy for the elimination of air pollution. This is an area beyond the circumference of one private lawsuit. It is a direct responsibility for government and should not thus be undertaken as an incident to solving a dispute between property owners and a single cement plant ....[50]

Several observations can be made here. The judge writes from the position that one should first expect to solve an air pollution conflict as a private problem. In this vein,

---

Ludwig Wittgenstein, *Philosophical Investigations*. Trans. G. E. M. Anscombe. 4th ed. West Sussex: Wiley Blackwell, 2009 *passim*.

[48] See Robert Barker, "Constitutional Comparisons Between the Law of the U.S.A. and Costa Rica," 27 *Latin American Law Review* (1992) 234.

[49] See Keith E. Wilder, "The 'Public Business' Conundrum," 3:2 *Kölner Schrift zum Wirtschaftsrecht* (April, 2012) 232–5.

[50] *Boomer v. Atlantic Cement Company*, 26 N.Y.2d 219, 223 (N.Y. 1970).

authors Subrin and Woo have commented that "It is to civil litigation that Americans frequently turn for redress of social ills; and it is a rights-based culture that has shaped and is reshaped by the process of litigation."[51] Only when that fails do they suggest that the problem ought to be one of public law and state enforcement. In other words, one should note that the default position is to solve a problem through private action, not through state control. By contrast, in looking for a book from which to teach German environmental law, I found that many books begin with a peculiar sort of disclaimer in which the author practically apologizes to the student for the fact that "there is no environmental law code."[52] Having said that, the authors go on to discuss all the public law statutes that do exist regarding air, water, waste and other environmental matters. What are we losing by not having all these norms in one code book? It certainly does not mean there is no environmental legislation, nor that the norms found in the legislation are any less valid because they are not in a code book. It also does not mean that the state will not enforce them. The non-existent code book is not a legal distinction, but a cultural distinction. One can find counterfactual examples contrary to the cultural assumption that law should be found in a code in even more common areas of the law than environmental law. For example, in Germany the "legally approved factual flexibility of relationships has, among other things, had the consequence that many contracts which are of central commercial importance receive no mention in the law of obligations of the Civil Code. Examples are leasing, factoring, and franchising agreements."[53]

Employing the Zweigert and Kötz notion of functionality, even if one has a particular source of law under consideration, such as a piece of statutory legislation, one cannot assume that such a source has only one function for all legal systems. One may typically think of statutes as being the primary norm emanating from the duly-elected law-making body. But the reverse could be true. In England, for example, statutes such as the Statute of Marlborough (1267), Statute of Westminster I (1275), the Statute of Gloucester (1284) and the Statute of Westminster II (1285) were used to correct excesses and corruption in the judiciary. The judiciary, up until that time, had largely been appointees of the king from among those whom he favored, regardless of their legal abilities or experience. The judiciary had been seen as the primary norm-giver, and the statutes were used to correct it, not vice versa:

> During or immediately after this period [of Statutory intervention] a practice arose of the utmost importance to Anglo-American law: judges were chosen not from the king's favorites, but from eminent sergeants-at-law. Henceforth practicing lawyers were to be the sole source of the higher judiciary. This meant that a community of interest between the bench and bar would exist to a closer degree than in any other legal system. When in 1292 legal education

---

51 Stephen N. Subrin and Margaret Y. K. Woo, *Litigating in America: Civil Procedure in Context.* New York: Aspen Publishers, 2006 7.

52 See for example Michael Kloepfer, *Umweltrecht.* 3rd ed. Munich: Beck, 2004.

53 Gerhard Robbers, *An Introduction to German Law.* 5th ed. Baden-Baden: Nomos, 2012 162.

was entrusted to judges, the system became totally inbred. Lawyers taught prospective lawyers, judges were selected from lawyers, and judges supervised legal education. This system proved to have a high degree of resistance to foreign ideas and to purely academic theorizing.[54]

Today, as common law lawyers, U.S. lawyers do not approach legal solutions from a comprehensive, top-down, rationalist hierarchy that a code might suggest. Instead, the law has developed, as U.S. Supreme Court Justice Learned Hand has famously said, as an accretion of cases, like the building of coral, one case at a time. Roscoe Pound adds:

> The actual legal order is not a simple rational thing. It is a complex, more or less irrational thing into which we struggle to put reason and in which, as fast as we have put some part of it in the order of reason, new irrationalities arise in the process of meeting new needs by trial and error. ... We must think not in terms of an organism, growing because of and by means of some inherent property, but once more, as in the eighteenth century, in terms of building, built by men to satisfy human desires and continually repaired, restored, rebuilt and added to in order to meet expanding or changing desires or even changing fashions.[55]

Even when "sources of law" are discussed as such, they are best considered after institutions, as historian Frederick Kempin does.[56] Just as custom is not to be taken lightly, customary law should not be dismissed by professional lawyers. As Montaigne reminds us, "there is nothing that custom will not or cannot do; and with reason Pindar calls her, so I have been told, the queen and empress of the world."[57]

The legal system that emerged during the eighteenth century in the United States still reflects its foundation in the values of both the Enlightenment and the Industrial Revolution. As these values took root and matured over the centuries that followed, their unique influence on U.S. jurisprudence became more and more enshrined—for good and ill. The Enlightenment's focus on secular first principles of society, coupled with the established "Rights of Englishmen," led to a unique constitutional experiment that is still playing itself out. In the commercial sphere, the influence of both John Locke and Adam Smith are also pervasive. What becomes evident is a legal system founded on the ideals of individualism. It is a legal system that envisions tying oneself to the soil and creating property where in the eyes of the early immigrants there was none. In addition, the system brings about a theory of contract tied to "bargain" not to "promise," with profound repercussions. It is a

---

[54] Kempin, *supra* note 9 at 91.
[55] Roscoe Pound, *Interpretations of Legal History*. Cambridge: Cambridge University Press, 1923.21. See also Coquillette, *supra* note 32 at 609.
[56] Kempin, *supra* note 9 at 95.
[57] Michel de Montaigne, *Essays*, Book I, "Of custom, and not easily changing an accepted law," (1572–74), trans. Donald M. Frame. London: Alfred Knopf, 1980 essay 23, page 100.

legal system that claims to reflect the values of self-determination, self-mastery and individual accountability. These values are expressed in a legal system that begins with individual conflict resolution, not the state's legislation.

3.2 A Note on Case Decisions

As with common law generally, the character of U.S. law is frequently overgeneralized as being limited to judge-made law, while the character of civil law is overgeneralized as being limited to statutory law. While in fact it is true that there are features for each of the two systems that point in these directions, there are many other differences between the two systems that are important precisely because they are more revealing about the ways that a lawyer from the other system might be thinking in a collaborative project or in resolving a conflict.[58] Nevertheless, since it is so often the case that one hears that "common law is case law and civil law is statutory law," one must confront rather than dismiss these claims, even if these features are over-emphasized. Each of these broad categories of world systems uses cases and statutes, as well as constitutions and regulations. Nowadays, most common law jurisdictions rely heavily upon statutory law as the primary source of law in most areas of legal practice, leaving what one might call "pure common law" (that is, judges deciding disputes for which there is no statutory authority) to almost only one area of private law in the United States—torts.[59] In public law, given the fact that the U.S. Constitution is a remarkably short text, its application relies heavily upon court decisions in cases of conflict, of course,[60] but nevertheless the courts are mostly basing their decisions upon some reading of the Constitution itself.

In civil law countries and international systems such as the European Court of Justice and the World Trade Organization's Appellate Bodies, more and more legal practice makes explicit reference to prior case decisions, even when the common law doctrine of binding precedent called *stare decisis* is not in operation. Moreover, taking Germany as just one example, practicing lawyers in civil law countries report that they often cite prior case decisions in cases they bring before a court.[61] While the crude comparatist might believe that common law systems exclusively build the rule of law from judicial decisions and only the common law systems do so, the more subtle comparatist would consider the civil law doctrine of *jurisprudence constante*, which is even practiced in a few parts of North America. All Canadian provinces except one—Quebec—are Anglophone and practice common law. Quebec

---

[58] Oscar G. Chase et al., *Civil Litigation in Comparative Context*. St. Paul, MN: West Academic Publishing, 2007.

[59] Coquillette, *supra* note 32 at 597.

[60] As has been true for much of the history of the common law, U.S. courts generally do not provide advisory opinions, whereas the European Court of Justice through Article 267 (ex Art. 234) of the Treaty on the Functioning of the European Union does, but instead are limited to deciding "cases" and "controversies" by Article III, Section 2 of the U.S. Constitution.

[61] Reinhold Zippelius, *Juristische Methodenlehre*. 11th ed. Munich: C. H. Beck, 2003.

is Francophone and unsurprisingly practices civil law in part. So too in the United States—the state of Louisiana was originally a French colony, part of the population retains a version of the French language, and unsurprisingly, it is the only U.S. state to use civil law in part. Thus, the courts of Louisiana must be versed in both systems. The Louisiana Supreme Court took it upon itself in the case of *Willis-Knighton Med. Ctr. v. Caddo-Shreveport Sales & Use Tax Comm'n* to note that although one case from a higher court would be sufficient to create a rule of law under the doctrine of *stare decisis*, one would require "a series of adjudicated cases, all in accord, [to] form the basis for *jurisprudence constante*."[62] And the Louisiana Court of Appeals reminds comparatists of a further refinement. In the case of *Royal v. Cook,* the court pointed out that *jurisprudence constante* is a secondary source of law and therefore is not of the same power as *stare decisis*.[63] Even so, this distinction between *stare decisis* and *jurisprudence constante* is a far more subtle distinction than the simple and false dichotomy of saying the common law uses *only* case decisions to develop rules of law and civil law *never* uses case decisions when developing rules of law.

3.3 Comparisons within the Family: English Law and U.S. Law

While comparative law usually rests upon the distinctions among the so-called "legal families" of the world,[64] there are differences even among the various states' employment of the common law system.[65] The legal system that emerged during the eighteenth century in the United States is not only distinguishable from civil legal systems, but intentionally distinguished itself from its English common law cousin. The first example comes from the very English area of the private law of property. In the famous case of *Van Ness v. Pacard,*[66] Pacard had constructed a building on the land of his landlords, Mr. and Mrs. Van Ness. At the end of his lease, Pacard tore the building down and removed it. Mr. and Mrs. Van Ness took a legal action against Pacard based upon the common law tortious cause of action known as "waste."[67] In support of their action, the plaintiffs cited English law that distinguished removing buildings built for agriculture from removing buildings used to house a trade. Justice

---

[62] *Willis-Knighton Med. Ctr. v. Caddo-Shreveport Sales & Use Tax Comm'n.*, 903 So.2d 1071 (2005).

[63] *Royal v. Cook*, 984 So.2d 156 (La. Ct. App. 2008).

[64] The notion of legal families is most often cited as it is developed by Konrad Zweigert and Hein Kötz, *supra* note 1, *passim*. It treats comparative law as the foundation upon which the study of U.S. law rests when the reader is a lawyer from any culture other than the United States.

[65] An excellent application of something resembling Matthias Reimann's four-part comparative system in the *Oxford Handbook of Comparative Law* is made by Queen's Counsel and Senior Dean of Oxford's All Souls College, Jeremy Lever, *supra* note 19, *passim*.

[66] *Van Ness v. Pacard* 2 Pet. 137, 7 L. Ed. 374 (1829).

[67] William B. Stoebuck, "Reception of English Common Law in the American Colonies," 10 *Wm. & Mary L. Rev.* (1968) 393; See David Brion Davis, *Antebellum American Culture: An Interpretive Anthology*. Lexington, MA: D. C. Heath and Company, 1979.

Joseph Story of the U.S. Supreme Court rejected the notion that U.S. common law must follow English common law:

> The common law of England is not to be taken in all respects to be that of America. Our ancestors brought with them its general principles, and claimed it as their birthright; but they brought with them and adopted only that portion which was applicable to their situation.[68] ... The country was a wilderness, and the universal policy was to procure its cultivation and improvement. The owner of the soil as well as the public, had every motive to encourage the tenant to devote himself to agriculture, and to favour any erections which should aid this result; yet, in the comparative poverty of the country, what tenant could afford to erect fixtures of much expense or value, if he was to lose his whole interest therein by the very act of erection? His cabin or log-hut, however necessary for any improvement of the soil; would cease to be his the moment it was finished.[69]

So here we can see that a legal culture that inherits its sources of law and norms from another legal culture may see fit to deviate at precisely the point where the availability and use of land differs. Some scholars even see the *Van Ness* case as demonstrating that colonial judges and their successors had a unified sense of at least basing their decisions on English common law, unless exceptions were justified.

Another example comes from the felony merger rule. The roots of this case help to explain why common law separates obligations into two distinct fields of torts and contracts. Private obligations that are not contracts—that is, torts—have historical connections to criminal law. Contracts do not. In the famous case of *Moragne v. State Marine Lines, Inc.*, the U.S. Supreme Court wrote:

> The historical justification marshaled for the rule in England never existed in this country. In limited instances American law did adopt a version of the felony-merger doctrine, to the effect that a civil action was delayed until after the criminal trial. However, in this country the felony punishment did not include forfeiture of property; therefore, there was nothing, even in those limited instances, to bar a subsequent civil suit. Nevertheless, despite some early cases in which the rule was rejected as "incapable of vindication," American courts generally adopted the English rule as the common law of this country as well.[70]

According to William B. Stoebuck, Chief Justice Lemuel Shaw of Massachusetts took a similar position in 1847 in *Commonwealth v. Chapman*. 54 Mass. (13 Met.) 69 (1847).[71] And in his Commentaries, New York's Chancellor Kent, about whom

---

[68] 27 U.S. 144.
[69] 27 U.S. 145.
[70] *Moragne v. States Marine Lines, Inc.*, 398 U.S. 375, 384 (1970) (case citations omitted).
[71] Stoebuck, *supra* note 67, at 394.

more will be said in Chapter 6 also agrees, saying: "It [the common law] was imported by our colonial ancestors, as far as it was applicable, and was sanctioned by royal charters and colonial statutes."[72] Stoebuck has found that an almost opposite position on the reception can be supported:

> Professor Paul S. Reinsch … denied that, at least in the colonial beginnings in the seventeenth century and perhaps along into the eighteenth as well, English jurisprudence was even a subsidiary force in the American legal system. Though conceding the colonists expressed adhesion to the common law, Reinsch says the actual administration of justice was "of a rude, popular, summary kind."[73]

There are of course other differences between the U.S. and English legal systems. In England, the general rule developed by the courts is that statutes should be read without reference to legislative intent.[74] Moreover, because Parliament is supreme, "[i]t is the considered opinion of the English courts that no court in England may declare a statute void on the ground that it is unconstitutional."[75] Not so in the United States. In the United States there is a general policy to try to interpret a statute in accordance with the intention of the legislature.[76]

Judicial review of legislation is foreign to most civil law countries; their legislatures make the ultimate decision as to whether legislation is constitutional.[77] Perhaps due to the heavy influence of the United States as an occupying power after the Second World War, Germany is an exception to this general rule. In addition, Brazil and Japan have a degree of judicial review and France has had a Constitutional Council since 1958, although it is not part of the judiciary.[78] Further, a defendant in a criminal case may waive the right to a jury trial and rely upon the judge as the finder of fact—a common practice in England, but not in the United States.[79] In addition, the civil jury, a subject of much criticism, was "virtually abolished in England, its birthplace, in the middle of [the twentieth century]. Australia and New

---

[72] James Kent, *Commentaries on American Law* 473 (quoted in William B. Stoebuck, "Reception of English Common Law in the American Colonies," 10 *Wm. & Mary L. Rev.* (1968) 393, 394).

[73] Paul S. Reinsch, "The English Common Law in the Early American Colonies," in *Select Essays in Anglo-American History*. Boston, MA: Little, Brown, and Company, 1907 367, 369 (quoted in Stoebuck, *supra* note 72 at 394).

[74] Kempin, *supra* note 9 at 16. As an example, in at least one of the United States (Pennsylvania), the state legislature itself, known as the "General Assembly," has passed legislation that requires courts and lawyers practicing before them to ascertain legislative intent. Volume 1 of the Pennsylvania Consolidated Statutes, §1921(a) states: "Legislative intent controls. Object and scope of construction of statutes. – The object of all interpretation and construction of statutes is to ascertain and effectuate the intention of the General Assembly. Every statute shall be construed, if possible, to give effect to all its provisions."

[75] Kempin, *supra* note 9 at 17.

[76] *Ibid.* at 16.

[77] *Ibid.*

[78] *Ibid.*

[79] *Ibid.* at 52.

Zealand followed England's lead."[80] The United States has not and continues to make juries available in civil as well as criminal cases, although the frequency of choosing to use them in civil cases has declined.[81]

Further the English "judge has in general considerable confidence in his own powers of judgement and in his own way of expressing things. One has the impression that, by and large, society regards this self-confidence as justified. The appointment of someone as High Court judge in England is still seen as a considerable vote of confidence in the powers of judgment of the person concerned."[82] Oliver Wendell Holmes, Jr. is often quoted as defining law to be experience, not rationality. This experience is the experience of the law in contact with the society it serves.

> Although social conditions, constantly changing, are the context within which law develops, it cannot validly be claimed that they are solely responsible for legal change. Ever since the legal profession developed the thinking of lawyers about the law has been the main source of change. In some historical periods lawyers' thinking about law was, it seems, totally isolated from social conditions. Thinking about law was sometimes nothing more than a game for its own sake, and law so developed as theoretically logical derivations from accepted legal propositions ... Lawyers are not necessarily dominant in the legislative process. The thinking of lawyers, however, does affect the way statutes are interpreted [during litigation]. Lawyers describe this process with the aphorism that "The law changes with its application."[83]

Thus the common law, as practiced in the courtroom involves both lawyers and the real experience of society, one case at a time, in the law-making. Holmes was likely thinking of this as distinct from relying upon legislative bodies to get it right during the law-making process, when he says that law is not "mathematical theorems."

There is a related category that distinguishes U.S. law from that of England. It is often and generally assumed that all that is U.S. law was first English law. Not so. For example,

> [the] habit of writing opinions that summarized both parties' arguments and sorted out the authorities struck [Chancellor James] Kent as distinctly American. But soon, a few English judges also began delivering elaborate written opinions. ... Suddenly, the carefully crafted opinion was an American form to which English decisions were compared.[84]

---

[80] *Ibid.* at 52–3.

[81] The U.S. Department of Justice reports that the number of civil cases going to trial is declining rapidly. Surveys reveal that in 1962, 11.5 percent of all civil cases in federal court went to trial. The survey revealed that by 2002, that number had dropped to 1.8 percent. From 1985 to 2003, the number of tort trials in U.S. district courts dropped nearly 80 percent, from 3,600 trials to fewer than 800 trials. See U. S. Department of Justice's Bureau of Statistics, National Center for State Courts, vol. 4, no. 1 (Spring 2000).

[82] Schiemann, *supra* note 15 at 743.

[83] Kempin, *supra* note 9 at 5–6.

[84] Daniel J. Hulsebosch, "An Empire of Law: Chancellor Kent and the Revolution in Books in the Early Republic." 60 *Ala. L. Rev.* (2008–09) 377, 403.

This simple chronological ordering has a further significance. The written judicial opinion, and the ability of lawyers to find them in some fashion such as official reporters, makes the scientific practice of *stare decisis* possible. And it was the U.S. lawyers who first invented official reports of the judicial opinions for the U.S. Supreme Court. By the U.S. civil war, which ended in 1865, nearly all state courts had done the same. "In England, semiofficial reports did not appear until 1865, although they appeared in some form considerably earlier in the same century."[85] Moreover, the U.S. Constitution already provided for a Supreme Court as the one highest court in the country in 1789, followed by the state constitutions. "In England there was no one highest court until 1873."[86] With the hierarchy of the courts clearly in place as well as the judicial habit of writing formal opinions and finally an official reporter system for recording the opinions in a way that could be researched and used by lawyers and judges all, the necessary tools were in place to enable the United States to change its position on *stare decisis* from that of believing that judges declared law to one of saying that judges make law. All that the United States needed was common law theory to back this up, and that came from Englishman John Austin's legal positivism.[87] "By 1825 some of the older states had started to stress the binding power of a single prior decision, and by 1850 the doctrine was firmly entrenched."[88]

In conclusion, after a consideration of why one should treat the study of U.S. law as the study of foreign law (Chapter 1) and a consideration of why one should treat the study of U.S. law as an exercise in comparative law (Chapter 2) and a consideration of why one should compare U.S. law both through its legal family of common law and in its distinctive sense even among other common law cultures (Chapter 3), we are ready to properly further compare the foreign institutions, processes and sources of law in the United States through the reference frames of history, social study, language, philosophy, disciplinarity and finally legal mechanics. In the next chapter, we will look at U.S. legal culture through the historical reference frame. Many of the most important lessons learned from comparative law, which focuses on comparing legal traditions across the earth today, apply equally to looking at legal history, which leads us to compare legal traditions across time. But before we look at the facts of history, we must be conscious of our own sense of the pattern of history, if any. That pattern is disputable, but is nevertheless present in all historical explanations as a reference frame.

CHECK YOUR UNDERSTANDING:

What is the difference between comparing common law and civil law sources from the "bottom up" (inductively) or from the "top down" (deductively)?

---

[85] Kempin, *supra* note 9 at 104.
[86] *Ibid*. at 104–5.
[87] *Ibid*. at 103–4.
[88] *Ibid*. at 105.

CHALLENGE YOUR UNDERSTANDING:

If you are from a civil law culture, try mapping out a description of your legal system starting with the persons of the legal system, then the institutions the persons have constructed, then the methods of conflict resolution. How does this differ from the way in which your legal system is usually described?

FURTHER YOUR UNDERSTANDING:

The various legal cultures of the world include more than common law and civil law jurisdictions. Some have religious systems, monarchies, local law or mixed systems. Do any of the differences between common law and civil law lend themselves to knowing the soul and spirit of other legal systems?

Literature

Berman, Harold J., *Law and Revolution: The Formation of the Western Legal Tradition*. London: Harvard University Press, 1983.

Chase, Oscar G., Helen Hershkoff, Linda Silberman and Yasuhei Taniguch, *Civil Litigation in Comparative Context*. St. Paul, MN: West Academic Publishing, 2007.

Coquillette, Daniel, *The Anglo-American Legal Heritage*. 2nd ed. Durham, NC: Carolina Academic Press, 2004.

Frankenberg, Günter, "Critical Comparison, Re-Thinking Comparative Law," 26 *Harv. Int'l L. J.* (1985). 411.

Holmes, Jr., Oliver Wendell., "The Path of Law," 10 *Harv L. Rev.* (1897). 457.

Kempin, Frederik G., *Legal History: Law and Social Change*. Englewood Cliffs, NJ: Prentice-Hall, 1963.

Lever, Jeremy, *Why Procedure is more Important than Substantive Law*, 48 *Int'l and Comp L. Q.* (April 1999). 285, 297.

Maine, Henry Sumner, *Ancient Law*. 10th ed. London: John Murray, 1884.

Markesinis, Basil, "Comparative Law—A Subject in Search of an Audience," 53 *The Modern Law Review* (1990). 1.

Sack, Peter G., "Law & Custom: Reflections on the Relations Between English Law and the English Language, 18 *Rechtstheorie* (1987). 421.

Schiemann, Konrad, "The Common Law Judge to European Judge," 4 *Europäisches Privatrecht* (ZEuP) (2005). 741–9.

Stoebuck, William B., "Reception of English Common Law in the American Colonies," 10 *Wm. & Mary L. Rev.* (1968). 393.

Suber, Peter, "Legal Reasoning after Post-Modern Critiques of Reason," 3 *Legal Writing* (1997). 21–50.

Suchman, Mark C. and Elizabeth Mertz, "A New Legal Empiricism? Assessing ELS and NLR," 6 *Annual Review of Law and Social Science* (2010). 561.

Tribe, Lawrence H., "Trial by Mathematics: Precision and Ritual in the Legal Process," 84 *Harv L. Rev* (1971). 1329.

White, James Boyd, "Law as Rhetoric, Rhetoric as Law: The Arts of Cultural and Communal Life," 52 *U. Chi. L. Rev.* (1985). 684.

4

THE HISTORICAL REFERENCE FRAME OF "KINGLESS COMMONWEALTHS ON THE OTHER SHORE OF THE ATLANTIC"[1]

Framing Issues

1. Do lawyers need to know history?
2. When one's theory of history changes, how does that change our practices in law?

The remaining six chapters each present a different reference frame through which to see the U.S. legal system. Each chapter begins by exploring the problems that are inherently part of that reference frame, and then applies the reference frame to the substance of U.S. law. Among the six reference frames, the historical reference frame can be seen as all-encompassing:

> [i]n law, as in other areas of human activity and learning, three valid questions may be asked: Where did it come from, where is it, and where is it going. Where the law came from can be traced through legal history; where it is now can partly be explained by legal history; where it is going may be indicated by trends and enduring principles revealed by the study of legal history.[2]

---

[1] The full sentence from which this title is taken comes from F. W. Maitland: "Those few men who were gathered at Westminster round Pateshull and Raleigh and Bracton were penning writs that would run in the name of kingless commonwealths on the other shore of the Atlantic Ocean; they were making right and wrong for us and for our children." F. Pollock and F. W. Maitland, *The History of English Law Before the Time of Edward I.* Ed. S.F.C. Milsom. Vol. II. 2nd ed. Cambridge: Cambridge University Press, 1968 674.

[2] Frederick G. Kempin, *Historical Introduction to Anglo-American Law.* St. Paul, MN: West, 1990 5.

4.1 The Problems of History

The U.S. legal system today belongs to what Zweigert and Kötz have called the "Anglo-American family,"[3] noted for its system of common law, an orderly species of the genus customary law. All references to the common law invoke a legal system that originated in England, was widespread over the world through the colonies of the British Empire (and therefore always practiced in the English language) and has been in place for centuries. But to know *where* it originated is just one of many points with which one could begin a narrative for understanding the U.S. legal system.

We have the habit of assuming a rational basis for existing institutions. History teaches us that, in fact, few extant institutions were created to address today's people or problems. To know whether they should be kept, one must know their histories:

> The rational study of law is still to a large extent the study of history. History must be a part of the study, because without it we cannot know the precise scope of rules which it is our business to know. It is part of the rational study, because it is the first step toward an enlightened skepticism, that is, towards a deliberate reconsideration of the worth of those rules. When you get the dragon out of his cave on to the plain and in the daylight, you can count his teeth and claws, and see just what his strength is. But to get him out is only the first step. The next is either to kill him, or to tame him and make him a useful animal.[4]

A common example where observation of a current fact, coupled with rationalism alone, might lead a person to state false conclusions would be to conclude that the twentieth-century "small claims court" in the United States is a descendant of the thirteenth-century shire courts of the United Kingdom. History shows that the small claims jurisdiction of the shire courts was instead a result of the very inception of the idea of an attorney at law:

> The shire courts retained jurisdiction over many civil disputes as well as lesser crimes. The decline in prestige of the shire courts, however, can be seen in the practice, starting in 1236, of permitting its suitors, who had been important men, to send attorneys to the shire courts in their stead. In the late 13th century the rule arose that the shire courts could not hear cases for amounts over forty shillings. The inevitable reduction in the value of money due to inflation over the years meant that the shire courts ultimately could hear only the smallest claims.[5]

---

[3] Konrad Zweigert and Hein Kötz, *An Introduction to Comparative Law*. Trans. Tony Weir. 3rd ed. Oxford: Oxford University Press, 1998 *passim*.
[4] Oliver Wendell Holmes Jr., "The Path of Law," 10 *Harv L. Rev.* (1897) 457.
[5] Kempin, *supra* note 2 at 25.

Such examples support the insistence of the empiricist that one has observed facts from which to build norms. According to the empiricist, without correct facts from history, pure rationalism is just guessing.

Too often we speak and write of history as if it is a neatly-packaged section on the bookshelf or course of study at the university. In this unreflective mode, we might well then say that the topic of history is something like "the facts of the past." Even the least critical ear should hesitate upon hearing this description, however. Even if we were to limit ourselves to narratives of past humans, this would mean the facts of approximately 107 billion human lives[6] would need to be told. This is impossible of course, but this difficulty illustrates the point that the telling of any history, even just human history, is a series of choices, and the way in which the choices are made reflects the preferences, goals and even prejudices (as the historian Harold J. Berman notes) of the story-teller. Historians know this. But the rest of us seem to ignore it, if we ever knew it.

This brings us then to how we select the facts of a culture to call "legal history." At this juncture, we learn that different cultures select different types of facts to call "legal history." My review of legal histories shows that very often, that which is called "legal" history begins with the attempt to locate a time when either a state was founded or a text was discovered or written, and then tell a narrative forward to the present using that state or that text as the glue bonding the "facts of history" together. The former, I would call a political history and although the latter is a legal history, it is one that usually does not justify why the date of a text should be the starting point for telling the story of a people. For example, the history of the law of the United States would often begin with the Declaration of Independence in 1776 and the written constitution thirteen years later. Another example would be the history of the civil law told as the history of the *Corpus Juris Civilis*, either by theorizing its inception in Rome, or by discussing its rediscovery and use by Irnerius.[7] For the civil law, with its focus on the text of the civil code, this telling of history is the most comfortable, makes the most sense, and has the most impact, just to consider three possible criteria. But there are alternatives. Berman writes, for example, that "[t]here was a time not long ago when a good lawyer was required, in a similar way, to know the story of the development of legal *institutions*."[8] And, at least for the common law, I tend to agree with Frederick Kempin when he writes that the history of the

---

[6] See www.livescience.com/18336-human-population-dead-living-infographic.html (last accessed 9 September 2014).

[7] It is usually stated that when a copy of the *Digesta* from the *Corpus Juris Civilis* was discovered in Italy in the eleventh century, "Roman law became the subject of renewed attention from such scholars as Irnerius." Howard D. Fisher, *The German Legal System and Legal Language*, 4th ed. Oxon, UK/New York: Routledge (2009) 1. What is not so often stated, however, is that Irnerius was first a teacher of the liberal arts, not law *per se*, and likely first incorporated the *Corpus Juris Civilis* into his teaching of rhetoric in Bologna. Little of his own written work survives, but to the extent he is known today, it is as a glossator of the *Corpus Juris Civilis*, rather than his work as a lecturer.

[8] Harold J. Berman, *Law and Revolution*. London: Harvard University Press, 1983 7 (emphasis added).

common law may best be said to begin when lawyering became an independent profession.[9] Understood as the story of human beings, history ought to describe the humans in that story when describing the law. And especially for the study of law by professional lawyers or by soon-to-be professional lawyers (current law students), it makes sense to study the point at which law became a profession, rather than perhaps some other category of anthropological study. Kempin goes on to note that it was the conditions of institutions that enabled the lawyer to become independent; not just a matter of will for those persons wanting to be a profession. He asserts that "[c]hanges in customs controlling the constitution of government, including the courts, created the legal profession."[10] We can relate Kempin's assertion to the words of Oliver Wendell Holmes, Jr., when he wrote that "[t]he prophecies of what the courts will do in fact, and nothing more pretentious, are what I mean by the law."[11] This famous statement is often read by focusing on prediction, but it is just as important to note that in characterizing what law "is," he focused on courts and not on statutes or legislative bodies.

4.2 Framing the Questions of History, U.S. History and U.S. Legal History

When Holmes claims that by "the science of law" he means our ability to predict how judges will rule in the case at hand,[12] he is reminding us that ours is a science of prediction. For the common law lawyer, prediction, as a science, must be based upon experience, which is to say that we predict the future based upon a path of trajectory from the past. These trajectories are the observation of histories, both personal and cultural. The first thing for lawyers to learn from history is simply that legal systems have one. Rules of law and institutions of law go in and out of existence. Neither the rules nor the institutions were always as they are today. A second thing for anyone—including lawyers—to learn from history is that it would be foolish arrogance to believe we have arrived at some endpoint of perfection today such that no further change will, or needs to, occur. So it is not a question of whether things will change, but rather a question of what will change next, when and why?

A framing concept to study history is the concept of time. Although we often take the concept of time for granted, given that we are studying law through history, it is worth pausing on the notion of time for just a moment. When speaking of time, the ancient Greeks had at least two distinct words, χρόνος (chronos) and καιρός (kairos). Chronos treats time quantitatively as though each minute were exactly the same, resulting in a view of history that is simply the ordering of those uniform minutes. This is the time used in the everyday sense by science and technology, for example. Kairos, on the other hand, is a qualitative sense of time in which we look

---

[9] Kempin, *supra* note 2 at 2.
[10] *Ibid.* at 95.
[11] See Holmes, *supra* note 4.
[12] Oliver Wendell Holmes, Jr., *The Common Law*. Boston, MA: Little Brown and Co., 1881.

for the significance of particular moments in the past. Keeping that in mind, we see that history does not come to us divided into minutes that were all experienced uniformly. It depends upon how we inquire, it depends on who is inquiring, and it depends upon the materials that the inquirer uses to create past events and give them meaning. That said, one may see that history often does not even come to us in chronological order. And when it does, chronological order is not even naturally associated with the spatial sense that many languages give to it today. Consider for example that for the Romans, the past was said to be "before" us and the future "behind" us.[13] So an additional lesson from problematizing history is to realize that history tells its narratives not using chronos, but instead using kairos as the nature of time.

Yet, we can do no other when we talk of history than to stand in the present and think about another time. In doing so, we must be careful, however. In consideration of the Middle Ages, for example, "[w]e should not see ... the medieval perception in an isolated way or according to our current world view."[14] Thinking back to Chapter 2, we should also note that insofar as we are standing in one age and looking at another, our practice of history is in and of itself always and already a comparative practice by comparing things not from one place to another, but from one time to another. Just as it is hubris to regard all other places being important only in their relevance to one's own, it is naïve to regard all other times as being worthy of consideration only in comparison to one's own.[15]

It is difficult, if not impossible, to look at a different time through the historic reference frame without loading that frame with particular preconceptions about history. Most notably, we might treat history as though it were a pre-written narrative that leads inevitably to the present, a dangerous concept leading to romantic notions of destiny and fate that are mistaken for historic projections. The contingencies of history show us that what we regard as the present would be, and is, different if we are simply a different person constructing the narrative. Moreover, how we view the possible histories upon which we look—the choices of which I wrote earlier—is in large part telling our view of history. If we treat history as a reference frame, it helps us to see the problems embedded in many of our unreflective assumptions about history. There are at least six views of history that provide us with reference frames. To most easily understand them, we can plot arrows on simple graphs where the horizontal axis represents time and the vertical axis represents change. If indeed our common law science should enable us to predict how a judge will decide the case, then we must consider our sense of the patterns of history (those lines with arrows) that would enable us to do so.

---

[13] Maurizio Bettini, *Anthropology and Roman Culture. Kinship, Time, Images of the Soul.* Trans. J. van Sickle. Baltimore, MD: Johns Hopkins University Press, 1991.

[14] Bernhard Grossfeld, *Core Questions of Comparative Law.* Durham, NC: Carolina Academic Press, 2005 183.

[15] See Roscoe Pound, "Comparative Law in Space and Time," 4 *Am J. Comp. L.* 1 (1955) 70.

FIGURE 4.1   The Static View

The following snapshots should enable the reader to see that there are a variety of views of history. These are only snapshots designed to provide the reader with a heuristic catalogue of possibilities, not to provide a considered study. From among these six views, I shall begin with the static view of history.

4.2.1 The Static View

In the static view of history, nothing ever changes (see Figure 4.1). The human experience today is much as it was a thousand years ago and much as it will be a thousand years from now in the future. There may of course be different technologies around us, but the essence of who we are and what we do does not change. One might have a static view of history only as to one sector of life's experience. For example, "Why should I vote?" my grandmother would ask rhetorically. "They are all the same and when one is done doing his dirt the next one will come and do the same." My grandmother held the static view of history for the political sector of human experience.

4.2.2 The Circular or Cyclical View

In the cyclical view of history, things do change over time, but ultimately return to a point where they have been in the past. The German philologist and philosopher Friedrich Nietzsche borrowed the ancient idea of "the eternal recurrence of the same" from Asian and Greek cultures to describe this view.[16] Graphically, the cyclical view would look something like Figure 4.2.

---

[16] For Nietzsche's most concentrated discussion of history, see Friedrich Nietzsche, *Vom Nutzen und Nachteil der Historie für das Leben* (1874) which was originally published as one of four *Untimely Meditations* (*Unzeitgemässe Betrachtungen*), translated by R. J. Hollingdale as "On the Uses and Disadvantages of History for Life," and edited by David Breazeale, Cambridge University Press, 1997. See Graham Parkes, *Nietzsche and Asian Thought.* Chicago, IL: University of Chicago Press, 1991.

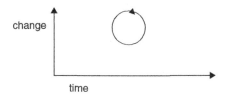

FIGURE 4.2 The Circular or Cyclical View

4.2.3 The Progressive or Enlightenment View

In this view, which generally has been regarded as being "true" or at least normal in the West since the age of the Enlightenment, the further along we go in time, the more progress we make. Such a view of course must assume that today we are more advanced than we were in the past and that in the future we will be more advanced than we are today. Ancient civilizations from which we claim to get our Western pedigree did not labor under this notion, however. "Heraclitus did not know progress. Neither did Plato or Aristotle, who saw the circle as the image of perfection: the beginning is also the end."[17] What the Enlightenment view through progress does not indicate is the nature of the point to which we are progressing, such as a destiny, fate or even τέλος (purpose), nor whether there even is such a point. Rather, it is concerned with whether our position today, *relative to yesterday* is better, insofar as we can measure, record and represent yesterday, and from that, make the assumption that things will continue as such. Oliver Wendell Holmes Jr.'s notion of predictability based on experience in the common law is rooted in this theory of history as progress. The quality of what it means to progress is not often examined. The progressive view does not usually make clear the criteria by which we can evaluate progress. Often, either technological or medical progress is cited. This brings the reader to a challenging question. Rather than frame progress in terms of science or technology, what would it mean to say that a legal system has made progress? It could mean that more persons in a legal system have access to courts, that more people actually receive just treatment, or that the quality not the quantity of justice is improved. The progressive view most often assumes that the engine that drives progress is human reason and rationality. In the

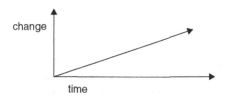

FIGURE 4.3 The Progressive or Enlightenment View

[17] Octavio Paz, *In Light of India.* Trans. Eliot Weinberger. New York: Harcourt, Inc., 1997 188.

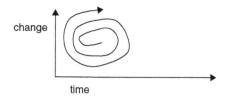

change

time

FIGURE 4.4 The Spiral View

present era, western culture seems to be so thoroughly soaked with this perspective of history that it is taken as the only or even the "normal" view of history. The progressive view of history could be charted as shown in Figure 4.3.

4.2.4 The Spiral View

If we were to combine the circular and progressive views, we would get something like the spiral view. This theory of history, sometimes associated with the philosopher Georg F. W. Hegel,[18] can be represented in our simple graphs as a spiral (see Figure 4.4). Adherents to the spiral view hold that although we do progress, we also return to the same places in human existence, but at slightly more "advanced" levels.

4.2.5 The Cataclysmic View

In the fifth Western theory of history presented here, change does seem to occur, but it has no pattern and is therefore unpredictable, as illustrated in Figure 4.5. It is a view from the perspective of nihilism or chaos, in which history consists of only random events. It would be very difficult to imagine the operation of any legal system, whether at the point of conflict resolution, law-enforcing or law-making, that could operate if there was no sense whatsoever that persons would obey or accept the law, or that judges or legislators would create law through patterns of conflict resolution consistent with the past, or by fitting current resolutions into norms through a demonstrated rationality.

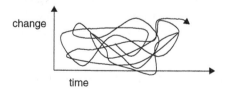

change

time

FIGURE 4.5 The Cataclysmic View

[18] See Georg F. W. Hegel, *Phenomenology of Spirit*. Trans. A. V. Miller. Oxford: Clarendon Press, 1977 (with a very useful analysis of the text and foreword by J. N. Findlay).

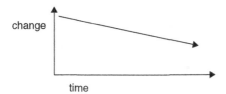

FIGURE 4.6 The Regressive View

4.2.6 The Regressive View

Finally, one should consider the regressive view of history in which the further we go in chronological time, the lower the quality value gets (see Figure 4.6). Some authors have used the second law of thermodynamics from physics as an analogy, thus calling this view "social entropy." In thermodynamic entropy, the world is tending to distribute energy irreversibly through systems that cannot do work ("work" in the sense of physics). One must be careful with the fit of the analogy, however, given that the second law of thermodynamics assumes a closed system. Given the permeation of legal borders by outside influences as well as law's own ability to change from within, it would seem this analogy is not so instructive. Even if the analogy is not instructive, the pattern should be taken seriously. What would a pattern of regression in history mean for legal systems over time? Cicero is reputed to have said that there is a direct proportion between the number of laws and the decay of a society living with those laws.

4.3 Proceeding from the Assumptions in the Various Views

So, the first thing observed about history in this chapter was that law *has* a history and lawyers should know it. "Your ultimate view of legal history will probably predict a great deal about the kind of lawyer you will become both professionally and politically, and your study of legal history may even influence this future."[19] A second thing we learn is that history makes use of a kairotic, not chronologic sense of time. Third, we saw through a study of six various views that there can be different assumptions about history that one makes even before one begins a particular historical narrative,[20] such as that of U.S. legal history. Different cultures and different individuals begin their narrative from different assumptions. For

---

[19] Daniel Coquillette, *The Anglo-American Legal Heritage*. 2nd ed. Durham, NC: Carolina Academic Press, 2004 600.

[20] For the role of narrative in history, see E. H. Carr, "History as Narrative," in *What is History?* Harmondsworth, UK: Penguin, 1987, 45–94. For a critique of the unitary discourse on history, see Michel Foucault, *L'Archéologie du Savoir*. Paris: Gallimard, 1969. An English translation by A. M. Sheridan Smith is available as *The Archaeology of Knowledge and the Discourse on Language*, New York: Pantheon Books, 1982.

the purposes of this book, the goal is that we become conscious of these assumptions. The U.S. legal narrative, beginning during the Enlightenment, predominantly assumes the prevalent view of history that was popular at that time—a progressive view of history. We can see, however, that "history is not unitary, but pluralistic."[21] "One, true answer" cannot be expected to questions of history. What we should instead try to do is understand why we choose to offer a particular history as a way of explaining the present. One could present more than the six views of history above, or one could dispute any of these six, but the point is that one must be aware of what view of history one has—and why—before one attempts to invent a history of any subject, including law. The English-trained barrister who would ultimately lead India, Mohandas K. Gandhi, noted that "[a] writer almost always presents one aspect of a case, whereas every case can be seen from no less than seven points of view, all of which are probably correct by themselves, but not correct at the same time and in the same circumstances."[22]

4.4 The Use and Abuse of History

A fourth learning point from history is that although we should be able to learn from history, we cannot use history to predict the future as though it is a mathematical extrapolation of the past the way a physicist might predict the location of a rocket or a moon, based upon mathematics and the presumed fixed laws of nature. This function is not possible with any theory of history! Even the straight lines of the static view or progressive view are misleading because past social events, no matter how regular, are never guaranteed to repeat in the same pattern.[23] The changing laws of states and human society are not the fixed laws of nature. One cannot predict with mathematical precision *when* human events will revisit themselves nor with which variations on the past. The cataclysmic view makes it all but impossible to predict, even under chaos theories in mathematics.

So if exact prediction is impossible, how can we use the experience we think we have gained through studies of legal history? How is the kind of prediction possible that Holmes, Jr. says defines the law? Most often in the studies of comparative law, legal history is studied through the histories of institutions and sources of law, a process that I call historical "reference framing." But what can be expected by only comparing the development of the courts, juries or legislation and codification

[21] J. W. Swain, "Theory of History by Frederik J. Teggart," 23 *The Journal of Philosophy* 25 (1926) 693–4.

[22] M. K. Gandhi, *An Autobiography or The Story of My Experiments with Truth*. Trans. Mahadev Desai. Ahmedabad: Navajivan Publishing House, 1927 30. Gandhi offers no reason for having used the number seven. Regardless of the absolute number, the point is that it is several, not one.

[23] See Ludwig Wittgenstein, *Philosophical Investigations*. Trans. G. E. M. Anscombe. 4th ed. W. Sussex: Wiley Blackwell, 2009 (in which he discusses how different interpreters will interpret even the pattern in a sequence of numbers differently, each calling his own pattern "natural").

from different legal systems? We might learn the differences in a very abstract way but the more important social information, such as how citizens settle disputes and shape their lives using these rules and institutions remains elusive, as do the ways in which the legal practitioners use the systems. To begin a look through the historical reference frame we must ask ourselves what we expect and what we can expect to achieve from looking at history at all, and especially U.S. legal history. The historical reference frame that follows tries to explain U.S. legal history not as inevitably leading to U.S. legal education and practices today, but rather as a frame within which today's social practices were possible.

4.5 Punished by Places and by Times: Establishing an Historical Narrative for U.S. Law

The historical approach is of course always limited to the historical evidence, for which too often insufficient data is available to arrive at a provable conclusion. Thus, the attitude that one takes to the limited available data matters a great deal. Historian of science J. E. McGuire has noted, for example, that the attitude of reifying texts defeats the project of history. On the contrary, a text must be read with the understanding of who wrote it and when, in the context of other texts, and in correspondence with the readers of the text, real or imagined.[24] For creating an understanding of legal history, we need at minimum an idea of the concepts, doctrines, and rules that have been used by the practicing lawyers and judges to keep order in a society. According to Frederick G. Kempin, ever since the legal profession developed, the best source of history has been the record of lawyers describing their own practices.[25] This is an advantage when it comes to studying common law because of the fact that so much of judicial decision-making has been recorded in writing. Those decisions originally read like a transcript of the lawyers' arguments[26] and to this day often still include explicit references to the words used by the parties in their arguments. Through the analyses of the recorded cases we have the chance to get an insight of the legal thinking at a certain period of time. The case decision opinions of common law judges give us facts, rules, the application of the rules and the reasoning behind new rules when they occur.

In addition to the stone records of past primary sources, such as the Code of Hammurabi or the Twelve Tables of Rome, we largely rely upon paper, vellum or even sometimes papyrus records of not only the laws themselves, but descriptions of the legal proceedings.[27] The Irish playwright Brian Friel connects our historical

---

[24] J. E. McGuire, "Reading Historical Texts," University of Ghent Sarton Medal Lecture, 28 April 2011 (notes on file with the author).

[25] Kempin, *supra* note 2 at 5.

[26] For an example of an opinion that is a bridge between the transcript model and the current scientific explanation model, see *Rylands v. Fletcher*, House of Lords, L.R. 1 Ex 265 (1866).

[27] J. H. Baker, *The Legal Profession and the Common Law*. London: Hambledon Press, 1986.

frame of reference to the language frame of reference, when he said about his play *Translations*: "It is not the literal past, the 'facts' of history, that shape us, but images of the past embodied in language."[28] In other words, for history to have meaning for us in the present the recorded "facts" must be connected through a narrative. And to this observation, I would add that the narrative itself is constructed using something like the assumptions that opened this chapter.

Regardless of the material of the source, we begin to realize that our ideas of the past are directed, enabled and limited by what is preserved from the past, and when it comes to law, that means written records in some medium. That record omits of course all that occurred that was unrecorded, including all that was only presented orally.[29] In the civil law tradition, for example, our narrative generally focuses upon the fact that when the *Corpus Juris Civilis* (C.J.C.) of Justinian was unearthed at Bologna, it enabled legal scholars to create a unified legal science, because there was a unifying legal text, even if it was one that was not at all the actual law in practice at the time. That same common narrative then tells us that scholars indeed did flock to study this text because already in the twelfth century, the work of the glossator Irnerius became indispensable for anyone wishing to systematically study all the interpretations of the C.J.C. that had already accumulated. Coincidentally, at nearly the same time, the decisions of the judges of England began to be recorded by William's men in Year Books, and these Year Books were eventually indexed through Abridgements and Reporters. Thus, we can see that in both the civil law and common law traditions, as soon as we speak of legal history, we must rely upon the written "facts" of history, and in the case of law, those facts are in the primary literature of the laws or authoritative interpretations of the law. But our narratives based upon these facts could be many and varied. Simple histories tend to suggest that the texts dictate only one possible narrative, and that narrative is often a political one, describing history as the acquisition of land by men through military force. Such a narrative would do little to tell us about domestic law or private law practices.

Recalling Chapter 2, when it comes to legal narratives, why choose the one that neatly distinguishes the world into only two systems—common law and civil law—and does so based on the facts of legal texts? Does this forced parallelism tell us something? On the contrary: The common law history of England has been continuous and uninterrupted for more than eight hundred years, whereas the civil tradition has been divided and reinvented in several different cultures and many different languages.

The method of this chapter is to place the history of U.S. legal culture in the context of the histories of English law and U.S. culture generally, with the forewarning that history of any sort is not a natural science, reducible to one "correct" narrative. With that in mind, we ask a question that demonstrates a *kairotic* rather than chronologic sense of history: How do we set up a date when we can say

---

[28] Brian Friel, *Translations*. New York: Samuel French, 1981 80.
[29] See Walter Ong, *Orality and Literacy. The Technologizing of the Word*. London: Routledge, 2002.

English law "began?" I follow the opinion of Kempin who feels the best answer to that question is when lawyering became a separate profession.[30]

> [The] Anglo-American system of law has been relatively mature (in the sense that it has been the object of study by a separate legal profession) for the past eight hundred years. It was preceded by the archaic and almost lost legal system of the Anglo-Saxons and finds its remote origins in the laws of the Germanic tribes which settled in England in the middle of the first millennium.[31]

This answer assumes that legal practices, not principles or ideas, or the text of statutes, are the stuff of the "law." By comparison, historical approaches usually assume that the starting point in British legal history is the Norman Conquest in 1066 and the changes to the Anglo-Saxon system by the Normans, which assumes principles or ideas are the law, not persons. Keep in mind that if we use the Norman Conquest of Saxon England as a starting point, it is we who have chosen where we begin to draw the line of history and should be able to say why.

4.5.1 The Birth of the Common Law

As the narrative is usually told, Anglo-Saxon law prevailed in England from the sixth century until the eleventh century. Then, in 1066 at the Battle of Hastings, William, Duke of Normandy, defeated the Saxon King Harold II and claimed for himself the crown of England.[32] The Norman Conquest in 1066 did not end Anglo-Saxon law, but it did change it. The changed system remained based upon custom.[33] This basis in custom continues in the common law right up to the present and it might well be the element that has been most responsible for common law's longevity.[34] If the law applied by judges is based upon the customs of the people they observed, then the law is already known to the people, not forced upon them. *One might even say that law based upon custom is of* the people. Thus, change occurs only slowly, case by case, even as governments change.

In addition, we should keep in mind the legal nature of William's claim to the throne. William's claim to the throne was as a matter of right, as the insider who was to have properly succeeded King Edward (the Confessor), not as an outsider who overthrew Harold II. Therefore as an insider who had a right to the throne, he also

---

[30] Kempin, *supra* note 2 at 5. There are alternatives, of course. For example, it has been suggested that the common law began with the twelfth-century elaboration and standardization of rules governing the term by which land was held, or the regular observance of custom by a feudal court. Kempin, *supra* note 2 at 28; Goldwin Albert Smith, *A Constitutional and Legal History of England*. New York: Charles Scribner's Sons, 1955. 70–1.

[31] *Ibid.* at 2.

[32] See for example Plantagenet Somerset Fry, *The Battle of Hastings 1066 and the Story of Battle Abbey*. London: English Heritage, 1990.

[33] Kempin, *supra* note 2 at 11.

[34] The exception would be the eleven-year rule by Oliver Cromwell in the seventeenth century, during which time he made what one might call "legislative changes." With the

honored the system of which he claimed to be the legitimate heir, and kept elements of the legal system in place. This did not change customary norms in England. "The Norman conquerors made certain changes in administration which, although they were to have radical effects, did not greatly alter existing English customs."[35]

It cannot be denied, however, that by installing an administrative system based on feudalism with the king as the owner of all land at its top, the Normans exerted a rather strong force on the Anglo-Saxon law. So, for example, in return for an oath of loyalty, the king granted large tracts of land to privileged chief lords. Thus, through the wise use of land, the lords could economically support themselves.[36] A further legal concept of the Norman feudal system was the idea that a feudal lord has jurisdiction over his tenants.[37]

The idea of feudal lord jurisdiction facilitated a new kind of private court in which the system of observed custom known as "common law" can be seen to have originated. By comparison, the *curia regis* (king's court) advised the king on matters of state, made agreements between the church and state, resolved conflicts between the tenants and acted as a type of legislature.[38] The *curia regis* mainly promoted the unity and consistency of the common law.[39] It enjoyed a special position: "over and above everything stand the pleas of the royal court, which preserves the use and custom of its law at all times and in all places and with constant uniformity."[40] Thus, the common law could be presumed to apply everywhere until a different local custom could be proven. Originally, the common law did not include substantive rights but rather only procedural remedies.[41] The custom of the realm became the custom of the courts, growing and intensifying the interactions between the customary law and the judges and lawyers who interpreted it.[42] But to ensure the feudal system the king's administration necessarily had to take over parts of the judiciary. When government became centralized near London, a bureaucracy was built up and written records maintained that enabled the facts of a legal history to be established. Parts of the pre-existing Anglo-Saxon system did survive, such as the jury, trial by ordeal and writs. The Norman king and his court of the *curia regis* did not stay in one place and the king's court necessarily followed the king.[43] However, a group of

---

restoration of the Stuart monarchy, Cromwell's body was disinterred and publicly hanged. Thus, one sees the relative failure of a forced legislative override of custom!

[35] Kempin, *supra* note 2 at 9.

[36] Kempin *supra* note 2 at 11; Smith, *supra* note 30 at 39.

[37] Kempin *supra* note 2 at 28; Smith, *supra* note 30 at 70–1.

[38] Kempin, *supra* note 2 at 28; Smith *supra* note 30 at 47.

[39] Baker, *supra* note 27 at 13.

[40] J. H. Baker, *An Introduction to English Legal History*. 4th ed. Oxford: Oxford University Press, 2002 13.

[41] See for example Michael Lobban, "*The Common Law and English Jurisprudence.*" Oxford: Clarendon Press, 1991 257–90 (cited in Robert Kagan et al. (eds.), *Legality and Community: On the Intellectual Legacy of Philip Selznick*. Lanham, MD: Rowman & Littlefield, 2002 128).

[42] Smith, *supra* note 30 at 118.

[43] Baker, *supra* note 27 at 17.

administrators did settle in one place, usually the Palace of Westminster in London, while the king was away.[44]

If one allows the Battle of Hastings to be the marker of the beginning of the English legal system as we know it today, one can, for purposes of understanding U.S. legal culture through the historical reference frame, divide the chronology of events into the three periods of early, middle and modern.

4.5.2 Early Period: Eleventh–Thirteenth Centuries

After William, the greatest changes in the early period happened during the reign of Henry II (1154–89). One commentator has said "[t]here is probably no court of common law on which the light of his reign has not fallen."[45] One of the most important overall changes was Henry II's royal claim to ownership of all the land in England.[46] But more specific to the practice of law was the use of the writ by Henry II's court. Although writs can be found as far back as Anglo-Saxon kings, the assertion has been made (not without eliciting some controversy) that the use of the writ for judicial matters did not begin until the Norman kings.[47] The writ, which at that time was nothing more than a written letter, was used as an order for the court to hear a case.[48]

As a consequence of the use of the writ, the young legal system quickly became overloaded. As a reaction to this, Henry II invented at least three writs to give quick and clear verdicts. They were: the possessory writ, which enforced recovery of the possession of land, the writ of Mort d'Ancestor, which decided whether the ancestor of a plaintiff had in fact possessed an estate, and the Darrein Presentment (that is, the "last presentation"), which decided who in fact had last presented a benefice to a church. It was the judges themselves who "spread the use of the elaborated technical system of forms of action."[49] But in recognition that speed may cause error, the verdicts produced by the three writs were also made subject to later revision. In addition to his development of the writ, Henry II accomplished the legislation known as the Assize of Clarendon in 1166, which established criminal procedure.[50]

If we focus upon the institutions of the time, we find that during the second half of the twelfth century the *curia regis* joined its administrators who were already in

---

[44] Smith, *supra* note 30 at 84; Baker, *supra* note 27 at 17.
[45] Smith, *supra* note 30 at 81.
[46] Kempin, *supra* note 2 at 31; Smith, *supra* note 30 at 84.
[47] Kempin, *supra* note 2 at 31; But see comments by Sidney Packard in 36 *Speculum* 2 (1961) 357, 358 in his review of R. C. van Caenegem, who maintains that the older theory of Giry and Brunner that the writ and the jury were brought to England by the Norman kings is no longer valid. See R. C. Van Caenegem, *Royal Writs in England from the Conquest to Glanvill: Studies in the Early History of the Common Law.* (Selden Society, LXXVII) London: Bernard Waritch, 1959, xlix, 556.
[48] Kempin, *supra* note 2.
[49] Smith, *supra* note 30 at 118.
[50] *Ibid.* at 97.

London at Westminster[51] and London became the center of all aspects of English law. Writs had become the medium of pleading and the courts were now centralized. The trial by ordeal had been replaced by the trial by jury. Juries resolved disputed facts and justices declared the principle and practices of the central courts at Westminster.

According to legal historian J. H. Baker, the emergence of the common law of England was more or less coincident with the appearance of professional judges, who were soon followed by practicing lawyers.[52] This is in line with Kempin's assertion that the independent profession of practitioners marks the beginning of the common law. On the relatively minor issue of whether professional judges or practitioners were first recognized, Kempin differs from Baker:

> Today we say the judge determines the law; this has been true for the past seven hundred years. But until long after the Conquest, judges were unknown. There were 'courts,' but they were composed of lay persons called suitors, who answered questions of 'law' on the basis of their knowledge of local custom. The heads of these bodies—the reeves, sheriffs, lords, and stewards—merely presided. Law was not yet a specialized body of knowledge that needed professional judges.[53]

While scholars may disagree as to whether it was the emergence of judges or practitioners that began the common law, it remains the case that these scholars agree on something more important, and that is that we mark the beginning of the common law with the emergence of professional persons, not with the discovery of a text. The invention of the independent practitioner emerged out of practical necessity. At first the individual represented himself before the king. But with Henry II's introduction of the writ for judicial matters, it became possible for a litigant to appoint someone to do his technical pleading. However, this appointee, as the first person to appear before the court and not himself be a party, was called the "*responsalis*," and was not a member of a separate profession.[54] The historical record does not indicate that the *responsalis* regularly appeared before the court. His role might be best understood as someone with a limited power of attorney in today's U.S. legal terminology, similar to what other Saxons—the Germans—would today call a *Vollmacht*. We cannot speak properly of a legal "profession" until such time as men were following the law for a living. That profession only recorded a size sufficient to be visible around the middle of the thirteenth century.

---

[51] Baker, *supra* note 27 at 17.
[52] *Ibid.* at 155.
[53] Kempin, *supra* note 2 at 22–3. How far urban society has gone from the expectation that a person could do all things for himself, and needed specialists only for areas of uncommon knowledge, to people who can do nothing for themselves, and need specialists to carry out even simple tasks such as walking their pet dog or planning their wedding!
[54] Kempin, *supra* note 2 at 78.

In addition to attorneys,

> [b]y the time of Henry III (1216–1272) judges had become professionals, and the courts had started to create a body of substantive legal knowledge as well as technical procedure. The narrators, or pleaders, came into being to speak for litigants in court and to perform the function of advocacy.[55]

Part of the evidence that lawyers were indeed an independent profession is the fact that there was some regulation of them in the law.[56] During the time of Edward I, who reigned from 1272 to 1307, the relatively new legal profession was in a rather bad condition. That which was now formally regarded as the business of lawyers had increased considerably, but preparation for the new profession was very weak. There were no independent law schools and the universities only taught ecclesiastical law—they considered the law of daily practice to be too vulgar for scholarly investigation. As a consequence, in 1292 Edward issued an order that addressed the situation. The order directed the courts of Common Pleas to choose certain "attorneys and learners" who would be permitted to take part in the business of the court. So although the direct effect of the order was to get legal training and education into respectable condition, the indirect effect of the order was to create a monopoly of the legal profession. "The effect of putting the education of lawyers into the hands of the court cannot be overestimated. It resulted in the relative isolation of English lawyers from Continental, Roman, and ecclesiastical influence."[57] This point cannot be overemphasized as we consider practices from comparative law. Henry III's reforms and contributions to the legal system served to create more unity and consistency in the system, which was well received by the public:

> Lawyer taught lawyer, and each learned from the processes of the courts, so that the law grew by drawing on its own resources and not by borrowing from others. It became insular. Whether this was good or bad for the development of the law is a debatable question, but it did create a unique system with a minimum of foreign ideas.[58]

A further point needs to be made here. Edward I's order not only cemented the difference between civil law and common law training, but also separated the secular lawyer from the ecclesiastical lawyer in England. That distinction today might seem obvious, but at the time, when a wrong was committed, it was not clear to the wrongdoer whether he or she would appear before a secular court or an ecclesiastical court.[59]

Edward I's reform of the legal profession did not stop with naming who would be the educators. Edward I in fact provided the texts for education when he organized the disarray of the common law by instituting the reporting of cases in Year

[55] *Ibid.*
[56] Baker, *supra* note 27 at 156.
[57] Baker, *supra* note 27 at 81.
[58] *Ibid.* at 79.
[59] Berman, *supra* note 8, *passim.*

Books. Prior to Edward I, only very informal notes of cases taken by lawyers and students made up the records of the common law. Even this collection of cases was essential for a system that would bind its judges to prior interpretations of the law, and consequently needed to be organized for judges and practitioners.[60]

With improved organization, subjects came to trust the power of the crown more, which in turn resulted in more use of the crown's courts. The increased use of the courts, with the concomitant fees, were, in turn, a benefit for the king.

4.5.3 Middle Period: 1340s–1640s

Since the second half of the twelfth century, all disputes were heard by the monarch in London, thus requiring that many travel far for conflict resolution. It is not only coincidence therefore that the lawyers themselves would all be in London. The features of the middle period that enable us to understand U.S. legal culture through an historical reference frame of course remain English and center around the concentration of legal study at the four Inns of Court—Lincoln's, Gray's, Middle and Inner. There is some discrepancy over when the Inns were founded, but the orders of Edward I from 1290 and 1292 could be used to establish that the Inns have been in existence for well over seven hundred years.

The Inns of Court not only educated lawyers, they influenced educated society generally. "Perhaps as many as one-third of the gentry of England passed through them, something which can by no means be confidently asserted to the universities in this period."[61] Education at the Inns of Court meant inductive education by observation of trials during the day, and discussions with professional lawyers at dinner in the Inns at night.[62] Education followed the oral tradition. Eventually, practice trials and procedures that today we would call "moot court" began to be included in education.[63] Trainees ate meals with their masters. Today, eating meals together is still required for barristers.[64] At least six different types of professional lawyer existed in this period, although only the barrister and solicitor survive today.[65]

Evidence of the importance of the Inns in legal thinking is plentiful. As late as 1573, Inns were recorded as "disagreeing" with courts, thus showing that they regarded themselves at least as an equal voice of authority to the courts on issues of

---

[60] *Ibid.* at 99.

[61] Baker, *supra* note 27 at 98.

[62] See Robert Richard Pearce, *A History of the Inns of Court and Chancery*. London: Richard Bentley, 1848 78.

[63] *Ibid.*

[64] See Alex Aldridge, "Barristers' Dinners – a Bit of Fun or One Upper-Class Indulgence too Many?" *The Guardian* 12 May 2011 online edition. Available at www.theguardian.com/law/2011/may/12/barristers-dinners-fun-indulgence (last accessed 8 July 2014).

[65] The different types were known by different names depending upon the record. They were: barristers; apprentices; and sergeants; to which later were added benchers or masters of the bench; masters of the utter; and masters of the inner bar. See Wilfrid Bovey, "The Control Exercised by the Inns of Court over Admission to the Bar in England," 3 *Am. L. Sch. Rev.* (1911–15) 334.

the law. The relative independence of the Inns of Court contributed to this ability to take an authoritative position on legal issues that differed from the courts. From our understanding of authority in the common law system today, it seems rather arrogant that an informal educational institution like the Inns of Court could be acknowledged as more authoritative than the courts themselves.

According to Baker, the Inns did eventually relinquish the authority to speak for the law. The three main reasons for this shift began with some inherent difficulties in transmiting common learning through the oral tradition within an Inn and to an even greater degree, between the Inns. Then in 1440, with the invention of printed books, the narrow limits on the transfer of legal knowledge through the oral tradition and the handwritten documents of lawyers diminished even further this function for the Inns. And finally, in continuation of Edward I's trend, the monarchy began to increase the authority of the judges to act on the monarch's behalf. This delegation process was extended when in 1474 the Courts of Chancery became separate from the courts of law, thereby providing a forum that allowed the remedies of equity to be distinguished from that of law and delegating some power from the court of the crown to the court of chancery.

We also know that although no precise dates are available "before the middle of the fourteenth century they [the Inns] had passed from voluntary associations of law students to close quasi-corporations of practicing master-lawyers, in a transition analogous to that of the halls of Oxford and Cambridge into colleges."[66] In the 1400s, legal education consisted of the four Inns of Court and ten Inns of Chancery. The university was still not involved.

Other important changes that occurred during the middle period concerned the methods of recording the decisions of the courts. Although in the fifteenth century the Year Books improved in quality and organization, by 1535 the Year Books ceased to be compiled.[67] Private printers picked up the task immediately thereafter, however, and began reporting on cases through what they published as "reports." It seems that there was such a need in the practice of common law for case decisions and rationale to be recorded that when the Year Books ceased to be compiled, an essential tool for legal practice was removed and needed immediate replacement.[68]

Yet we are reminded that all of these developments were remedies to problems perceived by the public, the practitioners, the judges or the crown. There was no grand plan for the legal system's structure or functions. Consequently, notes Baker, "No one expected a gradual accretion of law [in the fourteenth to fifteenth centuries] from case to case, any more than we now expect new rules of chess to

---

[66] Malcolm Fooshee, "The English Inns of Court: Their Background and Beginnings," 46 *ABA Journal* (1960) 616.

[67] Kempin, *supra* note 2 at 99.

[68] See Richard J. Ross, "The Commoning of the Common Law: The Renaissance Debate Over Printing English Law, 1520–1640," 146 *U. Pa. L. R.* (1998) 323.

emerge from each season of chess matches."[69] And to see this accretion grow, we can only look through the historical reference frame at the recorded evidence of the time.

A final note should be added that this system of legal education was not without strong political influence. The Inns of Court stopped teaching law due to the English Civil War. And despite the fact that the war ended in 1646, legal education did not resume until 1846—a full two hundred years later.[70]

4.5.4 The Modern Period: The Eighteenth Century Until Today

Jumping forward to the independent United States of America, it would be misleading to suggest that all of the fifty U.S. states had somehow begun as English colonies with English law and then evolved into something "American." Texas, for example, declared its independence not from Britain, but from Mexico in 1836 and only joined the United States in 1845. While part of Mexico, it was in a Spanish civil law jurisdiction, and thus evolved from it, not directly from English law. Louisiana, which at the time of its purchase from Napoléon Bonaparte by President Thomas Jefferson constituted nearly one-third of what is now the continental United States, was governed by French law and is a civil code jurisdiction still, just as the province of Quebec in Canada is a civil law jurisdiction in the midst of common law Canada. Moreover, even when the English common law system made its way to the U.S. during English colonization of North America, one should not assume that English jurisprudence was fully embraced after U.S. independence. "It is clear that early American courts were unwilling automatically to apply English precedents. ... Indeed, during the War of 1812 some American courts forbade English cases to be cited in court at all."[71]

With that in mind one might well ask how and why many other states, with their considerable degree of political independence from one another, nevertheless accepted and developed the common law of England? The answer lies in part with the fact that the undeveloped state of U.S. jurisprudence meant that general principles had to be relied on. In 1809, the Virginia Chancellor Creed Taylor wrote that "[i]t was the common law we adopted, and not English decisions; and we should take the standard of that law, namely, that we should vie honestly, should hurt nobody, and should render to everybody his due, for our judicial guide."[72] Furthermore, as states joined the Union, lawyers from other states emigrated to the new states, bringing their common law training with them.[73] Again we see that

---

[69] J. H. Baker, *The Common Law Tradition: Lawyers, Books and the Law.* London: The Hambledon Press, 2000 25.

[70] Kempin, *supra* note 2 at 81.

[71] *Ibid.* at 107.

[72] *Marks v. Morris*, 14 Va. 463 (1809).

[73] Daniel Hulsebosch, "An Empire of Law: Chancellor Kent and the Revolution in Books in the Early Republic," 60 *Ala. L. Rev.* (2009) 377 *passim.*

the practicing lawyers of the common law, not the legislated texts, formed the legal thinking throughout the United States of America. In reflecting on Indian home rule, Mohandas Gandhi reminds us that "[t]he chief thing, however, to be remembered is that without lawyers courts could not have been established or conducted and with the latter the English could not rule."[74]

It would equally be a mistake to talk about the reception of English common law in "America" as it would be to talk about a unified system of "American law" today. One might better understand the situation by analogy to the "reception" of colonial law in the various states of Africa today, and how, to varying degrees, each of those states has rejected, accepted or modified the law of its former colonial master. Each North American colony received English law in a different way, with the spectrum spanning from Massachusetts hardly receiving English law at all[75] to South Carolina receiving nearly all of English law,[76] except in those circumstances where American cultural sensitivities, to the extent they could be expressed by a judge, could differ.[77]

After the period during which the courts in the new states "received" the common law, it is worth taking a look at the official state acts of receiving the law of England so that one can sense just how differently each of the states received the common law. Taking a position consistent with what William Stoebuck calls the "standard" position of Justice Story in the *van Ness* case,[78] in 1777 the Pennsylvania General Assembly enacted a statute that says in part:

> The common law and such of the statutes of England as were in force in the Province of Pennsylvania on May 14, 1776 and which were properly adapted to the circumstances of the inhabitants of this Commonwealth shall be deemed to have been in force in this Commonwealth from and after February 10, 1777.[79]

In maintaining the "standard" position, the statute uses the condition "which were properly adapted to the circumstances of the inhabitants of this Commonwealth" (in reference to Pennsylvania), just as Story wrote in the *van Ness* case.

Wherever the British flag has flown over its former empire in the world, it took with it its language and legal system. And when British rule retreated, either

---

[74] M. K. Gandhi, *Hind Swaraj or Indian Home Rule*. Ahmedabad: Navajivan Publishing House, 1938 50.

[75] William E. Nelson, *Americanization of the Common Law: The Impact of Legal Change on Massachusetts Society, 1760–1830*. Athens, GA: University of Georgia Press, 1994 *passim*.

[76] William B. Stoebuck, "Reception of the English Common Law in the American Colonies," 10 *William and Mary L. Rev.* (1969) 242, 401. "The assumption that colonial law was essentially the same in all colonies is wholly without foundation." *Ibid.* (quoting George L. Haskins, *Law and Authority in Early Massachusetts*. New York: The Macmillan Co., 1960 114–15).

[77] Stoebuck, *supra* note 76 at 401.

[78] *Van Ness v. Pacard.* 27 U.S. (2 Pet.) 137 (1829).

[79] 1 Sm.L. 429 §§ 1 to 3, 8; became 46 P.S. §§ 151 to 154 and is today still in force as 1 Pa. C.S.A. §1503(a).

voluntarily or by force, it often left its language and legal system behind. Such was the case in North America. The fact remains that in its legal practices, the United States did not invent for itself a wholly different legal system. For example, in reference to the style of its judicial opinions, the famous U.S. judge, pandectist and Chancellor of New York, James Kent, noted that "[p]olitical independence did not bring full independence of legal culture."[80]

There is also a point to be made that relates law to language:

> [T]he law's imperial function refers to the role that law played as a language allowing people to communicate across political boundaries, whether interstate or international. Legal reasoning and discourse transcended politics in the basic sense that they allowed people to communicate, or argue, or agree to do business, across borders. Law had played this role in the British Empire, which was divided into a variety of kingdoms, colonies, and dominions.[81]

Thus, one can say that common law came into existence as a "system" in the British Empire out of necessity, because it was one legal system to talk across varying pieces of the empire. Eventually, this would suit U.S. federalism, with powerful independent states taking the roles that the various pieces of the British Empire would have played.

4.6 U.S. History

At this juncture it seems necessary to say a few words about U.S. history generally before proceeding to U.S. legal history, if only to make the point that a legal system is always part of a larger cultural fabric, and that for one to understand U.S. legal history, one must know a little about the broader picture of U.S. history. From the prior chapter on comparativism, one may recall that a useful and fair comparison to make among legal systems would be to estimate the degree to which any legal system meets the needs of the people of that culture. To that end, one must ask what the needs of the U.S. population have been over time.

In 1831, Alexis de Tocqueville and Gustave de Beaumont spent nine months travelling around the United States studying the prison system on behalf of the French government. During those travels, they collected many observations about U.S. culture in general, and political culture in particular. De Tocqueville identified several factors that he believed could help to explain the success of the United States— abundant and fertile land, opportunities for people to acquire that land and make a living, lack of a feudal aristocracy that blocked the ambitious, and the independent spirit encouraged by frontier living and individualism.[82] Some of those

---

[80] Hulsebosch, *supra* note 73 at 16.
[81] *Ibid.* at 17.
[82] Alexis de Tocqueville, *Democracy in America*. Trans. Henry Reeve. New York: George Dearborn & Co., 1835.

same traits today encourage citizens of the U.S. to even associate democracy with capitalism.

The culture of what is today the United States began long before what lawyers count as the beginning of the clock—the U.S. Constitution—and one should remain conscious of the fact that the constitution was written by people born into that already-functioning culture.[83] Histories could be told based upon geography or anthropology which would prominently feature the tribes of native Americans, many of whom were still thriving in the eighteenth century. But the history is usually told from the perspective of European colonizers. Even then, without looking beyond a history of common law practiced in the English language, one might overlook the early colonies of the Dutch, Portuguese, Spanish and French before English dominance.

Quite a different history would unfold if one were to follow the thread of slavery and its aftermath. Slaves made agricultural economies possible and provided an emotional touchstone for the American Civil War, in which more Americans were killed than in the two World Wars of the twentieth century combined. Today, 13 percent of the U.S. American population is at least in part of African descent. Like many European countries, the United States was socially changed in the 1960s when populations fought to come to terms with issues of race and civil rights, as well as to respond to social and environmental damage caused by unrestrained industrialism.[84] And although one might today think of the United States as capitalism in the extreme, trade unions and workers' rights have played a heavy part in U.S. industrialism. The May 1 holiday in Europe that celebrates labor was first celebrated in Chicago and, in the twentieth century, the Communist party was alive in the United States, even running a candidate for president well into the Cold War era.

The narratives often told to itself by U.S. culture are those of hard work, independent effort and social freedoms. The novels of Horatio Alger, Jr., epitomize the sense of the penniless European immigrant who can become a millionaire in the United States, or the humble man from Kentucky, born in a log cabin, who can become U.S. president. These narratives must be revisited, however, when one realizes that most presidents of the United States since the 1950s have been millionaires upon entering office.

4.7 U.S. Legal History

From these few short points on U.S. history in general, we turn to U.S. legal history. As I mentioned above, the first point to be made about U.S. legal history

---

[83] The already-functioning culture included the first "constitution," known as the "Articles of Confederation." For public lawyers, it is worth knowing the legal mechanics of how those articles went out of existence in order for the U.S. Constitution to come into existence. See Clinton Rossiter, *1787: The Grand Convention.* New York: W. W. Norton & Company, 1987 274–7, 299–300.

[84] Bernard Bailyn et al., *The Great Republic: A History of the American People.* Vol. II. Lexington, MA: D. C. Heath and Company, 1977 *passim.*

is simply that there is one. And part of knowing that there is a history teaches us that making the United States independent in legal thinking was not simple, complete, mechanical or automatic. In this sense, the United States needed its own pandectist like Blackstone, who could summarize and comment upon American law in a way that distinguished it from progenitors, be they French, Mexican or most of all, English. Chancellor Kent began that process. According to U.S. legal historian Lawrence M. Friedman, "Kent intended his huge work to be the national Blackstone."[85] As U.S. states changed their character from being part of someone else's empire to independence, they needed to demonstrate differences, including among sources of law. According to the Yale legal historian, John H. Langbein, "what Kent's *Commentaries* shares with European institutes of national law is the auspicious enterprise of giving character and definition to a newly self-conscious nation."[86]

The main features of the modern period that allow us to better understand U.S. legal culture today through the historical reference frame are first to keep in mind that before and during the modern period, a distribution of the practices of the common law takes place throughout the empire, including the United States. Second, the distribution of the common law in the United States is accomplished not through the Year Books or Reporters, which would have been too cumbersome to reproduce and likely too expensive to own for many of the colonists, but rather through the works of the common law pandectists—Blackstone, Littleton and Coke.[87].

Giving character to the new state was also a process of distancing the state from what it no longer wanted to be. According to New York University legal historian Daniel Hulsebosch, "[i]n continental Europe, the source to be distinguished was Roman law. In the United States, it was the English common law."[88] And it was during the modern period that U.S. law distinguished itself. The custom of writing opinions that summarized the parties' arguments and sorted out the authorities was a distinct feature of U.S. judicial opinions. When soon afterwards a few English judges also began delivering elaborate written opinions, they called them "American" in style.

By the time of the political theorists of the eighteenth century, the English constitutional system was well secure. That system, and not pure theoretical

[85] Lawrence M. Friedman, *A History of American Law*. 2nd ed. New York: Simon & Schuster, 1985 332.
[86] John H. Langbein, "Chancellor Kent and the History of Legal Literature," 93 *Colum. L. Rev.* 547, (1993) 591–3 (as quoted in Hulsebosch, *supra* note 73 at 4).
[87] For further reading in the history of the common law, see Pollock and Maitland, *supra* note 1, who pioneered the history of English law, and Christopher Columbus Langdell, the inventor of the American legal education "case study" system at Harvard Law School in the twentieth century. See also Paul Perell, "Stare Decisis and Techniques of Legal Reasoning and Legal Argument" (1987) found at http://legalresearch.org/docs/perell. html (last accessed 10 November 2010).
[88] Hulsebosch, *supra* note 73 at 4.

speculation, provided the basis for the separation of powers doctrine. The contribution of the theorists was to rationalize and provide a theoretical framework for that which already existed, and in the process to refine it into a new framework of government.[89] From this observation, we can see that practices are often not first rational proposals but rather actual practices that are then described rationally after the fact.

An example of this is the fact that the tripartite division of legal competencies in England, despite resembling Montesquieu's rational creation, was created backward from an all-powerful king. From *Bonham's Case*, we learn that the judiciary became independent from the king. And then in the *Case of Proclamations*, parliament was deemed to be supreme. Thus, from an all-powerful king, the competencies of law-making and law-adjudicating were taken away. As a result, the executive power came to the king not because of some rational tripartite division of competencies, but because after others removed themselves from the king's power, only his executive authority remained.[90]

The nineteenth-century English legal historian Henry Sumner Maine made the famous observation that "[W]e may say that the movement of progressive societies has hitherto been a movement from *Status to Contract*."[91] Looking ahead to the chapter on language, the truth of Maine's assertion can be seen in the English word for the legal act by which a person may transfer property at his death—the "will." In feudal law, one could not transfer land based upon one's will to do so, but rather only based upon one's status. Thus, the introduction of the notion that one could transfer land upon death was a shift from the legal basis being one of status to the will of the testator. Given the fact that Maine was well known, his writing widely read and this particular conclusion famous, upon reflection one can see that if such a statement had an impact on society, it could well lead to serious study of the social conditions by which one establishes a will to act, whether it is a commercial contract or the transfer of property to an heir. It is not surprising therefore that a "sociology of law" movement followed Maine's historical era.

Berman finds that many of the characteristics of the Western legal tradition "have been severely weakened in the latter part of the twentieth century, especially in the United States."[92] That weakening is based upon an ahistorical self-understanding of the law. "The law is presented as having no history of its own, and the history which it proclaims to present is treated as, at best, chronology, and at worst, mere illusion."[93] One might suspect that the U.S. tendency to dehistoricize during the second half of the twentieth century was due at least in part to the insistence by U.S. cold war opponents—China and the U.S.S.R.—that, according to Karl Marx, all state issues must be historicized. But there have been internal influences on

[89] Kempin, *supra* note 2 at 43.
[90] *Ibid.* at 92–3.
[91] Henry Sumner Maine, *Ancient Law*. 10th ed., London: John Murray, 1884 165.
[92] Berman, *supra* note 8 at 38.
[93] *Ibid.*

both sides of the Atlantic as well. English legal historian Frederic William Maitland famously wrote "The lawyer must be orthodox, otherwise he is not a lawyer; and orthodox history seems to me a contradiction in terms."[94] There is also a danger when one follows the progressive view of history to treat the past as incomplete, naïve, or without the benefits of full knowledge to which we have currently progressed. Holmes wrote:

> [w]e must beware of antiquarianism, and must remember that for our purposes our only interest in the past is for the light it throws upon the present. I look forward to a time when the part played by history in the explanation of dogma shall be very small, and instead of ingenious research we shall spend our energy on a study of the ends sought to be attained and the reasons for desiring them.[95]

That sort of self-centered view of reasons to know of other times is hardly better than a parochial view of reasons to know of other places.

4.8 Conclusion

"Where does that leave us and with what? Bereft of one universal truth and one universal path of (legal) development, we can no longer have only one historical explanation available but a multiplicity of developmental possibilities and explanations with which to deal."[96] A look through the historical reference frame such as this brings us to the present state of affairs in U.S. legal education, training and practice. While we could talk about the present in the context of history, to examine what the current state of affairs is, the focus turns in the next chapter to looking at U.S. legal culture through the social reference frame.

CHALLENGE YOUR UNDERSTANDING:

1. What would it mean to say that a legal system has made progress?
2. How would a narrative for U.S. legal history be developed differently if the model of history employed were cataclysmic or regressive, rather than progressive?

---

[94] See S. F. C. Milsom, "Introduction," in Pollock and Maitland, *The History of English Law Before the Time of Edward I.* Vol. I. 2nd ed. Cambridge: Cambridge University Press, 1968 XXIV–XXV.
[95] Holmes, *supra* note 4.
[96] Günter Frankenberg, "Critical Comparison, Re-Thinking Comparative Law," 26 *Harv. Int'l L. J.* (1985) 411, 454.

Literature

Bailyn, Bernard, Robert Dallek, David Davis, David Donald and John Thomas, *The Great Republic: A History of the American People*. Vol. II. Lexington, MA: D. C. Heath and Company, 1977.

Baker, J. H., *The Legal Profession and the Common Law*. London: Hambledon Press, 1986.

Bettini, Maurizio, *Anthropology and Roman Culture. Kinship, Time, Images of the Soul*. Trans. J. van Sickle. Baltimore, MD: Johns Hopkins University Press, 1991.

Coquillette, Daniel, *The Anglo-American Legal Heritage*. 2nd ed. Durham, NC: Carolina Academic Press, 2004.

Fooshee, Malcolm, "The English Inns of Court: Their Background and Beginnings," 46 *ABA Journal* (1960). 616.

Frankenberg, Günter, "Critical Comparison, Re-Thinking Comparative Law," 26 *Harv. Int'l L. J.* (1985). 411.

Friedman, Lawrence M., *A History of American Law*. 2nd ed. New York: Simon & Schuster, 1985.

Friel, Brian, *Translations*. London: Faber & Faber, 1995.

Fry, Plantagenet Somerset, *The Battle of Hastings 1066 and the Story of Battle Abbey*. London: English Heritage, 1990.

Grossfeld, Bernhard, *Core Questions of Comparative Law*. Durham, NC: Carolina Academic Press, 2005.

Holmes, Oliver Wendell Jr., *The Common Law*. Boston, MA: Little Brown and Co., 1881.

Holmes, Oliver Wendell Jr., "The Path of Law," 10 *Harv L. Rev.* (1897). 457.

Hulsebosch, Daniel, "An Empire of Law: Chancellor Kent and the Revolution in Books in the Early Republic," 60 *Ala. L. Rev.* (2009). 377.

Kempin, Frederick G., *Historical Introduction to Anglo-American Law*. St. Paul, MN: West Pub. Co., 1990.

Maine, Henry Sumner, *Ancient Law*. 10th ed. London: John Murray, 1884.

Ong, Walter, *Orality and Literacy. The Technologizing of the Word*. London: Routledge, 2002.

Pearce, Robert Richard, *A History of the Inns of Court and Chancery*. London: Richard Bentley, 1848.

Pollock, F. and F. W. Maitland, *The History of English Law Before the Time of Edward I*. Ed. S. F. C. Milsom. 2nd ed. Vol. II. Cambridge: Cambridge University Press, 1968.

Pound, Roscoe, "Comparative Law in Space and Time," 4 *Am J. Comp. L.* 1 (1955). 70–84.

Stoebuck, William B., "Reception of the English Common Law in the American Colonies," 10 *William and Mary L. Rev.* (1969). 242.

Swain, J. W., "Theory of History by Frederik J. Teggart," 23 *The Journal of Philosophy* 25 (1926). 693–4.

de Tocqueville, Alexis, *Democracy in America*. Trans. Henry Reeve. New York: George Dearborn & Co., 1835.

Zweigert, Konrad and Hein Kötz, *An Introduction to Comparative Law*. Trans. Tony Weir. 3d ed. Oxford: Oxford University Press, 1998.

5

THE SOCIAL REFERENCE FRAME: CULTURAL PRACTICES WE CALL "LAW"

Framing Issues

1. Why should any culture, including U.S. culture, want legal specialists?
2. What makes the practice of law a profession and how does the profession differ from other professions?

5.1 Introduction: Does Society Want Legal Specialists?

Through the social reference frame, we can view the legal actors, such as lawyers, judges, parties, legislators, police officers and others. It builds on Frederick G. Kempin Jr.'s point discussed in the previous chapter on the historical reference frame: we can say the common law begins when lawyers became an independent legal profession. In making this statement, we are saying that what law *is* or what a legal system *is*, is best understood by what its actors do in their interactions with society. A legal system is not a set of books or abstract principles—it is a set of social practices. Beginning with the legal realists, such as Oliver Wendell Holmes, Jr., and continuing through sociological jurisprudence advocates, such as Roscoe Pound, right up through the critical legal studies proponents such as Roberto M. Unger, the history of U.S. legal practice, training and education has rarely been without a forum in which reform was proposed. Often, the reformers have challenged the focus on texts and instituted instead the study and practice of social action. More will be offered on the philosophical elements of these "movements" when discussing the philosophy reference frame in Chapter 7.

At the beginning of his treatise, *The Common Law*, Holmes wrote:

> [t]he life of the law has not been logic; it has been experience. The felt necessities of the time, the prevalent moral and political theories, intuitions of public policy, avowed or unconscious, even the prejudices which judges share with fellow-men, have a good deal more to do than the syllogism in determining the rules by which men should be governed.[1]

Here, Holmes is clearly taking aim at the Roman tradition, excoriating the deductive rule-driven practices of the civil law, while at the same time supporting the inductive, experience-based practices of the common law. If one accepts Holmes' position, then the student and practitioner alike ought to raise the questions of how one studies experience and how one establishes practices from studied experience.

An additional lesson to be learned by looking at legal science through the social reference frame is to ask how legal science is shaped by social relations rather than by abstract principles or even substantive legal norms. To illustrate this additional lesson, one might look at such a simple social practice as naming in the common law: cases names ("*Smith v. Jones*," for example, not numbers), the names of legal practice areas ("landlord and tenant law," for example uses people's names, not case rent law), the names of statutes ("the Taft-Hartley Act"), the names of lawyers included in reported judicial opinions, and the names of judges, especially the U.S. Supreme Court, are well known. "They are like rock stars," says my colleague from the University of Bonn, when she compares them with the German Federal Court of Justice or German Federal Constitutional Court.

Usually law students and lawyers address *their* position in society by looking through the social reference frame from the inside out. When I ask law students why we even have the separate discipline of law, they answer "because we have specialized knowledge that the public does not have." This reason needs some interrogation, however. First, nearly everyone has some form of "specialized knowledge" that might help in the resolution of conflict. In fact the U.S. Federal Rules of Evidence allow someone to be qualified as an expert for purposes of trial testimony so long as he or she has some "special knowledge or experience."[2] That category includes car mechanics, babysitters, waiters, athletes, software hackers, and so forth, depending on the issue at trial. So specialization may not be so special. The question must refocus on why law is a separate discipline, and we will return to that in Chapter 8.

All too often the law student sees himself as a student among other students, and he will answer my question as though law is a university topic of study, just as philosophy or chemistry would be. If so, then the student might easily be led to think that society pays the lawyer for his services because he is an expert with knowledge in the particular field. Why then do most societies of the world require one to be licensed to be a lawyer, but not to be a philosopher or a chemist? We might do well

---

[1] Oliver Wendell Holmes Jr., *The Common Law*. Boston, MA: Little, Brown and Company, 1881.

[2] United States Federal Rule of Evidence 702.

to consider this licensing requirement as a strong indicator that society is directly interested in the education and training of the lawyer. Lawyers provide a direct service back to society that is necessary for that society to be civil, so society takes a direct interest in controlling how and what services are provided. In order to obtain these services, does a society need a professional class of lawyers at all? Or, as the Yale Law School philosopher Daniel Markovits asks, "What are lawyers for?"[3] In fact, would it not be far more democratic to allow any aggrieved citizen to appear before a judge and tell his tale of woe and allow the judge to do the work of determining whether these facts constitute a legal harm and if so, caused by whom and if so, remedied in what way?

The lawyer is not essential to the resolution of conflict in the way a surgeon is essential to surgery or a physicist is essential to send a rocket to the moon. While the specialized knowledge of a lawyer may make a transaction or trial more efficient, the transaction or trial could proceed without the lawyer. By comparison, surgery cannot proceed without the specialized knowledge of a surgeon. Individuals can and do exercise their rights and duties before courts in cases of conflict without lawyers. In fact, as we have seen in our study through the historic reference frame in Chapter 4, it has been the choice in some U.S. states not to have a professional lawyer, and although all U.S. states recognize the legal profession now, some states maintained their lawyerless societies even into the twentieth century.

A further analogy is perhaps instructive. Many countries require citizens to make a formal tax report each year of income taxes paid to the state during that year. Many countries have also made their taxation so complicated that the citizen finds it difficult to comply with the reporting requirement without the aid of a person who has specialized knowledge in tax report preparation. Still, we would not regard these tax preparers as necessary, had we ourselves not complicated tax reporting so much. Is the specialized knowledge of the law a specialized knowledge that we have created like that of a tax bureaucrat, or is it more like surgery or physics?

Again we circle back to Kempin's assertion that "[a] realistic point in time to begin a discussion of Anglo-American legal history, then, is with the common law as it stood when it first became the object of study by a distinct legal profession."[4] Thus, the common law should not be said to begin with the finding or writing of a particular text, but rather with the point at which lawyers became an independent profession. This assertion provides us with a good sense of what Roscoe Pound called the "spirit" of the common law as was discussed in Chapter 1.[5] And

---

[3] Markovits opens his discussion by asking "What are lawyers for? What social purposes do lawyers serve? What functions underwrite the special obligations and entitlements that accompany the lawyer's professional role?" Daniel Markovits, "What are Lawyers for?" 47 *Akron L. Rev.* (2014) 135.

[4] Frederick G. Kempin, Jr., *Historical Introduction to Anglo-American Law*. St. Paul, MN: West, 1990 3.

[5] Roscoe Pound, *The Spirit of the Common Law*. Francistown, NH: Marshall Jones Co., 1921 10.

in comparative law, while commenting on the problems of subjective bias, Günter Frankenberg adds that law is part of social life and not an added text:

> [d]efining law as an additive to and not … as a constitutive element of social reality confirms the domination of the text (dead or alive) over social experience and makes it difficult if not impossible to analyze legal ideologies and the rituals pervading social life.[6]

If lawyers are indeed not essential to resolving conflict, who is? The answer is referees or judges. But even then, one should note that we may not need professional jurists for that task. Judges are most often professional jurists, but commercial courts and other courts in Germany, for instance, use lay judges, and sometimes they outnumber the professional jurists who join them as judges on the panel. And in the United States, the lowest level of judges—the state magistrates, district justices or "justices of the peace" are often not professional jurists. So far, then, for conflict resolution, when we look to facts of social practice in society, we see that lawyers are not essential and judges may not need to be professional jurists!

After one considers judges and lawyers, what legal professionals remain for this examination? Law makers and law enforcement officers. Professional law makers themselves are often politicians, and in many countries, not professional lawyers. Although most members of the U.S. Senate are lawyers, the occupational make-up of the U.S. House of Representatives is much more diverse.[7] Most of the German *Bundestag* (parliament) are not lawyers. Only about 10 percent of the parliaments of India and Canada are lawyers. And while law enforcement officers are usually trained in the law, it is typically only one area of the law—criminal law—although it could also be tax law, environmental law or some other agency specialization. In the end, in various stages of conflict resolution in various cultures, none of the persons usually associated with the practice of law needs to be a professional lawyer with specialized knowledge. Having arrived at that realization, we still need to investigate what legal practice looks like, when seen from the outside.

As a subject matter of scholarly investigation for lawyers, this is a bit peculiar. After all, we usually look from the inside of law out to the social conflicts of other people, just as natural scientists usually take their scientific methods and apply them outwardly, on planets, birds, atoms, cells, other societies, the brains of monkeys, and a million things other than the scientists' practices themselves. Thus, during the so-called "science wars" of the 1990s, it was hotly contested whether sociologists could dare to explain science to scientists, who themselves either could not be bothered to explore their own behavior while working as scientists, or who insisted that only a scientist has the ability, and therefore the right, to explain scientists or

---

[6] Günter Frankenberg, "Critical Comparison, Re-Thinking Comparative Law," 26 *Harv. Int'l L. J.* (1985) 411, 424.

[7] See the Congressional Research Service report at www.senate.gov/CRSReports/crs-publish.cfm?pid=%260BL%2BR\C%3F%0A (last accessed 22 July 2015).

science. Turning science back on itself is a common move of self-reflection under the mantle of post-modernism and is meant to be a look at science and scientists using their own methods.[8]

Turning more directly to our own field of concern, do we invite or allow sociologists or other social scientists to explain the law and lawyers to the lawyers themselves? The sociology of law is a recognized sub-discipline of sociology, using its own methods and having its own goals.[9] This chapter looks only to social phenomena within the education, training and practice of law. Like the natural scientists of the 1990s, do we say that only lawyers can explain the law and lawyers? Here it might be wise to reflect for a moment on the old saying in U.S. law that "a lawyer who represents himself has a fool for a client." So if we compare the closed-door attitude of the natural sciences to this common saying of legal practice, does that mean we lawyers are more open to having our legal practices and persons examined and explained by the social sciences? Hardly. Rather than inviting sociologists to explain us to ourselves, we, as persons trained only in the law, feel entitled to claim knowledge of society when we "balance interests" (as when a court invents a decision rationale after considering the competing interests in the case "in balance"), become "legal pragmatists" or practice "sociological jurisprudence."[10]

We lawyers treat the practice of law as something from which we make a living, and as such, it is a business of everyday life. But the rest of society who are not lawyers look at law from the outside looking inward. And lawyers, as providers of legal services that are constitutionally guaranteed to citizens, must take account of how the society in which we work sees us. What does society expect from us? Why does society create a group of persons who are considered to be licensed legal professionals?

Already in 1922, Pierre Lepaulle, French *Avocat* at the Paris Court of Appeal told his Harvard Law School audience that "[w]e have come to a period when, in most countries, there is a real inadequacy in the law, a failure to reach scientific standards and meet social ends."[11] This double critique is significant for that which it explicitly criticizes, but also for something it implicitly questions. The implied question

---

[8] For a good example see Bruno Latour and Steve Woolgar, *Laboratory Life. The Construction of Scientific Facts*. Princeton, NJ: Princeton University Press, 1986. Latour and Woolgar became employed in a laboratory ostensibly to carry out the work of the laboratory, but were also observing, through the lens of social theory, what scientists do and how science is socially constructed.

[9] The sociology of law can be seen as inherently interdisciplinary, and include many of the issues that a discussion of "culture" includes, as was offered in the Preface *supra*. See e.g. Susanne Baer, *Rechtssoziologie: Eine Einführung in die interdisziplinäre Rechtsforschung*. Baden-Baden: Nomos, 2011.

[10] Sociological jurisprudence is also largely no longer accepted or practiced in the United States, but the theories of practice continue to be created and maintained by lawyers themselves who seem content to ignore the idea that trained sociologists should be conducting sociology. For a trenchant critique of sociological jurisprudence, see Pierre Lepaulle, "The Function of Comparative Law with a Critique of Sociological Jurisprudence" 35 *Harv. L. Rev.* (1922) 838, 839–42.

[11] *Ibid.*

is whether law students or practicing lawyers ever bother to engage themselves with whether their practices are scientific *or* whether they meet social demands. It would seem that rarely, if ever, does a law student or practitioner ask these questions. So the next question is whether we should expect them to do so, or whether we should find it peculiar that a legal scholar cares about such things if legal practitioners do not?

The present discussion aims to compare the understanding of law that U.S. lawyers have in comparison with other lawyers of the world. Perhaps because comparativism is a continental European invention, "[d]ifferent approaches to comparison have in common a core concept of law in which law is understood as a set of institutions, techniques and regulations designed and deployed to guarantee and vindicate individual rights in a neutral and rational manner."[12] Such an approach, often regarded as orthodox, rather ignores the profession of the lawyer and his or her practices. Would it not be more scientific to make explicit observations from cultural practice and what U.S. law *is* by describing what U.S. law *does*?

If one expects law to be a science, as will be discussed in Chapter 8, one might well also expect that it proceeds with a scientific method based upon facts determined through a scientific method. Lepaulle found too little of that happening even in the continental civil systems. The fault, he said, was largely to be found in the fact that lawyers deemed themselves capable of social science without having any training in it. By comparison to medicine, for example, he found law to be unscientific. And as to the other great concern—does law meet the needs of society—he concluded that legal systems are self-centered and focused on self-perpetuation, not scientific discovery. "Hardly anyone has tried to study inductively legal facts, in connection with other social facts, in order to discover the necessary laws of their relations."[13] In short, whether legal education or legal practice meet the needs of a society did not seem to him to concern lawyers on either side of the Atlantic. If his assessment was correct, has that state of affairs changed between then and the twenty-first century?

Law is a normative social practice: it purports to guide human behavior, giving rise to reasons for action. However, law is not the only normative domain in our culture: morality, religion, social conventions, etiquette and so on also guide human conduct in many ways that are similar to law.[14] Those other domains form part of our understanding of what law is and how it interacts with them. The intelligibility of the legal system depends on other normative orders, like morality or social conventions. In relying upon these social aspects, law becomes inextricable from culture and society. Therefore, neither a complete legal system nor any parts

---

[12] Frankenberg, *supra* note 6 at 421 (citing Konrad Zweigert and Hein Kötz, *An Introduction to Comparative Law*. Trans. Tony Weir. 3rd ed. Oxford: Oxford University Press, 1998, *passim*).

[13] Lepaulle, *supra* note 10 at 839.

[14] Marmor, Andrei, "The Nature of Law", in *The Stanford Encyclopedia of Philosophy*, Winter 2011 Edition. Ed. Edward N. Zalta, http://plato.stanford.edu/archives/win2011/entries/lawphil-nature/ (last accessed 2 April 2012).

of it can simply be transferred to other cultures. In other words, law is a social institution that shapes society, while also being shaped by it. Thus, when Holmes famously remarked that "[t]he prophecies of what the courts will do in fact, and nothing more pretentious, are what I mean by the law,"[15] we can see the strong role of social participation in conflict resolution. To prophesize a court's resolution is to anticipate more than the one right meaning of a text. The education, training and practice of U.S. lawyers reflect the thinking, skills and approaches to law from U.S. culture. And by doing so they shape the society in which they teach, publish or practice law. Therefore, a study of those influences in both directions goes far to aid understanding of U.S. legal culture when seen through the social reference frame by lawyers.

5.1.1 The Social Approach to the Legal Actors

While the United States did not copy English legal education, training and the organization of legal practice, those elements did influence U.S. legal culture. The types of lawyer who have studied and practiced law throughout history in England were far more numerous than today. At one time in the late Middle Ages, at least six different designations existed: the sergeant-at-law, the clerk, the attorney-at-law, the apprentice-at-law, the utter-barrister and the solicitor.

By the middle of the sixteenth century only two distinct types of lawyer remained in England, resulting in two branches of the profession, both of which are still fully in operation in England today: barristers and solicitors. A solicitor meets clients, drafts all manner of legal documents and advises whether a dispute should go before the court to be adjudicated. If the solicitor believes that a dispute will need to go before the court, then it is the job of the solicitor, not the party, to obtain the services of a barrister. It is the barrister who presents the dispute to the court using the advocate's skills of questioning witnesses and using their testimony to make other evidence admissible to the court. Although solicitors do today have some right of audience before the courts themselves, socially they have not yet begun to exercise the right to any great extent and still largely call upon the services of a barrister for oral advocacy in the courtroom. The client pays the solicitor for all legal services, and it is the solicitor who then pays the barrister when a barrister is needed. Barristers and solicitors are still educated and trained separately. Barristers may not work together in law firms and instead are tenants in chambers. The chambers may share secretarial services but not cases. By contrast solicitors usually work together in solicitors chambers. This requirement for barrister independence predictably

---

[15] Oliver Wendell Holmes Jr., "The Path of Law," 10 *Harv. L. Rev.* (1897) 457. Holmes was not only a U.S. Supreme Court Justice, but also a Massachusetts Supreme Court Justice and fought in the U.S. Civil War, in which he was twice wounded. He would often spend summers in London, and thus became familiar with the practices of his fellow common law lawyers and judges from both sides of the ocean.

results in a high failure rate among new barristers.[16] A barrister starting out can find it difficult to obtain work and clients from solicitors. Consequently, it has often been the case that new barristers had to have independent means. Thus, one of the historical social distinctions between solicitors and barristers was that only people of independent means could afford the difficult early barrister years when few cases or clients provide income. These independent means were often inherited or were the income from property.

5.1.2 Legal Practice and Training in the United States

Before their independence from Britain, the colonies in North America offered only a rather undeveloped legal education. There were nine universities in colonial America, but as with Britain's barristers and solicitors of the time, Americans did not need to study law at university in order to work as a lawyer. As in Britain, if one studied law at university, it was not the practical law in practice at the time, but instead was canon law. As a result, American colonists were admitted to the Inns of Court along with their British brothers and conducted their legal education overseas despite the difficulties and expense of travel. Another form of legal education was an apprenticeship (shadowing a lawyer while paying him a fee) with a member of the legal profession. By the end of the colonial period, a commercial need for professional lawyers began to grow. That need contributed to the establishment of formal legal education. The first bar exam in what is now the United States was instituted by Delaware Colony in 1763; it consisted of an oral examination before a judge.[17] The practice was soon adopted by other colonies and by the late nineteenth century overworked judges ceded the task of examining potential members of the bar to committees of attorneys. The oral examination was changed eventually to a written one.[18]

5.1.3 U.S. Legal Education and Practice Immediately After Independence

In achieving independence from English governance in 1776, U.S. society was eager to rid itself of the vestiges of class elitism that were part of the English culture. U.S. society had only primarily one type of legal professional: the attorney–at–law.[19]

---

[16] Richard L. Abel and Philip S. C. Lewis (eds.), *Lawyers in Society: An Overview*. Berkeley, CA: University of California Press, 1995 at 82, http://ark.cdlib.org/ark:/13030/ft8g5008f6/ (last accessed 11 November 2015).

[17] See The State Bar of California, "California Bar Examination, History and Information," at 3, http://admissions.calbar.ca.gov (last accessed 24 March 2015).

[18] *Ibid.*

[19] In addition, some states reserved the term "counselor" for attorneys practicing before the highest court of that state, but a counselor did not have different education or training from other attorneys at the time who existed only in some states for practice at the highest

Not long after U.S. independence, a practicing lawyer named Tapping Reeve began the practice of accepting university graduates as his apprentices. During their stay with him as apprentices, the university graduates were required to attend Reeve's formal lectures. Due in large part to the popularity of his teaching skills, Reeve attracted increasingly more students applying for apprenticeships. Consequently, Reeve founded what would be known as the first law school in the United States—Litchfield Law School at Litchfield, Connecticut – in 1784, with separate houses for his lectures and library. The curriculum was more than fourteen months long and used *Blackstone's Commentaries* as its teaching text. Before it closed in 1833, the Litchfield Law School had taught almost one thousand students. Relevant to the current legal education enrollment in the United States, the way in which Litchfield closed is nearly as important as the way in which it had opened. Litchfield Law School closed due to a dramatic drop in attendance, not unlike that being experienced by many U.S. law schools in the current decade of the twenty-first century. The drop today is largely due to exorbitant study fees coupled with a weak employment market. The reasons for the drop at Litchfield back in 1883 were different: first, after he started the law school, the charismatic Reeve eventually had become a judge and withdrew from teaching at the law school. Without his personal presence, part of the attractiveness of Litchfield was gone. Second, other competing private schools opened after Litchfield. Third, a combination of affordable publications of textbooks and commentaries, like those of Chancellor James Kent and Judge Joseph Story became available, thus ending a student's reliance upon a scholar to explain and teach from Blackstone's *Commentaries*.[20] And finally, bar admission standards had been lowered, thus reducing the need for such formal legal education as Litchfield offered. Some states even abolished bar admission standards altogether, thus enabling apprenticeship and self-education to be sufficient.

The ensuing years saw legal education vary to an extreme degree among the states. For example, the duration of legal education varied between three and seven years. Some states required fewer years if one had accomplished a university education in any discipline before studying law. Other states had an examination only and did not require any formal legal study or education. The new and enduring foundation in U.S. legal education was the establishment of the Harvard Law School, which opened in 1817 and which was only loosely connected to Harvard University itself. By comparison, at the University of Virginia legal education was included in the regular curriculum. An important by-product of these models was that both eventually enabled law-teaching to become a separate profession from legal practice. The establishment of a separate profession of law teachers was a necessary component to establish law as a separate discipline of study in the U.S. legal culture. (There will be more to say on law as a discipline in Chapter 8.)

---

court. The term "counselor" is still used by many U.S. judges in the courtroom to address attorneys simply to acknowledge that they are addressing an attorney-at-law.
[20] Frederik G. Kempin, *Legal History: Law and Social Change*. Englewood Cliffs, NJ: Prentice-Hall, 1963 86.

During wartime, education generally suffers. Schools close. During the U.S. Civil War (1861–65), some law schools were closed. After the civil war ended, some states struggled to reintroduce legal education. North Carolina, for example, ignored legal education and required only that men pay a fee of twenty dollars in order to acquire a license to practice law. In 1870 a change began that reshaped U.S. legal education in a way that is still with us in form today. One of the new professional law teachers, Harvard's Christopher Columbus Langdell, introduced the "case method."[21] At the time, neither Harvard nor many other U. S. law schools had any entrance require- ments. And until that time, most law teachers were only part-time teachers because they were still working as lawyers. Langdell's idea was that the law should be learned from the recorded case opinions, as written by judges. What might appear to be a simple measure of pedagogy in fact had several powerful effects outside the class- room. Written judicial opinions had both delivered the reasoning of the court to the parties and provided a binding interpretation of law for subsequent practitioners. But with Langdell's case method, those same opinions now also became the primary teaching texts for generation of lawyers up until, and including today. A second and related effect was that the judges, through their opinions, now held the position of official commentators on the law. Some judges even write their opinions in a pedan- tic, teaching manner, with the obvious expectation that their opinions will be used in the law school classroom.[22] So unlike the civil law tradition, with respected and standardized commentaries coming from commentators such as professors, or even common law, which until that time had relied upon pandectists such as Blackstone, Coke or Littleton, the U.S. law student now read the text of the judicial opinion and was instructed on its meaning by a professional law teacher. With the introduction of the case method, the roles of pandectist and practicing lawyer alike were greatly diminished in (some would even say eliminated from) U.S. legal education. At the same time, this dramatic change challenged teachers and students, who, even if they understood the change, predictably also resisted the change. Most students in fact refused to attend this type of legal study. So Langdell took an additional two steps to usher in his case method. He introduced entrance requirements for students, leading to a higher quality of student entering legal study and he began limiting the Harvard faculty to only full-time teachers.[23] Today, the accreditor of the legal practice stand- ards in the United States—the American Bar Association—still enforces the practice of both of those ideas as well as the case method of instruction itself.

[21] Some legal historians doubt Langdell's characterization as founder of the case method. These doubters assert that the real method was developed by Langdell's student, James Barr Ames, who joined the staff of Harvard Law School in 1873. It should also be noted that Harvard's case method in 1870 was not otherwise unheard-of. A similar method was used at the New York University of Law. Nevertheless, as Dean of Harvard, Langdell is normally credited with having institutionalized the system.

[22] For a good example of such a writing style, see *MacDonald v. Thomas M. Cooley Law School*, 724 F.3d 654 (6th Cir. 2013).

[23] As was the case with the introduction of the case method, these ideas were also employed elsewhere, namely at Columbia and Yale, which established similar steps at nearly the same time.

5.1.4 General Considerations for Admission to the Practice of Law

As previously mentioned, admission to the practice of law had been no more uniform among the states after the Civil War than legal education had been, and the differences persisted even later in many cases. States were not unified in their approaches to admission to practice law, and returning to the notion that access to the profession of legal practice should not be limited to an elite class, some states even eliminated all requirements except "good moral character." Within the spirit of the common law, this is not so surprising. Some states allowed one county's admission to be sufficient for a lawyer to practice in all counties of the state.[24] Some other states went to the opposite extreme and required separate admission to each administrative district or county within a state.

How is the practice of law different from other employment? One might begin to look at law by considering which areas of employment require education, training, examination and a license to practice. In law, typically one must first obtain the education and training in order to be examined. But a demonstration of substantive knowledge alone is usually considered to be insufficient. Two examples will help to address this issue. Pennsylvania, for example, kept the practice even into the 1960s of requiring a lawyer to be admitted separately to each county of a state. As part of what characterizes the spirit of U.S. legal culture, Pennsylvania still requires that a person be of "good moral character" among other things in order to be admitted to the practice of law. This sort of requirement is not required in other professions.

The Pennsylvania Board of Law Examiners explains:

> As part of the process of seeking a certificate for admission to the bar from the Board of Law Examiners, applicants must complete an application and provide background information for the purpose of enabling the board staff to conduct a character and fitness investigation and determination.
>
> The Board staff reviews the applications and may use other means of investigation to determine the fitness and qualifications of the applicant. For bar exam applications, the board staff begins a preliminary investigation of the application before the bar examination. However, the full investigation and determination of character and fitness is made only after the successful completion of the bar examination. For other applicant types, the board staff begins the investigation upon acceptance of the online application. The character and fitness determination process can take anywhere from three weeks to more than one year depending on the nature of the investigation, the issues

---

[24] Even in England, in order to qualify to practice law, formal legal education "was first required by the Solicitors Act of 1922, and required only one year of formal instruction. According to Kempin this legislation led a number of provincial universities to provide law courses. By the 1980s almost sixty institutions in the United Kingdom, both traditional universities and polytechnic universities, offered law courses that could qualify one to sit for the admission examination. Kempin, *supra* note 20 at 82.

involved, response to requests for additional information, cooperation from outside sources, etc.[25]

As a Pennsylvania lawyer who has employed candidates for legal practice in Pennsylvania, I have regularly received letters from the Pennsylvania Board of Law Examiners asking for a character assessment of a candidate. A recent such letter states:

> The Pennsylvania Board of Law Examiners conducts a background investigation of all applicants. As part of the investigation, please supply the Board with any information or knowledge that may indicate that the above-referenced applicant does not meet the character standards to become a member of the bar of the Commonwealth of Pennsylvania.

No definitive criteria are provided by which to assess what character standards are. Applicants cannot avoid having their character assessed, which is a further indication of a standard that is not driven by the state, but by a self-policing private bar. Further, applicants must waive the right to take civil action against a person who has assessed the character of an applicant. Rather, in addition to asking for the general character assessment, only several specific questions are included, among others:

> [w]as the applicant ever confronted, questioned, counseled, or approached by you or another supervisor, manager or colleague about … his or her truthfulness, … the manner in which he or she handled or preserved the money or property of others, … [or] his or her ability to maintain the confidentiality of information?[26]

Thus designed, lawyers themselves are the measures of all lawyers.

Other community members must also approve of lawyers. To be admitted to the practice of law in the State of New York, for example, in addition to proving that one has the required legal education and passed the bar examination, one must submit two affidavits from a rather strictly defined set of persons who are willing to attest to the applicant's good moral character. While the "good moral character" standard may be difficult to test or check, other professions do not even go so far as to formalize the requirement. The instructions from the New York State Board of Law Examiners provide, for example:

> The affidavits should be completed by reputable persons who have known applicant for not less than two years. The affidavits should not be completed by persons who also complete employment affidavits on applicant's behalf. The affidavits should not be completed by persons associated with applicant's present employer or persons related to applicant by blood or marriage or by

---

[25] See www.pabarexam.org/c_and_f/cfoverview.htm (last accessed 23 March 2014).
[26] Letter on file with author.

other applicants or by members of the faculty or administrative staff of any law school attended by applicant. Preferably, one affidavit should be completed by an attorney in good standing. The person completing the affidavit should return it to the applicant, who should file it with and at the same time as his or her application for admission questionnaire.[27]

Not long after the end of the Civil War, at about the same time that legal education was being constructed at Harvard in a pattern that would long be followed by many other law schools, practicing lawyers organized themselves in a national organization—the American Bar Association (A.B.A.). Founded in 1878, the A.B.A. wished both to "standardize" matters of law concerning the states and to raise the standard of practice in the legal profession once things had been standardized. Still today, in U.S. legal education, administrators refer not to the rules, statutes or regulations, but to A.B.A. "standards." To raise the level of practice, the A.B.A. strongly supported university-based legal education. They even published a memorandum to the state governments in which they recommended that the states should adopt a standard of three years of legal studies before being admitted to practice. Nevertheless, in all areas of study (not only law) education remains within the competency of the individual states to regulate. Similarly and somewhat surprisingly to many people, the admission to practice law is also managed at the state level, not the national level.[28] It is still the case today, as in 1878, that there is no one, national examination, the passing of which admits one to practice law in more than state.[29]

The A.B.A.'s presence is perhaps less felt when it comes to eliminating differences in substantive law among states. Because national legislation in any area must be enabled by the U.S. Constitution, the A.B.A. had to resort to a tool that was already part of the spirit of the common law—model statutes that could be adopted by the several states' legislatures, in whole or in part. "The thought was that a common statute would lead to uniform law."[30] Yet the power of an organization that is capable of unifying the profession remains quite high for a culture where the legal profession is largely self-organizing and self-policing. A number of uniform commercial statutes were adopted by many states in the period from 1896 to 1918, but it took until 1952 before the first draft of a uniform *code* of statutes was introduced. Even in these uniform and codified areas of the law, legal analysis and practice is still carried out through the traditional common law method and does not follow the civil law approach.

---

[27] www.nybarexam.org/Admission/Part%20II_MoralCharacter_10.01.13.pdf (last accessed 23 March 2014).

[28] As a consequence in the state of West Virginia, for example, because there was only one law faculty up until the 1980s, a candidate was automatically admitted to the practice of law in the state of West Virginia upon completing a J.D. degree with that law faculty.

[29] There is however a growing trend to make qualifying law examination uniform among the states. See the discussion of the Uniform Bar Examination below.

[30] Kempin, *supra* note 20 at 114.

In conclusion, a final cultural consideration is the fact that practicing law without a license is a crime. This is especially noteworthy when one considers that for many other jobs in the United States, unlike other countries of the world, it is only the market, and not the state, that controls the terms of education and training, and ultimately, employment for lawyers. The frequency of "at will" employment contracts and the relatively low numbers of civil servants indicates a preference for the individualism of private contract when it comes to employment, including the employment of lawyers. Yet, with the prohibition of practice without a license, we see that the state does exercise at least a minimal amount of control over the practice of law by making certain that lawyers are licensed. But unlike many other countries, the state itself does not exercise gatekeeping authority by legislating the conditions of licensing.[31] Each state, under the unifying guidelines and pressure of the A.B.A. accreditation of legal education, remains free to set its own requirements for admission to practice.[32]

5.1.5 Legal Education in the Twentieth and Twenty-first Centuries

At the turn of the last century, legal education followed legal practice and began to organize itself nationally. In 1900, the Association of American Law Schools (A.A.L.S.) was founded. The A.A.L.S., a non-profit organization with about 170 of the approximately two hundred law schools[33] in the United States as members, started as an association of law schools wanting to improve legal education and promote the case method. Over the years, the A.A.L.S. became very successful working with the A.B.A. to set higher standards for admission to the bar, thus helping the A.B.A. to achieve one of its two founding goals. The goal of legal education in the United States, as stated by the A.A.L.S. and the A.B.A., is to produce capable lawyers.[34] This may seem to be an obvious and banal statement, but it is different

---

[31] Kenneth M. Rosen, *"Lessons on Lawyers, Democracy, and Professional Responsibility,"* 19 *Geo. J. L. Ethics* (2006) 155, 167. Rosen is quick to point out, however, that "if lawyers are unwilling to recommit themselves to the regulation of their profession and their responsibilities to society, one might expect additional [external] regulations."

[32] Those requirements are not state legislation, and are most often state rules of court. To most people, this might seem like an insignificant difference between legislation and rules of court, but examined under the microscope of public law, it is the difference between the will of the people expressed through the state's legislative body, and the administrative rules promulgated by a state organ.

[33] Although most of legal education in the United States today is offered through university faculties of law, the common usage in U.S. English is still to refer to legal education as "law school". That moniker should not mislead the reader. Legal education is either part of a university at postgraduate level or is independent of a university, but nevertheless at a postgraduate level. In fact, as mentioned previously, one may only enter the study of law after one has completed a university education at the bachelor level in some area of study. Other professions, such as medicine, also use the term "school," as in "medical school," with medicine being a postgraduate program just as law is.

[34] A.B.A., "About the American Bar Association," www.americanbar.org/about_the_aba. html (last accessed 30 September 2014).

from the German system, as just one example of civil law education in which the form of legal education guides the student to think like a judge, and then rewards the top state examination performers with invitations to be judges. Ironically, most American lawyers are not litigators[35] and most German lawyers are not judges.[36]

In addition to the intentional reordering of legal education and practice, social forces such as industrialism had an impact. For example, with the invention of typewriters, secretaries were starting to replace apprentices to carry out scrivener functions within the law office. In addition, with gas and electric lighting, night schools became possible for part-time students. In turn, night school allowed the working class and immigrants to participate in legal education in the United States, whereas such technical changes would not have enabled those people in a more class-structured culture.

In 1923, the A.B.A. published its first list of law schools that it deemed to be accredited.[37] This act worked to do much more than just create a list. In addition, with this list, legal education was formally going to be recognized not just by the states, who controlled university education generally, and the universities them-selves, who controlled their own curricula in most subject areas, but by the practic-ing lawyers of the profession.

Into the 1930s, at least one state still allowed admission to practice law by simply paying a fee. But in 1931, yet another national organization in law, the National Conference of Bar Examiners (N.C.B.E.), formed to make part of the bar exami-nation uniform throughout the United States and thereby made sure of a more uniform legal education, thus further carrying out one of the goals of the A.B.A. By the middle of the century, due to the pressures of these private organizations—the A.B.A., the A.A.L.S. and now the N.C.B.E.—states became more uniform in their bar admissions practices, one by one requiring candidates first to complete an undergraduate degree in some other discipline before beginning the study of law, then requiring attendance of three or more years at law school, and then also requiring the bar examination itself. By the beginning of the Second World War, over two-thirds of law students in the United States studied law at an accredited law school. From its 1784 beginning at Litchfield, by the middle of the twentieth century, law school had become the "principal gateway to the profession."[38]

So what is the current picture of legal education in the United States? Today, in order to become a practitioner of law, one must obtain a license. The process of

---

[35] Edward Rubin, *Legal Education in the Digital Age*. Cambridge: Cambridge University Press, 2012 216.

[36] See the statistics published by the *Bundesrechtsanwaltskammer*, the German bar association, in which there are a total of roughly 164,000 registered lawyers as of January, 2014: www.brak.de/w/files/04_fuer_journalisten/statistiken/grmgstatisitik2014_korr.pdf (last accessed 13 June 2014). The number of judge positions in Germany, by comparison, is listed at roughly 21,000. For the precise number at any given time, one should consult the records maintained by the *Bundesamt für Justiz* (Federal Justice Office).

[37] Margaret C. Johns and Rex R. Perschbacher, *The United States Legal System – An Introduction*. 2nd ed. Durham, NC: Carolina Academic Press, 2007 8.

[38] *Ibid.*

obtaining a license begins by obtaining an undergraduate degree (bachelor's degree) from any faculty, domestic or foreign.[39] Subsequently, the candidate must score sufficiently on the Law School Admissions Test (L.S.A.T.). The L.S.A.T. is a uniform examination across the United States, and thus contributes to some sense of the nationalization and standardization of legal education. With an L.S.A.T. score and bachelor's degree in hand, a candidate may then apply for admission, by paying a fee, to any of the approximately two hundred law schools in the United States for entry into the degree program that enables a lawyer to sit for the bar examination. That degree program is usually entitled a "juris doctor" (J.D.) program today, but in the past, students completing an LL.B. or other degree could also take the bar exam. Indirectly, it is the A.B.A., through the accreditation of the law schools, that controls who is permitted to enter the study of law. So long as law schools work within the A.B.A. guidelines, they may tailor the profile of their students as they wish, but they cannot contradict A.B.A. guidelines. Thus, again we see that the profession is self-regulated, not state-regulated, even at the level of education.

With the above standardization developments in mind, the three-year curriculum of most A.B.A.-approved U.S. law schools runs approximately as follows: The first year curriculum consists mostly of compulsory courses such as; contracts, torts, property, criminal law, civil procedure and legal research and writing skills. In recent years, some of the more forward-thinking law schools have added international law to the compulsory first year curriculum. The second year curriculum may still include some compulsory courses, but many courses are selected by the student from such areas as taxation, decedents' estates, wills and trusts, constitutional law, conflict of laws, appellate advocacy, family law, Uniform Commercial Code, evidence[40] and business organizations. It often comes as a surprise to students, lawyers and even law professors from outside the United States to learn that U.S. law students often only begin to study constitutional law in the second year of legal education. But if one sees U.S. practice through the social and historical reference frames, one would be reminded that practice, not sources of law, defines the profession. Moreover, we know from history that many people who "read law" in England did so for only a year to gain practical knowledge to join a "nation of shopkeepers,"[41] not to practice law.

---

[39] As was mentioned back at the beginning of the book, there is no undergraduate study of law in the United States that qualifies one to sit for the examination to practice law. Often students of business will have a survey course called something like "business law," which is only a brief survey of all areas of law in just one or two courses.

[40] It is worth noting that in U.S. law there are both federal and state rules of evidence as well as federal and state bodies of substantive law of evidence. In an adversarial system, when the judge does not act as inquisitor but rather as a neutral and passive referee, far stricter rules must be observed by the adversaries in introducing evidence at trial. Therefore, at least one course in the law of evidence is necessary for anyone wishing to practice law and evidence is tested as a separate area of law on the bar examination.

[41] Adam Smith, then Napoleon I and others have referred to England as "a nation of shopkeepers." In *The Wealth of Nations*, Smith wrote "To found a great empire for the sole purpose of raising up a people of customers may at first sight appear a project fit only for a nation of shopkeepers. It is, however, a project altogether unfit for a nation of shopkeepers;

For daily business practices, knowledge of torts and contract were much more practical than a study of the constitution. It is also worth mentioning a final point on this apparent quirk in the U.S. curriculum. Given that even today the United Kingdom does not record its own constitution in one written document, it would have been rather abstract for the Inns of Court to have presented constitutional law as an area of study.

By the third year of legal studies, the curriculum is largely selected by the student, and might include such courses as federal courts, comparative law, international law, environmental law, legal philosophy, moot court competitions, admiralty law, legal history, civil rights law, animal law, landlord-tenant law, labor law, estate planning, clinics and practica. (In some states, third year clinic and practica students are even permitted to appear on behalf of clients in the courtroom, supervised by a practicing lawyer and certified by the court).

After three years of successful legal study, examined one course at a time, graduates are awarded the J.D. or equivalent degree. Remember that, with limited exceptions, only if the degree is from a law school that is approved by the A.B.A.[42] is the graduate permitted to attempt the bar examination. Further, the person must prove himself or herself to be of "good moral character" and usually at least one practicing lawyer must have attested that the graduate has the "fitness to practice law." The moral character requirement works to pay homage to the idea, if not carry out the practice, that the practice of law is regarded as a vocation, not simply as a job. Society tolerates lawyers being self-organized and self-regulated only insofar as they provide necessary legal services in a way in which the public approves. So long as their practices do not "frighten the horses,"[43] lawyers are left alone to govern themselves. As just one example, in 1895, the mere possibility of legislative regulation of the practice of law in Pennsylvania was the catalyst for the establishment of the Pennsylvania Bar Association.[44] Such a "soft" approval of the practice of law requires the self-discipline of a vocation. U.S. society, like so many others, has a Janus-faced relationship with its lawyers. When polled, U.S. citizens will rank the trustworthiness of lawyers near that of used car salesmen. But ask those same people whom they would hire to represent them in a divorce or contract dispute, and they will choose the most ruthless lawyer they can afford, so long as that lawyer has the reputation of winning cases.

---

but extremely fit for a nation whose government is influenced by shopkeepers." Adam Smith, *The Wealth of Nations*. Glasgow edition. Book IV, section vii.c. 1976.

[42] Some states such as California allow students to sit for the bar examination if the student has graduated from a law school approved by the A.B.A. *or* the state.

[43] The British actress, Mrs. Beatrice "Patrick" Campbell, who was the first person to play Eliza Doolittle in George Bernard Shaw's *Pygmalion*, when asked about certain sexually promiscuous behavior, is famously reported to have said "Does it really matter what these affectionate people do, so long as they don't do it on the street and frighten the horses?"

[44] Henry Thomas Dolan, "The Diamond Anniversary History of the Pennsylvania Bar Association," XLII *Pennsylvania Bar Association Quarterly* 2 (January 1971) 131.

5.2 The United States Today: Entry into the Profession of Practicing Law

Each of the fifty states, as well as other jurisdictions such as Puerto Rico, the American Virgin Islands or Guam, maintains its own rules governing the examination and admission of lawyers to practice within their respective borders. As there is no national bar admission, candidates are required to pass a bar examination in the particular state in which they want to work, or "practice law," as it is often referred to in the United States. Generally, a state bar association administers the exam or the exam is administered pursuant to the authority of the state's supreme court.

Beginning in 2010, some states adopted the Uniform Bar Examination (U.B.E.), which is prepared and coordinated by the N.C.B.E. While the number of states that have so far adopted the U.B.E. is a clear minority, it is too early to say to what extent this trend will expand.[45] The U.B.E. has as its advantage the facts that it is uniformly administered, graded, scored and produces a score that can be transferred to other jurisdictions that use the U.B.E. The majority of states do not use the U.B.E. For them, the bar examination is at least two days long, with a few states having three-day examinations. On one day of the examination, most students are examined on the Multistate Bar Exam (M.B.E.), administered by the state in which the student is sitting. The M.B.E. covers questions in the areas of constitutional law, contracts, criminal law and procedure, evidence, real property and torts and uses a multiple choice format. Those persons unfamiliar with the examination may mistakenly believe that multiple choice format questions are easy, assuming there is one correct and several incorrect answers among those offered. Instead, after a question that may itself run several pages, it is quite often the case that more than one of the possible answers from which to choose on the M.B.E. is correct; the student, however, must choose the *best* answer rather than simply identifying the single correct answer.

The second day of the bar examination typically is devoted to the law of the state in which one is taking the examination and therefore wishes to be admitted to practice. These questions are to be answered in longer answers or "essays." The subject areas tested differ by state,[46] and may include business organizations, employment discrimination, professional responsibility, civil procedure, evidence, real property, criminal law, family law, torts, conflict of laws (among the U.S. states), federal constitutional law, uniform commercial code sales, contracts, federal income tax, decedents' estates, wills and trusts.

---

[45] As of March 2015, fifteen of fifty U.S. jurisdictions have adopted the U.B.E. See www.ncbex.org/about-ncbe-exams/ube/ (last accessed 24 March 2015).

[46] It is a good indicator of the independence of each U.S. state that each state regulates legal practice within the state independently of other states. As Jonathan Goldsmith, Secretary General of the Council of Bars and Law Societies of Europe has noted, "it is easier for a German lawyer to practice in France, than a Pennsylvania lawyer to practice in Ohio." Interview with Goldsmith conducted on 3 August 2004 conducted by the author and Wayne J. Carroll, Esq. (Notes on file with the author.)

As further evidence of the fact that the profession wishes to see itself as more than a job, in addition to passing the bar examination, applicants in most states must pass a separate Multistate Professional Responsibility Examination within one year (before or after) of taking the bar examination.[47] In total, students are typically tested three times on the topic of professional responsibility (sometimes called "legal ethics"): it is examined as a required course in the law school curriculum that ends with examination, it is woven through other subject areas on the bar examination (questions on contract or constitutional law, for example, might also contain professional responsibility issues) and it is the only topic that merits a separate multistate examination that a student must pass within a year of the bar examination.

Due in no small part to its development as a profession that regulates itself, the common law legal practice has been likened to a guild or trade union or even a club. If we make use of lessons learned from comparative law, we are reminded that "[c]ompared to medicine or engineering, the particular social position of the legal profession and the nature of law as a field of study create a unique situation for legal education ... Unlike physicians or engineers, legal professionals act as social regulators."[48] But there is more. "The bar is not simply a guild or trade association. Those admitted to practice assume an official public role," featuring especially judges and government lawyers, but, given that all lawyers are officers of the court, meaning that, "in principle, lawyers have obligations to see to the proper functioning of the institutions of the law."[49]

5.3 Foreign Lawyer Practice in the United States (LL.M. and Foreign Legal Advisor)

Samuel Johnson, notable for, among other things, having published the pre-eminent dictionary of the English language in 1755, is reputed to have once said that "lawyers are a clubby lot." This character of lawyers comes through in their self-organization of legal practice. Just as each state has legal competency to establish its own rules for obtaining a license to practice law, each state is free to set standards for foreign lawyers to practice foreign law within that state. First, one should keep in mind that because there is no national bar examination, even U.S.-born lawyers with a license to practice in one state (say, Florida) cannot practice in another state (Texas, for example) without either passing the Texas bar examination or by being admitted to practice in Texas based on sufficient experience practicing law in Florida (many states require five years of such experience). But even with the required experience

---

[47] Some states, such as Connecticut, waive the requirement if the candidate completed an ethics class in law school with a satisfactory grade. See for example www.jud.ct.gov/cbec/faq3.htm (last accessed 25 March 2015).

[48] William M. Sullivan et al., *Educating Lawyers: Preparation for the Profession of Law*, Hoboken, NJ: John Wiley and Sons, Inc., 2007 82 (also known as the "Carnegie Foundation Report").

[49] *Ibid.*

in one's home state, one typically needs a lawyer in the second state (Texas, in this example) to make a motion to the court on behalf of the foreign (Floridian) lawyer, in order to have him or her admitted to Texas. This requirement continues to demonstrate the social need for one group of lawyers (in Texas) to accept another lawyer (from Florida) into their midst, over and above the neutral acts of having passed a foreign bar examination and having practiced in a foreign state. The practice of law is woven into the culture that produces its norms. The norms in much of U.S. law are produced by state culture (such as that of Texas). Texans, like any other local legal culture, want to be sure a Floridian *fits* in their local legal culture; high bar examination scores alone are not persuasive enough.

Currently, thirty-two states have adopted rules permitting persons who received their license to practice law in a foreign country to become "foreign legal consultants."[50] While law professors and commentators have advocated federal legislation that would provide for the uniform regulation of these consultants, the licensing of foreign lawyers in the individual states as a consultant has remained an area organized by the states.

An assessment of any legal practice and education system must be driven by whether the system fulfills the needs of the society it serves. The more heterogeneous a society, the less likely it is that all members will have the same needs from the legal system. Even in the rough geographic division of the country into states, there is variation. For example, the historical record shows that some U.S. states wanted to have no professional lawyers whatsoever, and functioned without them for varying periods of time. When professional lawyers do exist, what needs do they meet? Like many occupations, once established, both the occupation of the lawyer on the whole and any individual lawyer's practice has, as one of its main functions, to perpetuate itself. The practice of law might be especially capable of creating its own market. This phenomenon is illustrated in the story of the small U.S. Midwestern town in which there is only one lawyer. There is not even enough work to keep the one poor lawyer in business. And then, just when it seems business for the lawyer could not get any worse, another lawyer moves to the same town. Within a short time, both lawyers are doing quite well! The complexity of legal practices may well mean a citizen needs a lawyer to work through the labyrinth in resolving a conflict. But often it is the lawyers themselves who foster this complexity.[51] "The longer a case, the less it is worth, except to your lawyer," wrote Mark H. McCormack in his observations of the profession.[52]

---

[50] American Bar Association Center for Professional Responsibility Policy Implementation Committee, "Foreign Legal Consultant Rules," 24 June 2014: www.americanbar.org/content/dam/aba/migrated/cpr/mjp/for_legal_consultants.authcheckdam.pdf (last accessed 19 November 2015).

[51] My own study concluded that delay in the courts is not alleviated by adding more judges to the bench or many other administrative measures designed to quicken the pace of litigation, because lawyers benefit from, and therefore foster delay.

[52] Mark H. McCormack, *The Terrible Truth About Lawyers.* New York: William Morrow, 1986 (as quoted by Peter McGargee Brown in the *ABA. Journal*, 1 December 1987, at 126).

Rather than engage in lengthy and expensive litigation, parties may pursue an alternative means to resolve their disputes. Those alternatives include settlement before trial, arbitration and mediation, among others. Together they are referred to as "alternative dispute resolution" or just "A.D.R." In fact, if one considers how many cases are settled once litigation has begun, one could say that proceeding to final resolution through trial is relatively rare in the United States today. There will be more to say about A.D.R. in Chapter 9, when the discussion turns to the mechanics of trials.

While the nature of private legal practice might be such that lawyers dare not forget to perpetuate their business, one would not expect that same distraction among state lawyers or judges. With judges, it seems that there are instead ideological distractions away from serving social needs, rather than the distraction of perpetuating their business. In Chapter 7, when I discuss the philosophical reference frame, I will say more about legal realism and critical legal studies. But here in the social reference frame, it is worth mentioning that the legal realists of the 1920s, and the critical legal studies movement at the end of the twentieth century:

> both press the post-Enlightenment critique asserting that the reasoning of judges and legislators is largely the rationalization of interest and ideology. This charge is backed by a disturbing amount of empirical evidence. For example, in one study, Republican judges were found significantly more likely than Democratic judges to oppose the defense in criminal cases, to oppose administrative agencies in business regulation cases, to oppose the claimant in unemployment compensation cases, to oppose the finding of constitutional violation in criminal cases, to oppose the government in tax cases, to oppose the tenant in landlord-tenant disputes, to oppose the consumer in sales of goods cases, to oppose the injured party in motor vehicle accident cases, and to oppose the employee in workplace injury cases.[53]

Peter Suber points out that there are two very different ways to interpret this problem of bias in adjudication and therefore how one would correct for it. First, we could say that the law is okay, but our system for electing or appointing judges is flawed. Second, we might say that there is an inherent problem in the notion that judges could be apolitical. If the judge is politically constituted, we can expect

---

[53] Peter Suber, "Legal Reasoning After Post-Modern Critiques of Reason," 3 *Legal Writing* (1997) 21–50, 36 (quoting Joel B. Grossman, "Social Backgrounds and Judicial Decision-Making," 79 *Harvard L. R.* (1966) 1551–64). Although Suber uses the word "substantial" in his article, he provides only the Grossman article as support. Further, this study is now more than fifty years old. It would seem, however, given the more heightened claims of political bias in the judiciary, as illustrated in 2000, when the conservative majority of the U.S. Supreme Court intervened in Florida election law to stop a recount of the U.S. Presidential election and thereby gave the election to Republican candidate George W. Bush. The vote by the court was 5:4, with five justices appointed by Republican Presidents voting in a way that gave Bush the presidency.

no other than political judging. Legal realism, which will be discussed more in Chapter 7, says that rather than deny this truth and pretend judges are apolitical, we should acknowledge them as being political, and try to build their political nature into the adjudication system.

From the perspective of the outsider looking inward at legal practice and education, one expects to see not only the practice of law as a job like any other job, but as a service to society. That outside observer, however, might see a number of lawyers working in law as just another job. When that happens, the danger is that the enterprise becomes a daily routine of employee doing work for employer, and not the client or in service to society. It is easy to slip into such a workplace mentality. After all, unlike perhaps the barristers of old, the lawyer is working in an occupation from which he or she does make a living. And because of the high cost of legal education in the United States, regardless of how public-spirited the lawyer is, he or she is likely in great debt from the legal education for a considerable period of time while practicing law.

The relentless economic reminders are present in legal education, too. In the past twenty years, legal education providers have worked together with the government and banks to provide enormous loans to students without the collateral that any other loan would require, assuming instead that a lucrative future as a practicing lawyer is collateral enough, and furthermore, relying upon the fact that educational loans are not dischargeable in bankruptcy, unlike most other types of debt. While university education in the United States is expensive in general, for at least two reasons it is especially expensive to study law. First, one can study law only as a postgraduate discipline. Therefore, one must first pay for the undergraduate degree, and thereafter only begin the study of law as a second university course of study. Second, the fees charged for law study are often high in comparison to other courses of study, and therefore the amount of money a student must borrow is much higher than most other educational paths, except perhaps medicine.[54] Students in both fields are led to feel more comfortable accepting such large debt burdens because they are led to believe they will earn enough money to repay the loans.

Some economically-focused persons in the United States have always insisted that paying four or more years of big university fees for undergraduate education (even without the additional fees of law school education), is not a wise choice in comparison with shorter and cheaper training in a trade or industry and working

---

[54] See Shawn O'Connor. "Grad School: Still Worth the Money?" *Forbes*, 9 July 2015. O'Connor explains that while business schools may charge more than double the amount that law schools charge for yearly tuition, the law school curriculum, spanning three or four years, will likely accrue higher overall costs to the student. It is also important to note the difficulty in actually calculating the "costs" of education. One variable is yearly tuition, but another variable is "lost wages." The lost wage calculation is especially difficult because one must speculate concerning the level of income the student could earn without the very education he or she is pursuing. If the student were not in postgraduate university education (also called "grad school" in the United States), should the lost wages be calculated as if he or she were a lawyer or business manager, or as an entry-level business associate?

and investing during those early years of one's working life.[55] I had always resisted those arguments, even when the mathematics favored the proponent, because the purposes of a university education, as conceived and developed since the eleventh century, are not limited to getting a job and an income.[56] But most recently, the university-bank-government structure of guaranteeing loans for high-priced education has escalated the cost of legal education so rapidly and it has so completely outstripped the ability of many practicing lawyers ever to repay the loans that a variation of that old simple economic argument has begun to make sense. Why invest in a legal education that, when costs are compared with statistically demonstrated median income, cannot pay for itself? Student loans, issued by banks and guaranteed by the state were originally the very mechanism that enabled working- and middle-class students to attend university and law school. But eventually, the very mechanism that had at one time ushered in the democratization of educational opportunities—the government-guaranteed loan—now serves to burden the student so severely that the economic argument has begun to drive students away from the study of law.

I have made an informal study of how Deans, Associate Deans and Professors of law around the United States interpret the large-scale decline in law school applications (and consequently in admissions). Most agree that U.S. legal education is not going through a temporary phase, but is in fact undergoing a significant historical sea change. "We're not going back to 2006 anytime soon," according to James G. Leipold, Executive Director of the National Association for Law Placement (N.A.L.P.), a non-profit corporation comprised of law schools and legal employers.[57] The sector shed 60,000 jobs just during 2008 and 2009, and only 15,000 of those positions have returned, he said. Nearly 9 percent of associates at U.S. law firms were laid off in 2009 and some of them are still trying to make their way back into full-time law firm work[58] at the time of this writing.

---

[55] Evidence in support of this objection can be found in an extended report in *The Economist* that purports to measure the entirety of university education worldwide based (unsurprisingly) only upon the contributions to the personal and national economies that university education offers to its graduates. Such a treatment renders *Paideia, Bildung,* or *la formation humaine,* as naïve roadblocks on the path to the "glorious wealth" dangled by Deng Xiaoping: "Academics' resistance to change gains added strength from their belief that education is not an occupation, but a calling; and that to defend it against barbarians is not self-interest but moral duty." *The Economist,* "Special Report: Universities," 28 March 2015, at 16.

[56] During my own undergraduate education, Professor Robert Hauser, well aware that his audience of freshmen and sophomores had largely arrived from working-class high schools, made a very clear assertion early in our first semester at university. He told us that two shames of a university education are that afterward one could not get a job and equally, that afterward all that one could do in life was to function in his or her job.

[57] Jennifer Smith, "Law Firm Entry-Level Hiring Unlikely to Return to 2006 Levels," *Wall Street Journal LawBlogs,* 11 April 2014: http://blogs.wsj.com/law/2014/04/11/law-firm-entry-level-hiring-unlikely-to-return-to-2006-levels/ (last accessed 16 March 2015).

[58] *Ibid.*

To the degree that an extremely market-driven society can hope for a so-called "market correction" to the crisis, experts agree it will be only a partial return.[59] In short, legal education will not be graduating the large number of students it once did any time soon. It took several years for students to realize that costs of legal education had truly outstripped their ability to repay loans on the median practicing lawyer's wage. But now that that fact is treated as common wisdom among students, it will take another sea change to redirect them back to mass legal education in numbers near those pre-2008.

5.4 Legal Science

If one were to consult the historical record, one would find many and varying claims on what the content of legal training and education should be and how it served society. Back in the sixteenth century there were already recorded complaints that there were too many lawyers in Nottingham, England. Opinions have varied on the content of the U.S. legal curriculum since the U.S. legal system invented itself. As recently as 1995, one could find critics complaining that U.S. legal education was teaching a craft-side of law that is associated with the power of language, with reason, logic and analytical skills, abilities said to "reign supreme" at "our" law schools.[60] If U.S. legal education really wanted only such skills, why would admissions offices not limit themselves to students who had completed their undergraduate study in engineering, logic or physics? They asked "Is there a natural connection between the left sides of our brains and law or is it a cultural restriction which we take for granted?"[61] In disagreement with that criticism, the A.B.A. has in fact most recently changed the standards for education to require even more practical training, and to require that it take place in the field of practice, not in the law school, looking much like a return to the U.S. preceptorship, or a turn to the pupillage (for barristers) or training contract (for solicitors) of the United Kingdom or the period of mandatory practical training outside the classroom, such as that in Germany.

This chapter is devoted to understanding U.S. law through the social reference frame. One of the key differences between the common law and civil law is the way the law itself is defined or seen both as a discipline of study and in practice, and thus one must investigate how the social elements constitute the nature of the law. (As previously mentioned, there will be more on this in Chapter 8, which is devoted to the topic of disciplinarity.) Whereas Holmes famously said that law is experience, a

---

[59] See generally "Cooley Law School Plans to Close its Ann Arbor Campus at Year's End," www.abajournal.com/news/article/cooley_law_school_plans_to_close_its_ann_arbor_campus_at_years_end (last accessed 10 November 2014). The Western Michigan University Thomas M. Cooley Law School closed its Ann Arbor campus in 2014, reacting to a 39 percent decrease in enrollment in between 2010 and 2013.

[60] Jack A. Hiller and Bernhard Grossfeld, "Comparative Legal Semiotics and the Divided Brain: Are We Producing Half-Brained Lawyers?" 50 *Am J. Comp. L.* (2002) 175, 179.

[61] *Ibid.* (citing Tony Weir, *Wise Men's Counters* (1998) and Bernhard Grossfeld, *Unsere Sprache: die Sicht des Juristen* (1995)).

civil lawyer may well argue that law is logical science, known from a legislative rule which applies generally to the various real fact situations brought to the court. This difference is highlighted quite clearly by the role and reputation of a judge in each of the systems. As one cannot study experience, a judge in the United States will most often have been a practicing lawyer for some time before being appointed or elected to become a judge. In the civil law system, as, for example, in Germany, those who scored best on the state licensing examination would have the chance to apply to become a judge, whereas average or weaker performers would not. As a result, one finds thirty-year old judges on the bench of a trial court or even a lower appeals court. By comparison, in the United States, regardless of whether judges are elected or appointed, they do not apply for the positions directly after passing the bar examination. If appointed, the judges' appointments are usually partly political, in that whoever has the power to appoint—a governor of a state for state courts, or the U.S. President for federal courts—will appoint only persons from his or her political party. While this may seem overly political, the alternative—the general election of judges—has its own inherent problems. The general electorate may feel it knows what a law-maker does and therefore knows why or how to vote for a law-maker, but to know what a judge does, one has to be almost an insider of the legal profession, working in the courts. This fundamental difference is the outcome of how a legal system understands the law. In the United States, law—in the broadest possible meaning—is a "heterogeneous medley of rhetorical thrusts and parries," which is deemed best judged by the elders with the wisdom of experience.[62] Whether appointed or elected, judges in the United States have experienced the practice of law.

5.5 Lawyers and Law Students by the Numbers

According to Matthias Riemann, it is widely recognized that "there is almost no empirical research [in comparative law] worth speaking of and there is even less interest in sociological studies today than there was a few decades ago."[63] Nevertheless, it is worth attempting empirical descriptions of the students and professors of law in order to see the practice of law through the social reference frame. For instance, during the era of 1880 to 1947, the ratio of lawyers to citizens in the U.S. remained relatively constant at about 1:790.[64] There were a total of 169,489 lawyers in the United States in 1947. Approximately eighty years later (2014), the total number of

[62] Richard Posner, "The Material Basis of Jurisprudence," 69 *Ind. L. J.* 1, (1993) 2.
[63] Mathias Reimann, "The Progress and Failure of Comparative Law in the Second Half of the Twentieth Century," 50 *Am. J. Comp. L.* (Fall, 2002) 671, 693.
[64] See The American Bar Association, the Lawyer Statistical Report, 1985, 1994, 2004, 2012 editions, incorporated into the American Bar Association's Lawyer Demographics, www.americanbar.org/content/dam/aba/administrative/market_research/lawyer-demographics-tables-2014.authcheckdam.pdf (last accessed 20 May 2015). See also Robert MacCrate et al., "Legal Education and Professional Development – An Educational Continuum," *A.B.A. Sec. Legal Educ. & Admission to the Bar* (1992) 15 (hereinafter "MacCrate Report").

lawyers had risen to 1,281,432, resulting in a ratio of 1:402. From these three simple data points we can see that while the U.S. population more than doubled from 1947 to 2014, the number of lawyers multiplied nearly eight-fold. How could a country that originally functioned in some states with no professional lawyers need a lawyer for every 402 of its citizens?[65]

Not only has there been a growth in the number of lawyers disproportionate to the population in general, lawyers in the United States are unevenly distributed. An overwhelming number of persons below the poverty level in the United States cannot obtain legal services for civil disputes.[66] As of 2005, for example, there was only one legal aid lawyer to provide free or low-cost legal services for every 6,415 persons in poverty, while the overall average was closer to one lawyer for every 402 persons, fourteen times higher than lawyer availability for those in poverty.[67]

5.5.1 Gender

A further comparative social demographic frame in the practice of law is gender. In 1971, less than 3 percent of lawyers in the U.S. were women. By 1980 that number had increased to 8 percent and by the year 2000, 27 percent of lawyers were women. This appears to be a healthy trend, but one must further consider that in the year 2014, 47 percent of law students were women, but only 34 percent of lawyers in practice were women. Without investigation, the "common sense" response to the substantial reduction in the number of female lawyers compared to female law students is that women quit practice to raise children. However, just a little investigation shows such facts as, on average, a female lawyer earns $20,000 less per year than her male counterpart. Moreover, only 25 percent of federal judges, 20 percent of law school deans, slightly more than 20 percent of law firm partners, and just 4 percent of law firm managing partners are female.[68] Coupled with the same financial burdens as their male counterparts, female lawyers may well seek better pay outside the practice of law.

---

[65] American Bar Foundation, *supra* note 64 at 15.

[66] One must be careful to distinguish the availability of legal services for those accused of crimes from those in need of legal counsel in civil matters. Legal representation is constitutionally guaranteed to those accused of crimes, whereas there is no clear guarantee of legal representation for civil litigants. Nevertheless, most states have broadly interpreted the constitution, granting legal representation in a number of civil legal areas. For example, the Pennsylvania Supreme Court, in the case *In re Adoption of R.I.* 312 A.2d 601, 602 (Pa. 1973), applied a string of U.S. Supreme Court cases that stand for the principle that an individual is entitled to counsel in any proceeding that may lead to the deprivation of "substantial rights," such as a termination of parental rights. See www.americanbar. org/groups/legal_aid_indigent_defendants/initiatives/civil_right_to_counsel.html   (last accessed 11 November 2015).

[67] Legal Services Corporation, *Documenting the Justice Gap In America. The Current Unmet Civil Legal Needs of Low-Income Americans, An Updated Report of the Legal Services Corporation.* Legal Services Corporation, September 2009 21.

[68] American Bar Association Commission on Women in the Profession, "A Current Glance at Women in the Law 2014," available at the A.B.A. website, www.americanbar.org (last accessed 11 November 2015).

5.5.2 Race

Since Europeans landed in North America, racial differences have formed part of the fabric of the legal systems imported from Europe. In the U.S. Constitution itself, slaves (who were mostly brought from Africa) and the Native American "Indians" were counted for voting proportions and taxation as only three-fifths of a person. The three-fifths formula is found in Article 1, Section 2, Paragraph 3 of the U.S. Constitution:

> Representatives and direct Taxes shall be apportioned among the several States which may be included within this Union, according to their respective Numbers, which shall be determined by adding to the whole Number of free Persons, including those bound to Service for a Term of Years, and excluding Indians not taxed.

The importation, enslavement ("those bound to service") and eventual emancipation of Africans were all accomplished through measures permitted by law. Ultimately the abolition of slavery was also accomplished through the law. Once slavery was abolished, the culture began to address a litany of questions regarding race relations, including whether law needed to be invoked at all, and then processing to the many ways in which law could help to achieve racial justice. The refining of the law in the plan to achieve more racial equality includes measures for equal educational opportunities.

In 1971, among law students in the United States, there were a total of 5,568 racial minority students enrolled in the study of law. By the year 1991, 19,410 racial minority students were enrolled in the study of law. A more detailed review would show that in 2011, 11,327 Asian American students, 10,173 African American students, 6,514 Latino American students, and 1,273 Native American students were all enrolled in the study of law. If one compares the number of those enrolled in the study of law to the number of those in the practice of law, however, for African Americans alone, in 1970 only 1 percent of lawyers were African American. By 1990 that percentage had grown to 3.3, but 20 years later, in 2010, the growth had rather stagnated and rose to only 4.8 percent of lawyers.[69] At the same time, African Americans are approximately 13 percent of the U.S. population.

After the American Revolution, legal education suffered from the ongoing fight against elitism within U.S. culture. Still today, U.S. society would not call itself a class system. However, as far as legal education is concerned, only the most intellectually and economically able students have the opportunity to study law. Only after one has done well in secondary school, in university undergraduate education, and on the L.S.A.T., is the door to law school opened. If one compares the U.S. system

---

[69] The source of these statistics is the American Bar Association, "Resources for Lawyers: Profession Statistics" (2013), http://www.americanbar.org/resources_for_lawyers/profession_statistics.html and www.americanbar.org/resources_for_lawyers/profession_statistics.html (both last accessed 19 November 2015).

to systems in which one can study law as an undergraduate university student, the study and practice of law in the U.S. system may well be identified as open only to a select part of the population. By comparison, in the United Kingdom or Germany, for example, good A level or *Abitur* scores, respectively, are sufficient to be accepted at law faculties.

5.6 A New Millennium for Common Law Education, A New Century for U.S. Legal Education

During much of its history, formal legal education has been criticized for being antiquated and reform has been demanded from the public,[70] the profession, law students, professional associations, teachers themselves,[71] or any combination of these. Yet at the same time, legal education in the United States has continued to grow and expand, leading one to believe that education under criticism is just business as usual. Therefore, when a real change in education is at hand, one might well mistake that situation for more of the usual level of criticism and response. Are we now experiencing a significant change, or is it just more of the usual? In 2002, there were 187 law schools in the United States approved by the A.B.A. By 2010, the number of A.B.A.-approved law schools had swelled to 200,[72] an increase of nearly 7 percent in just eight years, although U.S. population over an eight-year span twenty-two years earlier (producing the students likely to take the law school seats in 2002 and 2010), rose only 300,000 with a growth rate of only about 1.3 percent. At the end of the twentieth century, the A.B.A. commissioned a task force to study the connections and gaps between legal education and legal practice. The product of that task force, the McCrate Report,[73] has been influential not only in U.S. legal education, but abroad as well.[74] A further report, "Educating Lawyers: Preparation for the Profession of Law"[75] (popularly known as "the Carnegie Report"), published in 2007, has also been influential in U.S. legal education. One might have been content to include

---

[70] Not only the practice of law, but legal education has been criticized for being political. See Russell G. Pearce, "The Legal Profession as a Blue State: Reflections on Public Philosophy, Jurisprudence, and Legal Ethics," 75 *Fordham L. Rev.* (2006) 1339.

[71] See Michael Hunter Schwartz, "Teaching Law by Design: How Learning Theory and Instructional Design Can Inform and Reform Law Teaching," 38 *San Diego L. Rev.* (2001) 347.

[72] Catherine L. Carpenter, ed. "A.B.A., A Survey of Law School Curricula 2002–2010," Executive Summary 14, fn. 8.

[73] American Bar Association, *supra* note 64.

[74] See for example in Germany, "*Abstimmung des Reformmodells mit den im McCrate – Report genannten Kompetenzen eines Volljuristen,*" on the University of Hagen website http:// wiki.fernuni-hagen.de/modjuristausb/index.php/ Abstimmung_des_Reformmodells_ mit_den_ im_McCrate_-_Report_genannten_ Kompetenzen_eines_Volljuristen, or Andreas Bücker and William A. Woodruff, "The Bologna Process and German Legal Education: Developing Professional Competence through Clinical Experiences," 9 *German Law Journal* (2008) 575.

[75] Sullivan et al., *supra* note 48.

these reports in the long continuum of justified criticism and response by legal education and the profession. But then the sham world of Wall Street finance and the housing finance market bubble collapsed in late 2008. It took a few years for the ripple effects of the economic collapse to reach legal education, but eventually it did, and an educational system that played on the vagaries of the marketplace now fell into the same recession as other sectors of that marketplace. By 2011, many law schools had reported a 30 percent decrease in their number of applications, and in 2012 through 2014 they experienced the same.[76] Is this just an adjustment or a sea change in U.S. legal education? When education is a market commodity, one might find it easy to talk about "market adjustments" and "market corrections." By comparison, would the state, providing education in an area of public services—law—speak in such terms? Does anyone study law simply to be educated in law without wishing to practice law? Not often, although a culture might well think that education is a good idea for its citizens, even if it is not job training. "It is common in French, though not in English, to talk about education as 'formation,' as in *la formation medicale* or even *la formation humaine*."[77] To this observation one might add the example of German, with Humboldt's famous notion of "*Bildung*," which means both "education" and "formation."

The reputation of law schools is heavily driven by their ability to produce graduates who pass the bar examination at the first attempt. The A.B.A. conducted a survey of U.S. law school curricula. Just as students can take preparatory courses for the L.S.A.T. while they are undergraduates, as of 2010, "49% of respondents offered a bar preparation course for credit. The range of topics included multistate essay, multiple choice, state essay, and performance practice. For most law schools, the course was voluntary."[78]

"It's probably not a huge surprise that starting salaries dropped substantially for the Class of '[20]10 law grads nationwide,'" according to the N.A.L.P.[79] The median starting salary for new law school graduates dropped nearly 13 percent, according to research released by the N.A.L.P. The mean salary fell approximately 10 percent according to the same report.[80] The national median salary for those working full time and reporting a salary was $63,000, compared with $72,000 for the class of 2009. The national mean was $84,111, compared to $93,454, falling nearly 10 percent from the previous year. The private sector was especially hard hit, according to the report.[81]

---

[76] See American Bar Association, "ABA Section of Legal Education reports 2014 law school enrollment data," 16 December 2014: www.americanbar.org/news/abanews/aba-news-archives/2014/12/aba_section_of_legal.html (last accessed 24 March 2015).

[77] Sullivan et al., *supra* note 48 at 84.

[78] Catherine L. Carpenter, "Major Findings of the 2010 Survey," in "A.B.A., A Survey of Law School Curricula: 2002–2010," American Bar Association, 2010 16. The survey used the previous A.B.A. 2002 study as the baseline to track changes.

[79] Hillary Mantis, "Starting salaries down for Class of 2010," *The National Jurist*, 7 July 2011: www.nationaljurist.com/content/starting-salaries-down-class-2010 (last accessed 5 August 2013).

[80] *Ibid.*

[81] *Ibid.*

The graduates working in the public sector did slightly better, according to the report. Median salaries for government and public interest jobs were almost unchanged from 2009 — at $52,000 and $42,900, respectively. And the median salary for judicial clerkships even increased. The median for clerkships was $51,900, compared with $50,000 in 2010. "This downward shift in starting salaries is not, for the most part, because individual legal employers were paying new graduates less than they paid them in the past," according to N.A.L.P.'s James G. Leipold. "Aggregate starting salaries fell because graduates found fewer jobs with the high-paying large law firms and many more jobs with the smallest law firms, those that pay the lowest starting salaries."[82]

When legal education is a product for consumption on the market, just as shoes, houses or financial "derivatives" are, one should expect to find the same treatment as these other items when it comes to marketing, advertising, and product performance. And we do. Making what might have once been a noble profession into a consumer market product is unsurprising in American culture. Would it be different if the profession were state controlled rather than independently self-policing? To answer that would require a mountain of presumptions and speculative conclusions, but we can begin. "The numbers that have become problematic were intended, said Ms. Rotenberg [spokeswoman for the A.B.A.'s Section of Legal Education and Admissions to the Bar] to provide 'consumer information' to prospective students and aren't required by the U.S. Education Department."[83] If one pauses a moment to reflect on this statement, it would appear that the A.B.A. is distinguishing that which must be reported to the state from that which a law school may use as advertising. That might suggest that in a consumer economy, private and state law schools alike are permitted to use all of the puffery to which we have become accustomed when buying underarm deodorant when advertising to the student, but not when they report to the state. Here one is reminded, however, of the advertiser's promise that a consumer product will perform as promised "or your money back." What is legal education promising?

The method and forum through which legal education makes its promises not only of concern to law school applicants, but already in 1992, to the A.B.A. itself. In the McCrate Report, the A.B.A. recommended more transparency in the process of becoming a lawyer through legal education. Specifically:

> The [A.B.A.] Section of Legal Education and Admissions to the Bar, in cooperation with the Law School Admission Council and the Association of American Law Schools, should seek to assure that prospective law students who are selecting a law school can obtain information about all law schools relating to admission statistics, tuition, costs and financial aid, enrollment and graduation statistics, curricular offerings and class sizes, library resources,

[82] *Ibid.*
[83] Carl Bialik, "Job Prospects for Law Grads? The Jury's Out," *Wall Street Journal*, 19 March 2012 11.

physical plant, housing availability, financial resources available to support educational programs, and placements and bar passage statistics.[84]

A series of lawsuits by recent law school graduates have alleged that the marketing that induced them to go to law school, and the particular law school chosen, was intentionally misleading and therefore the graduates want their money back.[85] Kyle McEntee, co-founder and executive director of a non-profit organization called "Law School Transparency," said he has no doubt that "misleading statistics were provided," but he raises a question also posed by lawyers for the defendants: *how* to determine whether damage has been done to the students, and, if it has, how much tuition should be refunded.[86] During these lawsuits, at least two law schools admitted submitting false data to the A.B.A. concerning the credentials of students who had been admitted to the study of law. Commenting on that revelation, Professor Brian Tamanaha of Washington University in St. Louis said "it would be naïve to assume that no law schools have falsified employment numbers," for their graduates.[87] If one puts that comment in the broader context of what legal education has been in the United States or elsewhere, it becomes its own cultural criticism. In a culture that commodifies education, the student market pressures toward cheating are to be expected even by those in charge of teaching people to care for the rights and liabilities of its citizens. Even if the plaintiffs in these lawsuits do not win any of their legal actions, it is worth noting as a matter of social science that at this point in the history of legal education and practice, such lawsuits are being filed at all. In response to the issues raised in these lawsuits and in many blogs, newspaper articles[88] and other media, the A.B.A. has changed Standard 509 of its *Standards for Approval of Law Schools*, through which it requires law schools to file annual reports. Further changes have already been proposed and are under discussion within the A.B.A.[89]

In response to the pace of all education, including legal education, outstripping the rate of earnings increases across the United States, President Barack Obama issued a Memorandum in March 2015 that the White House has called a "Bill of Rights for Students." While the document does not rise to the level of legislation, nor even to the legal status of an executive order, it still makes a number of U.S. administrative agencies the watchdogs over fair information and availability practices for student loans and their repayment.

---

[84] MacCrate et al., *supra* note 64 at 329.
[85] See *MacDonald v. Thomas M. Cooley School of Law*, 724 F.3d 654 (6th Cir. 2013).
[86] Bialik, *supra* note 83 at 11.
[87] *Ibid.*
[88] A particular article in the *New York Times* unleashed a torrent of discussion of the issues. See David Segal, "Is Law School a Losing Game"? *New York Times*, 8 January 2011: BU1.
[89] See www.wsj.com/articles/law-schools-face-new-rules-on-reporting-graduates-success-1426629126 (last accessed 11 November 2015), discussing a new rule adopted by the accrediting arm of the American Bar Association that will tighten claims, giving law schools less credit for jobs that they subsidize. These so-called "bridge-to-practice" fellowships typically pay graduates $1,000 to $4,000 a month for jobs in the non-profit or public sectors that often expire within a year.

5.7 Conclusion: Are the Horses in the Street Frightened Yet?

On the day it is printed, this book hits the barrier on what one might say is the "present" state of social concerns in legal education and practice in the United States. If one adopts either the spiral or Enlightenment models of history from Chapter 4, however, past conditions and current conditions might be defensibly connected to predict a trajectory for the future. With an educational system that is so expensive to the student, the ups and downs of the economy generally have a direct impact on who can afford legal education. And in a prolonged weak economy, even if one does complete the education, the number of jobs available to law graduates are fewer. Potential clients do not avail themselves of optional legal services when they are concerned with their own empty wallets. This state of affairs has clearly been felt by the approximately two hundred A.B.A.-approved law schools in the United States.[90]

History in general should teach us that society, culture and its institutions change over time. All of us are a little biased toward thinking that the state of play when we are born, or at least when we become conscious adults, is somehow the way it always has been, as though the Enlightenment view's arrow of history had an endpoint that coincidentally was the era of our birth. Moreover, it is relatively commonplace for all of us in old age to believe that the state of play at our birth was the best era—the "good old days"—and things just get worse now. Maybe. Legal education and practice in the United States are changing. Whether the changes are good or bad will be determined by which historian is writing the narrative in the future, and whose situation is being told. A situation in which fewer students can afford to study law or find a job as a lawyer, but more of those students are women or minorities can be described in many different ways, both favorable and unfavorable. A situation in which fewer new lawyers can find jobs, but more low-income persons have legal services available to them will be described differently depending upon whether one is telling the story of lawyers or the availability of legal services. Were it to come to pass that only the most elite of the wealthy can have legal services offered by those wealthy enough to have studied law, then the horses in the street might well become frightened.

CHECK YOUR UNDERSTANDING

Do the features of the social organization of the U.S. legal profession give U.S. law any defining characteristics?

---

[90] Many law schools are scrambling to meet their budgets by filling seats with foreign LL.M. students, "flipping" the classroom to feature digital teaching supported by live teaching (rather than the reverse), and new and creative joint degree programs.

CHALLENGE YOUR UNDERSTANDING

What evidence is there to demonstrate that private market economics are sufficient mechanisms to assure U.S. citizens of adequate legal services?

Literature

Carpenter, Catherine L., "Major Findings of the 2010 Survey," in "A.B.A. A Survey of Law School Curricula: 2002–2010," American Bar Association, 2010.

Frankenberg, Günter, "Critical Comparison, Re-Thinking Comparative Law," 26 *Harv. Int'l L. J.* (1985). 411.

Hiller, Jack A. and Bernhard Grossfeld, "Comparative Legal Semiotics and the Divided Brain: Are We Producing Half-Brained Lawyers?" 50 *Am J. Comp. L.* (2002). 175.

Holmes, Oliver Wendell Jr., *The Common Law*, Boston, MA: Little, Brown and Company, 1881.

Holmes, Oliver Wendell Jr., "The Path of Law," 10 *Harv. L. Rev.* (1897). 457.

Johns, Margaret C. and Rex R. Perschbacher, *The United States Legal System – An Introduction*, 2nd ed. Durham, NC: Carolina Academic Press, 2007.

Kempin, Frederik G., *Legal History: Law and Social Change*. Englewood Cliffs, NJ: Prentice-Hall, 1963.

Kempin, Frederick G. Jr., *Historical Introduction to Anglo-American Law*. St. Paul, MN: West Publishing, 1990.

Lepaulle, Pierre, "The Function of Comparative Law with a Critique of Sociological Jurisprudence" 35 *Harv. L. Rev.* (1922). 838.

MacCrate, Robert et al., Task Force on Law Schools and the Profession: Narrowing the Gap, "Legal Education and Professional Development – An Educational Continuum." A.B.A. Sec. Legal Educ. & Admission to the Bar, 1992.

Marmor, Andrei, "The Nature of Law", in Edward N. Zalta, ed. *The Stanford Encyclopedia of Philosophy*. Winter 2011. ed.

Posner, Richard, "The Material Basis of Jurisprudence," 69 *Ind. L. J.* (1993). 1.

Pound, Roscoe, *The Spirit of the Common Law*. Francistown, NH: Marshall Jones Co., 1921.

Reimann, Mathias, "The Progress and Failure of Comparative Law in the Second Half of the Twentieth Century," 50 *Am. J. Comp. L.* (Fall, 2002). 671.

Sullivan, William M., Anne Colby, Judith W. Wegner, Lloyd Bond and Lee S. Shulman, *Educating Lawyers: Preparation for the Profession of Law*, Hoboken, NJ: John Wiley and Sons, Inc., 2007.

6

THE LANGUAGE REFERENCE FRAME

Framing Issues

1. What are the connections between comparative law and language?
2. What role do legal education, training and practice ascribe to language?

6.1 Introduction and Outline

Just as Chapter 4 began with some issues that we face when looking through the historical reference frame before we attempt to construct a typical chronology of historical facts, and Chapter 5 began with some issues that we face when we look through the social reference frame before attempting to describe the U.S. legal education, training and practice through numbers and categories, here at the beginning of Chapter 6 it will be helpful for us to look at some language issues before we begin to talk about examples of the relationship of language to law in practice.

In Chapter 5, I introduced the Carnegie Report on U.S. legal education. Its authors wrote:

> On our visits to law schools, we were repeatedly told by both students and faculty that the first-year experience typically results in a remarkable transformation: a diverse class of beginners somehow jumps from puzzlement to familiarity, if not ease, with the peculiar intricacies of legal *discourse*. The legal-case method, in all its variations, has dominated the first year of most legal education through much of the past century. Its purpose was described to us in straightforward terms: the case-*dialogue* method, pioneered by Langdell

and his Harvard Law School colleagues from the 1870s, is designed to prepare students to "think like a lawyer."[1]

But wait a minute. Even in this formulation of the Carnegie Foundation, learning to "think like a lawyer" is, in practice, learning to "talk like a lawyer." Recall from the historical reference frame that one of the methods of legal history is the method of tracing legal texts, including statutes, commentaries, the opinions of judges and the trial notes of practicing lawyers. To say that language carries law is equivalent to admitting that language is both conceptually prior to and essential to law. U.S. law professor David Mellinkoff rightly states in the preface to his often-cited book, *The Language of the Law*, that "law is a profession of words."[2] To appreciate the significance of this simple statement by Mellinkoff, we must understand words to be units of spoken or written language, and language, in turn, to be a system of such words. From that, we may conclude that there would be no law without language. It would be misleading to conceive of law on the one hand, and language on the other, as two separate, independent entities, as one might be tempted to infer when looking at the syntagms "language of the law" or "language and law" or "law and language," as expressed in terms of seemingly opposite pairs. If as Mellinkoff says, law is a profession of words, lawyers need to know something about how these words and language work. But as with most foundations, including those beneath a building or the bitmap of computer software, our daily practices might rely upon the foundation, yet not see the foundation. The quality of our daily practices may be measured by the degree to which they are cognizant of the foundations upon which they are based.

In the 1990s, during the so-called "science wars," some cultural theorists claimed that all human knowledge, even that of the natural sciences, is constituted by language. If that is true, it would not be so bold a statement to assert that "[a]ll law established and spoken by people is language become power,"[3] whether law is understood as a civil law social science or a common law *artes liberales*. Going a step further, if law is constituted by language, then comparative law would be a practice constituted by translation practices. This is a problematic concept, however, because, as Bernhard Grossfeld says, "[l]inguistic experiences consequently are not easily transferrable from one culture to another."[4] Grossfeld does not say linguistic experiences are impossible to transfer, but that they are not easy to transfer. What makes it difficult is just as an idiom from one language cannot be simply entered into an

---

[1] William M. Sullivan et al., *Educating Lawyers: Preparation for the Profession of Law*. Hoboken, NJ: John Wiley and Sons, Inc., 2007. 47. Also known as the "Carnegie Foundation Report." (Emphasis added.)

[2] See D. Mellinkoff, *The Language of the Law*. Eugene, OR: Resource Publ., Wipf and Stock Publ., 1963.

[3] Bernhard Grossfeld, *Core Questions of Comparative Law*. Trans. Vivian Curran. Durham, NC: Carolina Academic Press, 2005 83 (quoting Hans Fritz Abraham, *Vom Beruf des Juristen als Ausdruck seiner Persoenlichkeit*. Berlin: F.S. Pinner, 1932 8, 13).

[4] Grossfeld, *supra* note 3 at 50.

online translator and produce a one-to-one equivalent in another language, neither can legal concepts, or worse still, what Grossfeld calls a complete "comparison of orders"[5] be translated as simple nouns from one language to another.

This brings us to another issue of language that goes to the core of how one understands law. The positivist philosophers of law such as Jeremy Bentham, John Austin and Hans Kelsen said that law should be understood as the command of the sovereign backed by the threat of force. When we think of the phrase "law enforcement" from criminal law, we hear "force" in the phrase. Is legal enforcement limited to physical force, or what Max Weber called the state monopoly on violence? Do not people also obey the law because they want order, and there is likely to be more order if most of us are obeying the same rules? This latter idea is more like embracing order rather than fearing force, yet both can account for obeying the law. Once we consider this second concept, it is easier to see that one is persuaded to obey the law, rather than simply "forced" to obey the law with physical violence. Over-simplified skepticism of international law often threatens that international law is not law at all because there is no superior executive, such as a super police or military, that can enforce international law over all nations or members of all nations. The error in such a simple critique is that it takes no account of the great motive for compliance with the law—that motive being a desire for order. We see it and acknowledge it quite often in domestic law, but for some reason ignore it in international law. Grossfeld tells us that "The legal community is certainly first and foremost a community of persuasion, not of compulsion; it is a spontaneous order."[6] Issues of language are central to the study, training and practice of law. Lawyers are wordsmiths. We know that in the early days of the United States, oral argument skills were a significant part of the practice of law. The extremely influential judge, chancellor and author James Kent of New York "was not a great public speaker, and he confessed that he 'hated' the practice of law—so much of which required oral improvisation."[7] The legal philosopher Peter Koller formulates the connection not just with law, but with justice. Justice, he says, "seems to be an anthropological constant, but to a great extent is formed by culture. Justice has a lot to with linguistic communication."[8]

To begin to understand language issues in the law, one must do a little work to understand the nature of language, which is not obvious just because we use it everyday. After all, we use our brains, computers and governments, and most cannot claim to know how they work either. First, one must abandon some "common sense" notions of how language operates. The three most misleading common sense notions are (1) that words are labels for things, (2) that a speaker communicates his or her intentions through language, and (3) that speaking to a listener is

---

[5] *Ibid.* at 10.

[6] *Ibid.* at 84 (citation omitted).

[7] Daniel Hulseboch, "An Empire of Law: Chancellor Kent and the Revolution in Books in the Early Republic," 60 *Alabama Law Review* (2008) 377, 389.

[8] Peter Koller, "Das Glück in Kooperation schmieden," an interview with Alois Pumhösel in *Der Standard*, 14 March 2015, p. A3, trans. this author.

a reified transmission, just as if one were sending an electronic signal to a receiver. These problematic notions are themes to be addressed from four different language approaches[9] throughout the rest of this chapter.

Of the four approaches to law through language two—literature and philosophy—will be mentioned only briefly and two others—linguistics and rhetoric—will be discussed in some detail. The outline is as follows: In the law and literature movement (6.2), one can observe that in the writing and reading of literature, themes develop for the law that may reflect or create the role of law in that culture. The second approach is through the field of linguistics (6.3), and grows from a simile that I mentioned earlier—studying a foreign legal system is like studying a foreign language. We do not learn a second language in the manner that we learned our own native language. The insights as to precisely how we do learn a second language have much to say about how we learn a second legal system as compared to how we learn our native legal system. Grossfeld, in his critiques of comparative law practice, advocates that in fact comparative law ought to model itself on language translation studies and practices. In translation studies, one focuses upon linguistics. One of the most enduring lessons in linguistics comes from structuralism, in which linguistic theory teaches us the way in which meaning is created in language. Opposite from law and literature, the linguistic approach may seem to the lawyer to be the most remote from what he or she knows about language in the practice of law, but when connections are made, it is the most profound.[10]

Third, we look for some insight from the approach of the ancient art of rhetoric (6.4), with emphasis on the fact that rhetoric was part of general schooling and education at the time of the inception of the English common law system, and secular law was in fact not part of English university education at the time.[11] While the linguistic approach may seem to be remote, but profound, the study of rhetoric's

---

[9] See Penelope Pether, "Language," in Austin Surat, Matthew Anderson and Catherine O. Frank (eds.), *Law and the Humanities: An Introduction.* Cambridge: Cambridge University Press, 2010 315–39, in which she writes at page 318: "Beyond registering that the body of work on law and language that proceeds from the premise that language is but a medium of transmission for the substance of law has been left methodically behind by contemporary law and language scholarship, this much might also be said: This survey of the state of contemporary humanistic Law and Language scholarship suggests four main conclusions. The first is that much of value in this body of work involves applying linguistic humanities and/or critical linguistic sciences methodology to the work of legal institutions, discourses, and texts […]. Next, some of it […] is about the unique or distinctive relationships between law and language […]. [T]hird […] much is yet to be done in the subdiscipline of scholarship concerning itself with the unique or distinctive insights that might emerge from interdisciplinary inquiries into 'law.' […] [F]ourth […]: to the extent that there is an aspect of language scholarship that is presently significantly underdeveloped, it is the theories of language, of subject formation, and of law." See also Peter Tiersma and Lawrence Solan (eds.), *The Oxford Handbook of Language and Law.* Oxford: Oxford University Press, 2012.

[10] See Grossfeld *supra* note 3.

[11] See, for example, Barbara J. Shapiro, "Rhetoric and the English Law of Evidence," in Victoria Kahn and Lorna Hutson (eds.), *Rhetoric and Law in Early Modern Europe.* New Haven, CT: Yale University Press, 2001 54–72.

practices can be done quite simply and nevertheless be as profound in explaining a legal worldview as philosophy. But for the common law, it is essential that one understand even the basics of rhetoric that historically formed the practice of law. With this book's focus on culture in mind, a simple categorical syllogism may be employed to place language in the context of the study of law:

> Major Premise: Language carries Culture
> <u>Minor Premise: Law is a function of Culture (not a function of Nature)</u>
>
> Conclusion: Language carries Law

The fourth approach will not be heavily emphasized here, but in writing the chapter I found it to be unavoidable, and that is the approach of the philosophy of language (6.5). In the philosophy of language, the reader will be asked only to consider a few points on the nature of language and what that means for our legal–cultural worldview. Regarding issues of language in general, there are further, far-reaching and deeply serious implications for the nature of knowledge here. In the study of the communication of scientific knowledge to various publics, research has shown that "having information" and "knowing facts" alone does not change peoples' thinking to align with scientific facts.[12] We like to emphasize that we have more information available to us through more different media than ever before. But the research shows that the extra information does not change beliefs. And among all that extra information, the facts of science seem to be least capable of changing beliefs.

6.2 Law and Literature

Although I am only mentioning it briefly, I will begin with literature because this approach is most accessible for lawyers who may not have previously studied issues of language. Approaching law through literature has attained what some have called the status of a "movement." It should be said from the beginning that one might rightly question whether there is any topic separate from law or literature that lies at the intersection of law and literature.[13] Yet given the focus of this book, when it comes to understanding a culture, law and literature can help one to understand how the culture understands the role of law in its midst[14] and how literature forms part of that cultural understanding. Film, television and other graphic media do so as well, of course, but this chapter is limited to approaches from language, and does not include multi-media.[15] In introducing his two-volume set, *The Law in Literature* and *The Law*

---

[12] See Eileen Scanlon, Roger Hill and Kirk W. Junker (eds.), *Communicating Science: Professional Contexts*. London: Routledge, 1999.

[13] See Jane B. Baron, "The Rhetoric of Law and Literature: A Skeptical View," 26 *Cardozo L. Rev.* (2005) 2273.

[14] See Catherine O. Frank, *Law, Literature, and the Transmission of Culture in England, 1837–1925*. Burlington, VT: Ashgate, 2010.

[15] See, for example, Michael Asimow and Shannon Mader, *Law and Popular Culture: A Coursebook*. New York: Peter Lang, 2007.

as *Literature*, Ephraim London writes that "the term 'literature' is merely a judgment of the quality of writing. Court proceedings, testimony, arguments, pleas and judgments, and the discussion of legal theories—all … may be read as literature. … Even statutory law can attain the level of literature. Great literature should ignite or inspire; but whether it does depends in part on the reader."[16] Yet a little reflection tells us that London must feel the need to make this statement because he feels that most readers will think of literature as prose fiction, not the documents of the law. Most of the law and literature movement concerns itself with prose fiction in seeking how and when and why law is shaped by, and shapes, a culture. The reader of literature is like the citizen in law—meaning and acceptance of values are as much or more for the reader and citizen as for the author and law-maker. And when the reader or citizen interprets the meaning of a literary or legal text and puts it into practice, then we have the full cultural context of law and literature.

Beyond this rather "democratic" development of values and the two-way street between the lawmaker and citizen, and author and reader, there are some authoritarian practices as well. The language of the law like the language of literature has a history and goes through periods when its use and our attitudes towards its use changes. The high-modernist notion of privileging an author's intent goes some way to explaining the orientation of law to its language. Lawyers may even have been conscious of an expansionist, if not imperialist use of language in the past and perhaps still in the present. For example, on March 3, 1885, David Dudley Field, who is known for having moved New York from common law civil pleading to civil code pleading, addressed the graduating class of Albany Law School on the topic "Reform in the Legal Profession and the Laws." During the speech, he said "[t]he language we speak, the institutions in which we participate, are to spread with our dominion."[17] In addition to the fact that language can show us the influence of the common law, we can look to how it is that language matters for understanding the legal culture in which it operates. To do so, we need first to understand how it is that language—any language—creates meaning. Incorporating the historical reference frame, we can see that the very notion of how language creates meaning itself has a history. According to Austin Sarat, "theorists of law and literature have established the fundamentally linguistic nature both of law and literature and their shared

[16] Ephraim London, ed. *The World of Law, Volume I, The Law in Literature*. New York: Simon and Schuster, 1960 xi; and *The World of Law, Volume II: The Law as Literature*, New York, Simon and Schuster, 1960. See also Sanford Levinson and Steven Mailloux (eds.), *Interpreting Law and Literature*. Chicago, IL: Northwestern University Press, 1988; and Richard Weisberg, *The Failure of the Word*. New Haven, CT: Yale University Press, 1984; and the journal *Law & Literature*, published quarterly since 1988 by the University of California Press for the Cardozo School of Law. For rhetorical considerations, see James Boyd White, *When Words Lose Their Meaning*. Chicago, IL: University of Chicago Press, 1984; Gert Ueding, ed. *Rhetorik. Begriff – Geschichte – Internationalität*. Tübingen: Niemeyer, 2005; and Katharine Swabota, "The Rhetorical Construction of Law," 5 *Int'l J. for the Semiotics of Law* 1 (1992) 39.

[17] As cited in Daniel R. Coquillete, *The Anglo-American Legal Heritage*. 2nd ed. Durham, NC: Carolina Academic Press, 2004 603 fn. 26.

ability to reflect and create reality through language."[18] All too often, lawyers, as well as other people, use language under assumptions that scholars largely dismissed by the end of modernism. Up to and including that era, we assumed such things about language and meaning as "the author's intent is the best way to know what a text means," and "a written (or even oral) text has one right meaning," and "words are labels for things." Moreover, literature scholars assure us that even if a meaning is treated as fixed in a text, the meaning will change over time, and according to the audience. This lesson ought very much to tell us something about how citizens read the text of a constitution, statutes, regulations and court decisions:

> [T]he ability of the black letter to convey one meaning only and forever—to achieve both transparency and permanence through language—can conflict with the spirit of the law, with the intentions of the writer, as well as with the interpretive frameworks governing its problem of preserving meaning over time, the gaps created by history have their analogue in those created by the attempt to translate meaning from one language to another (a problem for international law), from one discourse to another (from law to other discip-lines), and from one constituency to another (interpretive communities).[19]

The desire to fix meaning in symbols continues, however. Logicians and natural scientists use mathematics rather than natural languages in attempting to express one meaning only and forever.

The study of literature helps us to understand how texts can enable meanings.[20] What literature scholars have concluded is that the audience, not the author, makes meaning from a text. It is of course true that an author can hope to steer the readers' possible interpretations of meaning, but that is not a precise science. When the audi-ence does make meanings from a text, each reader brings his or her own experiences to the text and consequently makes his or her own meaning from the meeting of the text and the reader. Convention would have it that there are limits of course. A reader who reads "silently snow falls" to mean that "the unemployment rate in China rose 2 percent" will need to do a lot of work to explain the connection of the text to his interpretation or else his words will be called nonsense. But between having only one meaning and having any meaning whatsoever, there is a great deal of room for mul-tiple acceptable interpretations of meaning. How can or does law make use of this insight in the interpretation of legal texts? As a purely textual matter, it does not. To fight against the possibility of citizens constructing a variety of meanings from legal

---

[18] Austin Sarat, Matthew Anderson and Catherine O. Frank, "Introduction: On the Origins and Prospects of the Humanistic Study of Law," in Austin Sarat, Matthew Anderson and Cathrine O. Frank (eds.), *Law and the Humanities: An Introduction*. Cambridge: Cambridge University Press, 2010 34.

[19] *Ibid*.

[20] A helpful introduction to literary theory, accessible to those whose primary focus is not literature, is Terry Eagleton, *Literary Theory: An Introduction*. Minneapolis, MN: University of Minnesota Press, 2008.

texts, the law injects the notion of an authoritative interpretation—that of a king or judge, as the final interpreter of meaning when the judge says whether the facts presented do constitute liability for a private wrong or criminal guilt for a public wrong. Even then, the judge does not say the text has one meaning only, but rather asks only what the proper interpretation of the rule of law for this set of facts is.[21] None other than Lord Denning, whom *The Guardian* called "the most celebrated English judge of the twentieth century,"[22] commented that "the principles of law laid down by the Judges in the 19th century—however suited to social conditions of that time—are not suited to the social necessities and social opinion of the 20th century."[23]

The importance of reducing customary norms to writing is exceptionally high in the creation of a legal system. In fact, it is a giveaway, to some degree, that we ever say that ideas, agreements or norms are "reduced" to writing. In English legal history, for the first one hundred years of the land conquered by William, there was no unified text of customary law. But when Henry II made the law a matter of his royal power, it was by writing.

> In that connection the very writing was a matter of importance. That royal law was set forth in writing gave it a certain dignity, perhaps even a sanctity. The writing also gave the law a certain fixity, a certain stability. In addition it laid the foundation for further elaboration.[24]

As regards the study of a foreign legal system, proper learning has never meant a "jug to mug" dissemination of facts, although those who have never studied education might think it is. This unexamined assumption is in fact driven by the electronic model of communication technology, not communication itself. Learning in the age of the internet is an extreme example of that fact. When all information is available instantaneously, learning becomes even more obviously an exercise in acquiring the skills and wisdom of valid judgment, not downloading information. We might note that the word "jurisprudence" is from the Latin meaning "judgment in the law." Thus learning the law is learning jurisprudence, not memorizing a grocery list of rules. Continuing the simile that learning foreign law is like learning a foreign language, one is reminded of Goethe's rhyming observation that "*Wer keine fremde Sprache spricht, kennt seine Muttersprache nicht.*" ("Those who speak no foreign language do not know their mother language.") Learning U.S. law is learning to become comfortable in speaking *law English*.[25] And the process for doing this is to

---

[21] See Reinnhold Zippelius, *Introduction to German Legal Methods.* Trans. Kirk Junker and P. Matthew Roy. Durham, NC: Carolina Academic Press, 2008.

[22] Clare Dyer, "Lord Denning, Controversial 'People's Judge', Dies Aged 100," *The Guardian,* 6 March 1999: www.theguardian.com/uk/1999/mar/06/claredyer1, (last accessed 4 May 2015).

[23] The Rt. Hon. Lord Denning, *The Discipline of Law.* London: Butterworths, 1979 v.

[24] Harold J. Berman, *Law and Revolution.* London: Harvard University Press, 1983 458.

[25] "Law French" was the term given to the use of French in English legal practice from the time of William the Conqueror until several centuries later. See J. H. Baker, *The Manual of Law French.* 2nd ed. Aldershot: Scolar Press, 1990.

read and listen and mimic the tone, style, usage and substance of what one has read and heard, which itself is a process of experience.[26] With this in mind, what does law English provide? Near the end of the nineteenth century and the end of his life, when asked during a press conference what had been the most important event of the century, the Iron Chancellor, Otto von Bismarck replied, "the fact that North America speaks English."[27]

6.3 Linguistics: Making Meaning through Language

The study and practice of linguistics is one of several disciplines concerned with the scientific study of language. Unlike the researchers in the law and literature movement, the researchers in legal linguistics are often not lawyers, but linguists.[28] Thus, lawyers are wont to ask how linguistics applies to the study of law. First, I am not speaking about linguistics in its disciplinary sense here. Rather, I mean simply that as compared to all the categories of the social or humanistic consideration of the law,[29] such as the philosophic, mechanistic, historic or social reference frames, this chapter focuses upon law's relation to and dependence upon language. The natural sciences, whose objects of study are the material things of nature and their relationships to one another, are said to therefore produce truths good for all times and places. By comparison, law is a cultural, not a natural phenomenon, and because language carries culture, language carries law as a sub-set of culture. To support that point, consider an historic look at the geographical distribution of the civil law and the common law. The civil law was distributed over the scores of provinces of the Roman Empire and Late Roman Empire. With the collapse of the empire, the civil law largely remained, but the languages of the civil law varied. By comparison, the common law was spread by the British Empire over scores of colonies, but as the empire has receded, both the common law and the English language have remained. With perhaps the exception of the Cantonese language in the city of Hong Kong, today one can say that the common law has only ever been practiced in the English language.

To understand the linguistic approach to the study of law, it is first necessary to reflect upon the notion of language as a system of signs. The Swiss linguist Ferdinand de Saussure (1857–1913) is widely considered to be the founder of modern linguistics. His ideas have had a persistent and significant impact on later scholars

---

[26] See Kirk W. Junker, "What Is Reading in the Practice of Law?" 9 *J. L. Soc'y* (2008) 111.

[27] John M. Swales, "Language, Science and Scholarship," 18 *Asian Journal of English Language Teaching* (1998) 1.

[28] There are persons who are both, however, such as Lawrence M. Solan. See Lawrence M. Solan, *The Language of Statutes: Laws and their Interpretation*. Chicago, IL: University of Chicago Press, 2010. Legal linguistics is sometimes recognized as a discipline in its own right. See for example, University of Cologne, European Legal Linguistics degrees of study at http://erl.phil-fak.uni-koeln.de/11925.html?&L=0.

[29] See, for example, Pether, *supra* note 9.

in the twentieth century, both in Europe and in the United States, including the U.S. linguists Leonard Bloomfield and Noam Chomsky. For our study as lawyers, there is a great deal to be learned from Saussure's general discussion and the first of his two principles concerning the nature of the linguistic sign. Saussure insists that language can be seen as a socially shared and psychologically real system of signs, each sign consisting of a link between an abstract concept, for which Saussure introduces the term *signifié* (in English, the "signified") and a sound pattern, which is called *signifiant* (in English, the "signifier"). These two parts together—the signified and the signifier, constitute the sign and become the basic unit of communication for Saussure. He calls the sign a "two-sided psychological entity." The insight that Saussure offers, and which counters so much of our common sense notions of language, is that communication is not "a link between a thing and a name, but between a concept and a sound pattern." The concept stands for a particular mental image and the sound pattern is not actually the sound itself, but is rather the "hearer's psychological impression of a sound as given to him by the evidence of his senses."[30] Therefore, one can understand how it is that in a French-speaking culture, one could say "*arbre*," in a German-speaking culture, one could say "*Baum*" and in an English-speaking culture, one could say "tree," yet on all three occasions the two pieces of the sign (the acoustic impression of these words with an abstract concept) somehow together usefully lead the speakers to a similar or same thing in the world.

From this observation, Saussure asserts two general principles that counter our common sense notions of language. The first of these is simple: "the construction of the linguistic sign is arbitrary." Given what Saussure means by "sign," this means that the relationship between the sound of our language and the psychological concept with which it is associated is an arbitrary relationship. It must be, because language groups all have different sounds. He supports this conclusion through his consideration of multiple contemporary languages, just as I have compared French, German and English, above. In Saussure's terms, the relationship of the signifier to the signified is arbitrary.[31] There is no natural connection between the sound (signifier) and the abstract concept (signified). The connection is a social custom only. The bond between them is arbitrary. Therefore meanings are connected to words (signs) by social agreement, custom and convention. Even though this is true, it does not mean that the sound (signifier) can be freely chosen by each single speaker of a community. Rather, it means that the link between the two parts of the linguistic sign is not intentionally created, for it has neither a natural nor a rational basis. To illustrate, consider that the idea of a sister is not linked by any inner relationship to the sequence of sounds "s – ö – r" (*sœur*) that serves as its signifier in French. In other words, it could have been different and could be represented as well by any other sequence of sounds as is proved by the differences among languages and by the very existence of different languages.[32] The result of these revelations on the

---

[30] F. de Saussure, *Course in General Linguistics*. Trans. Roy Harris. London: Duckworth, 1983 66.

[31] *Ibid.* at 67.

[32] *Ibid.* at 67–8.

working of language, according to Saussure, is that it is wrong to see language as a mere process of naming or designating "things" or even as a mechanism available to represent the world.[33]

The fact that a speaker cannot just freely choose a signifier is just the beginning of an understanding of the social nature of the creation of meaning in language. A second important step is to recognize that meaning is not first formed by a sender as "thought" and then sent like an electronic message to a receiver, who opens it to discover the precise "thought" of the sender. Most students, when reflecting upon language and communication, might resort to the non-scientific, common sense notion that language works as a unilinear system[34] in which a sender "forms" a message and then transmits the message to a destination. Such a sender–message–receiver notion may be useful to understand the technology of sending email and mobile phone texts, but it fails to give a proper account of how language works in face-to-face speech situations and of how meaning is created. Therefore we must rid ourselves of it if we want to know how law works to resolve conflict in the courtroom, for instance.

Recall the discussion in Chapter 1 on the relationship of common law to customary law. The U.S. legal historian Harold Berman has made the observation that:

> The rules and principles and standards and concepts to be enforced—the definitions of felonies, the concepts of seisin and disseisin—were derived from informal, unwritten, unenacted norms and patterns of behavior. These norms and patterns of behavior existed in the minds of people, in the consciousness of the community.[35]

This insight points out that when we say "law" in the common law tradition, we are using a signifier (the sound) to refer not to the statute of a text, but to how the public understands the law. Consider the so-called common law marriage. If two people consider themselves to be married under a description that aligns in their minds, and hold themselves out to members of their community as such, there needs not be an instrument of positive law, such as a marriage license document, to make the marriage "legal." In this sense, what the arbitrariness principle demonstrates is the social nature of language: as we have seen, the linguistic sign achieves its meaning because it is socially shared—one cannot invent any sound that he or she wishes and expect the sound to achieve the function of a signifier in a language community.

---

[33] By the 1960s, American literary critic Kenneth Burke was fond of making Saussure's structuralist point that much stronger by reversing the now-rejected "common sense" Modernist notion, and instead asserting that, "[t]hings are the signs of words." Kenneth Burke, "What are the Signs of What?: A Theory of 'Entitlement,'" 4 *Anthropological Linguistics* 6 (June 1962) 5.

[34] The unilinear system is the basis of the Bell Laboratory model, developed in the 1950s on the example of the telephone, which assumes that communication is a linear electromagnetic process.

[35] Berman, *supra* note 24 at 480–1.

Like a good lawyer, Saussure anticipated that critics would object to his assertion, citing examples such as onomatopoeia and exclamations. They claimed that these two linguistic phenomena showed that the sounds of their language (signifiers) are indeed connected in some non-arbitrary way to the concepts (signifieds). Onomatopoeia, claimed the critics, demonstrates that the sound made by a human is an imitation of the sound found elsewhere in nature, and is not interpreted through Saussure's notion of a psychological concept. Yet Saussure points out that if in fact we were directly mimicking nature, we would all do so the same, and clearly we do not. When a dog barks, an English speaker will mimic the dog with the English "woof-woof," but the French will hear the same dog and mimic it with "*ouaoua*." Similarly, a German will hear the rooster and mimic it with "*kik-a-ri-ki*," but the English, hearing the same rooster, will mimic it with "cocka-doodle-do."

The second objection to which Saussure responded was that of the exclamation. Those critics who wished to adhere to their common sense notion of language argued that an exclamation is not processed through a psychological concept, but is instead a pure production of nature due to one being frightened, angry or injured. But exclamations are not called forth by nature; so when the French speaker exclaims "*aïe!*" the German speaker would exclaim "*au!*"[36] and the English speaker would exclaim "ouch!" These exclamations had to be socially learned by the speaker from his language group—they were not put in place by nature.

At this point, it is worth pointing out that the "concreteness" of the linguistic sign, according to Saussure, lies in its being psychologically real and mentally accessible by all speakers of a language. The concreteness of the sign is not due to its materiality. Further, because it is accessible to all speakers of a language, the sign is part of a language system, not a singular atom. Thus it is the connections within the language system, not the language "atoms" that merit study. For Saussure, "it is clear that only the connexions institutionalized in the language appear to us as relevant."[37] This shift of emphasis from the linguistic atoms to the linguistic connections is a shift that applies to all signs of a language regardless of whether they have a concrete meaning, such as the French word "*arbre*" and its English equivalent "tree," or an abstract meaning, such as the signs "beauty," "love" "contract" or "property."

On these linguistic points alone—the social construction of a linguistic sign and its arbitrary relation to concrete things—what observations may we make for the practice of law? We all come to learn rather early in the study of U.S. law that "property" is a bundle of rights, not a concrete thing, and that a "contract" in private law is a relationship between persons, not a piece of paper, and a "constitution" in public law is the relationship between the state and its citizens, not a piece of paper. But there is more to be learned from language on that front. The socially determined meaning of signs means that it must be made by agreement. When

---

[36] At his time and position in culture, Saussure refrained from using the types of profane exclamations that one might even more often use, and that are even better at illustrating his point of "social learning."

[37] Saussure, *supra* note 30 at 67.

it comes to common daily life, the agreement needs only to be approximate and functional—to call the tree "green" is to distinguish it from "brown," but there are many shades to defining "green" that need not come into play in that context. To say the child is "big" is acceptable in reference to her since we last saw her a year ago, or perhaps also to her peers, but she is not big relative to adult humans or elephants. The law may attempt to fix one meaning to signifiers by defining them but those signifiers' definitions are subject to further socially agreed interpretations over which the law, as a "profession of words," does not have the complete control that one might expect from a common sense understanding of language.

A further observation is the danger in translating an abstract legal term from one culture to an abstract legal term from another culture—"contract" to "*Vertrag*," for example. When it comes to U.S. contract formation, we say there must be the elements of offer, acceptance, consideration, capacity and legality. If I were to expect something like "consideration" in a German *Vertrag*, just because I translated "contract" to "*Vertrag*," I would be inviting tremendous confusion that could not be saved by the sole corrective of functionalism from Zweigert and Kötz (see Chapter 2). Likewise when I, as a lawyer from the United States, speak of "remedies" in contract, and I think of money to replace the contract's performance, I will not at all be talking about the German lawyer's first thought of enforcing contract performance.

Saussure's second general principle is equally instructive for us, especially in understanding that communication is not a preconceived message sent by a sender to a receiver like an email or text message. This principle simply reminds us that in spoken language we speak one sound after the other in order to distinguish sounds and make some sense and meaning. The term for this linguistic phenomenon is "linearity." Spoken language is not written language.[38] Saussure focuses on the sign as a sequence of sounds rather than as a group of written letters. Language is not a mere collection of words expressing the meanings of things existing in the world. Even though meaning and word are closely connected and cannot be considered separately from each other, it would be inaccurate and misleading to think of a word's meaning as being expressed by a sequence of written letters. According to Saussure, language consists of sounds in the first place, not of written letters. The latter are of minor importance as they are used as labels or signs for the sounds themselves. Thus, the meaning of a word (sign) is not merely equivalent to its written form: rather, it stems from and is shaped by and in the mental process through which the perception of a sequence of spoken sounds (in the listener), as well as the production of the same sounds when a speaker utters a given word, is associated to a concept in both the speaker's and the listener's minds. Hence it follows that meaning is not something that may be said to exist prior to language: according to Saussure, meanings are created along with the formation of the linguistic sign itself. Furthermore, although

---

[38] More than fifty years after Saussure's work in linguistics, post-modern language theorists made strong points of how written language nevertheless influences how we speak. See Jacques Derrida, *Of Grammatology*. Corrected, ed. and trans. Gayatri Chakravorty Spivak. Baltimore, MD and London: Johns Hopkins University Press, 1997.

the linguistic sign cannot be changed by a single individual speaker of a community, time can prompt the linguistic sign to change by altering the relationship between the signifier (the sound's impression) and the signified (the abstract idea), in which case, a new linguistic sign is created out of an "old" one even if the signifier remains unchanged. Since the time of Saussure's structuralist approach, trends in linguistics have gone to post-structuralism and post-modernism, among others. But for our purposes here, it is sufficient to see that for scientific linguists, the unexamined "common sense" idea of how language works is rather naïve, and a real peril for the practicing lawyer.

In addition to those abstract and theoretical concerns, language issues make demonstrable and concrete legal distinctions as well. So far, I have been arguing against what I have called the "common sense" notion of language. As a further juxtaposition to how scientists describe how language works, one might consider how courts assume language works. In her review of civil rights litigation and "English only" policies in the United States, Janet Ainsworth has arrived at common errors regarding language that courts commonly make. Much of this litigation arises because employers require employees to use English in the workplace, despite the fact that there is no official national language in the United States.[39] The asserted impetus for the imposition of English-only policies is often a claim that monolingual English workers fear that fellow workers are saying insulting things about them when they speak in other tongues. In none of the reported cases was there any concrete evidence introduced that the non-English-speaking workers actually made derogatory comments about their English-speaking co-workers. This is how Ainsworth puts it: "Apparently a belief on the part of the monolingual speakers that those speaking in a foreign language are doing so in order to talk negatively about them is a common paranoid suspicion."[40]

In her examination of the cases, Ainsworth distilled flawed linguistic assumptions in the courts' reasoning in the challenges by employees to "English-only" rules.[41] Three of the reasons she provides might be best described as political, but one reason is clearly based upon the courts' assumed function of language. The courts' analyses

---

[39] There seem to be persistent fictions about languages other than English, most notably German, Greek and Dutch, being voted upon as official languages in the United States, but these are simply untrue stories. The closest the United States came to an official language was when the U.S. Congress voted on whether to have an official language. The proposal was defeated so there was never a need to consider which language would be the official one. According to the 2000 U.S. Census, approximately 80 percent of the population reports English as its first language. Because approximately 30 percent of the population reports that it can speak Spanish, the federal government produces its texts in English and Spanish.

[40] Janet Ainsworth, "Linguistic Ideology in the Workplace: The Legal Treatment in American Courts of Employers' 'English-only' Policies," in Maurizio Gotti and Christopher Williams (eds.), *Legal Discourse across Languages and Cultures*. Frankfurt am Main: Peter Lang, 2010 189 (citations omitted). This sort of fear is not limited to the United States. I have been personally told by a teacher of the Irish language in Belfast that she was surprised to have a local Anglophone taxi driver in her class. When asked why he was interested to learn Irish, he replied that he was "afraid they were talking about him" when passengers spoke Irish in his taxi.

[41] Ainsworth, *supra* note 40 at 182.

presumed that "languages are transparent media of referential communications, such that there is nothing that cannot be as easily and effectively said in English as in the workers' native languages."[42] That presumption has many serious implications, but especially if one treats comparative law as translation, as does Bernhard Grossfeld as discussed in Chapter 2, and as does James Boyd White, discussed later in this chapter.[43] "This assumption focuses on the literal referential meaning of language and assumes that every language maps seamlessly into every other language, without slippages or gaps. Linguists studying bilingualism have exposed the inadequacy of this assumption."[44] If we can say that comparing legal systems works in the same way as comparing languages, does that mean that these same courts, when confronted with foreign law, would assume that every legal system maps seamlessly onto every other legal system, without slippages or gaps? Ainsworth concludes that "[s]adly, when expert scientifically-based knowledge clashes with judicial 'common sense' ideological beliefs, ideology tends to beat out science."[45]

There are more general observations regarding law that are generated by linguistics as well. If one takes the admonition from comparative law seriously—namely, that to compare legal cultures is to conduct translation—then one should need to understand a little from the study and practice of translation. Just as one learns a second or third language in a different manner than one learns one's native language, so too one learns a foreign legal system differently than one's own legal system. "It is hard to translate textual, value and conduct systems; maybe we are in a language cage from which there is no escape."[46] On the one hand, to a student interested in becoming a practitioner of law, looking at U.S. law from a language approach might seem to be rather strange and remote from practice. On the other hand, if the student is coming to U.S. law from a language other than English, language may always be at the forefront of his or her mind, especially concerning translation issues.

One of the lessons here is that we mislead ourselves by beginning any new area of study with wanting to define terms. As we shall see in the next section of this chapter, definition in the ancient art of rhetoric was recognized as only one among several "common topics," with comparison, relationship, circumstances and testimony being the others. Yet somehow (perhaps through reductionist or atomist thinking), it has become common to treat definition as though words are the builder's materials that must be laid out, selected and known before they can be used. As we all painfully learn when studying the prepositions or idioms of another language, it is usage, not definition, that tells us what a word means, when to use it and how to use it. Rhetoric and linguistics both teach us that usage is just as important, if not more important than definition in the process of making meaning in language.

---

[42] *Ibid.* at 182–3.

[43] James Boyd White, *Justice as Translation*. Chicago, IL: University of Chicago Press, 1994.

[44] Ainsworth, *supra* note 40 at 183, citing Jeannette Altarriba, "Does 'Cariño equal 'Liking'? A Theoretical Approach to Nonequivalence between Languages," 7 *International Journal of Bilingualism* (2003) 305–22.

[45] Ainsworth, *supra* note 40 at 191.

[46] Karl Dedicius, *Vom Übersetzen. Theorie und Praxis*. Berlin: Suhrkamp, 1986.

One might profit from applying this first lesson from the language reference frame to the comparison of common law with civil law in Chapter 3. When it comes to making meaning from language, deducing from definition compared to inducing from usage yields a proportion in which definition is to civil law what usage is to common law.

One can go much further with this first lesson regarding definition. Consider, for example, the term "litigation." How shall we understand the sense and usage of the term? By definition? Perhaps due to our sense of post-Enlightenment natural science or analytic philosophy, we tend to think that we can best understand something if we can first define terms.[47] We define things in the same way that we dissect plants and animals in biology or break down elements in chemistry in order to find their "building blocks" and, with that method, seek to understand the whole by reducing it to its smallest, indivisible parts. (In Greek, "*a-tomos*" literally means that which is not divided.) Atomism may be helpful to understand things in the natural world (and may not be, if the focus is on systems), but it is without question extremely misleading when it comes to language. The Viennese philosopher Ludwig Wittgenstein opens his *Philosophical Investigations* with a critique of the atomistic understanding of language. He claims that one learns more about the meaning of a word by seeing how a word is used than one does by definition. And certainly for many of the parts of speech, such as articles and prepositions, definition is nearly useless. This observation not only says much about language in general, but also about understanding law and also about the practice of law. Does one expect that the practice of law is to define a norm in the abstract, and then see if one can match a particular set of actual facts to the norm, thereby subsuming them into the norm's definition, in the way a logician can make a covering law that entails actual facts? Even if one wishes to say that that is the model for the civil law tradition, it is certainly not for the common law tradition. In their treatise on the law of U.S. evidence, Roger C. Park and colleagues say that "The law of evidence evolved in the fashion of a language, influenced as much by the usage of lawyers and the on-the-spot rulings of judges in courtrooms as by appellate opinions."[48] The appellate opinion could "define" the meaning of a rule of evidence by using its authority to give the word or the rule an official definition, but in fact, since evidence issues are decided at trial and not on appeal, it is usage that determines their meaning.

And as a further point for law, we are reminded that even for the legal positivist, law cannot be understood as individual rules in the way that language cannot be understood as individual words. Hans Kelsen reminds us that law is a normative *system*. "Law is not, as it is sometimes said, a rule. It is a set of rules having the kind

---

[47] For a thorough discussion of the history of language in the natural sciences see Scott Montgomery, *The Scientific Voice*. New York: Guilford Publishing, 1996.

[48] Roger C. Park, David P. Leonard and Steven H. Goldberg, *Evidence Law*. St. Paul, MN: West Group, 1998, 10, making further reference to Ronald J. Allen, "The Simpson Affair, Reform of the Criminal Justice Process, and Magic Bullets," 67 *U. Colo. L. Rev.* (1996) 989, 995, in which the authors maintain that common law, like natural languages, is a grown order rather than a made order.

of unity we understand by a system."[49] In language too, Saussure and others have stressed that language cannot be understood through individual words (*paroles*), but rather in the context of the whole language (*langue*).

6.4 Rhetoric

After literature and linguistics, a third aspect of the language reference frame through which we can look at law, and in particular at U.S. law, is the ancient art of rhetoric. First we will need to have an idea of what we mean by the word "rhetoric" when we use it. Notice that I do not say that we are looking at the "definition" of the word. For although definition is a common practice in learning, rhetoricians themselves would be quick to point out that definition is only one way of inventing speech. It is difficult to break the habit of beginning a study by laying out definitions, as if they are hand tools on the work bench. Even those cognizant of language issues seem to be driven toward—and by—definition, as for example Bernhard Grossfeld and Jack Hillers, when they write "We should first define our terms" in an article that extols the virtues of law as an art, rather than a science.[50] What authors fail to provide to support this common opening move is a foundation beneath the "should" in that sentence. Why "should" we? Is it moral? Not likely. Instead, it is a should that comes about based upon cultural expectations of how we make meaning, and definition is a way of making meaning for atomists and scientists who feel that a larger thing is explained by breaking it into its smallest indivisible units, and then, in the case of language, assuming unfounded relationships between those atoms (called "words") and the world. Usually that unfounded leap sounds something like the statement "words represent things," or "words are labels for things." But we have all sorts of words that are not nouns—articles, prepositions, verbs, adjectives and adverbs—and they cannot be associated with things in the way a label is associated with a thing. One cannot point to a "the" in the world, or to a "blue" or to a "softly," yet they are assuredly words. Thus we learn that a definition is a set of words that helps the reader to locate the context and use of a word in the language, but does not provide a thing which is being labeled. We saw earlier that linguists do not accept the label explanation of words—neither do rhetoricians. As Saussure pointed out, language works rather by association of a word or phrase with a psychological abstraction, not with a thing.

In the ancient world, rhetoricians themselves were loath to define "rhetoric." They insisted that to understand language and communication, one could not rely upon the atomist's device of definition. For the rhetorician, definition is just one of

---

[49]   Hans Kelsen, *General Theory of Law and State.* Trans. Anders Wedberg. New York: Russell and Russell, 1961 3.

[50]   Jack A. Hiller and Bernhard Grossfeld, "Comparative Legal Semiotics and the Divided Brain: Are We Producing Half-Brained Lawyers?" 50 *Am J. Comp. L.* (2002) 175, 190.

the common topics by which humans invent (Latin, *invention*;[51] Greek, εὔρεσις) discourse, that is to say, a theme that is often used by a community of speakers at a place and time, but which has not demonstrated any rational extra power beyond common usage. So if one does not quickly and easily employ definition, how does one know the meaning of a word? The answer is, in fact, by usage in a language community, just as the linguists tell us. Even when law creates definitions in a contract or legislation, there is room for interpretation, and in fact, it is precisely because of the variability of interpretation that we often need lawyers and litigation rather than a computer and the "theorems of Euclid" (recall Holmes' discussion in Chapter 1) in order to arrive at a legal result. Definitions attempt to stabilize the word's semantic field, a field that is unstable by virtue of the evolving and changing of meanings and interpretations that are determined by usage.

It would be faithful to the art and practice of ancient rhetoric to say we can better know what something "is" by observing it, rather than by defining it. But critics like Plato said that denial of definition was an attempt by rhetoricians to hide the true nature of their art, because its true nature was not honorable. It was, according to Plato, an attempt to make the weaker appear to be a stronger argument and a formal practice of teaching and thinking that lacked any moral content. This is a charge that is made to this very day against lawyers, especially in the U.S., where, for example, a contract is said definitively not to be a moral obligation.

In addition to lessons in the making of meaning, rhetoric teaches us the importance of the distinctions between definition and usage, and with some reflection, we can use those distinctions to better understand the practice of common law. But we still want a definition for this art of rhetoric because we today are so thoroughly accustomed to establishing meaning through definition. To satisfy this craving, we might take Aristotle's definition of rhetoric—"persuasion using any means available"—as a comfortable starting point. Definition can be useful, even if it is not the best way to understand meaning. We should be able to discard the convenience of definition later, after gaining insight into the making of meaning. Wittgenstein treats definition as a heuristic device that can be discarded after one has understood language, just as one discards a ladder after reaching a height.[52] One could also employ the notion that definition is a personal choice to limit the scope of an investigation, as when one writes: "My definition of legal gesture purposefully excludes from the scope of this paper the many ordinary gestures used by lawyers

---

[51] See, for example, the treatise by Marcus Tullius Cicero (106–43 BCE), *De inventione* (*Concerning Inventio*). More of the Ciceronian canons of rhetoric will be discussed later.

[52] "*Meine Sätze erläutern dadurch, daß sie der, welcher mich versteht, am Ende als unsinnig erkennt, wenn er durch sie – auf ihnen – über sie hinausgestiegen ist.*" (My propositions serve as elucidations in the following way: anyone who understands me eventually recognizes them as nonsensical, when he has used them – as steps – to climb beyond them. He must, so to speak, throw away the ladder after he has climbed up it.) Ludwig Wittgenstein, *Tractatus Logico-Philosophicus*. Trans. C. K. Ogden. London: Routledge & Kegan Paul, 1922 6.54. Originally published as "Logisch-Philosophische Abhandlung", in *Annalen der Naturphilosophische*, XIV (3/4), 1921.

and other legal actors to express emotion or emphasis, but which lack an explicitly legal import."[53]

The philosopher and philologist Friedrich Nietzsche, himself quite familiar with the ancient discipline of rhetoric, wrote that nothing that has a history can be defined. If something has a history, then an attempt to define is a matter of selection and interpretation, and that has a large subjective element to it. The historian of law Harold Berman, after noting Nietzsche's observation, writes: "[n]evertheless, an author of nonfiction has an obligation to disclose at the outset some of his prejudices."[54]

We continue to be reminded of the difference between usage and definition. Consider the form of the most authoritative dictionary of the English language, the *Oxford English Dictionary*, or O.E.D. The O.E.D. is a book that provides meanings of words by tracing their historical usages. It is not a definition dictionary. For each entry, the authors will build meaning by giving examples of the usage of a word from its earliest records until the present, thereby inducing a meaning, like the inductive philosophy discussed in Chapter 7 on philosophical reference frames. Definition, by comparison, uses the authority of the dictionary authors, based perhaps upon the art of etymology, to define by fiat the meaning of a word. The difference between the ways of making meaning might seem subtle at first glance, but upon a moment's reflection, one might see the differences in appeal to the audience. In one, it is the precedent of usage, and in the other, the authority of the author that determines meaning.

In some ways, legal practice does recognize the danger of relying upon dictionaries and definitions as tools for understanding. During a meeting of the Association of American Law Schools in 2001, Professor Peter Tiersma of Loyola Law School in California reported on a research project "Language and the Criminal Law," in which some studies with instructions to juries by judges were conducted in the United States. Tiersma cites cases where jurors were caught looking up words in dictionaries to improve their understanding of the law. They looked up "assault," "culpable," "inference," "malice," "murder-premeditate," "preponderance," "rape," "wanton" and "willful."[55] "Technically a jury is not allowed to consult outside sources," Professor Tiersma reports.[56] He mentioned reports of a U.S. federal court setting aside the death penalty of a man who had spent twenty years on death row, in part because of evidence that his jury had looked up the words "mitigate," "extenuate" and "vindication."[57] Of great concern here is the concept that looking up words in dictionaries will improve a person's understanding of the law and so provide greater justice. Whereas the study concluded that legal terms of art confuse

---

[53] Bernard J. Hibbitts, "Making Motions: The Embodiment of Law in Gesture," 6 *J. Contemp. Legal Issues* (1995) 51, 53–4.

[54] Berman, *supra* note 24 at 1.

[55] Peter Tiersma, "Dictionaries and Death: Do Capital Jurors Understand Mitigation?" 1 *Utah L. Rev.* (1995) 20.

[56] Peter Tiersma, "Asking Jurors to do the Impossible," 5 *Tenn J. L & P* 2 (2014) 116.

[57] "Learned Language of Judges Confuses Juries, Meeting Told," *Irish Times*, 17 February 2001.

jurors (hence the scramble for the dictionaries), the study also failed to appreciate that changing legal terms of art into "plain language" removed the legal precision that might not only give them meaning for lawyers, but which might also be calculated to have impartial implications, rather than a bias in favor of the prosecution or the defendant. Furthermore, the study did not mention that the jury instructions may be and often are offered by the lawyers for the parties, or are themselves legislated or regulated as standard jury instructions. So in the name of impartiality and treating all defendants the same with similar charges to the jury, we seem to have arrived at fair and impartial instructions that the jury nevertheless does not understand. And the problem goes still further. What is the cultural understanding of the use and meaning of dictionaries and their entries? After all, judges use them as well.[58]

Rather than a mechanical reliance upon the definition of "rhetoric," look at how rhetorician James Boyd White begins a paragraph: "But I turn first to the meaning of 'rhetoric.'"[59] If a reader's first reaction to this comparison is to say, "I see no difference; definition and meaning are the same," then the reader is exhibiting that he too is a linguistic atomist who has come to understand language as words representing things and therefore believing words have meaning when defined by a description of those things.[60] White writes of the lawyer in general, but might mean only the common law lawyer when he claims that the narrative language practices of the lawyer are "not merely an art of estimating probabilities [as per Plato's role for rhetoric] or an art of persuasion [as per Aristotle], but an art of constituting culture and community."[61] This returns us to placing the common law into the notion of law as culture, which I discuss in the preface to this book. As White says, one should "want to start by thinking of law not as an objective reality in an imagined social world, not as a part of a constructed cosmology, but from the point of view of those who actually engage in its processes, as something we do and something we teach. This is a way of looking at law as an activity, and in particular, as a rhetorical activity."[62] One last point on the weakness of definition needs to be made here. Just as Saussure noted that for linguistics, a word gets its meaning in the context of the entire language, not in its relation to the material world, considerable research has demonstrated that meaning is developed most often in words clustered together, not individually.

---

[58] See, for example, William Safire, "On Language: Scalia v. Merriam Webster," *The New York Times*, 24 November 1994. Safire discusses Justice Scalia's use of a number of dictionaries to support his view of the proper definition of the word "modify."

[59] James Boyd White, "Law as Rhetoric, Rhetoric as Law: The Arts of Cultural and Communal Life," 52 *U. Chi. L. Rev.* (1985) 684, 687. Indeed, in the *Gorgias* dialogue of Plato, when Gorgias is challenged to define "rhetoric," he remains faithful to the sense of meaning in rhetoric and responds that he cannot, and his detractors claim that therefore he is hiding something.

[60] See C. K. Ogden and I. A. Richards, *The Meaning of Meaning*. London: Routledge & Kegan Paul, 1923.

[61] White, *supra* note 43 at 692.

[62] *Ibid.* at 688.

If all of this discussion of definition and rhetoric is still looking a bit puzzling to a student of law, returning to Aristotle's work can help. Although he was generally not a friend of the practice of rhetoric, especially not rhetoric as practiced by the sophists, Aristotle does provide us with a single text called *Rhetoric*, which for the twenty-first century reader looks remarkably familiar in its form and style. In *Rhetoric*, Aristotle describes the practice of rhetoric as the art or capacity of considering the available means of persuasion in any given case. Aristotle says that rhetoric applies to assertions that could be "otherwise." In so doing, he is adding a category beyond the facts that are established by logic or dialectic, and beyond opinion. He is establishing the idea that if dialectic or logic establishes facts inconclusively, and which are therefore still open to dispute, then rhetoric can be applied to influence or effect a decision. Building upon Aristotle's short description of rhetoric, Trevor Melia developed a helpful shorthand to distinguish Aritstotle's use of the word from multiple other uses of the word "rhetoric." Melia writes that "while the term *rhetoric* almost invariably refers to 'persuasion,' it usually fails to disambiguate three different orders of persuasion, namely rhetoric as the act of persuading, rhetoric as the analysis of such acts and rhetoric as world view."[63] We might simplify further by giving each of these three uses a different number—R1, R2 and R3, respectively.

Even Aristotle's definition—limited to the first sense of rhetoric—tells us several very concrete things (while it also placates our cultivated desire to define). First, Aristotle's definition tells us that the practice of rhetoric is an art. This characterization was in fact carried forward throughout the middle ages when the universities of Europe taught, as their basic course of study, the trivium—rhetoric, dialectic (more recently called "logic") and grammar. If one goes to the National University of Ireland Maynooth today, one still finds the physical reminders of this past—a Rhetoric House next to the Logic House (although the Grammar House seems to have been physically lost to time). Notice that these three areas are all language-based practices and that nothing about science or natural science is mentioned. The practices that support the natural sciences—arithmetic, geometry, harmonics and astronomy—were a quadrivium studied only after the trivium. The quadrium and trivium together comprised the seven liberal arts. The art of rhetoric was also then carried forward even into the so-called "liberal arts colleges" and universities of the United States, where rhetoric remained recognized as a course of study. So how does this matter for the practice of law? First of all, we know from history that "Legal dialectic, which was a product of humanism, took two typical forms: the manual on how to argue in legal practice, subdivided into those which focused on the topics, and those which covered the whole of dialectic; and textbooks reorganizing the law on the basis of dialectical principles."[64] The first of these is an example of the first sense of "rhetoric," and is to be distinguished from the second one, which uses "rhetoric" in the second sense. In trying to assess their impact, it must be admitted that none of these books went through many editions.

---

[63] Trevor Melia, "Essay Review," 83 *Isis* (1992) 100.
[64] *Ibid.* at 278.

Scholars suggest that is perhaps because of the relatively small target audience.[65] Nonetheless, there is a certain resilient appeal and persistence in a set of practices carried forward in law through rhetoric. For example, it is still recognized today that "Humanist legal educators expect that their pupils will have studied classical rhetoric. They recognize the overlap between rhetorical and legal studies in the field of invention, especially the status-theory and in Cicero's *Topica*."[66]

In ancient Greece, the whole practice of rhetoric was necessary and popular mostly because it was the basis of what we would today call legal practice. There were no professional lawyers then; any citizen who wanted to take a legal action, or who was required to defend himself, had to present his own arguments before a jury made up of his fellow citizens. To do so, those who could afford it would hire logographers to write persuasive arguments for them. By today's understanding, the arguments would appear to have been much more reliant upon facts than law, but that should not be surprising given that legal procedure was a very small set of affairs. This reliance upon facts is still a distinguishing feature of the common law today. If we jump forward to what we know of the history of English legal education, the training of a new lawyer was accomplished in the Inns of Court, very much in the way that training in the craft guilds of England occurred—a master, already skilled in a set of practices, taught that set of practices to an apprentice on the job, or in preparation for soon being on the job. The sense of legal education in the United States until the middle of the twentieth century continued this sense of legal training as practical training, and many states allowed apprenticeships (often called "preceptorships") to be the method whereby the skills of legal practice were handed down from one generation to the next. One can see quite a difference between that idea of legal education and legal education in the civil law tradition, which has largely taken place in the university, treated as a discipline like other university disciplines. As a result, today a civil law student may not hesitate to say that law is a science, whereas his common law counterpart will not have a ready answer when asked to characterize the study or practice of law—is it an art or is it a science?

We should return for a moment to the second and third things to be learned from Aristotle's definition of rhetoric as "persuasion by any means available." Rooted in the adversary system of legal practice, the primary role of the lawyer is to advocate by arguing a case on behalf of a client. The advocate's role is constrained by the simultaneous role of being officer of the court. This is a much different picture of the practice of law from a civil inquisitorial system in which a lawyer is first an officer of the court, and in which a judge has the power to question witnesses, seek evidence and generally direct the investigation of the case. Unsurprisingly, the training and education of the common law lawyer was focused upon the practical skills of advocacy, while the civil law placed legal education and training among other

---

[65] *Ibid.*

[66] Peter Mack, *A History of Renaissance Rhetoric 1380–1620.* Oxford: Oxford University Press, 2011 278. The work *Topica* is thought to have been written by Marcus Tullius Cicero in 44 B.C.E.

social sciences at the university. It is my contention therefore that to understand the common law lawyer today, one needs to recognize even what the common law lawyer himself may not be able to articulate about the history and current structure of his education and training—he is first an advocate, trained and educated through the ancient art of rhetoric.

I have purposely placed the aspects of rhetoric after those of literature and linguistics because for lawyers unfamiliar with the discipline and art of rhetoric, it might look something like philosophy. One must distinguish philosophy from rhetoric. The basic position of Platonic philosophy from Socrates' *Apology* is to know truth and distinguish it from opinion through open rational dialectic. The basic position of pre-Platonic rhetoric is perhaps best known from the alternative formulations of Gorgias in his work *On Nature*, in which he writes that there is no truth, or if there is truth, we cannot know it, or even if we can know it we cannot communicate it.

On the one hand, one might notice that Gorgias' position on the nature of knowledge may not line up well with the natural sciences. So it was that by the time of the Enlightenment, rhetoric, which had long been associated with the Christian church in European universities, was removed from the European curriculum. Nevertheless, Gorgias' position is echoed in the form of pleading alternative legal defenses in the United States today. United States Federal Rule of Civil Procedure 8(d)(2) states that "[a] party may set out 2 or more statements of a claim or defense alternatively or hypothetically, either in a single count of defense or in separate ones. If a party makes alternative statements, the pleading is sufficient if any one of them is sufficient."[67] Alternative claims or defenses permit a party in a court action to argue multiple possibilities that may be mutually exclusive, and even contradictory, by making use of a concept related to literature—the legal fiction. Thus a party may alternatively and simultaneously claim as defenses in a motor vehicle accident that: 1) there was no accident, or 2) there was an accident but he was not driving, or 3) there was an accident and he was driving, but it was dark at night, or 4) there was an accident, he was driving, but that he could not see because the sun shone in his eyes. On the other hand, perhaps Gorgias was correct about the nature of human knowledge, thereby explaining how it is that despite our great advances in science, according to the dictates of the progressive reference frame for history, we still get so much wrong.

Even within the formal study and practice of law, one comes across the law in Aristotle's division of the modes of persuasion—persuasion concerning events in the past, present and future—forensic, epideictic and deliberative rhetoric, respectively—one finds the explicit role for rhetoric in law. Finding out what happened is the crucial question in all cases. If the parties agree on the facts, the judge can apply the law and give a judgment. If the parties disagree on the facts, however, the fact-finding method developed by the legal system must be used. Another example of rhetoric's direct influence on law is in the practice of maintaining commonplace books. Long a part of the discipline of rhetoric, students introduced the

---

[67] U.S. Federal Rule of Civil Procedure 8(d)(2).

commonplace book to the practice of law when the number of cases in the Year Books began to grow. Recall from the historic reference frame that the Year Books presented the cases as transcripts of what was said at trial, arranged in chronological order. But as was noted in that same chapter, humans tend to make meaning from history—*kairos*—not just list facts over time. So Abridgements to the Year Books were created, organizing the Year Books by topic, not just chronologically. The topics that were selected as organizing ideas were the commonplaces of the time. The Abridgements compiled and condensed the cases reported in the Year Books, arranging them by subject matter in an apparent attempt to ease their study, and many of them were produced by students as "commonplace books" for practice in abstracting cases and in analysis.[68] The legal historian Frederick G. Kempin reports that "[c]ommonplace books were large folios in which a student would write extracts of cases under various subject matter headings as practice in classification and analysis."[69]

At this point in this presentation of rhetoric, a fundamental point must be made: rhetoric is a set of practices that do not have an essence. That being said, one can see kindred resemblances between the nature of rhetoric and the nature of the common law. These resemblances helps us to understand the spirit and soul of the common law. All practitioners and theorists of rhetoric, from Cicero to Fabri[70] to Kenneth Burke echo Aristotle's point that the goal of rhetoric is persuasion, and the goal of persuasion is to affect judgments. Aristotle also says that the substance of rhetorical persuasion are the enthymemes (from the Greek ἐνθύμημα).[71] One can understand enthymemes as forms of argument that keep at least one of the premises or conclusion unstated, allowing the audience to make an inference based on its own thoughts, prejudices and so on. This brings us back to commonplaces. Rhetoricians have a feel for what an audience is likely to infer based upon that particular audience's commonplaces. Consequently, we can see that both common law's Year Books and ancient rhetoric made use of commonplaces. The Year Books did so through the organizing concept of topics, and rhetoric did and does so through allowing audiences to use commonplaces to complete enthymematic arguments.

In an adversarial system, the practice of persuasion is conscious and open, and no one needs to suggest that "the evidence will speak for itself" in order to persuade a judge or jury to believe something.[72] Historically, even the civil law student received

---

[68] Frederick G. Kempin, *Legal History: Law and Social Change*. Reprint. London: Forgotten Books, 2013 41.

[69] *Ibid.* at 100.

[70] Pierre Fabri defines "rhetoric" as "[t]he political science concerned with deliberately speaking and writing well according to the teaching of the art to persuade or dissuade in its subject-matter and to organize it into parts and to apply good works to each part, to keep them in the memory and to deliver them well." *Le grant et vray art de pleine rhétorique* (Rouen, 1521), repr. Geneva, 1972, sig. A4, as translated and presented by Mack, *supra* note 66 at 285–6.

[71] Aristotle, *Rhetoric*, II. Trans. W. Rhys Roberts. Oxford: Bollingen Series, 1984 22–6.

[72] See, for example, Eric Oliver, *Facts Can't Speak For Themselves.* Boulder, CO: National Institute for Trial Advocacy, 2005.

training of some sort in logic and rhetoric.[73] Yet here we must be careful to point out the indirect way in which it may be said that rhetoric influenced the study of law. This does not seem, on the whole, to have been a particularly influential part of legal training on the continent.[74]

The Romans borrowed and continued many practices of the Greeks including those of rhetoric. Cicero provides us with the final point to be made from ancient rhetoric in this brief discussion of the foundations for the practice of law found in the practices of rhetoric. While rhetoric does have a large theoretical component that even provides for the alternative worldview offered by Gorgias, as mentioned above, it often survives the disfavor of churches, philosophers and scientists due to its simpler "handbook" tradition. Cicero provides the five "canons" of rhetoric that constitute the handbook by which anyone can make and deliver a speech. Those canons, drawn from the Greeks, were *inventio* (in Greek, εὕρεσις; in English, invention), *dispositio* (in Greek, τάξις; in English, arrangement), *memoria* (in Greek, μνήμη; in English, memory) *pronunciatio* (in Greek, ὑπόκρισις; in English, delivery) and *elocutio* (in Greek, λέξις, ἑρμηνεία or φράσις; in English, style).

One can easily imagine how such a handbook for oral presentation would be useful to a law student or lawyer whose practice is to advocate the position of a client before the court. These skills were eventually extended to written communication as well, and in fact today, a university student in an English-speaking education system is often trained in writing through "grammar and rhetoric," with grammar being the scientific rules, and rhetoric being the art through which one persuades a reader. From this pair, one might find it helpful to think of civil law's tendencies toward grammar and common law's tendencies toward rhetoric.

It is not the task of this short presentation to review all of the canons, but it is worth taking a few extra lines on the concept of style, which, without saying more, might be mistaken for just adding flowery language to prose. The concept of style, which a rhetorician would say means the choice of words, provides a connection between literature and rhetoric. Aristotle reminds us that it is not enough to know what to say, because in addition, the way in which a thing is said affects its intelligibility. Metaphor, says Aristotle, "gives style clearness, charm, and distinction as nothing else can."[75] In order to get the soul and spirit of the Napoleonic campaign of which he writes, the great French novelist Stendhal actually made a regular habit of reading the *Code Civil* when writing his novel, *La Chartreuse de Parme*: "*En composant la Chartreuse, pour prendre le ton, je lisais chaque matin deux ou trois pages du code civil, afin d'être toujours naturel; je ne veux pas, par des moyens factices, fasciner l'âme du lecteur.*"[76] And while one often thinks of literary study as the study of *belles lettres*, when literature or rhetoric concern themselves with aesthetics, there is something for lawyers to learn.

[73] Mack, *supra* note 66 at 278.
[74] *Ibid*. at 281.
[75] Aristotle, *supra* note 69, III. 2, 1405a8-9.
[76] "In writing the *Chartreuse*, to acquire the tone, every morning I read two or three pages of the civil code, so it would be natural; I do not wish, through artificial means, to fascinate the mind of the reader." Stendhal, from a letter to Honoré de Balzac, 30 October 1840.

Legal language is not only prose information. Legal language has its own style, and that style is not necessarily dry prose. The philosopher Martin Heidegger goes so far as to insist that pure prose is never prosaic and is as rare as poetry,[77] leaving one to recognize that most language is somewhere in between, and figurative in some way.

A further example of the importance of style is given to us by Judge Sir Konrad Schiemann of the European Court of Justice. Throughout a short article in which he was comparing the writing of judgments in England to writing judgments within the European Court of Justice, Schiemann used *style* as a comparative criterion in his explorations and explanations. In the end, Schiemann uses his comparison of style as a window into the insights of social purpose *relative to the stated purpose of the court*.[78] Style, as can be seen, is not after-the-fact adornment. It contributes to the constitution of the text.

Once the student of rhetoric has mastered the entire catalogue of possibilities in each of the five canons, he or she must then be able to bring those tools to mind for effective speech. Aristotle once again simplifies the types of speech to be made into three categories that are based upon time: the forensic (what happened in the past), epideictic (what should be done in the present), and deliberative (how shall we proceed in the future) speeches. One can easily see how these divisions of speech types lend themselves to the practice of law. Was there a contract? Did the blue car strike the red car or was it the other way around? Did the defendant form intent when she committed the act? These are all questions of the past and are covered by forensic rhetoric. How much should the liable party pay to the injured to bring the injured back to health? How long should the prison sentence be? These are questions that are covered by deliberative rhetoric. Through the formal study of rhetoric, one could well prepare to practice the common law.

What about actual exposure to rhetoric for students of law in England? Did they study formal rhetoric? If so, did they rely on the vernacular versions of the texts, or did they study rhetoric in ancient languages? Certainly the books were available, in English, and popular enough for reprinting and new editions. Some were treatises on the art of rhetoric (in the R2 sense), such as William Fulwood's letter collection *Enemie of Idlenesse* (1568). Many others were handbooks of rhetoric that instructed the reader in a set of practice skills, in the R1 sense. Of this latter type, there were seventy-two editions of twenty-two titles of books on rhetoric in the English language between the years 1550 and 1620, including seven editions of the dialectic *Rule of Reason* (1551) by Thomas Wilson (1525–81), eight of his *Art of Rhetoric* (1553), and six of Angel Day's letter-writing manual *The English Secretorie* (1586).[79]

---

[77] *"Reine Prosa ist nie 'prosaisch.' Sie ist so dichterisch und darum so selten wie die Poesie."* (Pure prose is never "prosaic." It is as literary and therefore as rare as poetry.) Martin Heidegger, *Gesamtausgabe.* Vol. XII. Frankfurt am Main: Vittorio Klostermann, 1985 28, trans. this author.

[78] Sir Konrad Schiemann, "From Common Law Judge to European Judge," 4 *Zeitschrift für Europäisches Privatrecht* (ZEuP) (2005) 741–9, 747.

[79] Mack, *supra* note 66 at 284 (citing W. S. Howell, *Logic and Rhetoric in England 1500–1700*. Princeton, NJ: Princeton University Press, 1956 and P. Mack *Elizabethan Rhetoric*. Cambridge: Cambridge University Press, 2002 76).

In addition to rhetoric in the vernacular in England, there were still the originals in Greek and Latin.[80]

The influence of rhetoric on the common law is not limited to the R1 and R2 senses discussed above. The ancient art of rhetoric also provided an entire worldview on the nature of knowledge and our relationship to it. For the Greeks, there were at least three different paths one could follow in acquiring knowledge—the practical (*techne*), the theoretical or algorithmic (*episteme*) and the experiential (*emperia*).[81] This last one is, in fact, our earliest social and intellectual knowledge, the knowledge we acquire as we first begin to move and act in our social universe and learn to speak and understand. It is the knowledge by which language and social relations are made. Writing contrary to the position of such intellectual heavyweights as René Descartes,[82] Thomas Hobbes[83] and John Locke,[84] the U.S. lawyer and rhetorician, James Boyd White, elaborates as follows:

> The rhetorician thus begins not with the imagined individual in imagined isolation, and not with the self, isolated from all of its experience except that of cogitation, but where Wittgenstein tells us to begin, with our abilities of language, gesture[85] and meaning… This knowledge itself is not reducible to rules, nor subject to expression in rules, though many analysts wish it were, rather it is the knowledge by which we learn to manage, evade, disappoint, surprise, and please each other, as we understand the expectations that others bring to what we say. This knowledge is not provable in the scientific sense, nor is it logically rigorous. For these reasons, it is unsettling to the modern scientific and academic mind. But we cannot go beyond it, and it is a mistake to try. In this fluid world without turf or ground, we cannot walk but we can swim. And we need not be afraid to do this—to engage in the rhetorical process of life—for all of us, despite our radical uncertainties, already know how to do it. By attending to our own experience, and that of others, we can learn to do it better if we try.[86]

White goes on to tell the reader what the effects of law as rhetoric are. One of them, very importantly, is that "The law is something that lawyers themselves make

---

[80]   Mack, *supra* note 66 at 284 (citing Mack, *supra* note 76 at 76–80). Mack concludes that overall this does not seem to have been a very influential part of legal training. His conclusion is based upon the number of editions of works in rhetoric that were produced.

[81]   We can understand law as craft practice from the ancient Greek, τέχνη (*techne*). See Janet Atwill, *Rhetoric Reclaimed: Aristotle and the Liberal Arts Tradition*. Ithaca, NY: Cornell, 1998, and Kirk W. Junker, "Rhetoric Demonstrates the Foundation of Law as Techne, Not Empeiria," in K. Boudouris, ed. *Philosophy, Art and Technology*. Athens: Ionia Publications, 2011 99–114.

[82]   René Descartes, *Discours de la Methode*. Leiden: 1637 4.

[83]   Thomas Hobbes, *Leviathan*. London: 1651 Chapter 13.

[84]   John Locke, *Second Treatise of Government*. London: 1690 Book II, Chapters 1–3.

[85]   See also Hibbits, *supra* note 53.

[86]   White, *supra* note 59 at 695–6 (internal footnotes added).

all the time, whenever they act as lawyers, not something that is made by a political sovereign."[87] It is perhaps understandable why those outside the law, such as journalists and social theorists, often begin—and perhaps get no further—by talking about the law as law-making by the legislative body. Indeed, many of my own students who are not lawyers want to talk in this way. But if one considers the number of law students around the world who every year become practicing lawyers and not legislators, and the fact that when someone has a legal problem he or she goes to a lawyer, not a legislator or judge, it becomes a bit odd to then talk about the law as that which occupies that elite corner of society elected to legislate. If we wanted to bake bread, would we talk to a wheat farmer?

> From the point of view of the non-lawyer, this way of regarding law as rhetoric invites a certain kind of reading and criticism, for it invites you to test the law in part by asking whether your own story, or the story of another in whom you have an interest is properly told by these speakers in this language. The basic idea of a legal hearing [in common law jurisdictions] is that two stories will be told in opposition or competition and a choice made between them. On the rhetorical view of the law suggested here, you are entitled to have your story told in your own language (or translated into it), or the law is failing.[88]

White may be convinced, however, that rhetoric is an ancient and super discipline that can explain all other disciplines, the way logical positivists would think that mathematics can, or academics of earlier centuries might have believed philosophy, as "queen of the sciences" could do. White himself tells us that by this kind of "conjunction with the law," rhetoric can be seen differently.[89] Rhetoric is not a substitute for science when science does not work, which Aristotle suggested nearly twenty-five centuries ago when he said that the role of rhetoric was to reason through probabilities when logic fails to provide certainty.[90] One must be reminded, however, that White's formulation is from observation and engagement with common law, and its methods of adversarial advocacy. It may well lose universal claims about law when it is applied to civil law or another legal "family," to borrow the Zweigert and Kötz term. In the light of this brief discussion of rhetoric we now have a basis upon which to answer the question of whether the common law is a science for the common law lawyer.

---

[87] *Ibid.* at 696.
[88] *Ibid.* at 697.
[89] *Ibid.* at 701.
[90] Aristotle, *Rhetoric*, Book II, Chapter 25, in Jonathan Barnes, ed. *The Complete Works of Aristotle.* Princeton, NJ: Bollingen Series, 1984 LXXXI.

6.5 Philosophy of Language

It would be an incomplete look at law through the language reference frame if the chapter were to end without acknowledging the important role that philosophy plays in the structure and function of the language reference frame. When I use the term "philosophy," I am using it in the limited sense of the discipline that I outline in the next chapter. By leaving until last the philosophy of language, I seek to have it function as a bridge to the next chapter. To locate philosophy among the other aspects of looking at law through the language reference frame, one may return for a moment to the two-part phenomenon of Saussure's linguistic sign. Recall that the sign links an abstract concept, the *signifié* (in English, the "signified") and a sound pattern, the *signifiant* (in English, the "signifier"). Further, if things are not labeled by language, they must have a different relationship to language. The relationship of the thing to language is for the thing to stimulate the mental creation or maintenance of abstract concepts, a process that W. V. O. Quine called commitment to a "shared ontology."[91] We can root the philosophy of language in the abstract concept, the signified, which Saussure explains as a "two-sided psychological entity."

The brief mention of the contributions from the philosophy of language are limited to two areas in this chapter—the micro role of the signified and the macro role of language in society for law or what Saussure has called *parole* and *langue*, respectively. Each is independent of individual users and exists before and after the individual user. Yet even this limitation is sufficient to serve as a check on the totalizing tendency of the philosophy of language. The opening sentence of Reinhold Zippelius' influential work, *Introduction to German Legal Methods*, reads "Overstatement is a child of fashion."[92] Some years ago, while I was teaching a course in the philosophy of science, a student—a good student—raised the question whether all the issues of the philosophy of science were in fact issues of language. I wanted to answer the student's question by saying no, but I recognized that at the time, much of his cultural thinking was going through what was called "the linguistic turn." A danger of any such turn is to believe that all of human experience can be reduced to any one discipline. Such a belief would lead serious inquiry to have, as a goal, simply arriving at the "eureka!" moment in which one discovers the one discipline to which all else can be reduced. In that vein, when one characterizes the practice of law as a "profession of words," one might be tempted to say that law is constituted by words.

A little study in the history of ideas demonstrates that many disciplines have had precisely that moment of claiming the ability to explain everything, including philosophy as the medieval "queen of the sciences" and mathematics as August

---

[91] W. V. O. Quine, "On What There Is," reprinted in Steven Lawrence and Cynthia MacDonald, (eds.), *Contemporary Readings in the Foundations of Metaphysics*. Oxford: Basil Blackwell, 1998 32, 36. For the legal application of Quine's notion of shared ontology, see Steven D. Smith, *Law's Quandry*. Cambridge, MA: Harvard University Press, 2004.

[92] Reinhold Zippelius, *Introduction to German Legal Methods*. Trans. Kirk W. Junker and P. Matthew Roy. Durham, NC: Carolina Academic Press, 2008 xi.

Comte's (post-Enlightenment) "most axiomatic"[93] of disciplines. With this caution in mind, one should also not go to the other extreme and dismiss the impact of the philosophy of language on law as being just a fad. One needs only to consult such seminal works in the philosophy of law as H. L. A. Hart's *The Concept of Law,* which opens with an explicit connection to language. There, "he made it clear that he saw philosophy of language as playing a foundational role in his theory of law."[94] The positivist Hart was not someone to be easily taken up by the breeze of fashion's latest child.

After spending much of his academic career in England, Wittgenstein opens his book, *Philosophical Investigations,* with a critique of atomistic understanding of language.[95] He begins by reflecting on the tale from St. Augustine in which Augustine claims to remember the process of his having learned language. Wittgenstein effectively dismantles Augustine's claim that one learns language by observing a speaker say a word and point to an object. Wittgenstein points out that in order for that simple act to function as such, one would first need to know that the sound from someone's mouth is in some way directed at the listener; second, that the sound is meant to be instructive; third, that it is meant to be associated with a thing; fourth, that finger-pointing is an act of identification, and so on. Only then, after all of these acts of communication have been taught and learned, could one learn that the sound is the name of the thing, rather than a reference to its shape, weight, color, taste, smell, sound or even who owns it. Moreover, human communication may occur in other forms, such as gestures, visual signals, and even silence, all of which may be relevant in the practice of law and which may even convey, under certain conditions, a specific legal meaning.[96] "Words are labels for things" looked like a rather shaky proposition in linguistics and rhetoric; and after Wittgenstein finishes his critique, it is just as shaky a proposition in philosophy. Perhaps this convergence in conclusions ought to tell us something about interdisciplinary thinking in the law.

In reflecting upon the connections of philosophy to language, James Boyd White rejects the philosophies of Descartes, Hobbes and Locke in favor of that of Wittgenstein. For White, the philosophies of Descartes, Hobbes and Locke remain too much wedded to the idea that language represents things. Wittgenstein writes that "The limits of my language mean the limits of my world."[97] If we apply his characterization of the personal intellectual world to the broader social world, we might reflect on the fact that the Roman Empire, with all of its many jurisdictions

---

[93] August Comte, *The Positive Philosophy.* Trans. Harriet Martineau. London: 1853, reprinted Cambridge, 2009.

[94] Andrei Marmor and Scott Soames (eds.), *Philosophical Foundations of Language in the Law.* Oxford: Oxford University Press, 2011 1. See also Christopher Hutton, *Language Meaning and the Law.* Edinburgh: Edinburgh University Press, 2011.

[95] Ludwig Wittgenstein, *Philosophical Investigations.* Trans. G. E. M. Anscombe. New York: MacMillan, 1958.

[96] Bernhard Grossfeld, *Core Questions of Comparative Law.* Trans. Vivian Grosswald Curran. Durham, NC: Carolina Academic Press, 2005 113–41.

[97] Ludwig Wittgenstein, *Tractacus Logico-Philosophicus.* Trans. D. F. Pears and B. F. McGuinnes. London: Routledge & Kegan Paul, 1961 56.

emanating outward from the Mediterranean Sea, ended at Hadrian's Wall, the remains of which still stretch from the appropriately named Wallsend on the east coast of England to Bowness-on-Solway on the west coast. Beyond Hadrian's Wall, the Scots, Picts, Gaels and others remained free from Roman colonization. In one of the many ironic turns of history, the British themselves eventually were considerable colonizers, taking their language and legal system with them to each colony. At its peak, the British Empire included 104 seperate jurisdictions that we would recognize today. As colonial politics began to wane, the British Empire established the British Commonwealth in 1949 (now the fifty-three member Commonwealth of Nations), through which the influence of its legal system and language was maintained.[98]

What may one conclude from this empire-building and colonization? As the British Empire spread and then receded, it left at least two clear markers behind—the English language and the common law. Consequently, although one might assume without a second thought that the common law is the strange legal system of the English, limited to the United Kingdom and perhaps other, well-known common law countries such as the United States, Canada and Australia, the fact is that the common law legal system touches much of the world, having been extended through an empire that was so extensive that at its peak, the sun never set upon it.

When philosophy approaches the topic of law, from the Greeks to the present, it often does so more often by considering those broader social concepts such as justice, and not the workings of language. In connecting the philosophy of language to law, philosopher Peter Suber makes the point that for the day-to-day reasoning of litigating lawyers, the commonly accepted criteria of truth and certainty are not determined by the individual but by the public, and even by institutions. "Law is clearly a product of reason in this sense, that is, a product of long-term, free public dialogue. But just as clearly, law is a producer of reason, one among many cultural forms that preserves the institution of long-term, free public dialogue. In short, law is both a cause and effect of reason—at least among a free people."[99] So at the broadest level, one can connect law, philosophy and language when one considers things like the method through which one achieves justice. In reviewing the role of reason in law, and in support of his point that "global reason" continues to exist

---

[98] The Commonwealth States and their years of accession are: Antigua and Barbuda 1981, Nauru 1968, Australia 1931, New Zealand 1931, Bahamas 1973, Nigeria 1960, Bangladesh 1972, Pakistan 1947–62 and1989, Barbados 1966, Papua New Guinea 1975, Belize 1981, St. Kitts and Nevis 1983, Botswana 1966, St. Lucia 1979, Brunei 1984, St Vincent and the Grenadines 1979, Canada 1931, Seychelles 1976, Cyprus 1961, Sierra Leone 1961, Dominica 1978, Singapore 1965, The Gambia 1965, Solomon Islands 1978, Ghana 1957, Sri Lanka 1948, Grenada 1974, Swaziland 1968, Guyana 1966, Tanzania 1961, India 1947, Tonga 1970, Jamaica 1962, Trinidad and Tobago 1962, Kenya 1963, Tuvalu 1978, Kiribati 1979, Uganda 1962, Lesotho 1966, United Kingdom 1931, Malawi 1964, Vanuatu 1980, Malaysia 1957, Western Samoa 1970, Maldives 1982, Zambia 1964, Malta 1964, Zimbabwe 1980, Mauritius 1968.

[99] Peter Suber, "Legal Reasoning After Post-Modern Critiques of Reason," 3 *Legal Writing* (1997) 21–50, 47.

despite post-Enlightenment critiques, Suber finds the common thread of the role of dialogue among three influential twentieth-century philosophers. He writes:

> global reason is ultimately nothing more than the dialogue of free people over time. The left wing version of this idea today is associated with Paul Feyerabend, the right wing version with Karl Popper, and a moderately liberal version with Jürgen Habermas. But in my view, all three versions derive from John Stuart Mill's 1859 book, *On Liberty*. On this view, reason is not a faculty created by God, or a transcendental source of authority. It is the disputatious and passionate dialogue of free people. What view does reason favor? To find out don't merely introspect or meditate.[100]

The philosophy of language spans the intellectual distance from analyzing the everyday dialogue of the courtroom to explaining justice through the notion of free people in open and public disputation. The above discussion was only a brief consideration of some of the ideas of the philosophy of language, intended only to show that the philosophy of language contributes to the construction and maintenance of the language reference frame through which one understands legal culture.

6.6 Conclusions

At this point, we might ask: what are some consequences of these observations of law through the language reference frame? First, "[i]f language does not express linear time ideas, then causal ideas of time's passage, of cause and effect are missing."[101] In looking ahead to the next chapter on the philosophical reference frame, we can begin to make some connections between philosophy and language. The most recent large "movement" in U.S. legal philosophy is arguably the critical legal studies movement. According to the historian Berman, one of the critical legal studies proponents, Roberto M. Unger, connects the "shift in 'post-liberal' Western legal thought with a change in beliefs concerning language. 'Language is no longer credited with the fixity of categories and the transparent representation of the world …'"[102] writes Unger. Berman adds "The language of law is viewed not only as necessarily complex, ambiguous, and rhetorical (which it is) but also wholly contingent, contemporary, and arbitrary (which it is not). These are the harbingers not only of a 'post-liberal' age but also of a 'post-Western' age."[103] Already in 1921 Kantorowicz scolded court decisions as a "science of words," whereas it is supposed to be a "science of values." "One did not consider that language is the most dangerous enemy

---

[100] *Ibid.* at 46. Suber goes on to note that Mill's own position on the matter was based upon that of Thomas Aquinas.
[101] Grossfeld, *supra* note 3 at 205.
[102] Berman, *supra* note 24 at 40 (citing Roberto M. Unger, *Law in Modern Society*. New York: Free Press, 1976 196).
[103] Berman, *supra* note 24 at 40.

of knowledge, this treacherous servant and secret master of thought."[104] The difficulty language poses is greater to law than to natural science. Language does not simply describe; it always serves the purposes of the one using it. Thus one should see that the science of words is a science of values—the values are always and already there, established, maintained and destroyed as words.

CHECK YOUR UNDERSTANDING:

1. How might the English language lend itself to the common law?
2. How do Year Books and Reporters make common law possible?
3. Is there a civil law equivalent to Year Books and Reporters?

CHALLENGE YOUR UNDERSTANDING:

1. How would structuralism be applied to law?
2. Would structuralism be applied differently to common law and civil law?

FURTHER YOUR UNDERSTANDING:

Is structuralism different for oral speech than written speech?

Literature

Ainsworth, Janet, "Linguistic Ideology in the Workplace: the Legal Treatment in American Courts of Employers' 'English-only' Policies," in Maurizio Gotti and Christopher Williams (eds.), *Legal Discourse across Languages and Cultures*. Frankfurt am Main: Peter Lang, 2010. 189.

Baron, Jane B., "The Rhetoric of Law and Literature: A Skeptical View," 26 *Cardozo L. Rev.* (2005). 2273.

Berman, Harold J., *Law and Revolution: The Formation of the Western Legal Tradition*. London: Harvard University Press, 1983.

Grossfeld, Bernhard, *Core Questions of Comparative Law*. Durham, NC: Carolina Academic Press, 2005.

Hibbitts, Bernard J., "Making Motions: The Embodiment of Law in Gesture," 6 *J. Contemp. Legal Issues* (1995). 51.

Junker, Kirk W., "What Is Reading in the Practice of Law?" 9 *J. L. Soc'y* (2008). 111.

Kempin, Frederick G., *Legal History: Law and Social Change*. Reprint. London: Forgotten Books, 2013.

Mack, Peter, *A History of Renaissance Rhetoric 1380–1620*. Oxford: Oxford University Press, 2011.

---

[104] Hermann Kantorowicz, *Einführung in die Textkritik: systematische Darstellung der textkritischen Grundsätze für Philologen und Juristen*. Dieterich, 1921.

Sarat, Austin, Matthew Anderson and Catherine O. Frank, "Introduction: On the Origins and Prospects of the Humanistic Study of Law," in Austin Sarat, Matthew Anderson and Catherine O. Frank (eds.), *Law and the Humanities: An Introduction*. Cambridge: Cambridge University Press, 2010.

Scanlon, Eileen, Roger Hill and Kirk W. Junker (eds.), *Communicating Science: Professional Contexts*. London: Routledge, 1999.

Schiemann, Konrad, "From Common Law Judge to European Judge," 4 *Europäisches Privatrecht* (ZEuP) (2005). 741.

Suber, Peter, "Legal Reasoning After Post-Modern Critiques of Reason," 3 *Legal Writing* (1997). 21–50.

Swales, John M., "Language, Science and Scholarship," 18 *Asian Journal of English Language Teaching* (1998). 1.

White, James Boyd, *Justice as Translation*. Chicago, IL: University of Chicago Press, 1994.

White, James Boyd, "Law as Rhetoric, Rhetoric as Law: The Arts of Cultural and Communal Life," 52 *U. Chi. L. Rev.* (1985). 684.

7

THE PHILOSOPHY REFERENCE FRAME

Framing Issues

1. What is the difference between wisdom in the natural sciences and wisdom in law?
2. What is the difference between information and prudence (as in "jurisprudence")?

7.1 Philosophy, Legal Philosophy and American Legal Philosophy

As with previous chapters that looked at U.S. law through the historical, social or language reference frames, this chapter begins first by looking at the reference frame itself—in this chapter, philosophy—and noting some of the issues of concern in talking about philosophy before turning our attention to the substance of U.S. legal philosophy. From at least three different levels of abstraction, we may look through the reference frame of philosophy at law. It is like wearing trifocal eyeglasses. While all three levels are relevant and important, the more immersed we become in studying or practicing law, the less we seem to see law through the more abstract levels of philosophy, and the further we find ourselves from the heart of seeing law through the philosophical reference frame. At the most abstract, we may study law through the philosophy reference frame by staying within philosophy on its own terms, and with no explicit reference to the topics of "law" or "justice" or other obvious terms through which we makes a connection to the study and practice of law. Here we might consider basic questions of metaphysics or ethics or ontology and relate them to law, or approach law obliquely, as in the work of Marjorie Grene.[1]

Second, we could also take a less abstract look at law through the reference frame of what we might call "doctrinal" philosophy, wherein the philosopher is discussing philosophy that is related to concepts such as law or justice, but not specifically legislation, enforcement actions or conflict resolution. At this more common second level of abstraction, philosophers such as John Rawls,[2] Lon Fuller[3] or Ronald Dworkin[4] often discuss theories of justice.

The third category, and one that is most directly related to the study and practice of law, is the least abstract, but which may therefore also be the least creative. In this third category, the philosophy of law is what some call "jurisprudence." The philosophy of law in this third category might not be conducted by philosophers, but by judges, for example, like Justice Oliver Wendell Holmes, Jr. of the U.S. Supreme Court, Judge Richard Posner or Judge Frank H. Easterbrook, both of the U.S. Court of Appeals for the Seventh Circuit.[5]

But now it is time to begin with philosophy proper, and that means to begin with the most abstract of ideas—philosophy itself. For the purposes of this study of U.S. law through the philosophical reference frame, we must consider what philosophy is and what it is not. Some writers wish to make some broad claims for philosophy that span all cultures, all times and all general ways of thinking about fundamental human problems. That method of categorization is so broad as to exclude nothing, or nearly nothing and is therefore not really a category. My delineation is much narrower because the object of study here is just one aspect of Western culture—the legal—and in one place—the United States. Thus we can trace the history of the word "philosophy" and practices of φιλοσοφία to the Greek thinking of the sixth century B.C.E. and the texts that survive from the fourth century B.C.E. As such, it has its roots in Western thinking. These texts and this way of thinking spread to Rome during Hellenization and from Rome throughout its empire. Thereafter, the Christian church, with its ancient Greek and Latin texts, contributed to the expansion and preservation of this form of Western thought. For the purposes of this examination of legal culture, that will be sufficient narrative from which to look at U.S. legal culture through the philosophical reference frame.

---

[1] See, for example, Marjorie Grene, "Tacit knowing-grounds for a revolution in philosophy," 8 *Journal of the British Society for Phenomenology* 3 (1977) 164–71.

[2] See John Rawls, *A Theory of Justice*. Cambridge, MA: Harvard University Press, 1999.

[3] Fuller's most famous work is perhaps *The Morality of Law*, 1964. His natural law position in that work sparked a series of printed and oral debates with the philosophical positivist, H. L. A. Hart, most notably in the *Harvard Law Review*, volume 71.

[4] Dworkin was a student of Fuller's at Harvard. His most influential work is *Taking Rights Seriously*, in which, among other things, he carries on Fuller's critique of Hart.

[5] Judges Posner and Easterbrook are listed as the second and third most-cited authors in the field of law according to HeinOnline, a large electronic repository of academic journals. See https://help.heinonline.org/2013/11/most-cited-authors-2013-edition/ (last accessed 18 April 2015).

7.2 Making Meaning through Definition

In returning to the problem of definition that we visited in Chapter 6, we are reminded that the process of defining means to make a border within that which is infinite, calling that which is on the inside of the border the "definite" or "defined." In the process, we ought not to forget that we have left many things on the outside of the border – the things that are not part of the defined are therefore not part of the definition. Philosophy is not opinion or theory, even though one might hear the word "philosophy" used as a synonym for either one, as when a football trainer says he has a "philosophy" of defense. Moreover, philosophy is not a worldwide phenomenon – it is a Western idea. One might hear someone talk of "Eastern philosophy." There are of course great thinkers and great thoughts in the Eastern tradition, but they do not trace the history of their ideas to fourth-century Athens, for good or bad.

Those who would say that all educated or disciplined abstract thinking can be called "philosophy" can see that nearly everyone is engaged in philosophy when thinking about such things as the meaning or purpose of life, whether knowledge is possible and if so, the means by which we can achieve knowledge. We might also observe that those who denigrate philosophy are usually denigrating others' philosophy, but in doing so, employ philosophy themselves. These people often call themselves "realists" and deny that there is any practical utility to engaging in abstract thinking. For the lawyer, it would be difficult to imagine law-making or conflict resolution without abstract and even speculative thinking. How else could one establish norms for human behavior or exercise discretion in the practices of conflict resolution?

7.2.1 Making Meaning through Etymology

Etymologically, φιλοσοφία ("philosophy") means "love of wisdom." If we take the lessons from the language reference frame seriously, we must admit that not all things are translatable and the limitations of simple idioms that we often learn in a foreign language tourism course also apply when learning a foreign language for abstract and disciplinary thinking, as in law. Some philosophers have taken this lesson from language and noted that by the latter half of the twentieth century, much of philosophy itself had begun to focus upon language. If indeed philosophy is limited and enabled by language, this particular notion of Western thinking might not be available to all languages. This was the point made by Martin Heidegger when he said that there was a "special inner relationship between the German language and the language and thinking of the Greeks."[6] This statement is presumably based on the grammatical affinities between ancient Greek and contemporary German. This narrow use of the word "philosophy" results, however, in philosophy being reserved for only a rather small group of a certain type of thinker.

---

[6] Martin Heidegger, *Der Spiegel*, No. 23, 31 March 1976, 193–219, 217.

For the purposes of this study of U.S. legal philosophy, philosophy is best located somewhere between the narrow notion of limiting "philosophy" to a pedigree from the fourth century B.C.E. and the broad and seemingly limitless sense of any and all educated or structured thinking. To help us to further narrow the location of philosophy in this spectrum, and see what it does in U.S. legal thinking, it will help to look at philosophical method.

7.2.2 Philosophical Method

As we learn from that most basic of philosophical texts, Plato's *Apologia*, philosophy is practiced by asking questions. So as to order and systematize philosophy, we can categorize the branches of philosophy by the types of questions it asks. So for example, among the various branches of philosophy, the branch known as "ontology" is concerned with the question "what exists?" Ethics asks "what is the good?" Aesthetics is concerned with "what is the beautiful?" Epistemology then asks *how we know* any of the above.[7] In answering this last question, there has developed something of a geographical divide within Europe between the continental Europeans and the "island" Europeans of the United Kingdom and Ireland. Broadly stated, the island Europeans proceed epistemologically through inductive empiricism and the continental Europeans proceed through rational deduction. This divide is consistent with what one may have observed through the comparative legal family reference frame of Chapter 3, the historical reference frame of Chapter 4, the social reference frame of Chapter 5, and the language reference frame of Chapter 6. When the reader arrives at Chapter 8, he or she should not be surprised to find that it is also consistent with the fact that in disciplines other than law, such as those of the natural sciences, the penchant for experiential natural science through empiricism is also found in the islands, while rationalist natural science is found on the continent.

7.2.3 "Schools" of Philosophy in the Study and Practice of Law

If one thinks about the spirit of the common law by focusing upon actors rather than concepts, lawyers rather than upon laws, it should seem obvious to ask the question, who conducts legal philosophy? Legal philosophy might be better done by philosophers than by lawyers themselves. Compare the point made at the beginning of Chapter 5, The Social Reference Frame, concerning the sentiment by many natural scientists during the science wars that only they, and not sociologists, may speak about natural science. Is it the specialized knowledge of legal practice that enables one to philosophize about law, or is it the training and education of the philosopher that enables one to philosophize about any subject, including law? My

---

[7] An excellent English language history of philosophy is Frederick Copleston, *A History of Philosophy*. London: Doubleday, 1985. (Nine volumes available in three paperback books in the Image edition).

answer to the question is that both philosophers and lawyers may and should speak on the philosophy of law, with the condition that either must have an understanding for the other discipline, a process that amounts to how we learn a foreign language. We learn a foreign language, as was discussed in Chapter 6, through the rules of grammar and syntax. We learn our mother language through usage. The lawyer knows law as a mother language, but before speaking on philosophy, must first learn its grammar. The same is true in reverse for the philosopher who wishes to philosophize on the law. Zweigert and Kötz say the same for those who wish to compare domestic legal systems in their *Introduction to Comparative Law*.[8] That is to say, if we want to learn a foreign legal system, we must learn it through grammar and syntax, unlike learning our own legal system through usage.

In addition to the branches of basic philosophy listed above, philosophy may be applied as well. Thus one finds medical ethics and environmental ethics, or more broadly the philosophy of natural sciences and legal philosophy. Furthermore, within the area of the present focus – legal philosophy – there are different "schools" of philosophy. These are schools such as Natural Law, Legal Positivism, Legal Realism, and Critical Legal Studies. In the English language, sometimes all the schools of legal philosophy together are known by the name "jurisprudence". This brings us to an important distinction in philosophy: the differences between prudence and wisdom, or φρόνησις (*phronesis*) and σοφία (*sophia*) and between the wisdom of the natural scientist and the wisdom of the philosopher. In the introduction to his work, *The Enduring Questions: Main Problems of Philosophy*, Melvin Rader makes those distinctions clear. Rader writes that:

> If philosophy is the pursuit of wisdom as contrasted with foolishness, it *is* marked off from ordinary science. The subject matter of science is facts, and science attempts to discover verifiable laws—regularities—among these facts. These laws give a *description* of facts. It is obvious that the physicist does not talk about wicked atoms or beneficent motions and even the sociologist, in his purely scientific role tries to *describe* rather than to *evaluate* the behavior of social groups. If philosophy, on the other hand, seeks wisdom as the opposite of foolishness, it must be a kind of critical activity concerned with appraisals.[9]

During our present information age, when "facts" are unverified and easily available through media such as the internet, it becomes even more important that we are able to engage in the critical activity that can enable us to discern the difference between statements of foolishness and statements of wisdom, which, without critical evaluation, may appear to be the same. In prior ages, including that of when Rader wrote the above, cultures relied upon the editorial process and peer review to make the critical evaluations that enabled the distinction. Now we must do so for ourselves.

[8] Konrad Zweigert and Hein Kötz, *Introduction to Comparative Law*. 3rd ed. Trans. Tony Weir. Oxford: Clarendon Press, 1998; see also Chapter 2, *supra*, on Comparative Law.
[9] Melvin Rader, *The Enduring Questions: Main Problems of Philosophy*, 3rd ed. London: Holt, Rinehart and Winston, 1976 5.

7.3 What Are the Attributes of "American" Philosophy?

Quite often, philosophy in the United States is generally known by the school of thought known as "pragmatism." In the journal *History of Philosophy Quarterly*, Robert F. Almeder asserted that "a fairly concise characterization of the principles of Pragmatism will go a long way in the direction of defining what is distinctively American about American philosophy."[10] Certainly by the nineteenth century and well into the twentieth century, pragmatism had taken hold. The most famous U.S. pragmatists of the era are C.S. Peirce, William James and John Dewey. Pragmatism is not simply following that which is practical. Roscoe Pound reminds us that "Pragmatism sees validity in actions, not in that they realize the idea, but to the extent that they are effective for their purpose and in purposes to the extent that they satisfy a maximum of human demands. ... The implication is that we need not fear to act."[11] For example, according to Peirce's maxim of pragmatics, when we are asking questions concerning the nature of an object or idea, such as justice, we must consider the effects that the object of our conception has. Peirce would argue that "[t]hen, our conception of these effects is the whole of our conception of the object."[12] This is a difficult line of reasoning to follow, even for trained philosophers. Put another way, one knows what something is by observing its effects. Applied to law, that could mean that knowing what justice is would be to know the effects of justice. U.S. law impliedly adopts this reasoning when the U.S. Supreme Court decides, for example, that a statute is unconstitutional not on its face, but in the results of its application; that is, in its enforcement, implementation or effects.

7.3.1 Realism, Pragmatism and Positivism

Continuing the theme from Chapter 6, if language carries culture, how might it have influenced philosophy? It is more than coincidental that philosophers so often refer to "Anglo-American" philosophy as though it were one entity. Along with the English language, English law and English thinking in other abstract areas such as philosophy came to North America. The positivist philosophy of English legal philosopher John Austin had more impact in the United States than in England. The influence of positivism convinced many that common law judges did indeed make law and not simply declare it from a general cultural feel for right and wrong. or from Platonic forms of justice.[13] The influence can be seen in application when, for example, the State of Georgia passed a statute in 1858 that equated judicial decisions with statutory law, upon certain conditions. The statute said that decisions of the

---

[10] Robert F. Almeder, "A Definition of Pragmatism," 3 *History of Philosophy Quarterly* 1 (January 1986) 79.

[11] Roscoe Pound, *Interpretations of Legal History*. Cambridge: Cambridge University Press, 1923 11.

[12] C. S. Peirce, "How to Make Ideas Clear," in *Selected Writings: Values in a Universe of Chance*. Ed. Philip Weiner. New York: Dover, 1958 24.

[13] U.S. Supreme Court Justice Oliver Wendell Holmes implied that his colleagues sometimes forgot the nature of the common law: "The common law is not a brooding omnipresence

Supreme Court of Georgia are law if three judges have concurred, and "shall not be reversed, overruled or changed; but the same are hereby declared to be, and shall be considered, regarded and observed by all the courts of this state, where they have not been changed by the legislative enactment, as fully, and to have the same effect, as if the same had been enacted in terms by the General Assembly."[14]

In the nineteenth and twentieth centuries, the pragmatic philosophy of Peirce and William James had a very direct access to legal practice. Both men were colleagues of one of the most influential figures in U.S. legal history, Oliver Wendell Holmes, Jr. Holmes himself had the experience of being a twice-wounded soldier, a justice of both the Massachusetts State Supreme Court and U.S. Supreme Court, and a frequent visitor to London. Holmes read broadly, not just from the law. He associated with a group of intellectuals known as "the Metaphysical Club" that included Peirce, James and Dewey.[15] Thus his scope of experience included law in the United States from both state and federal reference frames, common law from both sides of the Atlantic and the resolution of conflict from guns to the courtroom. Influenced by legal philosopher John Austin,[16] who was himself friends with philosopher Jeremy Bentham, Holmes' experience and reading convinced him of the separation of law from morals, a separation that lays the foundation for legal positivism. In an address to the Boston University School of Law in 1897, Holmes stated:

> I wish, if I can, to lay down some first principles for the study of this body of dogma or systematized prediction which we call the law, for men who want to use it as the instrument of their business to enable them to prophesy in their turn, and, as bearing upon the study, I wish to point out an ideal which as yet our law has not attained. The first thing for a business-like understanding of the matter is to understand its limits, and therefore I think it desirable at once to point out and dispel a confusion between morality and law. ... If you want to know the law and nothing else, you must look at it as a bad man, who cares only for the material consequences which such knowledge enables him to predict, not as a good one, who finds his reasons for conduct, whether inside the law or outside of it, in the vaguer sanctions of conscience.[17]

in the sky, but the articulate voice of some sovereign or quasi sovereign that can be identified." *Southern Pacific Company v. Jensen*, 244 U.S. 205, 222 (1917) (Holmes, J., dissenting; opinion published 21 May 1917).

[14] Frederick G. Kempin, *Historical Introduction to Anglo-American Law*. St. Paul, MN: West, 1990 106.

[15] For an excellent account of the group, see Louis Menand, *The Metaphysical Club: A Story of Ideas in America*. New York: Farrar, Strauss and Giroux, 2002.

[16] Holmes departed, however, from Austin's point of view, which was steeped in legal positivism, and became a proponent of legal realism.

[17] Oliver Wendell Holmes Jr., "The Path of Law," 10 *Harv L. Rev.* 457 (1897). Recall from the language reference frame that the process of defining is, as Holmes sets out here, to set limits.

However, even within the U.S. Supreme Court, just as within the highest levels of physical science at the time, there was disagreement.[18] In the same year that Holmes resigned from the court at age 90, Benjamin Cardozo was appointed to the court to fill Holmes' seat. Just as Holmes had served as a Massachusetts State Supreme Court justice prior to joining the U.S. Supreme Court, Cardozo had served on the New York Court of Appeals (New York's highest appellate court and court of last resort in that state) prior to joining the U.S. Supreme Court. Nevertheless, Cardozo countered Holmes' divorce of morality from law when he wrote that: "[e]thical consideration can no more be excluded from the administration of justice which is the end and purpose of all civil laws than one can exclude the vital air from his room and live."[19]

Using the example of Holmes alone, one can see the influence that legal philosophy may have on the law. Holmes lived his philosophy in deciding cases, in publishing his philosophy, and through public speaking engagements. Legal philosophy has paths by which it directly matters in the practices of law. One can connect Holmes' separation of law from morals to the historical reference frame. If one's theory of history is circular, spiral or cataclysmic, one could see that the relationship of law to morality is one that changes from time to time and place to place and in so doing, may serve the changing needs of the society at that time and place.

From academic philosophy, Holmes developed the legal philosophy called "legal realism."[20] Holmes' realism is perhaps best known through his statement that the life of the [common] law has not been logic, but rather experience. This, in his view, has been more significant than the syllogism in determining the rules by which men should live. Holmes' statement provides a good example of applying empiricism to the law—one proceeds to make norms and apply them inductively through experience, not deductively through rational deduction from more general norms. Holmes was not alone. Cardozo also famously said that law is "a principle of rule of conduct so established as to justify a prediction with reasonable certainty that it will be enforced by the courts if its authority is challenged."[21] By contrast, "[i]n principle the French judgment is structured as a syllogism where the result follows logically from the statement of the facts and the statement of the law, leaving no room for doubt as to the contents of the two statements or as to the result."[22]

---

[18] Here I am making reference to the Bohr-Einstein debates on quantum mechanics. See Niels Bohr, "Discussions with Einstein on Epistemological Problems in Atomic Physics," in *The Value of Knowledge: A Miniature Library of Philosophy*. Cambridge: Cambridge University Press, 1949.

[19] Benjamin Nathan Cardozo, *The Nature of the Judicial Process*. New Haven, CT: Yale University Press, 1921.

[20] See Menand, *supra* note 15.

[21] Benjamin Nathan Cardozo, *The Growth of the Law*. New Haven, CT: Yale University Press, 1924 52.

[22] Judge Ole Due, a former judge of the European Court of Justice, as reported by an English judge on the European Court of Justice, Sir Konrad Schiemann, in "From Common Law Judge to European Judge," 4 *Europäisches Privatrecht* (ZEuP) (2005) 741.

However, even expressed in its most general sense, U.S. legal philosophy does not end with positivism, pragmatism or realism. In the latter half of the twentieth century there was a turn from pragmatism and legal positivism to a moral legal philosophy.[23] Rawls is credited with reintroducing social and political questions into U.S. philosophy generally. Rawls based his theory of justice on Aristotelian principles. For the limited purposes of this brief introduction to U.S. legal culture, the Rawlsian theory of justice might be best described as fairness, but the fairness of which Rawls writes is to be understood as making an interpretation, not making an equation. In that way, he focuses upon the fact that fairness in one's original position guarantees the fairness of the principles chosen from that position. This device of "original position" sets Rawls against the utilitarian equation that justice equals a legal system that creates the greatest good for the greatest number of persons. The legal philosophy of Rawls and Dworkin was explicitly ahistorical. Dworkin said of himself and Rawls: "We're not concerned with the historical question here. ... We're not concerned about how principles are in fact chosen. We're concerned about which principles are just."[24]

Most legal systems, including that of the United States, forbid the retroactive effect of legislation. However, if judicial decisions in fact recognize principles of common law that are omnipresent in the sky, when judges make decisions and write opinions they are really just articulating that which is already the law. When working through pure customary common law, however, the problem is, of course, that apparently citizens did not know, or were not sure of the law until it was articulated through a judicial opinion. In effect, the judicial opinion could give retroactive effect to rules of law that were heretofore only inarticulately floating in the sky as Platonic forms. There is a way out of this unacceptable pronouncement, however. If judges really are articulating that which was already the law, and the law is based upon custom as common law, then the custom is the observed practice of its citizens, not a surprise norm created by the judge. There is of course also the advantage that if judges are making the law (not simply articulating that which is already in place), they do so without the political pressures that the legislatures feel through their constituents and lobbies,[25] and do so to solve a legally framed problem, not as normative speculation through legislation.

Philosophers,[26] psychologists,[27] and literary theorists[28] have long questioned the assertion that we can know an author's intentions just from examining a text. Yet in

---

[23] See, for example, Rawls, *supra* note 2, or the work of Ronald Dworkin.

[24] Stephen Guest, *Ronald Dworkin: Third Edition*. Stanford, CA: Stanford University Press, 2013 267, fn. 31.

[25] Kempin, *supra* note 14 at 109.

[26] See, for example, G. E. M. Anscombe, *Intention*. 2nd ed. Oxford: Basil Blackwell, 1972; Martin Heidegger, *The Basic Problems of Phenomonology*. Trans. Albert Hofstadter. Indianapolis, IN: Indiana University Press, 1982; Niels O. Benson, *Heidegger's Theory of Intentionality*. Trans. Hanne Vohtz. Odense: Odense University Press, 1986.

[27] Bertram F. Malle, Louis J. Moses and Dare A. Baldwin (eds.), *Intentions and Intentionality: Foundations of Social Cognition*. Cambridge, MA: MIT Press, 2003.

[28] I. A. Richards and C. K. Ogden, *The Meaning of Meaning: A Study of the Influence of Language upon Thought and of the Science of Symbolism*. London and New York: Kegan, Paul, Trench, Trubner, 1923; Roland Barthes, "The Death of the Author," *Aspen*, no. 5–6 (1967).

the law, we have somehow frozen our thinking about the idea somewhere in the period of modernism, and continue to believe that we can know the intentions of those who wrote constitutions, statutes, regulations and case decisions.

> The English judges rejected the idea of looking for the intention of the drafters and by 1904 we have Lord Halsbury's statement that "the worst person to construe" a statute "is the person who is responsible for its drafting." The assumption of interpretive power was of great importance in creating the independence of the judiciary, and vital to [the U.S.] doctrine of the separation of governmental powers.[29]

Often when persons are introduced to legal realism, they are made uncomfortable by its challenges and demands and as a result, regard it only as a negative or destructive enterprise. While it is true that realists often challenge formalists, rationalists or natural law adherents by saying such things as "your notion of law is shiny and pretty but false, and the reality is ugly and harsh," there are positive interpretations of realism as well:

> The caricature of the German judge is that he judges each case without regard to precedent and makes up his own mind afresh in each one. The caricature of the British judge is that he blindly follows every precedent. In real life I suspect that a judge of either tradition tries in general to produce a result which accords with his instinctive sense of the justice of the case and would meet with the approval of the vast majority of his colleagues. To do so otherwise is to waste the parties' time and money in appellate proceedings.[30]

7.3.2 Critical Legal Studies

The original notion of legal realism, made famous by persons such as Holmes, had a resurgence in the later part of the twentieth century in the United States. This newer school of thought is known as "Critical Legal Studies," and it has influences both from legal realism and Marxism. The philosophy of critical legal studies has a particular focus on the social impact of law and how law is integrated in social life and in turn, affirmed by social life. Günter Frankenberg takes a swing at functionalist comparativism when he states that:

> [b]y stressing the production of 'solutions' through legal regulations the functionalist dismisses as irrelevant or does not even recognize that law also produces and stocks interpretive patterns and visions of life which shape people's

---

[29] Kempin, *supra* note 14 at 117.
[30] Sir Konrad Schiemann, "From Common Law Judge to European Judge," 4 *Zeitschrift für Europäisches Privatrecht* (ZEuP) (2005) 741–9, 745.

ways of organizing social experience, giving it meaning, qualifying it as normal and just or as deviant and unjust.[31]

The difficulty then for critical legal studies scholars is how to proceed with legal science once prior methods have been rejected.

Critical legal scholars study the ideological role of law, applying the larger tradition of Marxist scholarship, a fact that might come as a surprise to those outside the United States. According to critical legal scholars, "[l]egal ideology maintains the social order by creating a belief in the legitimacy of state power and the justice of the system by which the power is maintained."[32] In the 1980s, critical legal scholars felt that "[b]y examining the impact of legal symbols and rules of behavior on the stability of the modern industrial state,"[33] their research would rejuvenate the study of legal culture. The novelty of applying Marx to U.S. law has since worn off, but work continues to be done in critical legal studies. An important point of critical legal studies is that the cycle of services by legal institutions to the public and expectations by the public of legal institutions feed upon one another. Legal institutions form what the public thinks it can expect from law, and the public is therefore not surprised at what it encounters in the legal system. When the citizen exclaims "I know my rights," the critical legal scholar might comment that the citizen knows his rights because he was complicit in defining[34] those rights as being a function of the state.

From that basic critical legal studies position, a scholar might well conclude that:

> Until plaintiffs have experience with the courts, they assume that the legal system stands ready and willing to protect these rights by sending those who violate them to jail. With experience, this orientation changes. The plaintiff takes a more pragmatic view of the court, in which he or she realizes that the court is not willing or able to protect these rights.[35]

This may well be true, but it is not a unique epiphany for one to realize the difference between theory and practice once one gets inside a set of practices. When asked when a scientist first notices that the work of the natural scientist in practice

[31] Günter Frankenberg, "Critical Comparison, Re-Thinking Comparative Law," 26 *Harv. Int'l L. J.* (1985) 411, 445.
[32] Sally Engle Merry, "Concepts of Law and Justice Among Working-Class Americans: Ideology as Culture," 9 *Legal Studies Forum* (1985) 59.
[33] *Ibid.*
[34] While critical legal studies might find this use of language to be inherently in the interest in the state, and therefore limiting to the individual, studies of rhetoric might show that there is no neutral use of language, so either the state or another interest is advantaged no matter what language is used. See James Boyd White, "Law as Rhetoric, Rhetoric as Law: The Arts of Cultural and Communal Life," 52 *U. Chic. L. R.* 684 (1985) and James Boyd White, *Heracles' Bow: Essays on the Rhetoric and Poetics of the Law*. Madison, WI: University of Wisconsin Press, 1985.
[35] Merry, *supra* note 32 at 67.

does not proceed as it is described in theory, Steven Rose answered "the first time the postgraduate student must design and run a research project."[36] This consideration from the natural sciences leads me to a final note on legal philosophy in the United States that nicely encapsulates the tough note that opened this chapter—proceeding from experience or reason.

7.3.3 Rationalism v. Empiricism in U.S. Adversarial Trial Practice

Philosopher Peter Suber, in discussing the uses and abuses of reason in the U.S. courtroom writes:

> What is remarkable is that in our legal system most cases do support well-argued stories on both sides. We ought to pause a moment and ask why this should be so. After all, it is not the case that the physical universe supports well-argued stories on both sides of arbitrary propositions of physical chemistry. But not only does this happen in law, we are so confident in its regularity that we put lawyers under a professional obligation of zealous representation without even asking whether the client's case has a leg for zeal to stand on. Why do most cases support well-argued stories on both sides? Is it due to the nature of human conduct? Is it due to the ambiguity of virtue and responsibility? Is it due to the flexibility of interpretation? Is every deed somehow intrinsically subject to morally polar interpretations? Or is it due to the content of our laws? Is it due to the ways that deeds, interpretations and laws interact? I don't know the answer.[37]

Suber's line of questions underscores the very thought process of the common law. In a 1952 report of the Joint Conference of the American Bar Association and the American Association of Law Schools, the importance of which was discussed in Chapter 5, Harvard legal philosopher Lon L. Fuller reported:

> These, then, are the reasons for believing that partisan advocacy plays a vital and essential role in one of the most fundamental procedures of democratic society. But if we were to put all of these detailed considerations to one side, we should still be confronted by the fact that, in whatever form adjudication may appear, the experienced judge or arbitrator desires and actively seeks to obtain an adversary presentation of the issues. Only when he has had the

---

[36] Personal interview with Prof. Steven Rose by author, The Open University, Milton Keynes, UK, September, 1997. Notes on file with author.

[37] Peter Suber, "Legal Reasoning After Post-Modern Critiques of Reason," 3 *Legal Writing* (1997) 21–50, at 34. Suber's reference to "zeal" and "zealous representation" are because lawyers of the time would have known that the Model Rules of Professional Responsibility required a lawyer to represent his or her client zealously. Specifically, the terms "zealous" and "zeal" were included in the Preamble, paragraph 2 and the comment to Rule 1.3, respectively, of the Model Rules.

benefit of intelligent and vigorous advocacy on both sides can he feel fully confident of his decisions.[38]

As the U.S. Supreme Court commented "[v]igorous cross-examination, presentation of contrary evidence, and careful instruction on the burden of proof are the traditional and appropriate means of attacking shaky but admissible evidence."[39]

> It is worth repeating that the game is not to bend logic as elegantly and persuasively as possible; it is to support one's conclusion with relevant legal premises without bending logic at all. If logical rigor were not part of the game, or if we could infer anything from anything with equal validity, then there would be neither art nor science to legal reasoning. The game is not cramped so much by logical rigor so much as constituted by it, just as sonnet-writing is constituted by certain metrical constraints, not impeded by them.[40]

Most recently, the French philosopher Bruno Latour generalized the notion of the superior quality of knowledge obtained through adversarial procedure when he said that the adversarial procedure is more true to nature than the inquisitorial procedure is.[41]

7.4 Conclusions: Philosophy for the Future

"So between these two chief systems—inductive empiricism and deductive rationalism—which way is 'better'?" the novice might ask. The answer can only be to say that the legal system that better meets the stated goals for legal practice in its respective society is better. But somehow, the question is more often answered as if it is asking about two competing sports teams, and one of the two must be demonstrably better than the other as though they are playing the same "game." If we do ask whether legal education or practice meet the needs of a society, then we might well need the services of the sociology of law, investigated by sociologists, rather than lawyers.[42]

In this chapter, I have presented some of the larger phases through which U.S. legal philosophy has passed. Some of the more well-known and popular thinkers even

---

[38] Lon L. Fuller and John D. Randall, "Professional Responsibility: Report of the Joint Conference" 44 *A.B.A. J.* (1958) 1159, 1161.

[39] *Daubert et al. v. Merrell Dow Pharmaceuticals*, 509 U.S. 579 589 (1993) (citing *Rock v. Arkansas*, 483 U.S. 44, 61 (1987)).

[40] Suber, *supra* note 37 at 35.

[41] Bruno Latour, "Climate Change: How to Make the Paris Climate Conference Work? An Alternative Procedure," Albertus Magnus Professorial Lecture, University of Cologne, 15 June 2015.

[42] See Susanne Baer, *Rechtssoziologie: Eine Einführung in die interdisziplinäre Rechtsforschung*. Baden-Baden: Nomos, 2011. For more on this, refer back to the discussion of U.S. legal culture through the social reference frame in Chapter 5.

change the features of their philosophic reference frames within their own lifetimes. Judge Richard Posner, for example, whom the *Journal of Legal Studies* says was the most-cited legal scholar of the twentieth century, is often cited for his books on legal thinking and jurisprudence.[43] Posner has moved some distance away[44] from being an economic determinist of the so-called Chicago School of economics, employing "rational choice" theory[45] to most recently returning to realism in which a judge should strive against formalism and complexity and want "judicial decisions to 'make sense' in a way that could be explained convincingly to a lay person."[46] Some things have remained consistent over time, however, and one of those is the reliance of the common law, including U.S. law, upon the philosophies of empiricism, rather than upon rationalism. As I will discuss in the next chapter, that preference might be seen across the disciplines of Anglo-U.S. culture, not just in the law.

CHECK YOUR UNDERSTANDING:

How is legal pragmatism different than simply "being practical?"

CHALLENGE YOUR UNDERSTANDING:

What consistencies can you see among legal empiricism, legal pragmatism and inductive reasoning?

Literature

Almeder, Robert F., "A Definition of Pragmatism," 3 *History of Philosophy Quarterly* 1 (January 1986). 79.

Cardozo, Benjamin Nathan, *The Nature of the Judicial Process*. New Haven, CT: Yale University Press, 1921.

Frankenberg, Günter, "Critical Comparison, Re-Thinking Comparative Law," 26 *Harv. Int'l L. J.* (1985). 411.

Fuller, Lon L. and John D. Randall, "Professional Responsibility: Report of the Joint Conference" 44 *A.B.A. J.* (1958). 1159.

Guest, Stephen, *Ronald Dworkin: Third Edition*. Stanford, CA: Stanford University Press, 2013.

Holmes, Oliver Wendell Jr., "The Path of Law," 10 *Harv L. Rev.* (1897). 457.

Kempin, Frederick G., *Historical Introduction to Anglo-American Law*. St. Paul, MN: West Pub. Co., 1990.

---

[43] Richard A. Posner, *The Problems of Jurisprudence*. Cambridge, MA: Harvard University Press, 1990.

[44] Richard A. Posner, *A Failure of Capitalism: The Crisis of '08 and the Descent into Depression*. Cambridge, MA: Harvard University Press, 2009.

[45] Richard A. Posner, *The Economic Analysis of Law*. New York: Aspen Publisher, 1973; Richard A. Posner, *The Economics of Justice*. Cambridge, MA: Harvard University Press, 1983.

[46] Richard A. Posner, *Reflections on Judging*. Cambridge, MA: Harvard University Press, 2013 120.

Kuklick, Bruce, *A History of Philosophy in America: 1720–2000*. Oxford: Oxford University Press, 2002.

Menand, Louis, *The Metaphysical Club, A Story of Ideas in America*. New York: Farrar, Straus and Giroux, 2002.

Merry, Sally Engle, "Concepts of Law and Justice Among Working-Class Americans: Ideology as Culture," 9 *Legal Studies Forum* (1985). 59.

Posner, Richard A., *The Economic Analysis of Law*. New York: Aspen Publishers, 1973.

Posner, Richard A., *The Economics of Justice*. Cambridge, MA: Harvard University Press, 1983.

Posner, Richard A., *Reflections on Judging*. Cambridge, MA: Harvard University Press, 2013.

Pound, Roscoe, *Interpretations of Legal History*. Cambridge: Cambridge University Press, 1923.

Rader, Melvin, *The Enduring Questions: Main Problems of Philosophy*. 3d ed. London: Holt, Rinehart and Winston, 1976.

Schiemann, Konrad, "From Common Law Judge to European Judge," 4 *Zeitschrit für Europäisches Privatrecht* (ZEuP) (2005). 741.

Suber, Peter, "Legal Reasoning After Post-Modern Critiques of Reason," 3 *Legal Writing* (1997). 21–50.

Zweigert, Konrad and Hein Kötz, *Introduction to Comparative Law*. 3rd ed. Trans. Tony Weir. Oxford: Clarendon Press, 1998.

8

THE DISCIPLINARY REFERENCE FRAME

Framing Issues

1. In the United States, how does thought in law resemble thought in other disciplines, as for example in the natural sciences or philosophy?
2. When one remarks that something is "typically American," what could that mean in the law, and why would it typify the culture of the United States?

8.1 Introduction

In this chapter, I am treating disciplinarity as a reference frame through which both the law student and practicing lawyer may view the law. "Disciplinarity" is the separation of one field of thought (in this case, law) from other fields of thought. For comparison to law as a discipline,[1] I will make mention of natural science and philosophy, which of course are different disciplines from law, but each of which exists within U.S. culture. Christopher Columbus Langdell and James Barr Ames, the first two deans of Harvard Law School, who began teaching at Harvard in 1870 and 1873, respectively, substantially changed legal education in the United States. But despite the efforts by Langdell and Ames from inside the academy, U.S. legal study still takes much of its direction from legal practice, not academic legal science. Moreover, the curriculum in law faculties is driven by the licensing examination

---

[1] Lord Denning references the *Shorter Oxford Dictionary* and uses "discipline" to mean "[i]nstruction imparted to disciples or scholars." Lord Denning, *The Discipline of Law*. London: Butterworths (1979) v. Here, I am extending that meaning to all the social forms necessary in order to construct and maintain any separate such area of instruction.

known as the "bar examination." True to the spirit of the common law, in looking at the changes made by Langdell and Ames, one should look also to the persons involved, not just to texts, in order to examine the disciplinarity of the enterprise.

> Langdell and Ames ... altered the concept of who should teach law. Rather than to enlist prominent judges and lawyers as teachers, they saw law teaching as a separate profession. The theory was that taught law is scientific law, not practical law, and that legal science could be better developed by those not in active practices. James Barr Ames never practiced law. The concept of law teaching as a separate profession continues [in the United States] to this day, but without the idea that law is a science. In recent years law teaching has come to be recognized as a separate profession in England as well.[2]

The disciplinary reference frame can be understood by using the metaphors of spatial thinking and thereby placing law in the context of other disciplines, all of which fit into the concept of culture. Disciplines are plastic. Even in the natural sciences, biology, for example, would not have been recognized as its own discipline until the nineteenth century. Psychology has only been recognized as its own discipline since the twentieth century. One must ask oneself what the functions of a discipline are and what the indications of an independent discipline are. The indications might be in education, societal organization, or the gate-keeping of who enters the profession, for example.

By using the spatial metaphor to understand what lies inside disciplines, one might also ask what lies *outside* disciplines? Previously, the answer could have been that popular culture lies outside disciplines. However, for nearly fifty years, even universities—the main gatekeeper for disciplinarity—have been taking popular culture seriously, especially if one is scientifically looking to see what the social markers of a culture might be.

History, language and social concern show why the disciplinary structure of much of civil law in Europe comes from the university. One may begin by making a quick comparison of the disciplinary method of civil law with the disciplinary method of common law, using German law and U.S. law as examples of each, respectively. German law, in seeing itself as a science, has its roots in university study and the system of law that one learns in that study. One begins with a norm, and then applies the facts of the particular case under consideration to that norm using the principles of subsumption and abstraction. The norm is what a philosopher would call a "covering law" from which we decide the outcome of a particular conflict. The norm functions in the same way as the major premise in a logician's categorical syllogism. From this process, one hopes to deduce a just result.[3]

[2] Frederick G. Kempin, Jr., *Historical Introduction to Anglo-American Law*. St. Paul, MN: West, 1990. 87–8.
[3] See Karl Larenz and Claus-Wilhelm Canaris, *Methodenlehre der Rechtswissenschaft*. 4th ed. Berlin: Springer, 2014. For a thoughtful analysis and critique of the method, see Reinhold

In distinction to the German structure with its roots in the university, the disciplinary structure of U.S. legal study has its roots in the courts, resulting in the inductive "case method" of conflict resolution being studied within the discipline. For representative statements on how this works, one can look to two well-known U.S. judges. Judge Learned Hand said that the common law "stands as a monument slowly raised, like a coral reef, from the minute accretions of past individuals, of whom each built upon the relics which his predecessors left, and in his turn left a foundation upon which his successors might work."[4] And we should not forget the words of Justice Oliver Wendell Holmes, Jr. discussed in the philosophical reference frame of Chapter 7:

> The life of the [common] law has not been logic: it has been experience. The felt necessities of the time, the prevalent moral and political theories, intuitions of public policy, avowed or unconscious, even the prejudices which judges share with fellow-men, have a good deal more to do than the syllogism in determining the rules by which men should be governed.[5]

The syllogism to which Holmes refers is of course that used in the deductive method of the civil lawyer.

To know whether these methods of conflict resolution are typical features of their respective legal systems, or whether they fairly represent the cultures in which they are employed, one can look to other disciplines in the same cultures. This is a comparative practice, with all the same concerns as a proper application of comparative law. Professor Pierre Schlag has remarked:

> [w]hen traditional legal thought goes traveling (in the footnotes) through the university, it never seems to encounter much of anything except itself. The interdisciplinary travels of traditional legal thought are like [an American's] bad European vacation: the substance is Europe, but the form is McDonald's, Holiday Inns, American Express.[6]

In asking the question of why one would make cross-discipline comparisons, the answer is to see whether there is some element of thought in a culture that is common among all the disciplines practiced in that culture. To begin the disciplinary comparison, one could look, for example, at the disciplinary structure of "continental" philosophy, as outlined in the philosophical reference frame of Chapter 7. As discussed through the philosophical reference frame, one might say that the disciplinary

---

Zippelius, *Introduction to German Legal Methods.* 10th ed. Trans. Kirk W. Junker and P. Matthew Roy. Durham, NC: Carolina Academic Press, 2008.

[4] Learned Hand, "Review of Judge Cardozo's *The Nature of Judicial Process*," 35 *Harv L. Rev.* (1922) 479, 481.

[5] Oliver Wendell Holmes, Jr., *The Common Law.* Boston, MA: Little Brown and Co., 1881 1.

[6] Pierre Schlag, "*Le Hors de Text, C'est Moi*: The Politics of Form and Domestication of Deconstruction," 11 *Cardozo L. Rev.* (1990) 1631, 1656.

structure of continental philosophy begins with the university. The structure of continental philosophy shows tendencies to quests for first principles. Beginning already with Plato, one finds that the universal exists apart from particular things, and is related to them as their prototype or exemplar.[7] For Plato, philosophic method means the descent from a knowledge of universal forms (or ideas) to a contemplation of particular imitations of these.

By comparison, the disciplinary structure of what is called "Anglo-American" philosophy more resembles a flat array of examples or even experiments from which one may induce more general rules, or covering model. This relationship can be observed both in pragmatism and analytic philosophy. Examples can be found in the works of Francis Bacon (who was also a Gray's Inn lawyer), David Hume, C. S. Peirce, John Dewey, William James, W. V. O. Quine and Wilfred Sellars.

By further comparison, the disciplinary structure of Anglo-American natural science is modeled on industry. The Royal Society, founded in 1660, enjoyed the confidence and official support of the restored monarchy, in part because the establishment wanted better control over the "new science," which was the experimental method of induction. The "New" or "Experimental" form of natural philosophy had been generally ill-regarded by the established Aristotelian academies, but had been promoted by Francis Bacon in his book, *The New Atlantis*.

Recalling the social reference frame of Chapter 5, in the law one can observe features of the U.S. disciplinary culture, such as the form and content of legal education being capable of independence from the university and note the role and function of organizations such as the Association of American Law Schools and the role and function of the law reviews (journals) within the law schools. In legal practice, one observes considerable independence from state legislative control, the manner in which licenses to practice are obtained and the function of the American Bar Association.

8.2 The Method of the Legal Discipline: More Than Textual Exegesis?

Looking back to the historical reference frame, we find a confluence of three important events in the twelfth century—the establishment of the European university the rediscovery of the *Corpus Juris Civilis* (C.J.C.) and the integration of the customary law as practiced in King Harold II's Britain into the Norman administrative system brought by William. Both the civil law and the common law systems founded the university discipline of legal study upon texts that were not the secular law of the time, a concept that, to some degree, is carried forward to this day in the case books used in the U.S. classroom. The first two of these coincidences—the

---

[7] One is here reminded that it was the ancient Greeks who also first recognized irrational numbers and imaginary numbers.

rediscovery of the C.J.C. in Italy and the founding of the first European university at Bologna—together made possible a place of study (the university) with a thing (the C.J.C.) to study,[8] and thus enabled a discipline (law) to rise up around it. But we should keep in mind that the C.J.C. was attractive for study precisely because it *could* be studied—that is to say, it offered a systematized body of civil law complete with codes, a digest and the "Institutes," which was a sort of textbook for teaching the law. But the C.J.C. was not important because it was the body of law in force at the time—it most certainly was not. That fact illustrates even more that having a text in law can create a discipline for study, even if the text is not the culture's norms at the time. So this exercise in textual study was not a study for practice as we would study law today.

Before going further I will divide the disciplinary concerns of this reference frame into four categories—the textual and non-textual study of law, and the textual and non-textual practice of law. In England, the practice of ecclesiastical law, like its study, was premised on the written text. Not so with secular law. Secular law was of course in practice in the community, but not studied at the university. The norms announced by judges were found in custom, not text. In fact, because the practice of secular law developed without the presence of a text,[9] the practice did not enable a discipline of study. Therefore, for example, at the university in Oxford one could study ecclesiastical law, but not the secular law in practice at the time. (Here it must also be remembered, however, that the clear distinction between ecclesiastical law and state law was not so clear as it is today, so to say that the university taught ecclesiastical law in that context is different than saying that a university would teach ecclesiastical law today.) Nevertheless, apart from this ecclesiastical law there was indeed a body of secular law in practice, and the point is that this body of secular law was not taught in the university and it would still be hundreds of years until the Inns of Court were established, where secular law could be taught.

Despite the emergence of common law from practice that was not text-based, the famous and influential Lord Camden, in response to an abstract argument made by a lawyer practicing before him in 1765, wrote a telling statement that equated the importance of the written text with law: "If this is law it would be found in our books, but no such law ever existed in this country."[10] One need not be a legal naturalist to wonder about the "it" in his proclamation and ask whether it is itself an abstract notion of a rule, and further ask whether the written statement is not just one form of evidence as to what the rule is. One could go so far as to say that the European faculty of law was invented because a text had been rediscovered—the C.J.C.—and thereby there was something to be studied as a discipline of law at

---

[8] For a thorough consideration of the need to have a text upon which to found a discipline, see Stanley Fish, *Is There a Text in this Class?: The Authority of Interpretive Communities*. Cambridge, MA: Harvard University Press, 1980 *passim*.

[9] Harold J. Berman, *Law and Revolution: The Formation of the Western Legal Tradition*. Cambridge, MA: Harvard University Press, 1983 274.

[10] Lord Camden in *John Entick, Clerk v. Nathan Carrington and Three Others*, 95 ER 807 King's Bench, Michaelmas Term, 6 Geor. III 1765.

Bologna in the twelfth century. In the common law as well, the written reports of judicial decisions made the study of law possible as a discipline.

The notion in the United States of reporting cases so as to enable the *stare decisis* doctrine was not brought into the world in one complete act. In England, the system to report the decisions of judges needed time to develop the concepts and time to develop the resources needed to produce reliable texts. "Until the reign of Edward I (1272–1307), there was no single place to look for cases. … In Edward I's reign, the compilation of Year Books began."[11] The Year Books of Edward I's reign were collections of the notes of lawyers and students, organized only by year, not by subject matter. When the Year Books became too numerous to be researched effectively, Abridgements began to appear which were organized by subject matter, "apparently to facilitate study."[12] The "compilers of abridgements had to use classifying terms for headings which, in turn, provided the opportunity for them and their readers to think about law in new ways."[13] By 1535, the printing of Year Books and their Abridgements had ceased and Reports began. Reports were still not the words of the judges in deciding cases, but rather the notes of lawyers and students, some of which were so unreliable as to cause judges to forbid lawyers from citing them.[14] Such was the state of play when the United States began.

The importance of texts in the creation of disciplines cannot be overstated. The creation or presence of a text not only helped to establish the discipline, it gave the discipline the character and method of craft practice for legal scholarship. The craft practice of law would treat a lawyer's work the way other crafts are treated—one trains with one already possessing the desired skills so that one can make useful products in a given industry—baking, brewing, smithing or law. Texts and their creation were also instrumental in separating U.S. law from English law as a discipline. Although the concepts of *stare decisis* were already developed in England, the development of resources that could facilitate *stare decisis* in the United States had to begin anew.

For an excellent example of the significance of these three disciplinary aspects—establishment, craft method and separation—one can look to the work of an influential jurist, James Kent of New York. In the late eighteenth century, Dublin, Ireland was a large printing center, and although still under English control, was not covered by English copyright law. Therefore U.S. jurists would obtain books at a far lower cost from Dublin than they could from Britain. "As Kent struggled to make use of these books, he developed an unusually print-oriented vision of the ideal legal order. He then transplanted what he learned—the substance as well as the vision—into his own reports and his four-volume *Commentaries on American Law* (1826–1830), which were available everywhere in the Union throughout the

---

[11] Kempin, *supra* note 2 at 98–9.
[12] *Ibid*. at 99.
[13] *Ibid*. at 100.
[14] Kempin, *supra* note 2 at 101.

nineteenth century."[15] Thus, even if entire book collections of cases were not available, Kent's books made the law tangible.

> Until the early nineteenth century, reporters were typically practitioners who took notes on court cases and wanted to make a bit of extra money by publishing them. Most trial lawyers kept notes. Before reports [of case decisions] were published regularly, that was the best way for a lawyer to learn the law and, afterward, to keep track of what the courts in one's own jurisdiction were doing. ... Up to the late eighteenth century, a lawyer needed manuscript notes of contemporary cases to know how his jurisdiction had resolved disputes.[16]

The designation of a person in the role of official reporter changed this relatively informal manuscript practice. But even if states had official reporters, many reports still had to be printed where printing was available, such as in New York or Philadelphia, meaning that much of the law that was reported from any state was available for review by someone such as Kent, when he wrote his *Commentaries*. Thus it is no surprise that those commentaries in turn found their way to most states and most lawyers and thus had tremendous influence on the development of American, as distinguished from English, common law.

The next significant change that occurred in reporting was that the judges themselves began reporting, rather than leaving the task to a reporter. That change began with the new state and federal constitutions of the revolutionary period:

> In several states and in the federal government, these new constitutions strengthened the relative power of courts in the new republic—relative to colonial courts, and relative to other political branches. Some constitutions did so by design; others did so as the legislators and judges construed and interpreted them. The process was never uncontroversial.[17]

With this new-found strength and recognition, the judges exercised their ability and right to state the case and interpret the law in their own writing:

> Anglo-American judges generally did not write opinions before the nineteenth century. Even when some judges began writing them, the product remained a script for oral performance rather than a draft for publication.[18]

---

[15] Daniel J. Hulsebosch, "An Empire of Law: Chancellor Kent and the Revolution in Books in the Early Republic, Meador Lecture Series 2007–2008": Empire, 2 *U. of Ala. L. Rev.* (2008) 1–2.

[16] *Ibid.* at 8 (citing John William Wallace, *The Reporters Arranged and Characterized with Incidental Remarks*. Boston, MA: Soule & Bubbee, 1882 9–12).

[17] Hulsebosch, *supra* note 15 at 24.

[18] From the script for oral performance emerged a script that looked much like the combination of a playwright's script and the minutes of a meeting written by the meeting's secretary. See e.g. *Fletcher v. Rylands and Another*, 3 H. & C. 774, 159 Eng Rep 737 (Ex. 1865).

The practice of transmitting written opinions to a reporter did not develop until reporters were appointed by the court or the legislature.[19]

8.3 The Substance of the Legal Discipline: Attitude?

Where does the history of the discipline bring us? What is this discipline that we today call the study and practice of law? Why is it separated from other disciplines at the university? Why was (and sometimes still is) the discipline found in independent "law schools" in the United States, and not at universities at all? Some have questioned whether law is in fact a separate discipline, asking whether instead, it is more like an onion, and once we have peeled away all the contributions from other disciplines, there is nothing remaining in the center. Law students often say that lawyers have specialized knowledge and that law is a separate discipline due to this specialized knowledge. If so, what constitutes this specialized knowledge? Does the ability to memorize and repeat the text of statutes constitute knowledge? Of course not—one must also be able to interpret and apply the texts to concrete fact situations. But textual memorization and interpretation are not the unique province of lawyers. Theologians and literary theorists also memorize and interpret texts and apply them to concrete fact situations. Is the discipline reducible to applied sociology, psychology or economics? If in fact there is no exclusive object of study to law, no *res* about which to know, then what does one learn when one learns the law? Rather than focus upon memorizing statutes, many lawyers and law professors in the U.S. legal profession make reference to "thinking like a lawyer."[20] That phrase raises its own set of questions. How does a lawyer think? How is it different from how other persons think (if it is in fact different)? Professor Philip Bobbitt of the University of Texas feels that:

> It is only because of the false model of decision–making as rule-following that we are disillusioned when we discover that something other than a rule has motivated a decision-maker—a fact that ought to be irrelevant as regards whether the decision is justified. It is because we cling to this false ideal that we refuse to grant to rule-following the axiomatic legitimacy it deserves, and attempt to augment rule-following with an insistence that it guided decisions also, thereby imperiling the legitimacy of wrong decisions and leading us to the search for "helpful" augmentations of legal rules that can indeed serve as guides to decision-making but which sacrifice legitimacy in the process. And it is owing to our attachment to this erroneous epistemology about how thoughts and decisions are related that jurisprudence continues to ignore the

---

[19] Hulsebosch, *supra* note 15 at 25–6.
[20] See, for example, Frederick Schauer, *Thinking Like a Lawyer: A New Introduction to Legal Reasoning*. Cambridge, MA: Harvard University Press, 2009.

progress made in twentieth century philosophy with respect to the empiricist model of mind.[21]

For many who are not lawyers, the more obvious marker of the lawyer that meets the eye is attitude, not knowledge. In contemporary usage, "attitude" is typically pejorative, as though one can always infer "bad attitude" when one uses the word "attitude." Before slipping into that prejudice, however, we ought to consider the more literal denotation of "attitude" in the physical world. "Attitude" is the angle of orientation that a pilot or captain has when approaching a destination. If we were to return to the notion of reference frames, we could add that attitude is the angle of approach that one takes to looking through the reference frame. In this case, that angle is the lawyer's angle. In the pentad of dramatistic elements through which he seeks to explain human motivation, the American literary theorist Kenneth Burke eventually[22] features attitude as being more important than scene, act, agent, agency or purpose[23] in explaining human motivation. Burke used the word "attitude" in a way that is not far from the physical denotation, meaning an angle of orientation toward something. He describes attitude as "incipient action."

Perhaps then "*thinking* like a lawyer" is behaving as if one is always ready to *act* like a lawyer.[24] During the science wars, when sociologists and other social scientists dared to claim that the practices of natural sciences were socially constituted and therefore properly studied by sociologists, one of the most concise comments made was that "science is too important to be left to the scientists."[25] The sociologists maintained that scientists did not have the ability or distance perspective that is necessary to describe how scientists conduct science. Might this be said of law? Do lawyers have the ability or perspective to describe and explain the practice of law? Harold Berman answers the question of whether law is a separate discipline by asserting that one needs to know who can answer the question. "[L]aw is too important to be left to the technicians [of law],"[26] says Berman. Is law indeed too

---

[21] Philip Bobbit, *Wittgenstein and Law*. Ed. Dennis Patterson. Aldershot: Ashgate, 2004. 6. Bobbitt calls Schauer a critic of the "common law system of rules and decision."

[22] For lawyers, it is worth noting that the *A Grammar of Motives* was originally written as a critical study of the U.S. Constitution, although the book is known for having produced this dramatistic pentad among literary scholars and rhetoricians. Here I say "eventually" because although it is called a "pentad" and focused upon the five terms listed when it was written, Burke later came to write that if he were authoring *A Grammar of Motives* all over again, attitude would not only have been added as a sixth term, it would have been the most important of the six in explaining human motives.

[23] Kenneth Burke, *A Grammar of Motives*. Berkeley, CA: University of California Press, 1969.

[24] The words "ready to act" are crucial here. Friedrich Nietzsche explained his use of the term "power" with the simile of the eagle with talons that he does not use, but knows he has them. The eagle is ready to act, but not acting. Michel Foucault, influenced by Nietzsche in his early career, makes the connection of power to law in *Discipline and Punish* (1977) and *Power/Knowledge: Selected Interviews, 1972–1977*, ed. C. Gordon (1980).

[25] See, for example, Malcolm L. Goggin, "The Life Sciences and the Public: Is Science Too Important to Be Left to the Scientists?" 3 *Politics and the Life Sciences* 1 (August 1984) 28.

[26] Harold J. Berman, *Law and Revolution II: The Impact of the Protestant Reformation on the Western Legal Tradition*. Cambridge, MA: Harvard University Press, 2006 ix.

important to be left to lawyers themselves to explain? What do law students and lawyers know about law that can be said from an analytic perspective, rather than just from an insider's view; that is, law looking at law? Traditionally, in comparative law, the chosen perspective from which to conduct one's analysis "depends upon the author's field of study, area of competence and preconceptions about law and comparison."[27] The U.S. system does require that a student complete a bachelor degree program of study in a discipline other than law before he is permitted to study law. That requirement could provide a law student with another perspective, but the historical reference frame allows us to see that the reason for this preliminary degree requirement grew out of the perceived vulgarity of common law, which denied it from being taught at university, rather than out of some grand liberal arts design.

Of course, when we look at other disciplines, they too are largely self-referential in constructing their own disciplines. Why should law be any different? One reason would be that in the nature of legal practice, law not only touches upon many other disciplines, but in fact tries to regulate practices in those disciplines. Law creates norms for medical practice, as well as on the creation and performance of arts and technology, and law sets limits on the biology that is permitted to be researched. So if law is going to be so invasive in so many facets of life, it would seem that law ought to take some responsibility for knowing as much as possible about those facets. Moreover, it ought to try to do so in a way that helps the lawyer understand the client in those other disciplines—looking through those disciplinary reference frames, so to speak. As a result of being trained to see law in their own ways, lawyers of the civil law and common law traditions will apply norms to social conflicts in their own ways. A civil lawyer will answer social conflict with norms made rationally appropriate. A common law lawyer will solve conflict with norms derived from applicable experience. In public life, citizens often demand more transparency in their politics, but when it comes to law, those same citizens feel excluded by law's self-created specialized language[28] and ritual practices from knowing their rights and liabilities:

> Unfortunately, the Civil Law and the Common Law, widely and inadequately understood, are essentially non-creative (perhaps anti-creative) due to a "scientific" approach towards codes on the one side, to the doctrine of precedent and the narrow view of rules on the other side. This view is best illustrated by the following statement by Fortescue, C.J. [during the reign of Henry VI]: "Sir the Law is as I say it is, and so it has been laid down ever since the law began; and we have several set forms which are held as law, and so held for good reason, though we cannot at present remember that reason."[29]

[27] Günter Frankenberg, "Critical Comparison, Re-Thinking Comparative Law," 26 *Harv. Int'l L. J.* (1985) 411, 430.

[28] Eventually, educators, lawyers and the public resist the specialized language. See, for example, Richard C. Wydick, *Plain English for Lawyers*. 5th ed. Durham, NC: Carolina Academic Press, 2005. Since the 1980s, there has even been a "movement" by the name of Plain English for Lawyers.

[29] Year Book 36 of Henry VI, pl. 21 (pp. 25–6) (quoted in Sir William Searle Holdsworth, *A History of English Law*. 5th ed. London: Sweet & Maxwell, 1931 626).

Approximately 400 years later, Justice Oliver Wendell Holmes, Jr. dismissed this sentiment by insisting that:

> [it] is revolting to have no better reason for a rule of law than that so it was laid down in the time of Henry IV. It is still more revolting if the grounds upon which it was laid down have vanished long since, and the rule simply persists from blind imitation of the past.[30]

Thus we can see that the spirit of legal realism demanded that the discipline justify its practices by more than saying "this is the way we have always done it, but we forget why."

Returning to the importance of the text in the creation and maintenance of a discipline, the third aspect of the law enabled by the text is the method by which one theorizes the nature of law itself. The extent of Kent's influence, like that of Blackstone's *Commentaries* (1765–69) makes one consider not only the substance, but also the method of his work.[31] "His collecting habits and interactive reading, memorialized in his library, show that he considered law to be something other than pure will or pure science. It was a matter of craft: a transatlantic enterprise to which American jurists could make valuable improvements."[32] This is not the first time that extended discussion resulted in steering an entire legal system to see itself as a craft practice. For the ancient Greeks, there was considerable discussion of the differences between those practices that one could call τέχνη (*techne*) which is translated approximately as "craftsmanship," and the set of practices based upon *empieria*, or experience, from *episteme*, which is speculative or rational knowledge.[33]

8.4 Putting Notions of Text and Science Together

A review of the creation of common law texts begins, but does not end the answer to whether common law is a science. Why does this question remain important? Here one needs to recall from the language reference frame the difference between definition and usage. Understood solely from its Latin root, the word "science" would seem simply to refer to knowledge. But that is not how the word is used. And in fact the word is not used the same way throughout all cultures. When the native English speaker hears the word "science," the association is most often with

[30] Oliver Wendell Holmes, Jr., "The Path of Law," 10 *Harv. L. Rev.* (1897) 457, 469.

[31] In fact, Lawrence Friedman has gone so far as to say that "Kent intended his huge work to be the national Blackstone." Lawrence M. Friedman, *A History of American Law*. 2nd ed. New York: Touchstone, 1986 332 (as quoted in Hulsebosch, *supra* note 15).

[32] Hulsebosch, *supra* note 15 at 3.

[33] We can understand law as craft practice from the ancient Greek, τέχνη (*techne*). See Janet Atwill, *Rhetoric Reclaimed: Aristotle and the Liberal Arts Tradition*. Ithaca, NY: Cornell University Press, 1998; and Kirk W. Junker, "Rhetoric Demonstrates the Foundation of Law as Techne, Not Empeiria," in Konstantine Boudouris, ed. *Philosophy, Art and Technology*. Athens: Ionia Publications, 2011 99–114.

the natural sciences. If one means to include social sciences, then one must add the word "social" before the word "science." "Science" alone would not include social thought in the common usage of the words. And it certainly would not include something like literature or philosophy, although to the French, for example "*la science*" would include those disciplines.

It is very telling to consider the reasons why a discipline should want to be considered a science. In so doing, we see that we may not have advanced beyond Plato's pejorative criticism of craft practices that were based upon experience because they were not practices that led to any truth, and only those practices capable of *episteme* were worthy of being called "philosophy."[34] Recently I was involved in an inter-faculty discussion of whether medicine should be categorized as a social or natural science. Just as to this distinction between social and natural sciences (and not whether it was a science at all), the physician in the group was adamant that medicine be included as a natural science. It seems that despite the fact that few would want to call himself a "positivist," our knowledge hierarchy still follows lockstep with that of August Comte's positive philosophy, placing mathematics in the position of being most axiomatic and least derivative, and social sciences (or social physics, as Comte called it) as being most derivative and least axiomatic, with astronomy, physics, chemistry and biology completing the spectrum in between.[35] Based on the character of being non-derivative, this hierarchy percolates into other regions of culture as well, including funding, prestige and entry restrictions, leading us all to want our practices to be called the most "scientific."

In many languages, calling something "scientific" certainly is a positive attribute, even if we have difficulty agreeing upon precisely which disciplines should be included as sciences.[36] And simply because it is a generally positive cultural attribute one might want his or her discipline or practices to be called a science or at least "scientific." This desire would appear to include the study and practice of law as well—at least for the civil lawyer. When asked whether law is a science, civil law students confidently respond in the affirmative. But when asked what makes law a science, those same students answer with considerable variety and some disagreement. In the first instance, when the students agree on the concept, they are of course thinking largely of legal education. Students learn statutes by rote and then "subsume" the facts of the case under the covering statutory law, much as a natural scientist would posit an hypothesis and then test the hypothesis with the facts

---

[34] Atwill, *supra* note 33 at 79.
[35] Auguste Comte, *The Positive Philosophy*. Trans. Harriet Martineau. New York: Blanchard, 1855.
[36] In U.S. law, consider the studied efforts in the federal courts in attempting to define science, and therefore admit certain types of evidence in the *Daubert v. Merrell Dow Pharmaceuticals* litigation and the U.S. Circuit Court and U.S. Supreme Court opinions adjudicating those cases. Likewise, the federal district court for central Pennsylvania took more than eighty pages to discuss whether creationism could qualify as a science, such that a school district could mandate that creationism be taught in science classrooms alongside evolution. See *Kitzmiller, et al. v. Dover Area School District, et al.*, 400 F. Supp. 2d 707 (2005).

produced from an experiment.[37] To the civil law student, that method of solving hypothetical legal conflicts makes legal study "scientific."[38] In civil law practice, the inquisitorial judge, who, in comparison to the common law advocate, has relatively few constraints on what he or she can ask of the witnesses or parties, is tasked with finding "the truth," a practice suggesting that the truth of the facts will determine the outcome of the case. For both the student and the practitioner, the process of the law is to produce an accurate narrative of the facts, which would have been the same answer had a different student or judge applied the facts to the law, because the method and process are replicable, if not predictable, and are therefore "scientific."[39]

By comparison, what might we say of the student or practicing lawyer in the common law system? The student of the common law learns that facts come first. And judges in the common law accommodate this expectation by first providing readers with the facts of the matter being adjudicated in their written opinions. The student of the common law is a student of the adversarial, not inquisitorial process, and so after the facts are presented, the student learns that in all litigation there is an issue, which is to say that the litigants have presented two different views of the facts or interpretations of applicable law, and due to those differences, the judge's job will not be independently to inquire further, but rather to determine which of the competing presentation of facts is more persuasive, which of the competing interpretations of the law is correct, or both.

> The tradition of the Common law has been to decide individual cases and then later when many cases have been decided by many judges over many years, to arrive at broader principles by a process of induction. By contrast, the tradition of the E.C.J. [European Court of Justice] is rather to state the principles and to leave the national judge to arrive at the answer to a particular case by a process of applying those principles. We find in Luxembourg much more frequent references to principles, freedoms and rights than was customary in England.[40]

---

[37] See Rheinhold Zippelius, *Juristische Methodenlehre*, 10th ed. Frankfurt am Main: C.H. Beck, 2006 (also in translation, see Zippelius, *supra* note 3).

[38] And yet, Rudolf von Jhering (1819–1892), the great German legal theorist of social and natural law, is often quoted as saying that even in the law "art has always preceded science," according to Jack A. Hiller and Bernhard Grossfeld, "Comparative Legal Semiotics and the Divided Brain: Are We Producing Half-Brained Lawyers?" 50 *Am. J. Comp. L.* (2002) 175, 176.

[39] For an extended discussion of the meaning of the term "science" in the law, see the U.S. Supreme Court opinion in the case of *Daubert v. Merrell Dow Pharmaceuticals*, 509 U.S. 579 (1993) in which seven U.S. Supreme Court justices agreed that they could not determine what constituted "science" without consulting philosophy and natural science itself. In the U.S. District Court case of *Tammy Kitzmiller, et al. v. Dover Area School District, et al.* 400 F. Supp. 2d 707, 2005, the thorough opinion of Judge Jones distinguishes science from religion.

[40] Sir Konrad Schiemann, "From Common Law Judge to European Judge," 4 *Zeitschrift für Europäisches Privatrecht* (ZEuP) (2005) 741, 742.

To repeat a point from Chapter 6 made by Lon L. Fuller, only when an experienced judge or arbitrator "has had the benefit of intelligent and vigorous advocacy on both sides can he feel fully confident of his decisions."[41]

For a variety of reasons, some of which are discussed previously through the social reference frame, the common law lawyer is far less likely than his civil law cousin to identify his practices as "science" (in its English usage). It would also seem that neither system even encourages its students to think along these lines, or to question their method of study, but rather inundates them with tales of how difficult all the technical rules of law are to master, and in so doing, deters the student from a more fundamental inquiry. If so, it is no wonder that the practicing lawyer in either system is equally as unconcerned. That leaves scholars to consider the connections of law to culture and question whether the nature of legal education and practice are sciences. In some civil law countries, those scholars might be respected and accepted, as when professors of law are looked to for explanatory commentary or legislation, but in common law countries, it is not the case. If one looks to Article 38 of the United Nations Charter, which provides the U.N. Court of Justice with jurisdiction, one finds that the opinions of scholars and judges are only to be considered in the same category as derivative sources.[42] Whereas the civil law scholar is permitted to explain the meaning of the civil law, in the common law, it is the judge whose comments are given legal significance.

8.5 Putting Notions of Practice and Art Together

There are many places throughout this book where one can see suggestions that the common law, as represented by U.S. law, is different than the civil law in ways other than the sources of law. It is here, when we examine whether law is a discipline—and if it is, in what ways—that we find one of the clearest insights into understanding U.S. legal culture. We return again to the question from Chapter 1: "is the practice of law a science or an art?" To answer that question, one must be clear what is meant by these two terms. Despite criticisms by Bernal[43] and others through the historical reference frame (as presented in Chapter 4) as to how Europeans have developed a sense of their own history, if there is indeed influence on that sense from ancient Greek thought, then we ought to look there.[44] As was discussed in Chapter 5, the common law has been taught as the art of advocacy, particularly oral advocacy, from the origins of the Inns of Court until the present. Moreover, training in oral

---

[41] Lon L. Fuller and John D. Randall, "Professional Responsibility: Report of the Joint Conference" 44 *A.B.A.J.* (1958) 1159, 1161.

[42] At the website of the International Court of Justice. www.icj-cij.org/documents/?p1=4& p2=2&p3=0#CHAPTER_II (last accessed 17 September 2009).

[43] Martin Bernal, *Black Athena: The Afroasiatic Roots of Classical Civilization, The Fabrication of Ancient Greece, 1785–1985.* Vol. I. New Brunswick, NJ: Rutgers University Press, 1987; *The Archaeological and Documentary Evidence.* Vol. II. Rutgers University Press, 1991; *The Linguistic Evidence.* Vol. III. Rutgers University Press, 2006.

[44] Junker, *supra* note 33.

advocacy, especially the *dissoi logoi* ("contrasting arguments") of ancient rhetoric (recall the language reference frame from Chapter 6), was a skill taught by rhetoricians before there was an exclusively legal text from which a discipline of law could be built.

Yet to best answer the question as to whether law is a science, one should distinguish legal education from legal practice. Consequently, the common law sits quite comfortably today in its professional practice as an art, with its set of skills originating in the ancient art of rhetoric. However, the common law could sit just as comfortably among social sciences when one considers that its establishment of norms as a legal system is a practice accomplished through the empirical and observable experiences of past trials and judgments.[45] By comparison, it would seem that when the civil lawyer learns his principle of subsumption for courtroom practice, he is learning something akin to a social science, but when the norms are created and discussed academically, the notion of empirical and observable facts is withdrawn. One of my assistants recently attended a funding seminar for social sciences at our university, which lies in a civil law jurisdiction. When the speakers had exhausted their discussion of all the social sciences, the assistant asked about law. "Law is not a social science," declared the speaker. "It is its own science." This leaves the puzzle to be solved—if civil law is not a social science or natural science, what is its character as its own science?

How does the art or science characterization of the legal discipline matter for the practical understanding of legal practice? What could possibly be at stake in making such a distinction? For this, we need to combine some of the ideas of the earlier reference frames of history, philosophy and sociology. One of the twentieth century's most renowned philosophers from England, Alfred North Whitehead, famously said that "[t]he safest general characterization of the European philosophical tradition is that it consists of a series of footnotes to Plato."[46] There are many criticisms to be made of such a position. However, one thing is rather clear—much of western philosophy is written *as though* it is a footnote to Plato or Aristotle either by citing one of them directly or by citing philosophy that in turn relies upon Aristotle or Plato.[47] And "[a]ccording to Plato, law counts as art, which has nothing to do with quantities, with counting, duration and breadth."[48]

If we consider the history of the practices Aristotle had observed—forensic oratory from speeches often written by another (a sophist, no less), we can get an idea of what the practice of law was.[49] It was not a separate profession but rather a set of oral practices by citizens seeking justice for themselves. Of course, even

---

[45] For considered reflection on whether U.S. law can benefit from social science, see W. Laurens Walker, "Improving Legal Procedures Through Social Science," 7 *Va. L. J.* (2007) 32.

[46] Alfred North Whitehead, *Process and Reality*. New York: Free Press, 1979 39.

[47] See Junker, *supra* note 33.

[48] Bernhard Grossfeld, *Core Questions of Comparative Law*. Durham, NC: Carolina Academic Press, 2005 187 (citing Plato, *Laws*, 757 B-E).

[49] Michael H. Frost, *Introduction to Classical Legal Rhetoric: A Lost Heritage*. Aldershot and Burlington, VT: Ashgate, 2005.

in the fourth century B.C.E., there were those who abused the legal system and rather than seek justice, sought only personal material gain.[50] The practices used for justice or personal gain were the practices taught by the sophists as the skills of rhetoric.[51]

The distinction we would easily make today between common law and civil law traditions would be anachronistic[52] if we tried to apply it to the fourth century B.C.E. Through the historic reference frame, we see Rome ruled by the Twelve Tables (449 B.C.E.). The recorded interpretation of the Twelve Tables[53] (529 B.C.E.) was for a time lost, but then long after the empire had ceased, the Code of Justinian was resurrected in Bologna in the twelfth century and began to be studied as the C.J.C. It is worth noting that it was during this same century that the option of the European University was begun and the C.J.C. was on hand as text to be studied at university. This textual study of the C.J.C. enabled law to function as an independent discipline. Ironically the C.J.C. was not the law in practice for anyone at the time.

By comparison, at the north-western corner of the empire, where Hadrian had built his wall to guard against the attacks of the Picts, Celts and Scots,[54] legal practices in Britain were based on local custom. Even after William defeated Harold at the famous Battle of Hastings, he brought only Norman administration to England, not the substantive law or norms of the continent. Not long after, when the University of Oxford was established, it was the canon law of the Christian church whose presence was known in the university, not the local customary law in practice. (Keep in mind, however, that the clear distinction one would make today between the norms of the Church and those of secular society was not such a bright line in Britain at the time.)[55] Instead, the texts that made possible the study of law as a discipline of practice were first the Year Books of written judicial decisions, then the Reporters of the judicial decisions. But consistent with the fact that the secular law was not studied in the university, these collections of written judicial decisions were also not housed in the university, but rather in the Inns of Court. For one to learn the skills of the practice of law, one therefore had to observe barristers and the other six types of lawyers[56] in practice. The nearest one could come to a catalogue of substantive norms was the Year Books and Reporters.

---

[50] See, for example, Aristophane's *Wasps*.

[51] Edward P. J. Corbett and Robert J. Connors, *Classical Rhetoric for the Modern Student*. 4th ed. Oxford: Oxford University Press, 1999.

[52] J. H. Baker, *The Common Law Tradition*. London: The Hambledon Press, 2000.

[53] Berman, *supra* note 9.

[54] See Baker, *supra* note 52; Daniel R. Coquillete, *The Anglo-American Legal Heritage*. 2nd. ed. Durham, NC: Carolina Academic Press, 2004.

[55] See Kirk W. Junker, "The Procedure of *Rhetorica Ecclesiastica* as a Common Worldview to the Church and to the Courts," in *Proceedings of the 16th Biennial Conference of the International Society for the History of Rhetoric, July 24–28, 2007*. Strasbourg: Laurent Pernot, 2007.

[56] See, for example, Baker, *supra* note 52.

When we focus upon the word "process" in the term "due process of law," we may well get the feeling that law is, or at least can be, scientific. Berman writes that "'[d]ue process of law' is, in fact, a fourteenth-century English phrase meaning natural law."[57] In making this observation, Berman is addressing the more difficult term: "due." "Due" according to what criteria or frame of how things ought to be? The law itself does not and very possibly cannot answer that question. To answer that question one must connect the law to cultural values. After one has done so once, thereafter in the law one may ignore the cultural values in future references and instead use the law referring back only to itself—in common law, to precedential cases. "What constitutes 'due process?'" is the question asked by a constitutional law professor in the common law classroom; the correct answer is the one that names a process and cites a case that established that process, not the answer that names a process and cites a principle of philosophy, religion, history, politics or economics, for example. In the end, the old adage of Marshall McLuhan that the "medium is the message"[58] ought to sit quite comfortably with U.S. lawyers who define "justice" (the message) as "due process" (the medium).

For a legal system that treats, or at least historically treated, the preparation for the practice of law as upper-middle-class training rather than university education, it should also come as no surprise that law students, and even lawyers, fail to consider whether their study and practice of law is at all "scientific" or can "meet social ends." Recall that not long after the Paris Exposition of 1908, Pierre Lepaulle wrote:

> [w]e have come to a period when, in most countries, there is a real inadequacy in the law, a failure to reach scientific standards and meet social ends. … What has been done in that social medicine which we call law? More than fifty years ago men began to study the social organism inductively, with scientific methods. Patiently, by monographs, some endeavored to discover the general laws which govern the mechanism or the function of this or that social institution, while others tried to establish methods and to evolve a program.[59]

One would be far less likely to find an appeal to conducting legal practice as a science in common law countries. While cases may be said to result inductively in building rules of law, there does not seem to be an appeal to synthesize it all into a unified whole that one might call a science.

The relatively late arrival at the English university of the study of secular law in practice coupled with the relative independence of practice of law in the United Kingdom and United States leads me to the assertion that the study and practice

---

[57] Berman, *supra* note 9 at 12.

[58] Marshall McLuhan, *Understanding Media: The Extensions of Man*. New York: McGraw Hill, 1964.

[59] Pierre LePaulle, "The Function of Comparative Law, With a Critique of Sociological Jurisprudence," 35 *Harv. L. Rev* 7 (1922) 838–9.

TABLE 8.1: The Disciplinary Structure of the University

Disciplinary Category	Object of Study	Method of Study	Goal of Discipline
Arts[a]	Human behavior	Varied—hermeneutics, for example	Varied—justice in the law. Beauty, if arts reflect the ancient Greek cultural divisions of transcendental values—truth, beauty, goodness.
Natural Sciences	Material objects of nature	Hypothetico-deductive	Truth
Social Sciences	Human behavior	Hypothetico-deductive	Justice

[a] As Hiller and Grossfeld remind us, "in France we have faculties of 'droit et lettres.'" (above note 38 at 186).

of common law has grown from a liberal arts tradition, with emphasis on oral advocacy skills. By comparison, the civil law developed as textual expression of the C.J.C. and with its practices focused upon judicial inquiry to resolve disputes, treated the practice and study of the law as a social science. Though it was not always the case, the European university concept is today divided into its broadest divisions based upon this distinction of sciences from the arts; a distinction that has some resonance with the ancient knowledge distinctions of truth, beauty and goodness. In the United States an extra category has been invented outside the traditional university structure—that of the "professional school." The category of "professional school" usually includes business, medicine and law, although in a pure sense other "professions" such as engineering, psychology, architecture and the natural sciences are still at home in the traditional university departments. Table 8.1 illustrates the differences and relations among the three major disciplinary categories in the university.

When asked, students and practitioners from both the common and civil law traditions readily claim that the advantages of his or her respective method and system are expediency, truth-finding, justice, fairness and so on. And each from the outside of the other system can then rationally theorize how the other system does not reach those values and goals, at least not as easily as his or her own system does. But that is the key to recognizing that one learns a second legal system as a part of the culture and thus inherently carried by language in the manner that one learns a spoken language.[60] Just as a native speaker of English can find inefficiency and apparently

[60] See, for example, Vivian Grosswald Curran, *Comparative Law, An Introduction*. Durham, NC: Carolina Academic Press, 2002; James Boyd White, *Justice as Translation*. Chicago, IL: University of Chicago Press, 1990.

unnecessary complication in a more fully declined language, whether it is a romance language or a Saxon language, and a Romance language speaker finds the nuance of English vocabulary overwhelming, these same views from one's base can make it seem that a foreign legal system is inefficient and irrational, or even unjust and unfair.

To be truly scientific, one could survey the actions of common law and civil law systems and create a calculus of variables to compare System A and its citizens' life within it with System B and its citizens' life within it in respect of their desires and expectations, rather than only in respect to the desires and expectations of legal practitioners. Moving the citizens or the system across the equation to the other system would be an unhelpful mixing that suggests that law is somehow detached from the people of the culture that produced it.[61]

In short, common law lawyers are advocates whose historical and contemporary skill development has a pedigree in the discipline of rhetoric, while civil law lawyers are inquirers whose historical and contemporary skill development is social science. The fact that both can claim to be fair and advance justice with these differing systems is because the citizens in these differing systems have themselves different cultural expectations of their legal systems, based upon the history and social fabric of the respective cultures. This audience-centered way of determining meaning is of course itself from a rhetorical worldview.[62]

We might answer the question of what lies at the center of our discipline by saying it is an attitude—a "legal-centric attitude," which itself could be defined as having an orientation toward social problems that comes only from the law itself. When I taught U.S. law students a course in legal ethics, I told them that when a person comes to them and explains a problem, one of the potential answers must be "sorry, I cannot help you with this problem," because the law provides no solution. If that is not a potential answer, then he or she was practicing law unethically. Assuming that a lawyer can find a solution to all problems is an attitude problem of legal-centrism, but may be at the same time an attitude that defines the discipline. In some ways, this critique of U.S. legal practice is not new. The legal realism of Holmes and others,[63] of which I spoke through the philosophical reference frame, connected law with "social purposes, political interests and problems of language/writing."[64] After legal realism, it was sociological jurisprudence that made similar critiques and demands on the practice of law and on legal education.

8.6 Conclusion

August Comte concluded his famous work on positive philosophy with the notion that after we have reduced all of human thought from social physics to the most

---

[61] See Brian Friel, *Translations*. New York: Samuel French, 1981 and White, *supra* note 60.

[62] See, for example, Kenneth Burke, "Rhetoric Old and New," 5 *Journal of General Education* 3 (1951) 202; Trevor Melia, 83 "Essay Review" *Isis* (1992) 100.

[63] See Jerome Frank, *Law and the Modern Mind*. New York: Brentano's, 1930; Karl Llewellyn, "Some Realism about Realism," 44 *Harv. L. Rev.* (1930–31) 1222.

[64] Frankenberg, *supra* note 27 at 446.

axiomatic—mathematics—we are still left with the need of a person and discipline that can speak among the disciplines and coordinate their communication. While many people may operate according to the ideology of positivism, they likely have not digested it as a complete program. Consequently, we have not heeded that final requirement of Comte's positivism and instead, delve further and further into specialization. While one cannot claim to have avoided the perils of being a specialist of one sort looking into a phenomenon from areas that are not in his specialty, one can at least do some work in those foreign areas. In short, a lawyer's perspective looking at law is not enough, not even for the daily practitioner of law. On a more personal note, having been a member of natural science, social science, law and humanities faculties, I learned from perspectives at faculty meetings and professional meetings, as well as from literature, colleagues and students, even if I am not schooled to the terminal degree in so many fields.

CHECK YOUR UNDERSTANDING:

1. Where and when was the trivium, taught in the English university?
2. How often did a practicing barrister study rhetoric before going to the inns?
3. When did law join the English university?
4. Was law in the English university when the United States developed?

Literature

Baker, J. H., *The Common Law Tradition*. London: The Hambledon Press, 2000.

Berman, Harold J., *Law and Revolution: The Formation of the Western Legal Tradition*. Cambridge, MA: Harvard University Press, 1983.

Berman, Harold J., *Law and Revolution II: The Impact of the Protestant Reformation on the Western Legal Tradition*. Cambridge, MA: Harvard University Press, 2006.

Bernal, Martin, *Black Athena: Afroasiatic Roots of Classical Civilization, Volume I: The Fabrication of Ancient Greece, 1785–1985*. New Brunswick, NJ: Rutgers University Press, 1987.

Bernal, Martin, *Black Athena: Afroasiatic Roots of Classical Civilization, Volume II : The Archaeological and Documentary Evidence*. New Brunswick, NJ: Rutgers University Press, 1991.

Bernal, Martin, *Black Athena: Afroasiatic Roots of Classical Civilization, Volume III : The Linguistic Evidence*. New Brunswick, NJ: Rutgers University Press, 2006.

Bobbit, Philip, *Wittgenstein and Law*. Ed. Dennis Patterson. Aldershot: Ashgate, 2004.

Coquillete, Daniel, *The Anglo-American Legal Heritage*. 2nd ed. Durham, NC: Carolina Academic Press, 2004.

Corbett, Edward P. J. and Robert J. Connors, *Classical Rhetoric for the Modern Student*, 4th ed. Oxford: Oxford University Press, 1999.

Curran, Vivian Grosswald, *Comparative Law, An Introduction*. Durham, NC: Carolina Academic Press, 2002.

Frankenberg, Günter, "Critical Comparison, Re-Thinking Comparative Law," 26 *Harv. Int'l L. J.* (1985). 411.

Friedman, Lawrence M., *A History of American Law*. 2nd ed. New York: Touchstone, 1986.

Frost, Michael H., *Introduction to Classical Legal Rhetoric: A Lost Heritage*. Aldershot and Burlington, VT: Ashgate, 2005.

Holmes, Oliver Wendell Jr., *The Common Law*. Boston, MA: Little Brown and Co., 1881.

Holmes, Oliver Wendell Jr., "The Path of Law," 10 *Harv. L. Rev.* (1897). 457.

Junker, Kirk W., "Rhetoric Demonstrates the Foundation of Law Practice as Techne, not Empeiria," in Konstantine Boudouris, ed. *Philosophy, Art and Technology*. Athens: Ionia Publications, 2011. 99–114.

Kempin, Frederick G. Jr., *Historical Introduction to Anglo-American Law*. St. Paul, MN: West, 1990.

McLuhan, Marshall, *Understanding Media: The Extensions of Man*. New York: McGraw Hill, 1964.

Schauer, Frederick, *Thinking Like a Lawyer: A New Introduction to Legal Reasoning*. Cambridge, MA: Harvard University Press, 2009.

White, James Boyd, *Justice as Translation*. Chicago, IL: University of Chicago Press, 1990.

Whitehead, Alfred North, *Process and Reality*. New York: Free Press, 1979.

9

THE MECHANISTIC REFERENCE FRAME

Framing Issues

> 1. What substantive law does a U.S. Federal Court apply when it is adjudicating a state law case through diversity of citizenship jurisdiction?
> 2. What is the legal relationship among the states once a law is made or a conflict is resolved?

9.1 Mechanics

Here in the last chapter, this book will end where books that summarize the laws and legal institutions of the U.S. begin.[1] And so if I have been successful, after someone from outside the United States is comfortable with the cultural concepts presented in this book, he or she should be ready to learn and study those rules of law and institutions in the context of U.S. legal culture. This book began by making the point that if the practice of law is founded upon the ability to predict outcomes of conflicts, then one might well expect the law to work like a social science with theories (if not hypotheses), facts, applications and outcomes that produce reliable guides for prediction. But as we have seen in the preceding chapters, there is much that is necessary to the practice of law that is based upon the culture in which the law operates, not upon social science mechanics. If we found the social science

---

[1] See e.g. Margaret Johns and Rex R. Perschbacher, *The United States Legal System, An Introduction*. Durham, NC: Carolina Academic Press, 2007; Peter Hay, *Law of the United States*. Brussels: Bruylant 2010; Alan B. Morrison, ed. *Fundamentals of American Law*. New York: Oxford University Press, 1996; Gerald McAlinn et al, *An Introduction to American Law*. Durham, NC: Carolina Academic Press, 2005; Alberto Benitez, *An Introduction to the United States Legal System*. Durham, NC: Carolina Academic Press, 2006.

elements upon a base of cultural elements, we might get some way toward a predictive legal science, but will we produce a confidence level high enough to generate real predictability? How can we know culture in such a way that we are able to predict how conflict is resolved? Through the tool of cultural reference frames, this book has been an attempt to allow the reader from outside U.S. culture the opportunity for some cultural insights, so that he or she can better understand the cultural base upon which the mechanics of the social science of the law are based when resolving conflict. Having considered history, society, language, philosophy and disciplinarity as being the reference frames through which one can study U.S. legal culture, one may begin to apply concrete examples from the mechanics of legal practice to them.

If we had ignored those cultural features and had proceeded instead directly to the application of U.S. constitutions, statutes, regulations and cases to facts, we would be using the common technique of lawyers looking at the social phenomenon of conflict through only the reference frame of the law itself. In short, it would be law looking at law. I call this application the mechanistic reference frame. It is law explaining itself in such a way that the understanding of a legal system is treated as a matter of knowing the sources of law and institutions of law and it is the way of seeing law through a sense that law is mechanical—law is the application of facts to rules. For the U.S. legal culture, however, the reader who has read the preceding chapters will have far more tools available for understanding the cultural context of the mechanisms, rather than just memorizing the mechanisms themselves.

In this final chapter, I want to look at "U.S. law," artificial though the category may be, through the legal-mechanistic reference frame, but in doing so, use some of the themes from the other cultural reference frames to help the reader to approach U.S. legal mechanics with some cultural understanding. Further, rather than look at those mechanisms with a top-down deductive approach, I will present those elements of legal practice from the bottom up, that is, from the perspective of conflict resolution as encountered by the practicing lawyer. To do so, rather than attempt to offer the litany of substantive law that even survey books offer, I offer here only several examples that are both significant to the legal practitioner and that lend themselves to better understanding through the previous background in U.S. legal culture. In respect of my own admonition earlier in the book that common law lawyers work inductively and begin from conflict resolution, rather than first abstract principles, I will present the following selection of mechanics from that position, beginning with pre-trial discovery, and then proceeding to the lay jury, the trial, the doctrine of *stare decisis*, and finally, federalism. There are many others that could be included as well, such as class actions, oaths, the lawyers' fee structures, plea bargaining and the bail system in criminal cases. These should be investigated by the student as well and the need for that study would fit into the natural scientist's common phrase at the end of an investigation—"more research is necessary." The final point of introduction that needs to be made regarding these mechanisms is that the treatment of the mechanisms that follows is not meant to be exhaustive of all aspects of each mechanism as such, but rather to be illustrative of how one can see a legal culture's various reference frames within the mechanisms of the practice of law themselves.

9.2 Discovery

Part of the adversarial system is the notion that justice is best served when both parties to litigation can present the best case possible. To assist that process, the common law provides for "discovery" in the United States and a related process called "disclosure" in England and Wales. In these processes, the discovery or disclosure of the facts known to the other parties in litigation is made possible before trial. The adversarial legal culture values the idea that for a fair trial to proceed, each side should know the full picture of the facts. There are several purposes for permitting the practice of pretrial discovery, including to preserve evidence of witnesses who may not be available at the time of trial; to reveal facts; to aid in formulating the issues; to freeze testimony in writing prior to trial so as to prevent perjury during trial, and to prepare a case for the practice known as "summary judgment." Summary judgment is a practice through which a court may end a case before trial when the parties agree on the facts or disclose all relevant facts during discovery. In such cases, the court has no need of a trial, and can apply the discovered or agreed facts to the law and make a decision without trial.

One of the goals of discovery in the U.S. system is to make trials more efficient. This is a concept that is in fact quite consistent with the original idea of the English writ system of standardizing and regularizing pleading so as to limit and streamline legal practice before the crown. The legal culture's value of judicial efficiency is also served by discovery, as announced in Rule 1 of the Federal Rules of Civil Procedure (F.R.C.P.), wherein it states that the Rules are to be interpreted for judicial efficiency. Since discovery is governed by the F.R.C.P. (specifically F.R.C.P. 26–36), discovery is therefore to be interpreted to serve, among other values, judicial efficiency. So the twin aims of discovery are to provide for a fair method by which the parties can know as much of the facts as possible before trial (thus encouraging settlement of the conflict) and if settlement is not possible, to make litigation as efficient as possible (thus using fewer of the state's resources). Is discovery effective in attaining its goals? We know that the overwhelming number of cases settle or are otherwise disposed of rather than actually going to trial.[2]

The U.S. concept and procedure of discovery is often discussed by practitioners from outside the U.S. system for several reasons. First, U.S. Courts will allow U.S. parties to serve discovery requests on alien parties both inside the U.S. and outside the U.S. Consequently, many non-U.S. lawyers are faced with being told by U.S. Courts that they are required to provide data to a party opponent in the United States. At this point of course the non-U.S. lawyer needs to know whether he or she must do so, and if so, what information must be provided. Another reason that

---

[2] See generally Marc Galanter, "A World Without Trials," 2006 *J. Disp. Resol.* (2006) 7.

U.S. discovery is often discussed is less practical and more scholarly—why does the United States have such a system when other countries do not? Even the common law mother ship—the United Kingdom—has only the disclosure of documents, and does not extend disclosure to depositions, interrogatories, requests for admissions, mental or physical examinations, or the entry and inspection of land, as does U.S. discovery.

The mechanics of discovery are easy enough to name and understand. In the U.S., disclosure is the mandatory process by which a party is required to make known to the other parties the facts known prior to trial that support allegations made in the pleadings, without having to be asked by an opposing party. A deposition involves the questioning of a witness under oath by opposing counsel, at the demand of the opposing party, prior to trial and recorded in what is referred to as a transcript. Interrogatories are written questions asking for an opposing party to provide the factual evidence that supports the legal claims made in that party's pleadings before trial. A request for production of documents is usually attached to interrogatories and functions as a request to a party who answers interrogatories by reference to documents to provide copies of those documents to the opponent. A request for admissions is a set of statements of fact asserted by an opposing party, which the responding party must either admit or deny. There are many, many sources to which a lawyer or law student can turn for a thorough and extended discussion of these mechanics. F.R.C.P. 26(b) describes what may be discovered under the Federal Rules. Unless discovery has been otherwise limited by a protective order of the court, a party may discover any matter that is (1) relevant to a claim or defense; (2) reasonably calculated to lead to discovery of admissible evidence; (3) not privileged; and (4) does not constitute the lawyer's work product. As of December 2015, the F.R.C.P. were amended to restrict discovery and place it more closely under judicial management. This is only the latest in a series of changes to restrict discovery.

As was mentioned in prior chapters, cultures tend to think that the features of their legal cultures are in some way "normal" or "natural," and the U.S. legal culture is no exception to this tendency. Thus, within U.S. legal culture, the concept of discovery seems to be normal or natural. That tendency in general, and the surfacing of that tendency during discovery in particular, raises some important questions for an alien[3] party who finds himself compelled to U.S. litigation due to having visited or done business in the United States. It is generally the case of course that if one volunteers to enter another jurisdiction, for business or pleasure, one has implicitly "volunteered" not only to obey that jurisdiction's laws in the sense of prohibited

---

[3] While "alien" may seem like an exaggerated choice of words here, it is a legal term of art needed in the U.S. federal legal system, and the fifty state legal systems, when one needs to distinguish citizens from other U.S. states from parties who are not U.S. citizens. The reason reminds us of the legal power and independence of U.S. states: in U.S. law, especially concerning jurisdiction, one uses the term "foreign" to refer to a person from another state, so that for example a Virginian is "foreign" to Maryland. That leaves U.S. legal language with no alternative but to call persons from outside all of the states and the federation something different—hence, "alien."

acts, but also in the sense of observing procedural norms if there should be some conflict to settle. Persons of the twenty-first century seem to become more and more oblivious to this fact the more easily we are able to travel to, trade with and communicate with persons in other jurisdictions. It leads us to expect that some sort of "legal Esperanto" is at work in those other places in which we travel and do business, or even worse, we just feel we can take our home legal system with us abroad, because it is "normal" or "natural." And as if all this were not enough to present litigation surprises to people travelling or working internationally, the United States has a particularly strong idea of how legitimate the "long arm" of its law may extend beyond its own borders. With all this in play—implicit subjection to alien jurisdictions, legal globalization assumptions, and long-arm control outside the territory—the U.S. discovery tool, regardless of how odd it may seem to persons outside the United States, will be used as aggressively as permitted once one is subject to U.S. jurisdiction.

The states of the world have pondered this situation longer than the casual tourist or superficial business, however, and attempted to solve it through international private law; specifically The Convention on the Taking of Evidence Abroad in Civil or Commercial Matters,[4] Article 1 of which allows a judicial authority of one state to request the competent authority of another state to request assistance in obtaining evidence. Article 9 of the same convention provides that the authority executing the request "shall apply its own law as to the methods and procedures to be followed." In practice, that means an alien litigant could make use of U.S. discovery if litigating against a U.S. party who has discoverable evidence in the United States.

As a signatory state to the Hague Convention, the United States transposes its obligation through federal statutory law, 28 U.S.C. §1728, which allows a litigating party in a legal proceeding outside the United States to apply to a U.S. court to obtain evidence for use in the non-U.S. proceeding.[5] Specifically, §1782(a) provides:

> The district court of the district in which a person resides or is found may order him to give his testimony or statement or to produce a document or other thing for use in a proceeding in a foreign or international tribunal, including criminal investigations conducted before formal accusation. The order may be made pursuant to a letter rogatory issued, or request made, by a foreign or international tribunal or upon the application of any interested person. ... The order may prescribe the practice and procedure, which may be in whole or part the practice and procedure of the foreign country or the international tribunal, for taking the testimony or statement or producing the document or other thing. To the extent that the order does not

---

[4] Hague Convention on the Taking of Evidence Abroad in Civil or Commercial Matters, 23 U.S.T. 2555; T.I.A.S. 7444; 847 U.N.T.S. 231; reprinted in 8 I.L.M. 37 (1969).

[5] Looking back to the lessons from comparative law in Chapter 2, the various ways in which the signatory states to the Hague Convention have transposed its obligations into national law would be a worthy and practical project in comparison both for the practitioner and the student who wishes to see the limits of functionality.

prescribe otherwise, the testimony or statement shall be taken, and the document or other thing produced, in accordance with the Federal Rules of Civil Procedure. A person may not be compelled to give his testimony or statement or to produce a document or other thing in violation of any legally applicable privilege.[6]

But more commonly, a problem occurs when an alien party is brought into U.S. litigation, and a request is sent to alien authorities asking that they follow U.S. discovery procedure. U.S. litigants and courts will often take the typical legal position that if one has found it of benefit to be in the United States for work or pleasure, one has submitted oneself to U.S. jurisdiction, should litigation arise. And if one subjects oneself to U.S. litigation, one will be required to participate in discovery, regardless of whether the discovery procedure is contrary to an alien's expectations at home. So long as the U.S. maintains this practice through its F.R.C.P., as its legal-cultural sense of long-arm jurisdictional reach, U.S. litigants and courts will expect aliens to comply with discovery requests. It remains in dispute, however, whether under the Hague Convention U.S. litigants and courts must adjust expectations even when litigating at home, or whether they are justified in expecting compliance with F.R.C.P.-governed discovery.[7]

Regionally, the attempts of U.S. litigants and courts to obtain facts through discovery are rejected most explicitly by European data protection law. Chapter IV, "Transfer of Personal Data to Third Countries," of European Directive 95/46/EC on the protection of individuals with regard to the processing of personal data and on the free movement of such data is most relevant. The Article 29 Data Protection Working Party was organized under the first article of Chapter IV of the Directive to consider reform of EU legislation. This has become an especially sharp disagreement concerning electronic data. Legislation has been proposed to change the Directive.[8]

9.3 Lay Juries

As was foreshadowed at the end of Chapter 3, we now return to a discussion of the lay jury in U.S. legal culture. To understand the lay jury in U.S. law, one must compare it in the context of the role of the laity in other legal systems, rather than in some sort of rational bubble removed from the facts of other times and other places. So, for instance, in the German and Austrian legal systems, lay persons are routinely part of the court, and in panels of two laity to one professional judge, or three laity to two professional judges, can outvote the professional judges in criminal and civil

---

[6] 28 U.S.C. §1728(a).

[7] Anke Meier, "U.S. Discovery: The German Perspective," *Zeitschrift der Deutsch-Amerikanischen Juristen-Vereinigung e. V*, 10 (March 2012).

[8] See Article 29, Data Protection Working Party, 00339/09/EN, WP 158, Working Document 1/2009 on pretrial discovery for cross-border civil litigation, http://ec.europa.eu/justice_home/fsj/privacy/index_en.hm (last accessed 13 November 2015).

cases.[9] In the common law system, Frederick Maitland defined the jury as a body of neighbors summoned under oath by a public official to answer questions.[10] In the United States, "trial by jury continues to play a critical role in the civil justice system in resolving intractable disputes and in promoting public trust and confidence in the courts."[11]

Professor Stephen Goldstein has gone so far as to say that in his view, the explanation for the extraordinary nature of the common law trial, "is the use—or at least the historic use—of the jury in the common law procedure."[12] The connection between the jury and the spirit of the common law trial has been recognized by a number of different scholars. However, the literature as a whole has not given sufficient emphasis to the fact that the common law trial, as we know it, is a direct result of the use of the jury. Without the common law jury, there would be no common law trial. Jeremy Lever, who as Dean of Oxford's All Souls College and Queen's Counsel, wrote that upon reading this characterization of the connection between jury and trial by Professor Goldstein, "the scales fell from my eyes."[13]

What is especially impressive about the importance assigned to the jury in this discussion is that it comes at a time when the role of the jury, especially in England, is at an all-time low:

> At least in England and other common law jurisdictions that have largely if not entirely abandoned jury trial in civil cases, the jury is a phantom limb which, though no longer present, profoundly affects the behavior of the body of which it used to be a part.[14]

Judge David Edwards concludes that the "the inherent characteristics of the jury system explain why common lawyers are so 'fact-oriented.'"[15]

Given the fact that the United States does use lay juries, and that the theater-like drama performances of lawyers, witnesses and judges before these juries is fertile ground for screenwriters and film directors, it is not surprising that U.S. citizens

---

[9] While in practice the *Schöffen* (lay judges) most often agree with, or even defer to, the professional judges, that does not alter the construction of the legal system. American judges may guide a lay jury with instructions or set aside a lay jury's conclusion (judgment non obstante verdict).

[10] Frederick G. Kempin, *Historical Introduction to Anglo-American Law*. 3rd. ed. St. Paul, MN: West Publishing, 1990 54.

[11] National Center for State Courts, "Civil Action," volume 6, no. 1, (Summer 2007) 1.

[12] Stephen Goldstein (as quoted by Jeremy Lever, in "Why Procedure is More Important Than Substantive Law," 48 *Int'l & Comp. L. Q.* 285, 295 (April 1999)).

[13] Jeremy Lever, "Why Procedure is More Important Than Substantive Law," 48 *Int'l and Comp. L. Q.* (April 1999) 285, 294, fn 10.

[14] *Ibid.* at 296.

[15] David Edwards, "Fact-Finding: A British Perspective," in D. L. Carey Miller and Paul R. Beaumont (eds.), *The Option of Litigating in Europe*. London: United Kingdom Committee of Comparative Law, 1993 54.

and foreigners alike might believe that most conflict in U.S. legal systems ends with a trial by jury. That is clearly not true. There are many important legal ideas about which one must be clear in order to understand the use of the jury. First one needs to be clear about the path of a case. Criminal cases and civil cases have different paths, although both might eventually be put before a jury. Second, one must keep in mind the federal structure of the United States and the dominant presence of the state judicial systems. When considering juries, although the U.S. Constitution does make minimal provisions, the one federal and fifty state court systems, divided by civil and criminal divisions, produce 102 interpretations of how and when juries are provided. Moreover, the simple fact that a jury might be available in a given case does not mean it must be used—the parties will decide, and those decisions, as well as local nuances of court administration, mean that even if two states had the same jury system, the actual use of it might differ considerably.

The U.S. constitutional guarantee to a trial by jury is only in Amendments VI and VII. Amendment VI provides as follows:

> In all criminal prosecutions, the accused shall enjoy the right to a speedy and public trial, by an impartial jury of the State and district wherein the crime shall have been committed, which district shall have been previously ascertained by law, and to be informed of the nature and cause of the accusation; to be confronted with the witnesses against him; to have compulsory process for obtaining witnesses in his favor, and to have the assistance of counsel for his defense.

Amendment VII continues the English practice of distinguishing cases in civil matters that must be heard by a jury from those that can be heard by a judge alone. It applies only to federal courts, not state courts:

> In suits at common law, where the value in controversy shall exceed twenty dollars, the right of trial by jury shall be preserved, and no fact tried by a jury, shall be otherwise reexamined in any court of the United States, than according to the rules of the common law.

Amendment VII does not apply in a state court even when a litigant is enforcing a right created by federal law. However, the state constitutions may, and usually do, provide the right to trial by jury in civil cases.

These provisions leave many issues to be answered by legislatures or courts: What does the Amendment VI right to a trial by jury in criminal cases mean? What is "a jury"? Must a jury have twelve members, or is six or fewer sufficient? Must juries be unanimous in their decisions to convict a criminal defendant? Could someone be convicted instead by a vote of seven jurors against five who wish to acquit?

In addition, some of the U.S. constitutional guarantees are granted to persons in state court through Amendment XIV, which states in paragraph 1:

All persons born or naturalized in the United States, and subject to the jurisdiction thereof, are citizens of the United States and of the State wherein they reside. No State shall make or enforce any law which shall abridge the privileges or immunities of citizens of the United States; nor shall any State deprive any person of life, liberty, or property, without due process of law; nor deny to any person within its jurisdiction the equal protection of the laws.

This paragraph has been used by the U.S. Courts to "incorporate" the rights of the Sixth Amendment to the persons appearing before state courts.

So that is the doctrine. But despite the books and books that are written on various interpretations of what the doctrine is or should be, there are the empirical facts of how often Americans do in fact make use of juries, as opposed to the depictions one might see in popular culture. Once a complaint is filed (or one of the other less common methods of commencing litigation), it is possible to begin keeping statistics. Based upon its own survey, the National Center for State Courts' Center for Jury Studies[16] revealed some important facts. State courts conduct an estimated 46,200 civil trials annually and federal courts conduct an additional 2,100 civil jury trials. Combined, these comprise slightly less than one-third (31 percent) of all jury trials in the U.S. courts each year. That means the other 69 percent are criminal. The statistics alone generally do not tell us "why?" although "[o]verall, the civil and criminal jury trial rates are strongly correlated, which suggests that state court rules, local practices, and the prevailing legal culture in each state do not disproportionately encourage or discourage civil trials relative to criminal trials in most states."[17] Different state cultures do use civil jury trials with great variation, however. Hawaii, for example, has only 24 trials per 100,000 persons and Alabama has 59.2 trials per 100,000 persons on average.

Furthermore, in federal courts, tort trials between 1970 and 2003 steadily declined from 2,526 to 768, but the total number of tort cases steadily increased from 25,451 to 49,166.[18] Melding the two trends together, we see that the percentage of tort cases in federal court that actually go to trial fell steadily from 10 percent in 1970 to just 2 percent by 2003.

But how many cases go to trial at all? A recent U.S. Department of Justice report shows that in state trial courts (where most civil trials happen) only about 4 percent of all tort cases begun were concluded in trials. If, however, tort cases did make it to trial, 90 percent were heard by juries. Still, that means legal conflicts are most often disposed of without juries (97.4 percent of the time, to be precise).[19] Also of interest

---

[16] The full report of the State-of-the-States Survey of Jury Improvement Efforts is available at www.ncsc-jurystudies.org/State-of-the-States-Survey.aspx (last accessed 19 November 2015).

[17] National Center for State Courts, *supra* note 11.

[18] Bureau of Justice Statistics, Key Facts at a Glance, Federal Tort Trials and Verdicts, 2002–03, NCJ 208713.

[19] Thomas H. Cohen, "Tort Bench and Jury Trials in State Courts, 2005," U.S. Department of Justice, Office of Justice Programs, Bureau of Justice Statistics, Bureau of Justice Statistics Bulletin, November 2009, NCJ 228129, 1.

from this Department of Justice study are such statistics as: nearly 60 percent of tort trials were automobile cases, plaintiffs won about half of all tort trials, half of plaintiff winners in tort trials were awarded $24,000 or less in damages (contrary to the conservative talk-show favorite theme of "runaway juries" and the need therefore of tort reform), and punitive damages, a U.S. oddity, were sought (not necessarily awarded) in only 9 percent of tort trials. The median punitive damage award was $55,000.[20] The United States Department of Justice found:

> [t]he number of tort trials concluded in state courts in the nation's 75 most populous counties declined by about a third from 10,278 trials in 1996 to 7,038 trials in 2005.[21] Within that timeframe, data from the two most recent Bureau of Justice Statistics civil trial surveys revealed stabilization in the number of tort trials. From 2001 to 2005, the number of tort trials concluded in the nation's 75 most populous counties declined by only 12%, which Cohen regards as "a decrease that was not statistically significant."[22]

9.4 The Trial

When U.S. lawyers talk about a "trial," what exactly do they mean? At first glance, this might seem like a banal question. But my experience and that of my colleagues in civil law cultures demonstrates that the U.S. lawyer's notion of a trial is very different from the proceedings before the court in a civil law state. One of my German colleagues recently reported his frustration at having arrived in court only to have the case postponed. When I asked why the case was postponed, he reported that when the judge asked if everyone had read the expert report, one of the parties' lawyers said he had not because he "had not had time" and the judge responded by delaying the proceeding, saying it did not make sense to proceed until everyone had read the report. That relaxed nature of proceeding would be unthinkable in U.S. legal culture. With such anecdotes in mind, another colleague with experience in both the U.S. and German systems has gone so far as to describe German civil litigaton as a "series of semi-formal meetings," when compared with U.S. civil litigation.

The U.S. system's use of advocacy makes the observance of rules of evidence and procedure[23] strictly enforced to ensure fairness to both sides of the conflict. The driving and guiding force in U.S. legal practice is to question what will happen if this issue of conflict proceeds to trial. This sense of hard and formal testing is in the back of the mind of both litigation lawyers and transaction lawyers. Transaction lawyers know that if their transaction runs into problems or conflict, they cannot avoid trial if

---

[20] *Ibid.*
[21] *Ibid* at 12.
[22] *Ibid.*
[23] A useful project for comparative law would be to examine why the United States has separate codes for evidence and procedure, whereas Germany, for example, combines the ideas in one code.

the other party pushes to exercise that right. Once while working for a state agency's Bureau of Litigation, I reflected with my colleagues on how many cases we settled compared to the relatively few number that went to trial. We concluded that a more accurate title of the office might have been the "Bureau of the *Threat* of Litigation." We were not alone in our experience of settling conflicts more often than taking them to trial, nor were we alone, however, in our forever-conscious sense of what would happen if the matter did not settle and did go to trial.

By the time a case gets to trial, it is too late to go back and do the proper and binding preparation through discovery, pleadings and pretrial motions. Often these pretrial processes in litigation function to encourage one or both parties to settle the litigation because one or both parties have the weaknesses as well as the strengths of their positions made clear. Consequently, as was mentioned in previous chapters, relatively few disputes in the culture are ultimately resolved at trial. Settlement is just one alternative. Rather than go down the path of litigation at all, parties may instead choose other alternatives such as mediation or arbitration. Collectively, they are referred to as "alternative dispute resolution," or simply "A.D.R." These alternative processes, especially negotiation, are used far more frequently. Even disputes among lawyers themselves are more often resolved by negotiation than litigation.[24]

Given the variety of alternatives to litigation some of which might even be informal, it becomes nearly impossible to quantify the frequency with which alternatives to litigation are chosen. It is clear, however, that the advantages of A.D.R. have even been recognized by the courts themselves. Thus, in one form or another, A.D.R. was formally offered by more than two-thirds, or 63 of 94, of the federal district courts in 2004. At the appellate level, all thirteen federal districts implemented mediation or settlement programs.[25] And the process of mediation (sometimes referred to as conference or settlement conference) is explicitly included in Federal Rule of Civil Procedure 16, regarding pretrial conferences.[26] Generally, mediation is a consultation, by the parties,

---

[24] Stephen J. Ware, *Principles of Alternative Dispute Resolution*. St. Paul, MN: West Academic Publishing, 2007 § 1.5.

[25] Mediation & Conference Programs in the Federal Courts of Appeals, https://bulk. resource.org/courts.gov/fjc/medicon2.pdf (last accessed 21 May 2015).

[26] Federal Rule of Civil Procedure 16, in relevant part states:

  (a) **Purposes of a Pretrial Conference.** In any action, the court may order the attorneys and any unrepresented parties to appear for one or more pretrial conferences for such purposes as:
    (1) expediting disposition of the action;
    (2) establishing early and continuing control so that the case will not be protracted because of lack of management;
    (3) discouraging wasteful pretrial activities;
    (4) improving the quality of the trial through more thorough preparation; and
    (5) facilitating settlement....
  (1) *Attendance.* A represented party must authorize at least one of its attorneys to make stipulations and admissions about all matters that can reasonably be anticipated for discussion at a pretrial conference. If appropriate, the court may require that a party or its representative be present or reasonably available by other means to consider possible settlement.

with a neutral mediator, seeking a settlement, thus sparing the time and expense of litigation. Arbitration, a process agreed by the parties through contract, can be legally binding; therefore, whatever decision the neutral arbitrator comes to, will likely be enforced by all courts.

Alternative dispute resolution is most common in commercial, family, employment, bankruptcy, foreclosure, and elder law cases. Commercial disputes are the most common to be put into mediation: in the U.S. Court of Appeals for the Third Circuit, for example, nearly all cases are eligible for its mediation program except for cases where parties are not represented, are original proceedings, prisoner petitions, social security cases, immigration cases or black lung cases.[27] Because family law is handled at the state level, the means can vary from state to state, but oftentimes court-appointed masters and magistrates are used to expedite family court cases. Alternative dispute resolution also provides the opportunity for parties to state their personal feelings to the neutral mediator or arbitrator; this can be especially useful in resolving often emotional employment and elder law issues where, going outside the traditional courtroom, parties may be willing to come to a settlement sooner.

While mediation exists in commercial, employment, bankruptcy, foreclosure, and elder law, it also has a role (though limited) in criminal law. The goals, within at least the civil law areas, are to settle cases through facilitated negotiations, help litigation achieve more dynamic outcomes, conserve judicial resources and improve case management. In the sphere of criminal law, formal A.D.R. exists primarily in the form of "victim-offender mediation."[28] Like the peace and reconciliation process made internationally known from South Africa, these programs, unlike litigation, allow the victim actively to participate in his or her own interest to resolve the conflict, rather than just to act as a witness for the state's interest in prosecution. The mediation allows victims to open a dialogue with offenders, thereby granting a feeling of security to the parties, and assisting the parties in creating a restitution plan. While these programs sometimes offer case facilitation and closure for victims, they are distinguished from other forms of A.D.R. programs because of the fact that they are used in criminal matters. The use of A.D.R. in criminal matters presents the problem of whether an accused receives his or her constitutionally guaranteed "due process" of law. The constitutional due process guarantee might be violated if the A.D.R. is not genuinely voluntary or if offenders may not receive the same access to an attorney. In addition, the constitutional rights of the accused may be violated if the objectives of the mediation are unclear or not uniform or there is no guarantee of confidentiality. There can also be an unwillingness or refusal from the courts to enforce agreements due to sentencing or other legal requirements.[29] Nevertheless, there are over 120 such mediation programs in existence in the United States. Most

---

[27] Mediation & Conference Programs in the Federal Courts of Appeals, *supra* note 25.
[28] Jack Hanna, "Mediation in Criminal Matters," 15 *Disp. Resol. Mag.* (2008) 4, 5.
[29] See generally Jennifer Gerarda Brown, "The Use of Mediation to Resolve Criminal Cases: A Procedural Critique," 43 *Emory L. J.* (1994) 1247, 1283.

are found in state not federal criminal processes because the federal process has more fixed criminal sentencing requirements.[30]

Why is the threat of litigation such a driving force? A trial conducted by adversarial advocates is a very different animal than a trial conducted by a neutral inquisitor. The differences go far beyond simply identifying who is asking the questions. When we shift the burden of knowing the evidence that supports both sides to the role of the advocate, there is great pressure on him or her to discover the evidence, be able to prove the evidence within the rules, and defend the selection and presentation of evidence against an adversary, all the while remaining an officer of the court and supporter of a system that should provide justice to all parties. To accomplish this, an advocate must spend considerable time prior to trial interviewing witnesses, conducting discovery (in a civil case) and being ready for the moment when the trial begins to call witnesses through whom evidence is produced such that, when held against the rule of law, it will determine that justice favors his or her client.

Popular culture likes to use the adversarial trial as the scene of drama, and a disproportionate number of U.S. television shows and films concern themselves with trials. In fact, there are so many that the sub-genre of "courtroom drama" is now well known. The popular culture courtroom drama features almost exclusively criminal trials. Anyone who has ever participated in a civil trial would notice why. While crimes involve facts that everyone can understand and issues of morality that touch all lives, civil cases are often technical and perhaps even boring reviews of documents, and the rules for procedure and the admission of evidence interfere with a clean and fast-moving dramatic narrative. Yet popular culture does give a person who has never been in a U.S. courtroom some insight into the timing and pressures of the events of a trial in the U.S. litigation system. Unfortunately, the dramatic narrative is often framed in metaphors of sport or war. This might well be the inevitable outcome of a system that puts the power of selecting and proving evidence in the hands of the adversaries who must use the system both offensively and defensively to obtain justice for their clients. Recall from the language reference frame what Wittgenstein said: the limits of one's language are the limits of one's world. Could we lawyers conceive of an adversarial trial without using the framing metaphors of war or sports, which in turn limit our legal world?

9.5 The Doctrine of *Stare Decisis*

It is fitting to come nearly to the end of a book that concerns itself with common law before discussing the notion of *stare decisis*, to "let the decision stand," as we most easily translate the phrase into English. *Stare decisis* is based upon the inductive process of solving problems individually in order to arrive at some

---

[30] Carrie Menkel-Meadow, "Restorative Justice: What is it and Does it Work?" 3 *Annu. Rev. Law Soc. Sci.* (2007) 161, 168.

generalization, just as one might do after thinking through the cultural reference frames before looking to solve conflicts in the U.S. law cultural setting. In making the title of this subsection, I placed the words "*stare decisis*" in italics because of the convention in English to place foreign words in italics. But it occurs to me that it might be far more important to put the word "doctrine" in italics, instead of using the italics to emphasize, for it should indeed be emphasized that *stare decisis* is only a *doctrine*. Once a series of words have been written and gone through a culture's process of calling those words "the law," it will still be necessary when settling a conflict (the courts) or enforcing the law "as written" (the executive) to say what the law *means*. Legislative bodies attempt to control interpretation of their words through further legislative acts, called rules of statutory construction.[31] The courts have not only the rules of statutory construction, but also their own precedent from prior cases.

The full statement of the doctrine is "*Stare decisis et non quieta movere*," and means "to stand by decisions and not disturb the undisturbed."[32] However, as *stare decisis* is only a *doctrine*, courts can and do legally ignore precedent, especially when it comes to interpreting the U.S. Constitution. In a rather famous dissenting opinion in *Burnet v. Coronado Oil & Gas Co.*, U.S. Supreme Court Justice Louis Brandeis emphasized that "in cases involving the Federal Constitution, where correction through legislative action is practically impossible, this Court has often overruled its earlier decisions. ... This is strikingly true of cases under the due process clause."[33] Indeed, in the years 1946–92, for example, the U.S. Supreme Court reversed itself in about 130 cases. The U.S. Supreme Court has further explained its behavior as follows: "[W]hen convinced of former error, this Court has never felt constrained to follow precedent. In constitutional questions, where correction depends upon amendment, and not upon legislative action, this Court throughout its history has freely exercised its power to reexamine the basis of its constitutional decisions."[34] And in the famous case of *Erie v. Tompkins*, used above to point out the difficulties with federalism, Justice Brandeis wrote "the doctrine of *Swift v. Tyson* is, as Justice Holmes said, 'an unconstitutional assumption of powers by courts of the United States which no lapse of time or respectable array of opinion should make us hesitate to correct.'"[35] This sort of self-reversal makes it very difficult for an outsider, including a practicing lawyer, to predict the outcome of constitutional cases before the U.S. Supreme Court based on the mechanics of law—in this case the doctrine

---

[31] See, for example, the Rules of Construction for U.S. statutes found at 1 U.S.C.A. sections 1 et seq., and for a state example, the Rules of Construction (for Pennsylvania legislation) found at 1 Pa.C.S.A. section 1902 and the presumptions in ascertaining legislative intent, found at 1 Pa.C.S.A. section 1922.

[32] Cf. *stare dictis*, which means "to stand by or keep to what was said" and *stare rationibus decidendi*, meaning "to keep to the *rationes decidendi* of past cases." All of these formulations have been used in some legal system at one time or another.

[33] 285 U.S. 393, 406–07, 410 (1932).

[34] *Smith v. Allwright*, 321 U.S. 649, 665 (1944).

[35] Justice Brandeis quoting Justice Holmes in *Erie Railroad Co. v. Tompkins*, 304 U.S. 64 (1938).

of *stare decisis*—alone. One might study prior case opinions, including the dissents written by the Justices while on the Supreme Court and previously, if they sat on other courts. One might even look to see how these Justices answered questions during their U.S. Senate confirmation hearings to become Supreme Court members. But just as relevant are political beliefs along party lines, the gender, age, race, education and socio-economic background of the Justices, all of which together make it difficult, but not impossible, to have a high degree of confidence in predicting the outcome of a conflict placed before them.

This sense of ignoring precedent is not limited to U.S. Supreme Court behavior. In addressing a conflict in Washington State, the Washington State Supreme Court noted:

> [a]n exception to a rule will be declared by courts when the case is not an isolated instance, but general in its character, and the existing rule does not square with justice. Under such circumstances a court will, if free from the restraint of some statute, declare a rule that will meet the full intendment of the law.[36]

This of course represents a problem both for the statement of law and the practitioner of law—how does one know when a court will follow precedent and when it will decide that there has been "former error" or that the "existing rule does not square with justice?" This is especially troublesome if one accepts that the main test of the lawyer (and what Holmes said he meant by the term "law") is to be able to predict how a court will resolve a conflict brought before it. By sheer number of cases, the problem is not as large as it may seem in theory. While studying the law, U.S. lawyers often read the opinions of the U.S. Supreme Court, but the fact is that one rarely, if ever, appears before the U.S. Supreme Court—it is a court of almost exclusively appellate jurisdiction, and even then only accepts cases for appeal when it wishes to do so, most often based upon one of the old writs (refer back to Chapter 4, the historical reference frame) such as certiorari, to do so. All in all, the U.S. Supreme Court hears about one hundred cases per term with oral argument by lawyers, and writes about eighty to ninety opinions deciding those cases.[37]

Lower federal courts cannot operate nearly so freely to change precedent because on appeal, from District Court to a Circuit Court, or from a Circuit Court to the Supreme Court, the conservative nature of the law would easily allow the higher court to "conserve" past precedent and overrule the new, independent thought of a lower court. As was noted in the philosophical reference frame of Chapter 7, there is substantial empirical research that has questioned for some time the assumption

[36] *Mazetti v. Armour & Co.,* 75 Wash. 622; 135 P. 633, 636; 1913 Wash. LEXIS 1760 (Wa. 1913)
[37] See the U.S. Supreme Court website, www.supremecourt.gov/about/justicecaseload.aspx (last accessed 4 May 2014).

that precedent actually has the authority claimed for it. Many legal scholars have long held that judges respond "not only to legal stimuli but also to a wide range of political … stimuli."[38] A further study concluded, "Supreme Court justices are not influenced by landmark precedents with which they disagree."[39] What the empirical data tends to show, then, is that the classical model does not explain very well the way actual judges decide cases. Another study claimed an 85 percent success rate in prediction of future case decisions based upon a study of the judge's "values."[40]

The legal repercussion for refusing to follow precedent is to have one's judicial decision reversed on appeal. But in addition to the purely "legal" demand for "conservation of precedent," there are also disciplinary and social rules. Judges, like lawyers, must follow a Code of Judicial Conduct, and Rule 2.2 of the Model Code of Judicial Conduct requires that "[a] judge shall uphold and apply the law, and shall perform all duties of judicial office fairly and impartially."[41] A judge who fails to apply case law could face disciplinary actions as a judge, as though he or she had failed to apply statutory law.[42] Moreover, judges, lawyers, students and administrators are all socialized to accept the doctrine of *stare decisis*.[43] One could perhaps psychologize that phenomenon and say that we want predictability so we are complicit in supporting predictability measures that go beyond the rule of law. Were a U.S. law student asked whether a court is *legally* bound to follow precedent, chances are very high that he or she would answer "yes."

[38] Sheldon Goldman, "The Effect of Past Judicial Behavior on Subsequent Decision-Making," 19 *Jurimetrics J.* (1978–1979) 208.

[39] Jeffrey Segal and Harold Spaeth, "The Influence of Stare Decisis on the Votes of Supreme Court Justices," 40 *American Journal of Political Science* (1996) 971.

[40] "Legal Pragmatism," Internet Encyclopedia of Philosophy: A Peer-Reviewed Academic Resource, www.iep.utm.edu/leglprag/ (last accessed 21 May 2014), (citing David W. Rohde and Harold J. Spaeth, *Supreme Court Decision Making*, San Francisco, CA: W. H. Freeman, 1976). See also Jerome Frank, *Courts on Trial: Myth and Reality in American Justice*. Princeton, NJ: Princeton University Press, 1949 *passim*.

[41] The Model Code of Judicial Conduct was adopted by the House of Delegates of the American Bar Association in 1990, and amended several times, most recently in 2010.

[42] See, for example, *In the Matter of Hague*, 315 N.W. 2d. 524 (Mich. 1982). In *Hague*, a trial court judge in Michigan had refused on several occasions to apply the law as interpreted by the Court of Appeals of that state. The Supreme Court of Michigan, in a judicial discipline proceeding, found that the judge "violated his oath of office, engendered disrespect for the law and improperly interfered with the proper administration of justice." It then upheld the judge's suspension without pay for sixty days. *Ibid.* at 554. The Code of Judicial Conduct, Canons 2 and 3, according to the court, provided that a judge is not free to willfully refuse to enforce the law. The court wrote at page 552 that "[w]here, as here, a judge's decision striking down a law as unconstitutional is directly contrary to appellate precedent of which he is aware and obviously based upon his widely publicized personal belief about what the law should be rather than what it is, the public perception of impartiality of the justice system is seriously harmed. Code of Judicial Conduct, Canon 2(B)."

[43] *Anastasoff v. U.S.*, 223 F.3d 898 (8th Cir. 2000). (Discussion of Blackstone and Federalist paper's treatment of the obligation of judges to abide by precedent).

In order to use *stare decisis*, one must be able to distinguish questions of law from questions of fact during the trial process. In my own experience, this was one of the first lessons when learning common law method. Although the professors found it to be very clear from their perspective, the students, new to this distinction in the way common law study invents it, had difficulty. Perhaps the difficulty was that students new to the law would regard their abilities to distinguish law from facts to require only close reading and common sense. But "[w]hether a particular question is to be treated as a question of law or fact is not itself a question of fact, but a highly artificial question of law."[44] (One might note here that Isaacs' view was offered in 1922, a high point in the philosophy of legal realism, as discussed in Chapter 7. He therefore might be writing against the legal realists and their wish to remove legal abstractions from the law.) Perhaps the difficulty is in part due to the artificiality of the distinction. Anyone who has studied the famous *Erie Railroad* case and the subsequent cases that cite it (and are therefore called its "progeny") will recognize a similar artificiality in distinguishing issues of substantive law from questions of legal procedure. That same student will recognize that the substance or procedure distinction is likewise not one of common sense or fact, but a legal distinction that one can only know by studying the law itself. Likewise,

> [f]or the lawyer, the rhetoric of law and fact often says nothing about things perceived or policies preferred, but rather denotes function[45]—whether, that is, a question at trial (whatever its essential nature) is for judge or jury, or whether a question on appeal merits full or cursory review.[46]

The philosophy of legal realism can be seen applied to the *stare decisis* doctrine by Sir Konrad Schiemann:

> modern information technology makes it easy to search for precedents. You can usually find something which will point in the direction you want to go. Citing this will not only help to persuade your fellow judges but will also give the world at large the impression that you are applying the law rather than making it. But the scissors and paste approach to judgment writing seems to me to be greater [in E.C.J. decisions] than would be the case in England where, particularly the higher courts are much more accustomed to use precedents as broad inspiration rather than as suits of armour into which a judgment can be squeezed.[47]

---

[44] Nathan Isaacs, "The Law and the Facts," 22 *Colum. L. Rev.* (1922) 1, 11–12 (as cited in Kenneth Vinson, "Artificial World of Law and Fact," 11 *Legal Stud. F.* (1987) 311, 313).

[45] One should here keep in mind the notion of functionality in comparative law championed by Zweigert and Kötz and criticized by others, as discussed in Chapter 3 of this book on comparative law.

[46] Vinson, *supra* note 44.

[47] Sir Konrad Schiemann, "From Common Law Judge to European Judge," 4 *Zeitschrift für Europäisches Privatrecht* (ZEuP) (2005) 741, 745.

9.6 Federalism

In the history of world legal systems, kingdoms have evolved into states, empires develop as amalgams of kingdoms and states, and states have conquered and subsumed other states. As these various legal entities rise and fall, very different methods are attempted to keep expanding domains together and to defend the domain against would-be invaders. Viewing the various amalgams through the historical reference frame, Berman writes that:

> [p]erhaps the most distinctive characteristic of the Western legal tradition is the coexistence and competition within the same community of diverse jurisdictions and diverse legal systems. It is this plurality of jurisdictions and legal systems that makes the supremacy of law both necessary and possible.[48]

From the historic reference frame, one could understand why each of the fifty U.S. states is a sovereign of considerable independence. Thus, the United States is certainly not a unitary state like France, nor is it a "vertical" federation like Germany, in which there is a constitutional role for the *Länder* governments in the federal government. Rather, the United States is a "horizontal" federation,[49] which sets the federal government horizontally beside, rather than vertically above, the state governments. Therefore if one knows something of the public law of the European Union, I would maintain that to best understand the U.S. federation, one would be better served to make an analogy between the United States and the European Union, than between the United States and any one European state.

9.6.1 Federalism in the Making of Law

Within the U.S. federal or state governments, one finds Montesquieu's familiar tripartite division of legislative, judicial and executive branches. But in the United States, that basic division of powers leaves many questions unanswered for the legal practitioner, such as: (1) What is the law-making competence of the federal legislature compared to the fifty state legislatures? (2) What is the law-making competence of the federal judiciary compared to the fifty state judiciaries? (3) Given each state's sovereign powers, what is the legal relationship of each state's law to another state's law and each state's judiciary to another state's judiciary? Article VI of the U.S. Constitution contains a passage known as the "supremacy clause":

---

[48] Harold J. Berman, *Law and Revolution: The Formation of the Western Legal Tradition.* London: Harvard University Press, 1983 10.

[49] "Our unique form of federalism, which, as a former Canadian Supreme Court Justice put it, is the part of American constitutional law that has made 'the smallest impression elsewhere'." Mary Ann Glendon, "Comparative Law in the Age of Globalization," 52 *Duquesne Law Review* (2014) 1, 15 (citing Claire L'Heureux-Dubé, "The Importance of Dialogue: Globalization and the Impact of the Rehnquist Court," 34 *Tulsa L. J.* (1998) 15, 35).

> This Constitution, and the Laws of the United States which shall be made in Pursuance thereof; and all Treaties made, or which shall be made, under the Authority of the United States, shall be the supreme Law of the Land; and the Judges in every State shall be bound thereby, any Thing in the Constitution or Laws of any State to the Contrary notwithstanding.

To the person uninitiated in the limited legislative powers of the federation, Article VI might appear to construct a clear and familiar top-down hierarchy of power, just as would be the case in the United Kingdom, where the parliament is supreme, or as would be the case of Article 31 of the German Basic Law, which states simply that "*Bundesrecht bricht Landesrecht*," meaning that federal law is superior to state (*Land*) law. There is a difference, however. In the U.S. Constitution, the strong pronouncement of Article VI only applies to those areas of competence delegated to the federation in the event that one of the several states creates a conflicting norm. The fact that it was the several states, through their delegates, that formed the U.S. federation—and not the other way around—should not be forgotten. Amendment X to the U.S. Constitution reminds the reader that only the exclusive powers given to the federation by the member states are authorized, and that any powers not explicitly given to the federation remain with the states. It reads: "The powers not delegated to the United States by the Constitution, nor prohibited by it to the States, are reserved to the States respectively, or to the people." Having read Article VI and Amendment X, one is guided to see what powers were in fact delegated to the federation by the member states. U.S. Constitution Article I, section 8 states that:

> The Congress shall have the power to lay and collect taxes, pay debts, provide for common defense, borrow money regulate commerce with foreign powers and among the states, establish rules of naturalization, coin money, establish post offices, promote progress in science and the arts, constitute tribunals inferior to the Supreme Court, declare war, punish piracy, raise and support armies and navies, and to make all laws necessary and proper for executing the foregoing.

The U.S. Constitution therefore at the same time divides powers of the state among the legislative, judicial and executive branches and divides the powers in those branches between the states and the federation. Compared to many other states of the world, the U.S. federal structure is remarkable for the number and type of powers reserved for the states (such as making, enforcing and adjudicating the law of common crimes), while at the same time dividing the functions of the state along the tripartite lines of Montesquieu's model. To be sure, unlike many other countries of the world, the fifty U.S. states are emphatically *not* just administrative units of the federation. The name alone belies this: they are called "states," just as an independent sovereign of the world would be. As the reader may recall from the social reference frame, a further example of state independence is the fact that upon passing the bar examination, a lawyer is licensed to practice the law of only one state, the substantive laws of which differ from the other forty-nine states.

When a non-lawyer speaks of "American law" or "U.S. law," an artificial category of which I spoke above, it can only be properly understood as a cultural term that approximately refers to fifty-one systems, occupying the geopolitical space of the United States. Referring back to the language reference frame and the lessons of structuralism, one would be hard-pressed to identify clear boundaries to the mental "referent" for something called "American law" or "U.S. law." Once that fact is understood, one has begun to understand U.S. federalism. And it is precisely at that point that one sees that legally one might be better served to make the analogy between the European Union and the United States than between the latter and one of the member states of the E.U. To emphasize that point, consider the landmark European Court of Justice case in which it was concluded that E.U. law was superior to member state law, *Flaminio Costa v. ENEL,* Case 6/64 [1964] E.C.R. 585. Although the case does establish the general rule, just like in the United States, the rule only applies if otherwise it has been determined that the E.U. has legislative competency. The fact alone of being a "central" government does not make it a higher government, just as the U.S. federation, as a centralized government, does not make it a higher government.

9.6.2 Federalism and the Practice of Law

To understand U.S. federalism as a practicing lawyer, one must go further than law-making and attempt to understand that when it comes to resolving conflicts, one has a choice of forums among those fifty-one jurisdictions, a process popularly called "forum shopping." The choice of forum is limited by subject matter jurisdiction and the personal jurisdiction of the courts. To understand those jurisdictional choices, one must study not only the U.S. Constitution itself, but the binding case law that interprets the U.S. Constitution. Consistent with the points made above of the strength of the several states and their law-making competency, they also therefore hold jurisdiction over the subject matter and persons within their boundaries. Therefore, unsurprisingly, statistics show that conflict resolution is carried out almost 98 percent of the time in a state, not federal, court.[50] The state courts apply norms of law made in that state: the state's constitution, legislation, regulations and binding case decisions.

However, if a conflict arises to which one of the reserved competencies of federal law applies (called a "federal question, "as set forth in Article I, section 8), then one *must* go to a U.S. federal court for resolution of the conflict. In comparison to

---

[50] See Galanter, *supra* note 2 (citing Brian J. Ostrom, Shauna M. Strickland and Paula L. Hannaford-Agor, "Examining Trial Trends in the State Courts," 1 *J. Empirical Legal Stud.* (2004) 755).

conflicts that are resolved in state court jurisdiction, these federal question cases are by far a minority category.

But beyond exclusive state court jurisdiction and exclusive federal court jurisdiction, there is still one other category of case in which one *may* (not must) present one's conflict to a federal court. This third category is not to be confused with law-making competency. Here we are speaking of jurisdiction over conflict, not competency to make law. The third category is available when the citizens of more than one state are involved in the litigation, or when one or more of the litigants is from another country altogether, which is called citizenship "diversity." Article III, section 2 of the U.S. Constitution permits the federal courts in such cases to hear the claim and resolve the conflict. Again here, one has evidence of the relative strength of the states insofar as it was originally feared that a state court's judge or jury may be biased in favor of a litigant from its own state against a citizen from another U.S. state or even a foreign country.

One must keep in mind that with diversity of citizenship jurisdiction, however, it is a choice, not a requirement, for a plaintiff to bring an action before a federal court. That same injured party may also bring the action in the state court of the state where the injury occurred or before the state court in the state where the defendant resides. Given this choice, how does an injured person (or a lawyer) choose—federal or state; and if state, which state? The answer may be determined by the applicable sources of law between the states themselves. States have competency to make legislation in many areas and in so doing, are also free to vary and even disagree with other states, so long as they do not violate their own constitution or that of the United States. The fact that the several states do in fact make and enforce different substantive law makes it advantageous to "shop" among the available jurisdictions that have authority over a conflict and choose the one that best suits the party who brings the legal action, due to its substantive law, procedural law or even the convenience of its location.[51]

When a plaintiff chooses a forum state based upon advantageous rules of law that can be made by the legislature or, as is often the case of non-contractual obligations (known in the United States as "torts") made by judges through their precedent-setting case decisions, he is said to be shopping for the forum. Once the plaintiff has shopped for a forum and made a choice of state rather than federal, or of state X rather than state Y, the defendant is not without his own strategic maneuver, however. The defendant in those situations may "remove" the case to the federal court where the plaintiff filed the action, for the same reason (avoiding bias) that allows a plaintiff to file in federal court to begin with, in cases of diversity of citizenship.[52]

---

[51] The convenience of the location, known as the "venue" is beyond the scope of this presentation of jurisdiction.

[52] It is worth noting, however, that while diversity of citizenship jurisdiction is enabled by the U.S. Constitution, removal is enabled only by legislation, specifically 28 U.S.C. § 1441 et seq.

9.6.3 What Law Applies to a Conflict—Federal or State?

Whether a litigant finds himself in federal court because of plaintiff's choice in a diversity of citizenship action or by way of a defendant's removal, there remains a question to be answered that one might not expect, and that is the question of which substantive law should the federal court apply? Keep in mind that the litigants are not in court because their conflict is to be answered by applying federal legislation, but rather, because one or both parties feared bias in state court. The conflict to be resolved remains in the law-making competence of the state court where the federal court is sitting and the litigation is taking place. Federal legislation does not apply. If the United States were a civil law country, in which it is asserted that the law-making body has anticipated all conflict and provided a rule to resolve that conflict, then we would have no problem—the federal court would apply state legislation on the matter. But in a common law country such as the United States, the legislative body may well not have ever created legislation in this area of conflict. Even then, as is true in the cases of torts, which make up the majority of civil litigation decided by bench or jury trial,[53] one might well expect to find cases with binding precedential effect having been previously decided by courts of appeal or even the supreme court of that state. Those rules of law would answer the matter. In the famous case of *Erie Railroad v. Tompkins*, precisely that problem occurred.[54] It is completely accepted in common law thinking that when a competent legislative body has failed to legislate in a substantive area that would create a sufficient rule of law to dispose of a conflict before the court, the court may nevertheless resolve the conflict, and in so doing, establish a rationale that is valid in future cases as a binding rule of law. Considering U.S. federalism, that would mean that fifty different court systems could do so in fifty different ways in the areas of law-making competency reserved for the states in the U.S. Constitution, if the respective state legislature has failed to act in that area of competency, resulting in state common law. And it also means that the courts in the United States could do so in any of the Article I, Section 8 areas of competency if Congress has failed to act in an area of its competency, resulting in federal common law. But should a court in the United States, sitting in diversity jurisdiction over two parties whose conflict should be resolved through state law, make a rule of common law for that state, resulting in federal-made common law for a state? Somewhat surprisingly, up until 1938, there was disagreement on the answer to this question, and federal courts sitting in diversity jurisdiction felt free in situations where state legislatures had failed to act to invent their own norms for the state and call them "federal general common law." Famously, in deciding a dispute between an injured man from Pennsylvania and the railroad that injured him from New York, which the injured man filed in federal court in New York on diversity jurisdiction, Justice Louis Brandeis declared that

---

[53] Tort litigation made up 60 percent of cases adjudicated in state courts in 2005. See Cohen, *supra* note 19.
[54] *Erie Railroad v. Tompkins*, 304 U.S. 64 (1938).

"[t]here is no federal general common law."[55] Even if a state legislature has failed to legislate in a particular area of conflict, the decisions of the highest court of that state are themselves "law," Brandeis stated, and shall be used by the federal courts in deciding the conflict. So federal courts are to apply state substantive law, regardless of whether the state made that law through legislation or judicial precedent. That leaves one hole, however. One of the maxims from common law equity (recall the history reference frame) is *'ubi jus, ibi remedium,'* meaning there is no wrong without a remedy. But it is also part of the thinking of the common law that courts do not provide advisory opinions and in the United States it has been made part of the U.S. Constitution (Article III, section 2, clause 1) that courts will only decide actual "cases and controversies" brought before them. As a result of all of this, it is possible that a diversity case could be brought before a U.S. federal court for which there is neither state legislation nor a binding state court decision of precedent to decide the case. By 1938, there may have been few areas of the law remaining in any state in which neither the legislature nor the courts had made a rule. And by the twenty-first century, that is even more the case. In theory, however, it still might come about. If it does, what rule of law should a federal court use? In one of those rare situations, one would really begin to see the reasoning process of the federal judge in all of his or her common law heritage.

For the practicing lawyer, this short description concludes the application of some cultural reference frames to the mechanics of federal-state relations in U.S. federalism, but given that the fifty states are powerful independent sovereigns, further issues for reflection remain: What is the legal relationship between and among the states once a law is made or a conflict is resolved? Can a losing defendant escape paying on a civil claim because he lives in another state or has purposely moved to another state to avoid the court's jurisdiction?

9.6.4 Federalism and State Relations to Other States

Historically, as between two sovereign states, if a court were to exercise jurisdiction over a defendant of another sovereign state, and find him or her liable, the defendant could avoid payment on the claim if he or she moved to, or remained outside the state's jurisdiction. Given the respect given to the sovereignty of states, this presents a real problem, unless the two states have come to an explicit agreement on how each state will respect the judgments of other states and aid in their enforcement. The same situation would obtain between and among the U.S. states because each state can and does make its own substantive and procedural law, as discussed above, and each state constitutes its own jurisdiction over that law. However, rather than rely upon a treaty to make foreign judgments enforceable, the U.S. Constitution provides the rules for the U.S. states. Article IV, section 2, clause 1 of the U.S. Constitution says "[t]he Citizens of each State shall be entitled to all Privileges and Immunities

[55] *Ibid.* at page 78.

of Citizens in the several States." This constitutional provision has been generally understood to prevent any one of the states from treating a citizen of another state in a discriminatory manner. Furthermore, Article IV, section 1 of the U.S. Constitution provides: "[f]ull faith and credit shall be given in each state to the public acts, records, and judicial proceedings of every other state. And the Congress may by general laws prescribe the manner in which such acts, records, and proceedings shall be proved, and the effect thereof." Thus, after a court in one state completes a judgment in the case, the executive branch of another state is required to honor that judgment. A common situation would be, for example, that if a private civil action in State A is concluded in favor of the plaintiff and the property of the defendant is in State B, State B would be required to honor the judgment of the court of State A and facilitate the collection of the debt in State B. This may seem overly burdensome, and in a unitary state would be unnecessary, but in a federation of truly powerful individual states such as that of the United States, it is necessary to make the binding nature of this legal relationship explicit, if citizens are to move freely and easily from one state to another, confident of some level of shared legal protection. Again, this is quite similar to the goal of a borderless European Union, sought through the legal guarantees of free movement of persons, capital and goods within the E.U.

Within the realm of culture there is much to be said beyond the mechanics of any of these rules and norms. Whether making law, interpreting law or enforcing law, persons of that culture will feel that they have a "sense" of what is fair or just, and therefore a sense of what will be accepted as an interpretive practice. That sense can be understood in a positive way as being one's control of local knowledge, or could be understood in a negative way, as unconscious conformity to an ideology. To what degree that sense versus the operation of the mechanics can predict outcomes is difficult, if not impossible to say. What is worthy of study, however, are the differences in how cultures regard their legal systems beyond the mechanics of the law themselves. Only by knowing something of this cultural reception by the citizens[56] can one claim to be able to predict how a conflict will be settled. And that is the essence of law, if it is a social science.

9.7 Conclusions

So with this introduction of some of the mechanics of U.S. law, I hope that the reader can see the essential role played by legal culture for him or her to understand the mechanics and ultimately to aid the person in need of legal services in the

---

[56] In addition to how the citizens accept law and its procedures, one must consider how lawyers will use law and its procedures, if one is to predict the outcome of conflicts. In a related study on delay in the courts, I have found that practicing lawyers can, for example, create delay for use in their favor, even when the courts take measures to eliminate the backlog of cases filed waiting to be heard, by adding judges or panels, shortening the time for pretrial motions and discovery, and other practices. See also the classic work in legal realism by Federal Appeals Judge Jerome Frank, *supra* note 40.

United States. This chapter is only a sample of some legal mechanics and is by no means exhaustive of all the cultural understanding one must have to understand the legal system as it functions in these examples or the many others that a student or lawyer can find in other books or actual practice.

CHECK YOUR UNDERSTANDING:

If a U.S. federal judge sitting in diversity jurisdiction encountered a conflict to which no state statute or judicial precedent applied, what substantive law would he or she apply?

CHALLENGE YOUR UNDERSTANDING:

Through what mechanisms, procedures and cultural understanding does a trial produce its outcome?

Literature

Berman, Harold J., *Law and Revolution: The Formation of the Western Legal Tradition.* London: Harvard University Press, 1983.

Edwards, David, "Fact-Finding: A British Perspective," in D. L. Carey Miller and Paul R. Beaumont (eds.), *The Option of Litigating in Europe.* London: United Kingdom Committee of Comparative Law, 1993.

Galanter, Marc, "A World Without Trials," 2006 *J. Disp. Resol.* (2006). 7.

Goldman, Sheldon, "The Effect of Past Judicial Behavior on Subsequent Decision-Making," 19 *Jurimetrics J.* (1978–1979). 208.

Isaacs, Nathan, "The Law and the Facts," 22 *Colum. L. Rev.* (1922). 1, 11–12.

Johns, Margaret and Rex R. Perschbacher, *The United States Legal System, An Introduction.* Durham, NC: Carolina Academic Press, 2007.

Kempin, Frederick G., *Historical Introduction to Anglo-American Law.* 3d. ed. St. Paul, MN: West, 1990.

Lever, Jeremy, "Why Procedure is More Important Than Substantive Law," 48 *International and Comparative Law Quarterly* (April 1999). 285, 296.

National Center for State Courts, "Civil Action," vol. 6, no. 1, Summer 2007.

Schiemann, Konrad, "From Common Law Judge to European Judge," 4 *Europäisches Privatrecht* (ZEuP) (2005). 741.

Segal, Jeffrey A. and Horold J. Spaeth, "The Influence of Stare Decisis on the Votes of Supreme Court Justices," 40 *American Journal of Political Science* (1996). 971.

Vinson, Kenneth, "Artificial World of Law and Fact," 11 *Legal Stud. F.* (1987). 311.

Ware, Stephen J., *Principles of Alternative Dispute Resolution.* St. Paul, MN: West Academic Publishing, 2007.

INDEX